CITY AT THE CENTRE

A city on a plain: the eastern portion of Palmerston North, showing the city's relationship with the Manawatū River and its problematic 'Fitzroy Bend', historically prone to flooding. Steve Bicknell

CITY AT THE CENTRE

A History of Palmerston North

Tini whetū ki te rangi,
take rau tāngata ki te whenua

EDITED BY
Margaret Tennant, Geoff Watson and Kerry Taylor

MASSEY UNIVERSITY PRESS

This book is dedicated to historian and archivist
Ian Roderick Matheson (1946–2002)

CONTENTS

Tini whetū ki te rangi, take rau tāngata ki te whenua
As there are stars in the sky there are issues on the land

The title page of the book incorporates the well-known Rangitāne whakataukī (proverb) 'Tini whetū ki te rangi, ko Rangitāne ki te whenua', comparing the myriad stars in the sky with the multitudes of Rangitāne people on the land. This acknowledges both Rangitāne's place as tangata whenua and the many take (issues) discussed in the following chapters.

Robert Jahnke's *Ngā Huruhuru Rangatira* frames the entrance to Te Marae o Hine, looking towards the statue of Te Peeti Te Aweawe. Leith Haarhoff, Manawatū Heritage COMM 1481682432

The Palmerston North Borough Council 1921–23 and senior staff, all male. From left: Cr Frederick Needham, Cr Frederick Jackson, Cr Meldrum Elliot, Cr Stephen Lancaster, Arthur Spilman (abattoir manager), Roy Jordan (assistant town clerk), James Hardie (town clerk), Peter Black (curator of parks and reserves), Mayor James Nash, John Hughes (borough engineer), Edward Rabbidge (gas manager), George Healey (assistant gas manager), Cr Matthew Oram, Cr Archibald Graham, Cr Charles Spooner, Cr Ernst West, Cr Henry Canton. Manawatū Heritage 2010N_Cc5_3329

FOREWORD

This jubilee snapshot of Palmerston North marking 150 years of urban development is a wonderful achievement and a welcome addition to understanding and appreciating the city's origins and its subsequent development.

Rangitāne, the region's mana whenua, first settled here some 400 years ago, so why pick 1871 as our foundation year? It was in 1871 that the small North Island settlement of Palmerston — population around 200 — acquired a distinctive new label for having added the word 'North' to its name. For convenience, the settlement needed distinguishing from its South Island counterpart, inadvertently gifting us the longest English name of any urban centre in New Zealand. It was also the year that the first Scandinavian immigrants arrived, having sailed to New Zealand aboard the *Celaeno* to work as sawmillers, road builders, railway workers and farmers.

That year, George and Louisa Snelson, 'the Father and Mother of Palmerston North', opened the first store on The Square. As postmaster, George Snelson was the settlement's first registrar of births, deaths and marriages, and became Palmerston North's first mayor when the town gained borough status in 1877.

In 1871 came the first boarding house and establishment of the first factory — a sawmill powered by the town's first steam engine. Also arriving that year to the natural 400-hectare Papaiōea clearing in the forest were the settlement's first blacksmith, brewer and butcher; and its first cabinetmaker, carpenter, doctor, shoemaker, tailor and wheelwright. Within a remarkably short period those early foundations of urban life subsequently attracted a school, a newspaper, telegraph connections, more roads and a railway, and by 1877 Palmerston North had a population of 800.

An October 1871 edition of the *Wellington Independent* newspaper prophetically observed that '"Go-ahead Palmerston" will be our motto, I trust for some time to come'. It's fitting then, 150 years later, that Palmerston North can still be characterised by its 'go-ahead' opportunities and attitudes. With its diverse economic base, it is poised and predicted to continue growing both in size and stature as a city of significance.

Always a major transport hub and farming centre, the city has become a focus for logistics, higher education, agri-tech and agri-commerce, food science and research, manufacturing, health and defence. We are a thriving, progressive, multinational, multicultural boutique city, small by international standards but with big ambitions. We are well furnished with amenities, well served by infrastructure and facilities and, at the pivot-point of the lower North Island, well placed for expansion.

As the twenty-ninth mayor of Palmerston North, I wholeheartedly endorse 150 years of progress thanks to the invaluable partnerships established between council, communities, organisations, companies, institutions and central government.

But it has been the city's special and deep relationship with Rangitāne that has helped Palmerston North establish and prosper. From early days of friendship and trading to embracing Christianity and, more recently, development opportunities, Rangitāne have always been welcoming and have shared Palmerston North — Te Papaiōea — with us all.

I thoroughly commend the work that has gone into researching our story, making its various strands accessible, and bringing our past to life in such a comprehensive and readable way. In 50 years' time — 2070 — future historians will have added their interpretations to our rich and varied narrative.

As with the city's progress, those future reflections will be something for upcoming generations to look forward to.

Ngā mihi

Grant Smith
Mayor of Palmerston North

More diverse than its 1921–23 counterpart, the Palmerston North City Council elected in 2019 poses on the bridge over the butterfly lake in The Square. From left: Cr Zulfiqar Butt, Cr Renee Dingwall, Cr Rachel Bowen, Cr Lorna Johnson, Cr Karen Naylor, Cr Billy Meehan, Cr Leonie Hapeta, Cr Susan Baty, Deputy Mayor Tangi Utikere, Mayor Grant Smith, Cr Aleisha Rutherford, Cr Pat Handcock, Cr Bruno Petrenas, Cr Brent Barrett, Cr Lew Findlay, Cr Vaughan Dennison.
Palmerston North City Council

01
STORIES OF A CITY

MARGARET TENNANT & GEOFF WATSON

The city celebrates an anniversary: the arrival by canoe of Louisa Snelson and her ward, Mathilda Montgomery. Their welcome at the riverbank by George Snelson (later the town's first mayor) was re-enacted on 13 March 1971, with city councillor Ken Wynks playing Snelson. The Māori welcome party in the background included representatives of Rangitāne. The *Evening Standard* reported that 'Palmerstonians seemed to shed their traditionally conservative cloaks of inhibition and joined in the celebrations with abandon.' Manawatū Heritage 2011P_J35_004840

'Owing to its central position, its splendid means of communication, and the constant influx of strangers, Palmerston North has become an extremely cosmopolitan town. It has escaped the narrowness of thought and action which is begotten of isolation, and the newcomer who desires to cast in his lot with its inhabitants, will find them willing to extend to him a hearty welcome and a fair field for his energies.'[1]

Written in 1903, Lindsay Buick's penultimate paragraph of *Old Manawatu* encapsulates many key features of Palmerston North's past history and present aspirations. In an area initially settled by Rangitāne, Palmerston North has become home to peoples from many parts of the world. In this book we seek to explain why people chose to come to Palmerston North, and what they did when they were here: where they worked, how they played, who they chose to lead them, how they were schooled, the organisations they formed, and the ways in which they changed the environment and the environment changed them.

Palmerston North is a provincial, inland city with a university and a military base, and with strong links to its rural hinterland. It is a city which was part of a second phase of urban formations in New Zealand — occasionally subject to the condescension of its older counterparts and to apology from its own inhabitants — but which now proudly promotes its 'Small City Benefits, Big City Ambition'. Palmerston North offers a testing ground for historical generalisations derived largely from the four main centres, leavened by its own particularities — of time and circumstances of human settlement; of environment and place. Its centrality and key role as a transport hub, first by rail and road, and then by air, inform the title of this volume and so much of Palmerston North's development since colonial times.

Geography was part of Palmerston North's naming, one part of its title locating it within New Zealand, the other linking it to an empire based in a far-distant part of the globe. Palmerston North, like Auckland and Wellington, was named after a British luminary long since forgotten by most of its residents. The third Viscount Palmerston was twice prime minister, dominating British foreign policy at the height of imperial power. He was famous enough in his time to inspire the naming of two New Zealand towns, so to

ABOVE A Māori pageant was the star event of the city's 1937 diamond jubilee, but other events were more focused on the struggles faced by European settlers. Winston Davis and Leslie Verry wrote a play, 'The Precious Years', about 60 years in the lives of the fictitious 'Priestleys of Palmerston', 'a family in whom are typified all those hardy adventurers who founded the city'. Manawatū Heritage 2014N_T14_009097

LEFT Anniversaries provided ample opportunity to tell stories about place and history, usually with an emphasis on Pākehā pioneers. The illustration on the programme for Palmerston North's fiftieth anniversary in 1927 shows the transmission of the foundation story from old to young, with a heavy emphasis on progress. Manawatū Heritage 2016Pa_A175-20-1_013140 reduce postal confusion the North Island settlement's name gained the prosaic geographical qualifier 'North' in 1871. If the overall effect is one of blandness, by the 1890s there was general relief that another, more striking though equally imperial, label had been avoided. In 1871 the two British explorers David Livingstone and Henry Morton Stanley met at Ujiji in what is now Tanzania. It was suggested at a public meeting soon after that Palmerston North be renamed in commemoration of the encounter.[2] The suggestion was not supported: the settlement then and later was not to be characterised by the exotic.

At various times there have been attempts to change the name to 'Manawatu', most prominently in 1895 when the borough council put forward the suggestion. Although this was rejected by the Minister of Lands because of its association with the wider district, 'Manawatu' continued to surface as a possible name, especially in the 1920s when Palmerston North was on the verge of becoming a city, and again in the late 1990s as a new millennium approached.[3] But by then 'Palmerston North' was so well embedded that the difficulties of change seemed greater than any antagonism to a lengthy and increasingly obscure name. There were always those who felt it a pity that a Māori term had not been adopted from the start, and 'Papaiōea',[4] the name of the original forest clearing on which Palmerston North was built, also came up at various times.[5] Confusion over its spelling and meaning made Papaiōea secondary to 'Manawatu' as an alternative, although Papaiōea was adopted by a number of local sports teams by the 1900s.[6] The borough, and then the city, remained 'Palmerston North'. The affectionate abbreviation 'Palmy' has even been utilised recently in official campaigns such as 'Palmy Proud'.

Palmerston North may have had what the *Manawatu Standard* termed a 'not very euphonious' name,[7] but this never held its leaders back when it came to promotion and puffery. Historians sometimes use the concept of 'urban biography' when they turn their attention to individual towns and cities.[8] The characteristics claimed for Palmerston North by booster politicians and, more recently, by public relations personnel, form part of what might be termed its '*auto*biography', for they too involve forms of storytelling about place. Early in its existence the little settlement earned a reputation for progressivism, a label based largely on the borough's ambitious borrowing for development (involving a loan that, the newspaper of rival town Masterton noted, 'almost takes one's breath away').[9]

Many New Zealand towns were called the 'Chicago of New Zealand' at some point in the nineteenth and early twentieth centuries, but the label was especially bestowed on Palmerston North for its progressivism as well as its importance as a railway junction. The 1897 *Cyclopedia of New Zealand* used the term, seeing a parallel with the American city in the borough's annual agricultural show and weekly stock sales (the expansion of facilities for animal slaughter also giving weight to the claim).[10] Playing to a parliamentary audience, MP William Wood, a former mayor of the borough, noted in 1907 that letters were sometimes sent to 'the "Chicago of New Zealand" — viz., Palmerston North, the most progressive, prosperous, best laid-out, go-ahead, and up-to-date town in the Dominion', when they were intended for that 'dreary village' known as Palmerston in the south.[11]

Local body politicians did not hold back on further external comparisons after the establishment of Massey College. In 1927 Mayor Archibald Graham foresaw Palmerston North becoming the 'Cambridge of New Zealand',[12] and in 1966 councillor Brian Elwood anticipated the city's evolution into the 'little Oxford of New Zealand', if it could properly promote its image as a university city.[13] When a 1992 National Research Bureau study showed Palmerston North ahead of Hamilton, Wellington and Dunedin as the city with the strongest education and scientific research associations per capita, a new slogan was devised: 'Get in the Know', followed by the 'Knowledge City' branding which took the city into the early twenty-first century.[14] Subsequent assertions that Palmerston North was a 'defence city' were based on the economic contribution to the region of the Linton army camp and the nearby Ōhakea airbase, but this proved more contentious as a label.[15]

Identity was claimed through other slogans promoting the city to outsiders. Many of Palmerston North's promotional materials have successfully focused on its role as a central transport hub, the 'Crossroads of the North Island'.[16] When an outside publication like the *Auckland Weekly News* featured Palmerston North, it was with captions such as 'Palmerston North: A Thriving Inland Town and Important Railway Centre of the North Island' (1924).[17] In 1952 the city's seventy-fifth anniversary publication pointed out how the entire railway system of the North Island converged on Palmerston North. It also extolled the 'rural–urban cooperation exemplified in Palmerston North more strikingly than in larger centres where the tendency is to develop along lines more essentially secondary'. Manufacturers were assured Palmerston North offered 'the twin possibilities of farm and factory in the prosperity of the district and of the nation'.[18]

Another promotional thread plugged Palmerston North's 'liveability'. A publication for the 1940 New Zealand centennial emphasised transport *and* liveability, showing how 'All RAILWAYS HIGHWAYS AIRWAYS Lead you to PALMERSTON NORTH THE MODEL MODERN CITY'. After the inevitable image of the city fathers (all men in 1940), the lead photograph was of The Square, 'this beauty spot within the bustle of competitive trade', an inspiration to private citizens who had emulated its trees and 'gorgeous profusion of seasonal flowers': 'Many of the streets are lined with flowering cherries, chestnuts, planes and other trees which provide a pleasing setting to the cool green of the street lawns.' (There was little mention of native species, still seen in the 1940s as uncolourful past impediments to progress.)

The garden city motif was a common one from early twentieth-century urban contexts, a counter to wider views of cities as corrupt and crime-ridden.[19] Palmerston North was cautiously labelled 'A Garden City of New Zealand' in one publication from the 1960s, hardly a ringing claim to distinctiveness. The 'Rose City' logo devised in 1971–72 was a nod to the national rose trial grounds in the Esplanade, but this, too, was seen as insufficiently distinctive or progressive a decade later. Many of the representations of Palmerston North

You must come and see us too!
PACIFIC OCEAN
AUCKLAND
TASMAN SEA
NORTH ISLAND N.Z.
339 M.
GISBORNE
148 M.
NEW PLYMOUTH
136 M.
NAPIER
116 M.
PALMERSTON NORTH
87 M.
WELLINGTON
SOUTH ISLAND
All
RAILWAYS
HIGHWAYS
AIRWAYS
Lead you to
PALMERSTON NORTH
THE MODEL MODERN CITY

OPPOSITE This 1940 pamphlet emphasised Palmerston North's centrality by road, rail and air, but also picked up on the notion of modernity — accompanied by a plea to visit. Author's collection

ABOVE LEFT Although the Public Relations Organisation picked up on the established idea of a garden city in the 1960s, this brochure was aimed at attracting industry to Palmerston North, and argued that the city offered most of the advantages, and none of the disadvantages, attached to a metropolis. Manawatū Heritage 2012Pa_PNCC1-17-5_006569a

ABOVE RIGHT This tea towel from the 1960s depicted many of the standard features of a large urban centre, including public parks, a clock tower, an art gallery and civic buildings, but also featured the newly built Lido swimming complex. Te Manawa Museum

in this period seem anodyne compared with the extravagant claims of an earlier era: a 1962 brochure advertised 'The City of Friendly Charm'. If a centre's qualities are captured, partly at least, by tea towels issued with its name, Palmerston North's attributes were not of a dynamic kind. 'The City of Space and Grace' said one, probably from the 1960s; 'A Pleasant Place is Palmerston North' indicated another.[20]

City planners added a quantitative take on Palmerston North's stories with a series of citizen surveys in the 1970s. In 1973, for example, respondents were asked to elaborate on what they considered to be the good features of the city. The largest number (40 per cent) said its physical and locational advantages, 35 per cent its 'environmental good points' — quietness, cleanliness and the fact that it was a 'good place to bring up children' — and 35 per cent its amenities; a disaffected 8 per cent said there were no good points. Asked about the 'irritating or disturbing' features of Palmerston North, the largest number (45 per cent) loyally said there were none, 10 per cent focused on traffic problems, and 11 per cent on 'fellow citizens & their attitudes', with specific mention being made of 'students', 'boring people', 'small town attitude' and the 'bikie/mongrel mob element' (this was the year after a major bikie contretemps in The Square, largely featuring outsiders). It was more problematic that 37 per cent were unable to think of any unique features that made the city different from elsewhere, and that those who could, focused on The Square and the Esplanade and gardens, longstanding city amenities.[21]

'Pleasantville' emerged as one of the more dismissive epithets directed at the city, a double-edged descriptor, depending on one's stage of life. Like many provincial centres, Palmerston North had to cope with perceptions that it was boring for the young, at least compared with 'bigger smokes' such as Auckland and Wellington. And, in a country where the populace loves its sea and beaches and lakes, Palmerston North could suffer from its inland location. It was not located 'astride the river'[22] in the way that Hamilton was, and although the Manawatū River had been a transport route in the past, by the mid-twentieth century it was often used as a dumping ground and quarry, and was perceived as a flood threat. Palmerstonians did not fully embrace the potential of the Manawatū until the twenty-first century, after expansion into the Aokautere area had shifted Palmerston North's residential locus further south-east.

The Māori term 'manawa', meaning 'heart', and part of the river's name, provided a basis for the 'heartland' label. From the 1950s this had given a more emotive slant to the notion of Palmerston North's centrality.[23] In 2001, it was incorporated into a new slogan, 'Young Heart, Easy Living', the 'young heart' referring to the relatively young age profile of the city, with its student and army populations. As one of the slogan's promoters recalled, 'We talked to a lot of people from different clubs and the "Easy Living" was the obvious part because everyone was telling us [that] it's five minutes to get to anything.'[24] Something of this quality was also captured in the 2017 vision of 'Small City Benefits, Big City Ambition', which was bolstered by video clips of people extolling the ease, affordability and flexibility of living in a small city.[25]

Council vision statements of the twenty-first century also acknowledged Rangitāne as the local iwi, and expressed an appreciation of Rangitāne support in the ongoing development of the city. The Māori history of the area had never been lost to tangata whenua, but it had featured little in the city's twentieth-century promotions.[26] By the 1960s this history was sufficiently unsung for the important pā site Te Motu o Poutoa (also known as Anzac Park) to be flattened for a carpark. The 2019 opening of He Ara Kotahi, the bridge and pathway 'that brings people together', has, by way of contrast, brought Rangitāne history to a new audience: the much-viewed interpretive panels along the riverbank tell of villages, conflicts and relationships with the land and river, an important contribution to citizens' sense of place.

The term 'urban biography' has already been mentioned, and it is an apt enough concept, for approaches to urban history can be as various as the stories told of human lives. Just as some biographies focus on childhood as the underpinning of adult actions, many of New Zealand's urban histories are strongest on the foundation years of their subjects: Māori history has often been presented as a precursor to the colonial era and to Pākehā settlement, which generally attracted more attention than the twentieth century.

Palmerston North's 'childhood' has attracted far more coverage than its recent past. This was understandably the case in volumes such as Lindsay Buick's *Old Manawatu* (1903) and George Petersen's *The Pioneering Days of Palmerston North* (1952), for they were written when the nineteenth century was still within living memory. Even Petersen's expanded history for the 1971–72 centennial was published at a time when there were men and women who had direct experience of the colonial town. Written before the availability of online newspapers, and deserving of admiration for its tenaciously detailed research, the centennial history fades in coverage once it hits the 1930s. As well as providing important written material on tangata whenua of the area, Petersen featured the first Scandinavian immigrants to the 1870s township, as has a cluster of more recent publications by local historian Val Burr.[27]

The most significant twenty-first-century monograph on Palmerston North is Ian Matheson's *Council and Community* (2003). Brought to completion by Dorothy Pilkington, this work also has a particular focus, taking the city's history into the more recent past through the lens of local government — although, given both writers' deep immersion in the history of the Manawatū, it goes far

An example of Palmerston North push-back against external negativity. In 2005 British comedian John Cleese visited the city in 'grotty' weather and famously proclaimed it the 'suicide capital of New Zealand'. Another comedian, Palmerston North-born John Clarke of 'Fred Dagg' fame, suggested renaming the Awapuni rubbish dump as the John Cleese Memorial Tip. In due course a good-humoured sign appeared labelling the landfill 'Mt Cleese'. A view of the sign in 2019, appropriately embellished by lichen. Photograph: Simon Johnson

RANGITĀNE AND THE MANAWATŪ RIVER

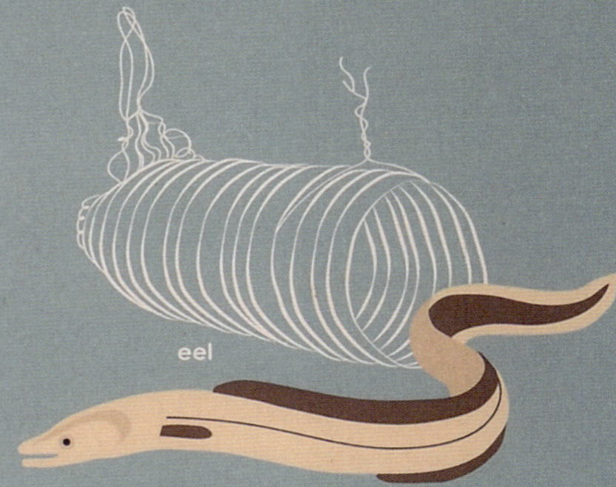

From as early as the 1300s to the late 1800s, there were as many as twenty villages along both sides of the Manawatū River between Awapuni Racecourse and the Manawatū Gorge.

The main Rangitāne hapū or sub-tribes who occupied these villages were Ngāti Hineaute, Ngāti Te Rangiaranaki, and Ngāti Kapuarangi.

The river was a vital and significant resource for Māori. It was their huarahi matua (main road), pataka kai (food store), and puna waimāori (freshwater supply). There were two types of waka (canoe) that were used on the river, the waka tiwai and the waka tētē.

Waka tīwai

Also known as waka kōpapa, was probably the most common. They were formed from a hollowed-out log, with no carvings, bow or stern pieces. They were ideal for moving small groups of people and their belongings up and down rivers.

Waka tētē (waka pakoko)

Was generally shorter and plainer than the waka tīwai. Some hulls were constructed from single logs, and some had joints. These canoes were used in many ways and were often not subject to as many ritual restrictions as waka taua. They carried goods, produce and people along many of the coastal and inland waterways. Local Māori used both of these waka on a daily basis to set and retrieve eel nets, go to fishing spots and also travel to the river mouth to collect shellfish.

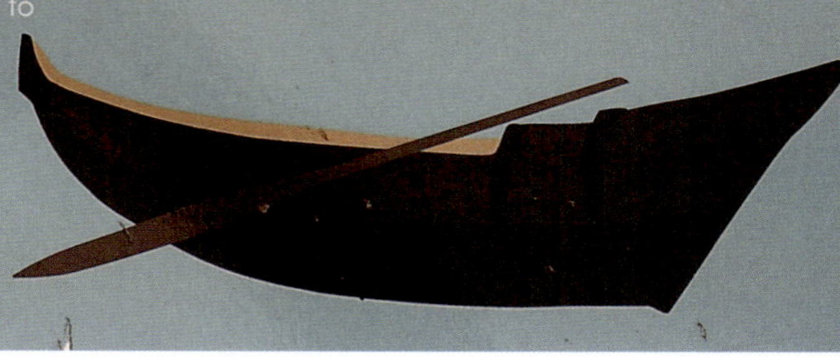

The sharing of Rangitāne stories has been a feature of the recreational development of the Manawatū River. This sign is one of a series of interpretive panels situated along the riverbank.
Photograph: Simon Johnson

beyond governance matters.[28] Matheson died before this book's publication, but following in his spirit was the *Manawatū Journal of History,* published annually since 2005.[29]

Not limited to the history of Palmerston North, the *Journal* has a relatively even spread of articles covering the nineteenth and twentieth centuries. Lively and varied, they drill down into the specifics of personalities, businesses, schools, organisations, buildings and sports. Just as biographies may focus on one aspect of a life — be it a person's work, relationships, creative outputs or public service — the *Journal*'s articles present many valuable but discrete strands of research. Other written contributions to the city's history have focused on its geographical parts, such as Garry O'Neill's history of Terrace End, Palmerston North's first suburb, and his subsequent contributions on Hokowhitu and West End; while the Savage Crescent state housing precinct has been the subject of displays, theses, oral histories and conservation plans. And there are the family histories, business histories and school histories. Individually they are of varying degrees of length and merit, shards of light into the history's past; added to a wider mix, they provide illumination beyond their original context.

City at the Centre draws on and expands the past work of local historians, and in passing (rather than as a sustained conversation) links it to the national and international. The volume is informed by questions raised in other urban histories, including Ben Schrader's award-winning overview history of city life between 1840 and 1920, *The Big Smoke: New Zealand Cities 1840–1920.* Schrader's study ends after the First World War and before a second wave of towns such as Palmerston North, Whanganui and Invercargill gained city status, but is important in asserting the centrality of urban life to New Zealand history.[30] Chapters in our history took inspiration from the social history approach in Schrader's book, but also attempt to bring Palmerston North's story into the twenty-first century on a broad front and in a way that reflects both the authors' interests and the need to fill gaps in earlier historical coverage.

City at the Centre offers a synthesis of existing work on Palmerston North, but also draws on that wonderful digital resource, *Papers Past*, as well as multiple forays into local and national archives to address the many gaps in the secondary literature. All of the authors greatly blessed former city archivist Ian Matheson for his own energetic gathering up of materials, and for persuading the city council to authorise the collection of community archives as well as those it is required by statute to retain. The two sides of the city archive complement each other, allowing research conversations between public and private residues of the city's past. There are still many deficits in the primary sources, including a lack of very early local newspapers, and copyright constraints that have prevented digitisation of

A series of photographs was taken from the top of St Patrick's Catholic Church, Broadway, during its construction in 1924. This view looks towards the city centre, The Square, top left. Auckland Libraries Heritage Collection AWNS_19241002_49_2

In 1952 Palmerston North celebrated the seventy-fifth anniversary of its proclamation as a borough. As this float by seed and fertiliser firm Hodder and Tolley shows, the city was still largely a rural service centre, linking itself to a heritage 'won' from the soil. But the vision was not simply local: some Palmerston North businesses saw themselves as linking into an international distribution system, sharing the Manawatū's bounty with the world.
Manawatū Heritage 2011_P-J54_004940

the remainder until 50 years have lapsed since publication. There is a need for further oral histories to be completed, and to encourage university postgraduate research into the history of the Manawatū, which was more vigorous in the 1970s and 1980s than it has been in the recent past.[31]

Our challenge was to bring together these many elements into a new overview history, recognising that there is more than one way to write about a place as it commemorates 150 years of permanent settlement and 90 years as a city. Many models were on offer from New Zealand and elsewhere, including histories of other provincial cities such as Hamilton and Hastings.[32] Rather than presenting a single authorial voice and chronological coverage, *City at the Centre* offers multiple lenses trained onto the city's past, and the input of several writers.[33] Some of the contributors come fresh to the history of the city, but have experience of studying New Zealand history on a national basis; some have long been involved in local heritage organisations and activities; nearly all have a long-term association with Palmerston North — and a number remember the smell of locomotives moving through the city centre!

The chapters which follow cover tangata whenua; the

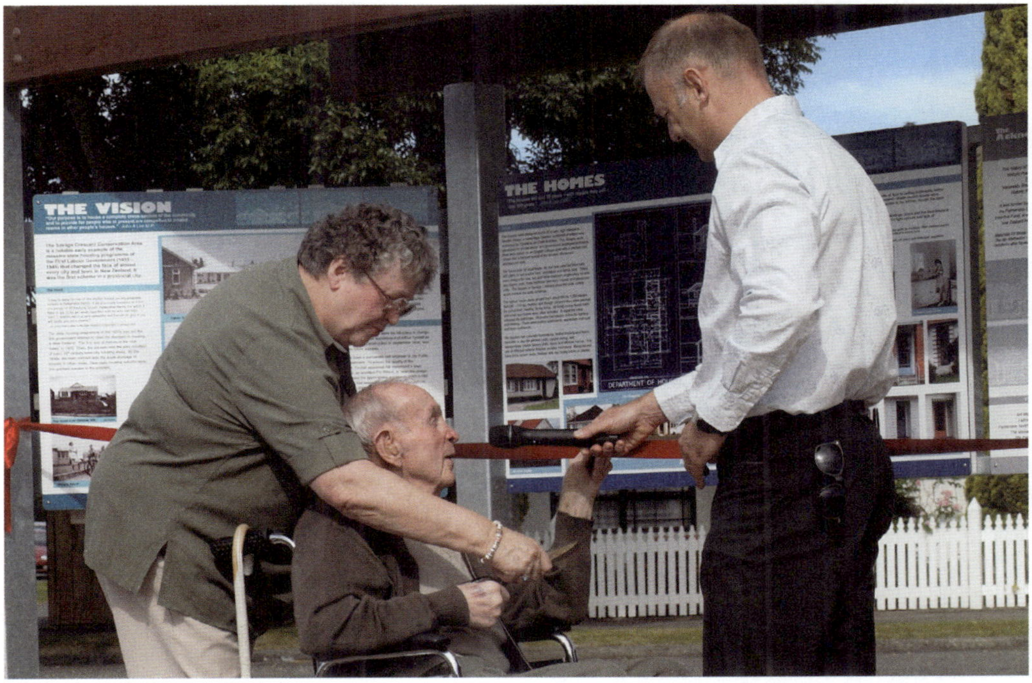

environmental history of the city; its settlement and expansion; working life; politics, local and national; education; sport and recreation; and community organisations. Thematic history of the kind offered here poses challenges, not least in the possibility of other, equally valid, areas of focus. (Indeed there are enough alternative themes for a second volume of this kind!) There was the challenge of writing overview chapters without turning them into lists of names and institutions. Individuals, businesses and organisations are more usually named when they represent some larger trend or relationship in the city's history. Where there was already published material on a topic, the authors of this volume often chose to focus on areas and people who have featured less fully in the written record, and to reference the work of other historians for those who wish to read further.

We saw ourselves as continuing a conversation begun by others, one which will continue in the future, in a variety of forms, and not just on the printed page. This book is not an end point, but, we hope, a spur to further inquiry. One of the joys of history is that there is always more to uncover and more fellow travellers in the search.

Historical signage has more recently started to tell the story of particular parts of the city, including the Savage Crescent state housing precinct. Interpretive panels were launched in February 2013 by the precinct's oldest resident, former Blind Association field worker Jack Shortt, seen here with his daughter Lesley Cranefield and Mayor Jono Naylor. Historic Places Manawatū–Horowhenua members Margaret Tate and Don Irvine played an important role in developing the display.
Photograph: Pat Scrivens

02

TANGATA WHENUA

Mā tātou e whakaoti

PETER MEIHANA
Ngāti Kuia, Rangitāne, Ngāti Apa, Ngāi Tahu
& HONE MORRIS
Ngāi Te Rangitotohu ki Rangitāne,
Ngāti Mārau ki Kahungunu

Rangitāne chief Kerei Te Panau and George Snelson, first mayor and first shopkeeper in Palmerston North. Kerei Te Panau, along with Te Peeti Te Aweawe and Hoani Meihana (Te Rangiotū), were the three great Rangitāne chiefs of the late nineteenth century. Each, in his different way, advanced relationships with the Pākehā settlers of Palmerston North, but nonetheless spoke out forcefully when they considered Pākehā and the Crown had behaved improperly. Kerei Te Panau was the only one of the three still living in 1900 when this photograph is believed to have been taken. When Snelson died in 1901, local Māori held a tangi for him and participated in his formal funeral. Kerei Te Panau died in 1908. Manawatū Heritage 2013N_Pi206_006897

Writing a Māori history of Palmerston North has in many ways never been easier. Historians can cast their eyes over the works of earlier historians, Māori and Pākehā; a significant amount of research has been carried out as part of the Treaty of Waitangi claims process; and there are databases that catalogue the huge amounts of information that are now at our fingertips. But how does the historian construct a narrative that reflects Palmerston North's Māori community, particularly when that community is so diverse? What events should be narrated? Whose voices should be heard? How do we write a Māori history of 'Palmerston North' when Māori occupation of the Manawatū pre-dates the establishment of the city?

One way of addressing these questions is to begin by saying Māori history is shaped by migration, first from Hawaiki and then within Aotearoa. It is organised around whakapapa, which helps to frame identity, and identity is inherently connected to land and mana. To this extent, the Māori history of Palmerston North reflects the experiences of Māori throughout Aotearoa-New Zealand. The tangata whenua of this area have, despite the impact of colonisation, retained a deep and unbroken connection to the land.

The city of Palmerston North sits within the takiwā of Rangitāne, the roots of occupation having been put down centuries ago. One account has Rangitāne's grandfather, Whātonga, following the encouraging words of Tūkapua at the launch of *Kurahaupō* waka.[1] *Kurahaupō* arrived in New Zealand sometime in the fourteenth century, landing first at Nukutaurua, on the Te Māhia Peninsula.[2] After establishing themselves there, the new arrivals set about exploring and naming the land. According to one tradition, Haunui-a-Nanaia, the grandson of Kupe, and son of Popoto, also the leader of a section of the Kurahaupō iwi, moved from the Hawke's Bay to Taranaki. It was here that Hau's wife, Wairaka, absconded with a commoner, an insult that demanded compensation.

Hau pursued the lovers as they fled south, naming prominent features of the landscape as he went. When he came upon a great river, he was in awe of what he saw and was unsure whether he would be able to cross it, declaring 'Ka tū taku manawa' — 'My heart stands still' — giving rise to the name Manawatū.[3]

Initially the descendants of Whātonga remained in the Heretaunga (Hastings) district, while the descendants of Ruatea, another leader of the Kurahaupō, moved to the Rangitīkei. Following a domestic dispute, Whātonga was compelled to take leave from his wife, Hotuwaipara, and he headed south along the Wairarapa Coast, across Raukawakawa Moana (Cook Strait) to the South Island, where his stay was brief. He then made his way up the Kapiti Coast and on to the Manawatū River, travelling inland as far as 'Forty Mile Bush' — Te Tapere nui o Whātonga. The descendants of Whātonga, his sons Tara and Tautoki, and grandson Rangitāne, came to occupy the lower portion of the North Island.[4] Whātonga's progeny also crossed Raukawakawa Moana and settled in the northern South Island, later meeting Abel Tasman and James Cook.

The eventual settlement of the Manawatū by the descendants of Whātonga took place following the arrival in Heretaunga of Ngāti Kahungunu under Rākaihikuroa and Taraia.[5] The migration of Rangitāne into the Manawatū took place under the leadership of Tamakere, Rākaumauī, Poutoa, and brothers Tāwhakahiku and Māngere. The migrants were checked along the way by already established communities, and, near what is now Dannevirke, battles were fought with Ngāti Māmoe and Ngāi Tara. Rangitāne were successful in the initial stages, but counter-attacks forced Tāwhakahiku and Māngere to abort their plans to enter the Manawatū via the gorge. Instead they passed through Pahiatua and Eketāhuna, determined to cross over the Tararua Range.[6]

Following a number of successful battles and having reached as far as Lake Papaitonga (near Levin), Tāwhakahiku and Māngere were killed. Utu for the death of the brothers was eventually exacted by Tamakere, in turn displacing Ngāi Tara and Ngāti Māmoe. The Rangitāne occupation of the Manawatū was preceded by fighting, and, according to custom, followed by intermarriage, a pattern that would repeat itself in subsequent generations. Initially pā were established under the leadership of Rākaumauī at Te Papaiōea, a forest clearing in which Palmerston North city would be built, and another, on the opposite side of the Manawatū River.[7] Other pā and kāinga were established nearby at Hotuiti, Tokomaru, Paparewa, Raewera, Puketōtara, Tiakitāhuna, Te Kuipaka, Awapuni and Te Wī.[8]

If the early European descriptions of the Manawatū are anything to go by, the land that the descendants of Rangitāne settled, some 200 years earlier, must have been a remarkable sight. A. E. Esler writes that the area was 'wealthy in resources', its dense forests were 'alive with the sound of birds'. Such abundance, however, brought Rangitāne into competition with neighbouring Kurahaupō relatives. Influential in the location of pā, then, was access to food-gathering areas, but also the ability to defend them and to retreat if necessary. The waterways of the Manawatū were also utilised:

Ngāti Toa chieftain Te Rauparaha, whose migration to the lower North Island and upper South Island in the 1820s led to conflict with tangata whenua, including Rangitāne of the Manawatū. Some of the consequences for mana whenua had a very long trajectory. Manawatū Heritage 2008Pa_Twl1-4_TWH_1902

> Rangitāne used the intricate river system to travel to the coast and it afforded Rangitāne a refuge in the time of war. Forest covered parts of the sand country, most of the Manawatū-Ōroua lowland, the rolling countryside, terraces, and the Ruahine and Tararua Ranges.[9]

This relative peace was disrupted during the 1820s. Hundreds of kilometres north of the Manawatū, Tainui peoples, the descendants of Hoturoa, were engaged in warfare that had spanned generations. This cycle of conflict culminated in Hingakākā, a battle that took place near present-day Te Awamutu in which many rangatira were killed. Hingakākā was particularly devastating for Ngāti Toa Rangatira, and the defeat weighed heavily on them. Te Rauparaha, who was born at the time of Hingakākā, searched for ways of reversing the defeat. Fighting between the Kāwhia and Waikato peoples continued, but ultimately Te Rauparaha and his relatives were compelled to migrate to the lower North Island and northern South Island.[10]

In 1819, Te Rauparaha took part in an early foray south. At Ōtaki, he met Māhuri and Te Aweawe, the sons of Rangitāne chief Tokipoto. Te Rauparaha tricked the brothers into leading him to their father, who he then killed.[11] It was at this time, too, that Te Rauparaha's eyes were opened to the benefits of relocating to the Kapiti Coast. The ever-increasing number of Pākehā frequenting the Cook Strait region meant trading opportunities — and muskets. This, along with the constant threat of attack from Waikato and Ngāti Maniapoto, provided Te Rauparaha and his Kāwhia and Taranaki relatives with reason to leave their ancestral lands. The migrations — Te Heke Tahutahu-Ahi and Te Heke Tātarāmoa — can be described as 'epic'. Subsequent migrations of Taranaki peoples followed, and, inevitably, the migrants came into conflict with tangata whenua, including Rangitāne of Manawatū.[12]

Te Rauparaha's invocation to migrate south was not taken up by all, at least initially. His mother's Ngāti Raukawa people were more intent on migrating to Heretaunga (Hastings district). However, a call from Te Rauparaha for reinforcements was answered by Te Ahu Karamū, who led a force of 120 to Kapiti. Te Heke Karere arrived a short time after Waiorua (1824), the battle that would secure the position of Ngāti Toa and its allies in the area.[13] Impressed with the land and its resources, Te Ahu Karamū returned home to Maungatautari, set on bringing his Ngāti Raukawa kin back with him. So determined was he that it is said he burnt the houses of those who refused to join him. Te Heke Whirinui,

the first major migration of Ngāti Raukawa, was so called because of the large woven mats that the heke brought south. A second migration, Te Heke Kariritahi, was led by Nēpia Taratoa, and was named after the type of musket that was carried.[14] Te Whatanui's initial plans to settle the Heretaunga were aborted, and his attention was also drawn towards Kapiti. Te Heke Mai-i-raro, the final migration, was led by Te Whatanui.[15]

Following the arrival of Ngāti Raukawa, land was redistributed among Ngāti Toa's allies. This was a delicate operation that in the end led to conflict, culminating in the battles of Haowhenua and Kūititanga. There is some debate as to who oversaw the land allocations, Te Rauparaha or his sister, Waitohi.[16] Also disputed is the extent of the allocations and the nature of the rights that arose from them. Issues of mana whenua would later complicate New Zealand Company and Crown purchases, and influence whose rights would be acknowledged, and abrogated. Until then, relative peace was restored.

Te Whatanui's people settled along the coast,[17] while Ngāti Kauwhata, under Te Ahu Karamū, established themselves at the confluence of Mangaone and Ōroua rivers.[18] The migration and settlement of hapū from Kāwhia/Waikato and north Taranaki saw a change in the geopolitics of the lower North Island. Ngāti Toa and its allies had gained a footing, although equally important was the fact that at the cessation of fighting Rangitāne were 'still in possession of the fruits of Whātonga's conquest'.[19] With the advent of colonisation Māori were confronted with new problems, and new opportunities. However, inter-tribal rivalry remained, a fact the Crown would exploit to its advantage.[20]

OPPOSITE Drawing of a meeting house, possibly Puketōtara or Raukawa pā, labelled 'drawn by R. Grindell Manawatu 1879'. Manawatū Heritage 2018Pa_JTStewart-S2F1_025406

FOLLOWING PAGES A suite of Māori place names was mapped on top of a copy of J. T. Stewart's 1859 survey of Te Ahu a Tūranga block. The map was compiled by Leslie Adkin, a Levin farmer later employed by the New Zealand Geological Survey. His Te Ahu a Tūranga block map dates from 1956, after he had expanded his interest northwards into the Manawatū. The detail on page 37 shows Te Papaiōea clearing with Hokowhitu and Awapuni lagoons. The old pā site is now usually written as 'Te Motu o Poutoa'. Palmerston North City Council

Early contact between Māori and Pākehā dates back to Jack Duff, a trader who in 1830 travelled up the Manawatū River and through the gorge as far as present-day Woodville, visiting a number of Māori settlements. The information gathered from this expedition was later passed on to Colonel Arthur Wakefield of the New Zealand Company.[21] The Company advanced the theories of Edward Gibbon Wakefield, who viewed immigration as a solution to Britain's present woes; furthermore, immigration would bring Māori into contact with British civilisation. Some saw the spread of this 'civilisation' as a moral imperative for a nation which regarded itself as the world's most advanced, but the Company's more immediate plan was predicated on the acquisition of cheap land.[22]

The New Zealand Company flagship, *Tory*, arrived in Port Nicholson (Pōneke) in August 1839. Its departure was hurried because the Company, and other land speculators, were aware of the British government's intention to intervene in New Zealand. The humanitarian lobby in Britain viewed the Company and colonisation as a threat to Māori, and so campaigned strongly against it. Despite this, the land rush had begun.[23] Within weeks of the *Tory* departing, the government dispatched William Hobson as Consul to New Zealand. By the time Hobson arrived, the Company had executed three 'purchases' — Port Nicholson (September), Kapiti (October), and Queen Charlotte Sound (November). Of particular importance here is the Kapiti deed. Signed by eight Ngāti Toa chiefs, including Te Rauparaha, it purportedly conveyed to the Company 20 million acres of land, straddling both sides of the Cook Strait, including the Manawatū.[24] Te Rauparaha later stated that he did not intend to sell the areas named in the deed;[25] the more likely case being that he was naming places he held rights to.[26]

Before arriving in New Zealand on 29 January 1840, Hobson stopped at Sydney, where New South Wales Governor George Gipps issued him with three proclamations. The first brought New Zealand, or any part in it, under Gipps's jurisdiction if or when sovereignty was acquired. The second proclamation declared that Hobson had been sworn in as Lieutenant-Governor of any aforementioned territory. The final proclamation stated that the Queen would 'not acknowledge as valid any title to land which either has been or

shall be acquired' in New Zealand, unless it was 'derived from or confirmed by' a Crown grant. The intention of this final proclamation was to put speculators on notice, but where land had been purchased commissioners would investigate and make recommendations.[27] While Rangitāne of the Manawatū were not a party to the Treaty, the Crown's undertaking to investigate the New Zealand Company 'purchases', and subsequently the Crown's own purchasing programme, would eventually draw Rangitāne into negotiations that would lead to the alienation of much of their territory.

It was not long until it became apparent that there was a shortage of suitable land for settlement at Wellington. Some hope of alleviating the Company's position appeared when a deputation of Ngāti Raukawa, led by Te Whatanui, travelled to Port Nicholson requesting that Colonel Wakefield send Pākehā to live among them.[28] In December 1841 Wakefield and a number of officials met with a gathering of Ngāti Raukawa at Ōtaki to discuss the matter further, for the earlier Kapiti 'purchase' had evidently not extinguished the interests of all. More problems appeared the following February when the Company returned to distribute gifts.[29] The immediate problem was that Te Rauparaha and Te Rangihaeata opposed the sale; another problem was that the area that had been offered up included lands belonging to people who had not participated in the negotiations, including those communities from the upper Manawatū.

Land Claim Commissioner William Spain met with Ngāti Raukawa in 1843. Te Whatanui, Te Ahu Karamū and Taratoa expressed their support for the sale; however, Taikaporua from the upper Manawatū opposed the sale. Spain proposed that compensation

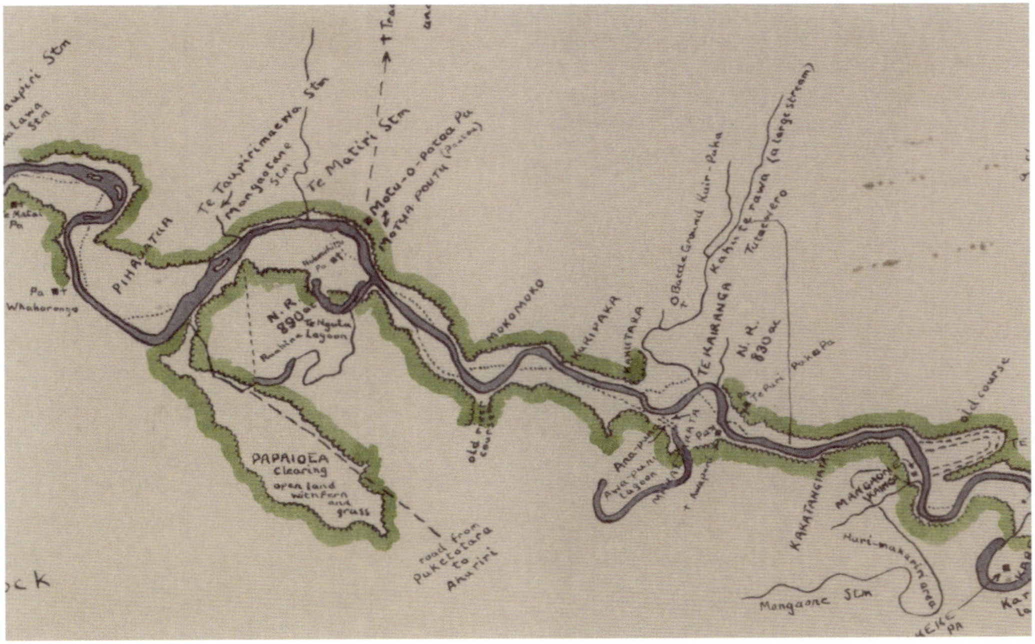

payments should be made, but when he, Wakefield, and Protector of Aborigines George Clarke returned in January 1844, Ngāti Raukawa refused to accept the money. According to Spain, this change in attitude was due to Te Rauparaha's presence.[30] With such opposition to the proposed sale and no post-1840 deed on which he could base a grant, Spain rejected the Company's claim.[31]

By the end of the decade, the Company was in dire straits. Failure to acquire enough cheap land was compounded by the fact that much of the land that was acquired was done for speculative reasons.[32] When the Crown took over responsibility for the dealings of the failed Company, it passed the Land Orders and Scrip Act 1858. This entitled settlers with a Company land order in the Manawatū to select land wherever customary title had been extinguished. This had the effect of placing pressure on the Crown to put the settlers in possession of land. The first block purchased in the Manawatū under this regime was Te Awahou at the lower north bank of the Manawatū River, near present-day Foxton. The next block was Te Ahu a Tūranga.

Historians have noted the varying tribal narratives associated with the sale of the 250,000-acre Te Ahu a Tūranga block, the land on which Palmerston North city was later built.[33] According to T. J. Hearn, the 'transaction revealed the complex and intricate inter-iwi and inter-hapū links'.[34] Hearn also observes that the Crown's desire to purchase land in the Rangitīkei and Manawatū led it to construct its own narratives. These narratives 'might be broadly termed a narrative of intervention, peacemaking, and purchase'.[35]

Negotiations for the sale of the block were complicated and protracted. Initially,

OPPOSITE Te Peeti Te Aweawe, c.1870. Te Peeti's leadership of his Rangitāne people extended across the musket wars and Pākehā colonisation. Requiring skills as a warrior and a negotiator, ultimately his actions were underwritten by a view of the best outcomes for his tribe. Manawatū Heritage 2008Pa_Twl-1_TWH_1084

Rangitāne chief Te Hirawanu Kaimokopuna offered the block up for sale as a way of encouraging Pākehā settlement, but an agreement could not be reached. Te Hirawanu said: 'before the land could be sold that it must be surveyed all-round the boundaries and then paid for at the rate of 30/- per acre — that [the] land was of immense extent and that it should not be sold in the dark'. The Crown's preference was to pay a lump-sum amount, offering £5000 and then £6000. When this was refused, negotiations broke down in 1859. So determined was the Crown to fulfil its obligations to the New Zealand Company settlers, however, that Te Ahu a Tūranga was exempted from the investigation of the Native Land Court when it was established in 1862.[36]

Te Ahu a Tūranga was eventually sold by Rangitāne in 1864 for £12,000, of which Te Hirawanu paid a portion to Ngāti Raukawa. The Rangitāne hapū that were in occupation at the time of the sale were Ngāti Hineaute, Ngāti Kapuarangi, Ngāti Rangitepaia, Ngāti Mairehau and Ngāti Te Rangiaranaki. With the purchase finalised, J. T. Stewart, chief district surveyor, completed the survey of the block. Reserves totalling 2370 acres (959 hectares) were set aside at Te Wī, Hokowhitu and Te Kairanga, and further Crown grants were issued between 1873 and 1879. An immediate problem arose when a number of significant sites were excluded from Rangitāne's reserves, including Raukawa pā, Awapuni Lagoon and kāinga, Te Motu o Poutoa, Maraetarata and Tiakitāhuna. Thus, between 1866 and 1873 Rangitāne sought to repurchase what they could as part of the Wellington Provincial Government's auctioning of Te Ahu a Tūranga. One hundred and sixty-eight acres (68 hectares) at Karere, which included the Tiakitāhuna kāinga, and 100 acres (41 hectares) opposite was repurchased. One hundred and five acres (42.5 hectares) at Te Awapuni was also repurchased, and would become, until the 1920s, the 'principal settlement of Rangitāne o Manawatū'.[37]

A year after the Te Ahu a Tūranga purchase, Kerei Te Panau and Huru Te Hiaro approached the government with a proposal that reserve land at Te Wī be exchanged for land at Te Papaiōea. In this way the Hokowhitu reserve would be connected to Te Papaiōea and 'held in one piece'. Moreover, Te Papaiōea had once been the site of a pā belonging to Rākaumauī. The Crown did not take up the offer, but it did purchase 71 acres (29 hectares) at Te Papaiōea from the Wellington Provincial Government in 1867.[38] The Crown then used the land to compensate Te Āti Awa for land that had been

Hare Rākena Te Aweawe (sometimes known as Harry Larkins), brother of Te Peeti Te Aweawe.
Manawatū Heritage 2013N_Pi150_007389

alienated from them in Lower Hutt and Wainuiomata in 1863 and 1864.[39] This has been a longstanding grievance for Rangitāne. The land was first administered by the Public Trustee under the 1882 Native Reserves Act. Then, in 1921, that responsibility was passed on to the Native Trustee. As a result of public works takings, sales conducted under freeholding legislation and land acquired for roads, only 36 acres (14.5 hectares) of the original 71-acre (29-hectare) block remained in Māori ownership by 1975. In that year a Commission of Inquiry recommended that a body representing the owners be established to administer the Palmerston North reserves, and four years later the Palmerston North Reserve Trust was created.[40]

The events of the 1820s and 1830s, followed by the arrival of Pākehā, created a new world that demanded new forms of leadership. A key figure at this time was Te Peeti Te Aweawe of Ngāti Hineaute. His grandfather, Tokipoto, and uncle, Māhuri, had been killed during the period of inter-tribal fighting. This would have a profound effect on Te Peeti. As Mason Durie writes, 'he did not hesitate to use a variety of means and agents to effect restitution from Ngāti Raukawa'. Te Peeti was himself a warrior, joining the Native Contingent in 1866 and taking part in the Taranaki campaign alongside Major General Trevor Chute, as well as the campaign against Tītokowaru.[41] Like other leaders during this period, Te Peeti aligned himself with the Crown as a way of safeguarding tribal lands from alienation.[42] The government honoured Te Peeti for his military service by presenting him with a flag and a sword. His support for the Crown was not absolute, however. His primary concern lay with his tribe, and he opposed the government when its actions impinged on the rights of Rangitāne. Te Peeti died in 1884 at Awapuni, and was buried at Puketōtara.[43]

Whereas Te Peeti maintained the martial traditions of his forebears, his Ngāti Rangitepaia cousin, Te Rangiotū, approached the changing world in a quite different way, but was nonetheless driven by the same desire to preserve the mana and authority of his people. An early convert to Christianity, he took the baptismal name Hoani Meihana (John Mason) and in the early 1840s became a lay preacher proselytising among the Ngāti Apa, Ngāti Raukawa and Rangitāne. He quickly acquired literacy and put it to customary use. In 1852–53 he convened hui at Puketōtara, bringing together 60 tribal leaders, and began recording the history and traditions of Rangitāne. Te Rangiotū devoted considerable time establishing better relations between Rangitāne and the newly arrived Ngāti Raukawa and Ngāti Kauwhata. When a land dispute between Rangitāne and Ngāti Raukawa erupted in 1868, Hoani was able to intercede; such actions earning him the title of 'peacemaker'.[44]

In 1878 Hoani and Te Peeti convened another hui, this time to discuss the naming of the Palmerston North town square. It was decided that Mātene Te Whiwhi of Ngāti

Raukawa would be asked to put forward a name.[45] The decision to approach Mātene Te Whiwhi, the nephew of Te Rauparaha, must have been a carefully considered one, especially when the events of the previous decades are taken into account. Mātene, at that time aged 90, put forward the name Te Marae o Hine — The Courtyard of the Daughter of Peace.[46] The name recalls the oral tradition of Te Rongorito, the sister of Maniapoto. Of aristocratic birth, she would become the ancestress of Ngāti Raukawa. She and her husband lived at Te Waka near Ōtorohanga where it is said conflict was forbidden, giving rise to the saying 'Kei hewa ki te marae o Hine' — 'Do not desecrate the courtyard of Hine'.[47]

In the eastern corner of The Square stands a monument erected in memory of Te Peeti Te Aweawe. Designed by local artist Harold Anderson, and commissioned by Te Peeti's sister, Ereni Te Aweawe, the Carrara marble monument was unveiled in January 1907 by then Native Minister James Carroll. The monument faces east, the direction from which the Rangitāne people originally entered the Manawatū. On the pedestal of the monument are engraved Te Peeti's dying words: 'Kua kaupapa i au te aroha, mā koutou e whakaoti' — 'I have laid the foundation of friendship for you to bring to completion'.[48]

The Hopwood clock tower at the centre of The Square also has a Rangitāne connection. The clock and chimes were originally housed in the post office on Main Street. At a ceremony held in

A gathering in The Square during a hearing of the Native Land Court, c.1881. Even where there were conflicting Māori claimants to land, The Square, Te Marae o Hine, operated as a place of sanctuary and civility. George W. Shailer, Manawatū Heritage 2008P_Tw2-3_TWH_1918

November 1906 the clock was set in motion and given the name 'Kerei Te Panau' in honour of the Rangitāne chief who once owned the land on which the post office was built.[49] In 1942, following the Wairarapa earthquake, both the tower and the clock were removed and placed in storage. Ten years later the city received a gift of £10,000 from Arthur Hopwood to build a new tower, and in 1957 the project was completed.[50]

The generation that followed Kerei, Te Peeti and Hoani faced new problems, mostly brought about by increasing numbers of Pākehā settlers and changes to the physical environment. Following the land purchases of the 1860s it took some time before settlers began to arrive. In 1871 there were an estimated 1000 Pākehā living between the Rangitīkei River and Ōtaki, with the Māori population numbering about the same and the only town in between being Foxton (Te Awahou). Ten years later the Pākehā population had grown to 9000, with more people living in Palmerston North than in Foxton. It is likely that the Māori population had declined by this time, a pattern seen throughout the country.[51]

To accommodate the growing settler population and New Zealand's burgeoning pastoral economy, the land and resources that had for centuries sustained Whātonga's descendants would be significantly altered. Between 1870 and 1910 wetlands were drained, inevitably leading to a decline in freshwater fish, and forests were cleared, likewise leading to the disappearance of

The death of Kerei Te Panau in November 1908 was widely reported around New Zealand, such was his standing. This image appeared in Auckland and Dunedin newspapers. At the centre is his wife, Ereni Te Aweawe, surrounded by prominent local chiefs. To her left is Ellen Wood and MP William Wood, who paid tribute at the funeral. Kerei Te Panau was interred at the Terrace End cemetery. E. Denton, Auckland Libraries Heritage Collections AWNS-19081203-2-4

The Awapuni Lagoon was one of five in the Palmerston North area, a rich source of eels, birds and karaka berries. The whare puni on the right was part of the Awapuni settlement on the north bank of the lagoon. In 1881 when this photograph was taken, there was still dense forest to the south in the vicinity of today's Maxwells Line. The lagoon was ultimately drained. Manawatū Heritage 2007N_Awa1_EPN_0252

birdlife.[52] These and other changes compelled Māori to adapt. Farming, dairying and horticulture were encouraged, and some were indeed able to farm their own land.[53] But, as was the case elsewhere, Māori were usually employed as labourers on settler farms, on the railways, in freezing works, or on public work schemes. A new generation of leaders carried forward the work of their forebears, taking up the challenge of negotiating a changing world.

Politics was one area in which Rangitāne were particularly astute. Rangiputangatahi Māwhete, or Rangi Māwhete as he was better known, had a distinguished career in politics. The grandson of Ereni Te Aweawe and Kerei Te Panau, Māwhete was the first Māori Labour candidate.[54] He contested the Western Māori seat in 1922 as an independent, and for Labour in 1925. Māwhete 'was fired by Labour's principle of equality between the races' and he saw an alliance with Labour as a means of achieving some long-held Māori aspirations, although as Claudia Orange

writes, 'the results under Labour were uneven'. In 1936 he was appointed to the Legislative Council, a position he held until 1952. During the passage of the Petroleum Act 1937, Māwhete was outspoken in favour of the recognition of Māori treaty rights. When war broke out in Europe, Māwhete opposed the conscription of Māori, but he was also a member of the select committee that oversaw the creation of the Māori War Effort Organisation. As was the case throughout the country, the Second World War took its toll on the Palmerston North Māori community. Two of Rangi Māwhete's sons enlisted in the armed forces, Allan in the 28th Māori Battalion and Joe in the RNZAF. Sadly, Joe died in Italy.[55]

The Māori Battalion trained in Palmerston North during the Second World War — here characterised as a 'fine type of men'. Auckland Libraries Heritage Collection AWNS-19410219-38-4

Palmerston North played an important role in the formation of the 28th Māori Battalion. From July 1940 the city hosted hundreds of young men from the four corners of New Zealand, who travelled to the Manawatū to undertake military training before they were deployed overseas. The streets of the city were regularly the scene of marching drills, and civic receptions were held in honour of the battalion. In March 1940, 400 soldiers and their partners

This Māori pageant in the form of a historical cavalcade was the most spectacular event of Palmerston North's 1937 diamond jubilee. With songs, haka, poi performances, a mock battle and 'brilliant lighting effects', it was under the overall direction of Rangi Māwhete (or William Moffatt, as he appeared in the publicity). It involved some 70 performers from a range of local tribal groups, and the *Manawatu Standard* pronounced it a huge success in conveying to Pākehā a 'deeper understanding' of the Māori people. Auckland Libraries Heritage Collections AWNS-19371201-51-2

Children performed kapa haka during the re-enactment on 13 March 1971 of Louisa Snelson's arrival in Palmerston North. The event took place at the river end of Albert Street. The welcome party included Rangitāne, and Mr Mac Whakamoe gave the speech of welcome on their behalf. MS, 13 March 2001, 2008P_Tw4-4_TWH_1936

were received at the Empire Hall by the mayoress, Mrs A. E. Mansford. On this particular occasion, composer Corporal Amohau formally presented the 28th Battalion with its marching song.[56]

Following the Second World War, increasing numbers of Māori moved to urban centres. This movement had in fact begun prior to the war, but by the 1960s it was 'clear a major demographic transformation was upon the Māori world'.[57] These modern migrations were motivated by a number of factors. One factor was a general increase in the Māori population that placed pressure on limited land and resources in rural areas. Government policy also promoted urbanisation by placing restrictions on rural housing assistance. These push factors, coupled with employment opportunities and education in towns and cities, increased the pace of migration.[58] The 1926 census, the first to include Māori alongside Pākehā, revealed that only 42 residents of Palmerston North were identified as Māori. By 1986 the figure was 9255.[59]

Urbanisation brought Māori from various tribal backgrounds into contact with tangata whenua — whose families had resided in the area since Rangitāne first settled — as well as families whose

ancestors had migrated south during the 1820s and 1830s. Reflecting on her life growing up in Palmerston North during the 1960s and 1970s, Debi Marshall-Lobb (Rangitāne, Ngāi Te Heiwi) remembers 'knowing every Māori family in the area'. The government's assimilationist policy of 'pepper-potting' Māori families seemed to have had the opposite desired effect. Rather than abandoning their communal 'ways', Rangitāne families simply formed new bonds with non-Rangitāne families. The terms 'Aunty' and 'Uncle' were redefined to meet the needs of a rapidly changing environment.[60]

Pita King and others have examined how Highbury, a low-income suburb heavily populated by Māori, 'became an enclave that has been actively cultivated by Māori for generations in an effort to reproduce Māori selves within the city'. In spaces such as sports fields, fish and chip shops, dairies and the homes of various 'aunties', as well as the urban marae, urban space was reconfigured to become familiar and homely in Māori cultural terms.[61]

Participation in activities such as kapa haka and work brought people together and helped to reinforce family bonds. They also enabled Māori to develop strategies to help mitigate against the potential negative impact of urbanisation. For instance, Te Waiora, a community-based kapa haka group, enabled its members to travel locally and further afield. It was in this way that the group became familiar with the history, whakapapa and customs of the wider Manawatū and areas from which some of its members originated. On one occasion Te Waiora travelled to Te Tai Tokerau, where the group met All Black Sid Going. For many Māori families in Palmerston North the Longburn freezing works was an important employer. The role of the works went beyond the immediate benefits of paid employment, however. For Debi Marshall-Lobb, her father's time at Longburn exposed her to lockouts, strikes and unions. All of this led to her own 'conscientisation'.[62]

Kapa haka has maintained an important position in the life of Māori in Palmerston North, with competitions catering for all ages taking place on a regular basis. Mokotini, a kapa haka event for kōhanga reo-aged children, has been running since 2010, while primary and intermediate schools take part in Te Pae Tamariki, a non-competitive event that began in 1993. In 2011, a new competitive event was organised: Ko Whiri Tika Mai included seven schools from Palmerston North and was held at the Regent Theatre. The strength and commitment to kapa haka in Palmerston North can be seen in the success of its groups on the national stage. In 2008, Te Piringa won the national secondary schools' competition and finished third two years later.[63]

In 2005, Palmerston North hosted Te Matatini, New Zealand's premier kapa haka festival, for the first time.[64] Formerly known as the Aotearoa Māori Performing Arts Festival, in 2005 the event was renamed Te Matatini — 'many faces' — by Te Wharehuia Milroy.[65] Twenty-nine teams from across the country as well as dignitaries, including the late Te Atairangikaahu, converged at Arena Manawatū. Here they were met with a wero led by Heemi Te Peeti (Rangitāne o Wairau, Ngāti Raukawa), and a 600-strong haka pōwhiri.

Mike Kawana, Jim Broughton and Manahi Paewai were the representative voices of the Rangitāne and Kurahaupō peoples on the day. According to Hēnare Kani, a member of the organising committee, Te Matatini 2005 was a source of pride for Rangitāne and the wider Māori community. As he put it, this was 'the first time since the late 1800s that Rangitāne have carried off a major kaupapa [event] such as this'.[66]

In order to meet the needs of Palmerston North's Māori community, a number of marae and other facilities have also been established. Opened in 1980, Te Kupenga o te Mātauranga was the first meeting house built at a tertiary institution in New Zealand. It was carved and decorated by the students and staff of Palmerston North Teachers' College under the direction of Cliff Whiting (Te Whānau-a-Apanui).[67] In 1996 the college became part of Massey University, and when it relocated from the Hokowhitu campus the guardianship of Te Kupenga o te Mātauranga was handed to Te Wānanga o Aotearoa during a ceremony in 2012.[68] Whiting had a distinguished career, and many of his art pieces are on public display in New Zealand and abroad, including at the Ethnological Museum of Berlin. He played a key role in the development of marae in Kaikōura and Bluff, and was integral in the building and design of Rongomaraeroa and Te Hono ki Hawaiki at Te Papa Tongarewa. In 1996 Massey University recognised his contribution to the arts by awarding him an honorary doctorate in literature.[69]

Another important community centre is Te Hotu Manawa o Rangitāne o Manawatū marae in Awapuni. The marae is home to the meeting house Tūturu Pūmau — 'cultural integrity forever'. The house, opened in 2004, does not carry an ancestral name as is often the case, but it implies that Te Hotumanawa o Rangitāne o Manawatū is a marae for all Māori who reside in Palmerston North.[70] The marae is also the base for Tanenuiarangi Manawatu Incorporated (TMI), the mandated iwi authority for Rangitāne o Manawatū. TMI's membership is made up of the five local hapū of Rangitāne o Manawatū: Ngāti Hineaute, Te Rangitepaia, Te Rangiaranaki, Ngāti Mairehau and Ngāti Rangitauira.[71] In 1998 TMI received a mandate to begin negotiating the settlement of Rangitāne's Treaty of Waitangi claims.

The 1964 opening of Te Rau o te Aroha, the Māori Battalion Hall on Cuba Street, brought to fruition many years of hard work. The idea of building a memorial to those who had lost their lives in the Second World War had been floated before war's end.[72] Responsibility for planning and fundraising for the memorial was assigned to the Raukawa tribal executive. Committee chair, John Mason Durie, would have preferred that memorial educational scholarships be established; however, he and Adelaide Poananga were supportive of the kaupapa and played key roles in the building and opening of Te Rau o te Aroha ('emblem of gratitude').[73] Hastings architect John Scott (Taranaki and Te Arawa) was commissioned to design the three-storey building that would 'be a harmonious combination of Māori and Pākehā architectural traditions'.[74] The 14 carvings on the building's façade are the work of Ngāti Raukawa carver Kelly Kereama. The building

The memorial alcove within Te Rau o te Aroha, the Māori Battalion Hall designed by John Scott. The names of members of the 28th Māori Battalion who died serving overseas are inscribed on the brass plates. The four figures in the left and right foreground represent the A, B, C and D companies of the Battalion. Evan Greensides, Manawatū Heritage 2018BD_IMCA-DigitalMaster_024686_002

was later taken over by Te Wānanga o Aotearoa.[75]

The 1970s was an important decade for Māori development. Simmering discontent boiled over into protest, putting the state on notice. Land marches and occupations placed Māori grievances squarely in the public eye. The Labour Government responded with the passing of the Treaty of Waitangi Act and the establishment of the Waitangi Tribunal in 1975. A particular focus of protest and agitation at the time was te reo Māori. The kōhanga reo movement was an outcome of the protest movement. The Māori community of Palmerston North was also driven by a desire to protect and revitalise the language. One of a number of initiatives that grew out of this context was Mana Tamariki o Manawatū. Although first opened in 1989 as a kōhanga reo, then a home-based kura kaupapa in 1995, Mana Tamariki o Manawatū, in its present manifestation, opened its doors in 2009.[76] It was the first total-immersion school in the country to teach kōhanga reo-aged children through to Year 13. The construction of Mana Tamariki also brought together architects Tennent Brown and Māori Visual Arts Professor Bob Jahnke. The result is an architecturally recognised building that expresses a child's educational journey while they are nourished by te reo Māori.[77]

Māori were also drawn to Palmerston North to further their education. Massey University is the largest tertiary provider in the city. When Massey opened its doors in 1928 its focus was on agricultural science. Māori were not considered in the university's establishment or the early stages of its development. This was not to say Māori were uninterested in agriculture and science; quite the contrary. Secondary schools promoted agriculture as the 'salvation' of Māori; bringing land into production was seen as a way of protecting it from alienation. Te Aute College and Hawkesbury Agricultural College had exchanged students as early as 1926. Four years later, one Māori student attended Massey on a scholarship, and Āpirana Ngata would also send his son to Massey.[78]

The introduction of Māori Studies led to an increasing number of Māori students attending Massey University. However, according to historian Michael Belgrave its introduction 'was driven more by the needs of non-Māori to find solutions for Māori problems than to encourage Māori students to become part of the university'. This focus arose out of a perceived need to address the problems arising from Māori urbanisation. But this was not the approach of Hugh Kāwharu, a social anthropologist who was appointed to oversee the programme. For Kāwharu, anthropology 'was a tool not for understanding the Māori past but for developing effective paths for Māori futures'. He returned home to Auckland in 1984, where he took up the chair of anthropology and the newly established chair of the Māori Studies programme at the University of Auckland.[79]

It was, however, under the leadership of psychiatrist Mason Durie that Māori advancement at Massey University reached new heights. In 1988 Dr Durie became Chair of Māori Studies, a position the university left vacant until he was able to take it up. Following his appointment, his responsibilities at Massey were expanded to the new role of Professor of Māori Research and Development, and between 2009 and 2012 he served as Deputy Vice-Chancellor. 'Māori@Massey', Professor Durie's policy for improving Māori educational achievement, saw a tenfold increase in Māori doctoral completions in a 10-year period, as well as the first doctoral and master's theses completed in te reo Māori. His influence extended well beyond the walls of Massey University; a fact recognised in the many accolades he received. In 2010 he received a knighthood for his contribution to Māori and public health. Two years later the Royal Society of New Zealand named one of its medals after Sir Mason, putting him in the company of Te Rangi Hīroa (Sir Peter Buck) and Sir Ernest Rutherford. Of Rangitāne, Ngāti Kauwhata and Ngāti Raukawa descent, Mason Durie has in many ways epitomised the vision articulated by those ancestors who faced the challenges of a changing world.[80]

Despite its location, Massey University was late in establishing a relationship with tangata whenua. By the 1970s there was little indication that the land on which the university was built was once part of the wider cultural landscape connected by the Manawatū River that included pā, cultivations and battle sites. What had survived, numbering just six, was the grove of karaka trees at the university's Number 1 Dairy Farm.[81] The restoration of the grove took place between 1982 and 1987. It included the installation of pou carved by John Bevan Ford (Ngāti Raukawa) and Warren Warbrick (Rangitāne), inaugurating the beginning of a relationship between Massey and Rangitāne.

After 30 years the grove was again in need of repair, and a community committee was established to attend to its redevelopment. According to custom, the original pou were buried and new pou, carved by Craig Kawana in memory of John Bevan Ford, were installed. A steel entranceway created by artist Israel Birch (Ngāti Rongomaiwahine, Ngāti Kahungunu, Ngāi Tawake, Ngāpuhi) and a sculpture by Clayton Tansley (Ngāti Maniapoto, Tainui) were included in the redevelopment. A pā harakeke consisting of local and national specimens also added to the grove's revitalisation.[82]

Palmerston North's Māori past has been remembered because in many instances individuals have deemed it important. Hoani Meihana certainly recognised this in the nineteenth century. However, people sometimes forget and need to be reacquainted with the past. When New Zealand commemorated the 150th anniversary of the Treaty of Waitangi in 1990, Mina McKenzie, with the support of Rangitāne, took the opportunity to revive Te Marae o Hine as the name for The Square. Of Ngāti Hauiti and Jewish descent, Mina's whakapapa speaks to the intent for which the name was originally given. In 1985 she donated to Te Manawa a sperm whale tooth pendant carved for her by Te Aturangi Nepia-Clamp (Ngāti Porou and Rongowhakaata). The pendant is aptly named Te Rongorito, after the ancestress who forbade acts of violence in her courtyard. Mina McKenzie was best known for her role as curator, and then director, of the Manawatū Museum from 1974 to 1994. She also took an active interest in educating those interested in museum work, and from 1994 taught in Massey University's Museum Studies programme. A scholarship recognising her contribution to the profession was established following her death in 1997, and the Mina McKenzie Memorial Lecture is held annually during Local History Week.

As with many other tribes throughout New Zealand during the late twentieth and early twenty-first centuries, Rangitāne attention was focused on their Treaty of Waitangi claims and settlement. On 14 November 2015, the Crown and Rangitāne o Manawatū finally signed a Deed of Settlement at the Te Hotu Manawa o Rangitāne o Manawatū marae,[83] some 25 years after Ruth Harris had filed the tribe's Treaty of Waitangi claim.

The path to settlement, much like the Te Ahu a Tūranga purchase itself, was protracted. The Crown recognised Tanenuiarangi Manawatu Incorporated's mandate to negotiate a settlement on behalf of Rangitāne o Manawatū in May 1998. Terms of negotiation were signed in July 1998, and in November 1999 Rangitāne and the Crown signed a Heads of Agreement; however, negotiations were stalled following a mandate dispute.[84]

Ko Te Pou Marangatahi o Rangitāne ki Manawatū, the group formed to challenge the settlement process, insisted that they were 'not critical of Tanenuiarangi Incorporated', rather, they considered that not all Rangitāne families were represented.[85] With the assistance of the Crown, the mandate was reconfirmed in 2005, but it would take another 11 years before the Rangitāne o Manawatū Claims Settlement Bill was introduced into Parliament. The time that it had taken to reach this milestone was acknowledged by

Minister for Treaty of Waitangi Negotiations Hon Christopher Finlayson during the first reading of the Bill in March 2016.[86]

When Māori enter treaty negotiations, they do so knowing that the settlement of historic claims are 'full and final', and that any settlement reached will not truly reflect the actual loss experienced as a result of the Crown's 'acts and omissions'. In lieu of what is actually owed, Rangitāne intended 'their foregoing of full compensation to contribute to New Zealand's development'. Thus, the settlement is seen as a means of enhancing the relationship between Rangitāne and the Crown.[87] Rangitāne's approach to settlement, then, is consistent with the actions of their forebears, who also endeavoured to create a community built on inclusion. Their contribution to this vision was immense, for the land on which the city is built had for generations been the home of Whātonga's descendants.

Following European settlement, Rangitāne tried desperately to participate in the new settler economy. To a very limited degree they achieved this. In more recent times Māori have sought to be included in the decision-making processes of their community as well. The first Māori city councillor was welfare officer Sam Mīhaere (Ngāti Mutuahi, Rangitāne), who served on council from 1962 to 1972, followed by teacher Waana Davis (Ngāti Awa, Ngāti Kahungunu ki Te Wairoa), whose term ran from 1984 to 1998, and, from 1989 to 1995, Yvonne Marshall (Rangitāne). Marshall, like Mīhaere, had a welfare background.[88]

These first Māori councillors had an impact beyond their numbers, often having to school their Pākehā colleagues on Māori issues. Sam Mīhaere had his hopes dashed on an issue dear to his heart when a planned urban marae in the Maxwells Line area succumbed to objections and a High Court planning appeal in the mid-1970s.[89] By the time Waana Davis came on to council, however, there was a wider community more open to Māori concerns, including some liberal Pākehā and church groups. In 1981 the *He Pātai* report had given city councillors a (reluctant) insight into the experience of being Māori in the city, and in 1982 the St Michael's Anglican church and marae was opened in Highbury. (Although, given previous opposition, city planner Ken Tremaine remembered advising that it be called a church as 'no one's prepared to appear to be godless enough to lodge objections to a church!') He also remembered that Davis, in particular, became 'a force to be reckoned with' on the council, correcting councillors' pronunciation of Māori words and quietly educating a key group of older male Pākehā councillors to the point where they were prepared to back Māori initiatives.[90]

Still, these Māori councillors were only three out of the 300 or so men, and a few women, who have served the city in this role since urban governance was instituted, though a later mayor, Mark Bell-Booth, was of Rangitāne o Wairau descent. Wiremu Te Awe Awe later became the first Māori to win a place on the Horizons Regional Council in 2016. In 2002 the Local Electoral Amendment Act gave councils the option of establishing Māori wards. Parliament introduced the ward option to address the reality that few Māori sit on

Palmerston North's major event for the 1990 sesquicentennial of the Treaty of Waitangi was the re-dedication of Te Marae o Hine. A multicultural parade preceded the ceremony to mark the significance of the marae. The replica of the Tānenuiārangi flag presented to Te Peeti Te Aweawe by the government flies prominently above the event. Ian Matheson, Manawatū Heritage 2017N_A175-71-1_0136

local councils. The Palmerston North City Council did not take up the option until 2017, in preparation for the 2019 elections. Following a period of public consultation, the council passed a resolution in favour of a Māori ward. There is, however, provision in the Act whereby a referendum can be called by voters. This is what transpired.[91]

The petition that triggered the referendum was organised by local resident Don Esslemont, although the campaign against a Māori ward will most likely be remembered because of the backing it received from a nationally organised body, Hobson's Pledge. Led by former Reserve Bank Governor and National Party leader Don Brash, Hobson's Pledge sought to remove what it sees as 'race-based privilege'. The Hobson's Pledge campaign espoused equality, but appealed to ideas rooted in nineteenth-century colonial thought, ideas that led directly to the dispossession and marginalisation of Māori. The outcome of the referendum suggested many Palmerstonians believed such thinking still had a place in modern New Zealand. The referendum saw a turnout of 37 per cent of eligible voters, 68.9 per cent (14,567) voting against Māori wards while 30 per cent (6530) voted for.[92]

Although the ward option was rejected, Mayor Grant Smith believed 'we had moved the dial . . . it has opened the conversation up to some decent debate'.[93] Other commentators noted the disregard for Maori cultural practices shown by some anti-ward campaigners. For instance, during a debate held at Massey University in the lead-up to the referendum, an anti-ward campaigner removed himself from the venue while the traditional welcome was taking place and returned once it was completed. This prompted Massey University academic Steve Elers (Ngāti Kauwhata, Ngāti Raukawa, Rangitāne) to suggest that the campaigner 'doesn't want a Māori voice at the council table. He doesn't want to hear a Māori voice, period.'[94]

In 2013 Māori made up 16.5 per cent of the city's population; the national figure was 14.9 per cent.[95] According to a 2011 Palmerston North City Council community profile, the largest iwi living in Palmerston North was Ngāti Raukawa, making up 13.7 per cent of the Māori population. This number included both northern and southern branches; the latter, those with whakapapa connections to Manawatū-Horowhenua, constituted 9.3 per cent. The Rangitāne population made up just 4.8 per cent; again, that figure comprised all Rangitāne, not just those with whakapapa to Manawatū. Overwhelmingly Palmerston

North's Māori population has tribal connections outside of the area. For instance, Ngāti Porou, Ngāti Kahungunu and Ngāpuhi collectively make up over 35 per cent of the Māori population. Significantly, the city's Māori population saw a marked increase at the turn of the twentieth century, growing by 24 per cent between 1996 and 2006. This growth is set to continue, presenting both challenges and opportunities.[96]

Rangitāne's generosity and commitment to building an inclusive community have been defining features of Palmerston North's history. This does not mean the iwi has resiled from defending its rights; indeed, over centuries of occupation the descendants of Whātonga have asserted their rights consistently and resolutely. What history does show is that the resolution of conflict was as much a part of the city's story as conflict itself. The arrival of Pākehā would have lasting consequences that compelled tangata whenua to search for new ways of engaging with settler-colonial society. Despite their efforts, they were dispossessed and marginalised.

Opposition to the creation of a Māori ward has indicated that the struggle is ongoing. Nevertheless, tangata whenua continue to work alongside like-minded people within the Palmerston North community. Following the 2019 local body elections, the Palmerston North City Council invited Rangitāne to nominate representatives with full voting rights onto the environmental sustainability committee, the community development committee and the economic development committee. In addition, a joint Rangitāne o Manawatū/Palmerston North City Council committee was established and tasked with the management of Te Motu o Poutoa (Anzac Park).[97] The significance of the kawenata (treaty/covenant) signed between the parties cannot be overstated. During the nineteenth century Rangitāne tried, without success, to retain ownership of the site. The joint management of Te Motu o Poutoa is, perhaps, a step towards the realisation of the hopes expressed by those ancestors who first welcomed Pākehā into the area.

The writers would like to thank Wiremu Te Awe Awe, Meihana Durie, Jon Proctor, Huataki Whareaitu, Mark Moses and Richard Bradley for points of clarification.

Te Tānenuiārangi Flag

The Rangitāne flag, emblazoned with the ancestral name 'Tanenuiarangi', was sometimes described by nineteenth-century Pākehā as the 'Rangitāne Union Jack' in recognition of its dominant presence at important Rangitāne events.[1] It was presented to Te Peeti Te Aweawe by Governor Grey in the late 1860s, acknowledging Rangitāne bravery during the campaigns of the New Zealand Wars. The flag became a treasured possession, raised for royal visits, tangi and other events until, by 1902, 'having braved the battle and the breeze' for too long, it had become too worn to hoist, and the government replaced it with a new one.[2] The original battle flag remained in the possession of Ereni Te Aweawe at Awapuni.[3] In the 1900s the flag was recorded as flying in The Square alongside the Union Jack and the Blue Ensign.[4] In recent years the Rangitāne flag has been raised between the New Zealand and Palmerston North flags on Waitangi Day, symbolising co-operation and ties between the Māori and Pākehā leaders of the city.

Rangitāne kaumātua Wiremu Te Awe Awe and his daughter Nuwyne Te Awe Awe Mohi are pictured holding Te Tāneniuārangi flag. In the background is a photograph of Te Rangimārie marae at Rangiotū. It was built to commemorate the peace between Ngāti Raukawa and Rangitāne following a meeting in 1858. *MS, 2 February 2015*

03 AN ENVIRONMENTAL HISTORY

MICHAEL ROCHE

Water and attempts at its control and mitigation are a major part of Palmerston North's environmental history. There is no shortage of images of flooded streets and dwellings. In May 1941 the home of nurseryman Richmond Harrison at 364 Albert Street (now the Village Inn) succumbed to floodwaters when a stopbank between Fitzroy and Jickell streets failed. Manawatū Heritage 2011P_IMCA-DigitalLibrary_005568

In 1947 grassland scientist Bruce Levy[1] addressed local Palmerston North horticulturalists on 'Lawns and Lawn Grasses', including seed mixtures and fertiliser applications.[2] Banal as this topic might seem, it is evocative of broader themes of 'design', 'order' and 'control' that frame the environmental history of the city.[3] Levy's early writing included articles on how to clear the bush and establish pasture; his later writings being codified in 'Grasslands of New Zealand'.[4]

Levy's talk on lawns, an arguably unremarkable part of New Zealand's urban landscape, is a reminder that the country was 50 per cent urban from 1911, and also that a mere 70 years earlier the Manawatū and much of the North Island had been covered in dense forest. In little more than a generation a town site had been selected and surveyed, the forest had been cleared, and a regional service centre and transport node created. As early as 1912 the residents were describing their town as 'a garden city'.[5] Levy also enjoyed an international reputation as a grassland scientist — the architect of New Zealand's grasslands revolution — a further reminder that the environmental history of the city is not entirely local in the making.

Here, we will look at the much-modified 'natural' environment, rather than the built environment,[6] concentrating on the rate and scale of transformation.[7] This involves examining critical moments in the vegetative de-cloaking and re-clothing of Palmerston North, the draining and preservation of various lagoons around which the city has expanded, consideration of the many gravel pits that accompanied the early growth of the city, some of which were repurposed, the engineering of the streams across which the city was sited (and which later posed a local flood hazard), and the establishment of Victoria Esplanade. These themes range across the city as well as through time.[8]

The city of Palmerston North lies across several alluvial terraces and now straddles the Manawatū River, although most of the city is on the western side. The river rises on the east of the Ruāhine Ranges and cuts through the Manawatū Gorge, which separates the Ruāhine from the Tararua ranges, before flowing over the alluvial plains to discharge into the Tasman Sea near Foxton.[9] The suburb of Summerhill sits on a remnant of an older uplifted marine terrace, and the old meander loops in Hokowhitu are on the Raukawa Terrace, which is of fluvial origin. The main portion of the city is situated on the older and higher Ashhurst Terrace surface, with Terrace End being part of the Milson Terrace.[10] The streams that previously bisected the plain have now disappeared, been channelled or even piped, and the series of old meander loops, former river beds, have in most cases been drained and subdivided for residential housing. Ashhurst Terrace, on which most of the town is situated, dates from around 18,000 to 24,000 years before the present. Milson Terrace at Terrace End is older, and dates from 27,000–60,000 years ago.[11]

Rangitāne occupied the area in the seventeenth century. The larger locality now occupied by the city was heavily forested, with some swampy areas and a number of lagoons, containing flax and replete with eels. Europeans first ventured up the Manawatū River in the early 1840s, and two decades later land sales and town development began. The rate and degree of environmental transformation stands out, even when compared to other New Zealand urban areas.

The site selected by John Tiffin Stewart for the town was Te Papaiōea, a clearing surrounded by heavy forest. The comparative ease of surveying and the relatively flat site would have drawn Stewart's eye. The fiftieth anniversary account of the city gives prominence to Charles Hartley — 'the trader-explorer who first set eyes on the clearing of Papa-i-oea' of about '600 acres' (242 hectares) in 1846.[12] In his centennial history of the city, George Petersen was doubtful of Hartley's claim, and favoured Stewart as the first European to see the clearing in 1859.[13]

The immediately surrounding areas were, however, neither unoccupied nor unmodified. Te Papaiōea would most likely have been produced by human-induced burning — its size would surely preclude it being the result of a 'natural' fire started by lightning strike.[14] Whatever the case, Hartley was guided to the clearing from Ruāhine pā in Hokowhitu where there were extensive gardens. The pā in the 1870s, Lindsay Buick noted, was 'famed for its gardens and peaches'.[15] Hokowhitu Lagoon in particular was a source of eels. There was an older unoccupied pā site — Te Motu o Poutoa — on the high terrace immediately across the river, and another, Kuripaka, where the Turitea Stream ran into the Manawatū River opposite Awapuni. An associated kāinga — Mokomoko — also unoccupied in the 1860s, lay near to the river, with the surviving remnant of the Karaka Grove[16] opposite the Esplanade.

Large areas were 'intensively tilled as kumara gardens' on the shingle terraces by the river.[17] Eels were harvested from Awapuni Lagoon, and there were abundant karaka trees nearby.[18]

Geographer L. L. Pownall has divided the urban centres of New Zealand into 10 types, based on their origins. One of them, termed 'colonial settlements', is a cluster of townships planned as a result of government policies. Pownall includes Palmerston North in this cluster, as it was laid out by the government in 1866.[19] Palmerston North was part (along

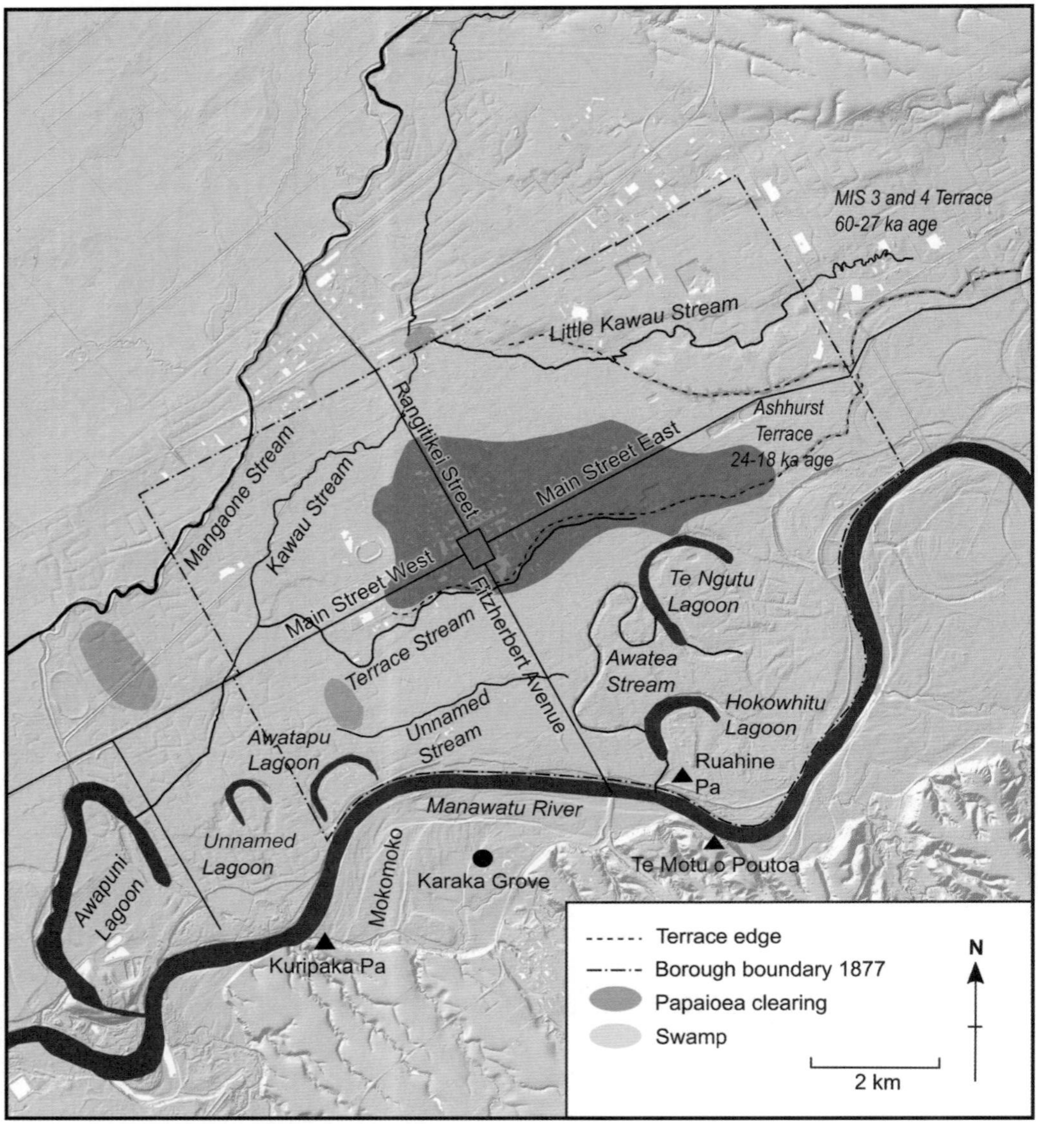

At the time J. T. Stewart surveyed the Palmerston North town site in 1866, the immediate area was neither unoccupied nor unmodified. Orienting his plan to the landscape, Stewart laid out the town in the Papaiōea clearing of some 600 acres (242 hectares). Covered in flax, fern, mānuka and other vegetation, it was a 'clearing' only when compared to the encircling heavy tōtara forest.
Redrawn with modifications from Matheson, 1986

with nearby Feilding and Masterton) of a later group of inland colonial towns located away from navigable rivers, which were established to facilitate 'the development of rural land from an urban base'.[20] These new inland towns were characteristically on sites free from forest cover.

The lay of the land nevertheless influenced the surveyors, notably in the orientation of the town. Stewart did not, for instance, orient the main street along the long axis of Te Papaiōea. Nor was The Square situated in the middle of the clearing. The long axis of the streets lies further to the north-east, because Te Papaiōea lay across a river terrace and was not completely flat. Rather than have streets run over these undulations, they typically follow them or cross at right angles, still obvious, for instance, at the Pitt Street/Main Street intersection.[21] The surrounding forests were a barrier but also a resource for the early residents, and the gravels below the surface were initially critical to the improvement of the urban road network. The waterways flowing along the eastern border and through the town both affected, and were affected by, urban development. In Palmerston North, as elsewhere, the price of selecting a flat, non-forested site was periodic flooding, poor and muddy roads, and mosquitoes.[22]

Unsurprisingly, sawmilling was one of the settler town's earliest industries. The first mill was established by Peter Bartholomew and Peter Manson in 1871. The second plant was that of John Richter, Jacob Nannestad and Frits Jenssen, erected in 1874. Other mills cutting on the edge of the town included those of William Summerhays in Hokowhitu (1877), Charles Nee at Brightwater in Terrace End (1877), and Gillies and Henderson at Kelvin Grove (1879).[23] Buick also noted a Māori-owned sawmill cutting from forest in the Hokowhitu Native Reserve in the early 1870s.[24] Nee succumbed to financial troubles, while Gillies and Henderson survived being burnt down in 1881, before dissolving the partnership in 1884.[25] The late 1870s saw the sawmilling frontier move northwards along the railway line.[26]

Bartholomew and Manson, and Richter, Nannestad and Jenssen were larger concerns, and operated for longer at several locations on the edges of the town, and later further afield as the bush was cleared.[27] Bartholomew and Manson situated their original mill on the western edge of the Te Papaiōea clearing (near the corner of Main Street and Cook Street), but in 1872 relocated to Terrace End (Fitzroy Street), cutting the durable tōtara for government railway contracts, and supplying timber for house construction in the town.[28] When this sawmill was destroyed by fire in 1875, it was not rebuilt. Manson began farming the cutover land, although the partnership established new mills at Halcombe and Kiwitea.[29]

In 1874 a partnership of Norwegians, Richter, Nannestad and Jenssen, began milling operations in Albert (then Scandia) Street (between Grey Street and what is now Broadway

Avenue), and extracted logs from the bush by means of an expanding system of tramways. Other sawmills were erected in Hokowhitu (Albert Street and Stewart Crescent), and further afield in heavy forest at Bunnythorpe. By 1879 they owned 600 acres (242 hectares) of forest land in Terrace End and what is now the suburb of Roslyn, westward from Vogel Street to North Street, and leased another 900 acres (364 hectares) in Milson.[30] The Hokowhitu mill was sold to the Palmerston North Sash, Door and Timber Co. in 1892, and operated thereafter as a sash and door factory, drawing timber supplies from the Pohangina Valley and Hawke's Bay.[31] By 1890 the town site was largely cleared of forest.

The Manawatū River rises to the east of the Ruāhine Ranges and flows through the Manawatū Gorge into the Tasman Sea near Foxton.[32] Between the 1860s and the 1880s the river was effectively a town boundary, the river being unsuited to navigation other than by canoe, not bridged at Fitzherbert until 1877, and prone to flood.[33] Significant early floods occurred in 1880, 1897 and 1902.

Of immediate concern to the landowners and council was riverbank erosion at Fitzroy Bend, at Hokowhitu and along parts of the Esplanade and beyond. In 1888, Te Tiera Te Panau had lost 30 acres (12 hectares) from the 101-acre (41-hectare) Section 1 of the Hokowhitu Native Reserve.[34] The initial response by some riverside landowners was exemplified by George Slack at Awapuni, who around 1899–1900 created a structure of piles driven deep into the river bed and laced together with willows where his riverbanks had 'crumbled like sugar'.[35]

The council also constructed groynes at several points along the riverbank; one still survives by the Fitzherbert Bridge.[36] Their concern, shared by residents of Hokowhitu, was that floodwaters breaching the riverbank at Fitzroy Bend would cut a new channel through to the old meander loops of Te Ngutu Lagoon and continue on to Hokowhitu Lagoon before returning to the main river channel. In 1907 borough engineer Samuel Jickell recommended constructing up to 10 groynes south of the Fitzherbert Bridge to protect the Esplanade's riverbanks.[37] In 1908 the government engineer recommended four groynes to protect the town at Brightwater Terrace, at Fitzroy Street, at the old rifle range adjacent to Hokowhitu Lagoon, and south of the bridge.[38] Earlier, the *Manawatu Evening Standard* presciently expressed the opinion that such efforts only minimised damage, and could not prevent it.[39]

An attempt in 1910 to form a river board, which would have enabled a more co-ordinated approach, foundered.[40] Finally established by the 1920s, the board's efforts were immediately frustrated by injunctions to prevent it cutting a new overflow channel.[41] Not until the Manawatu Catchment Board was established in 1943, under the 1941 Soil Conservation and Rivers Control Act, was regionally co-ordinated action possible. A major flood of the Manawatū River in 1953, which inundated parts of the city and

Timber groynes on the Manawatū River, c.1909–10. These were built in a vain attempt to prevent erosion at Fitzroy Bend as the river moved south-westward.
Manawatū Heritage 2014N_St30_008742

the surrounding districts, further galvanised efforts, and resulted in a major regional stopbanking and river-engineering effort, featuring a set of sluice gates and a spill-way at Ōpiki, onto which up-stream water can be diverted during large floods: the Lower Manawatu Scheme.[42] As a consequence of these engineering works, the city was not affected by the floods of 2004.[43]

In recent times the river has attracted attention for different reasons. In 2009 it made headlines as one of the 300 most-polluted rivers in the world on the basis of dissolved oxygen fluctuations.[44] A Manawatū River leaders' forum — comprising local government and agricultural, environmental, iwi and industry groups — signed an accord in 2010 pledging to clean up the river.[45] The government contributed $5.2 million in 2012 for upgrading sewage treatment, developing land-based effluent treatment and the restoration of indigenous vegetation.[46]

Symbolic of a new relationship between the city and the river was a set of steps opened in 2011 by the Fitzherbert

Over the course of several decades the Kawau Stream was straightened and stopbanked in order to reduce the risk of flooding. These initial efforts were not particularly effective until the mid-twentieth century. By the 1970s, it was increasingly referred to as the 'Kawau Drain', and was regularly polluted by industrial discharges as well as being congested by rubbish. From Matheson, 2003

Bridge, providing safe public access to the river and named Okatia after the taniwha who, Rangitāne say, guards the river.[47] Another stairway, Te Arapiki a Tāne — the Stairway of Tāne — was created in 2018 on the slope formed from major modifications to the cliff near Anzac Park as part of the Vaucluse Heights subdivision, and is a segment of the riverside walkway.[48] With investment in the development of river walkways and parklands, the city planner by 2018 could observe 'people are seeing the river less as a barrier and threat and more as their urban backyard' and playground.[49] This is reinforced by the cycleway and pedestrian bridge, He Ara Kotahi, reaching across the river at Dittmer Drive and opened in 2019, which connects with pathways on the Massey side of the river stretching to Linton.[50]

Localised problems for residents and council were posed by the streams that flowed through the forest around Te Papaiōea. The expanding town grew around their banks, and flooding was a major problem until the 1940s. In the 1880s Kawau Stream flowed sinuously across the forested landscape and into Awatapu Lagoon. Maps from the 1900s reveal how the stream had been subsequently engineered, being straightened and becoming more channel-like, and re-routed to take stormwater and prevent local flooding as the town expanded around it. These engineering works were initially undertaken by the borough, then by the drainage board, and later became the responsibility of a catchment board.[51] The Mangaone and the Kawau streams[52] have their sources beyond the city boundaries, and responsibility for their management was consequentially divided.

As early as 1881 the town clerk was corresponding with the Railways Department's district engineer over the clearing of Kawau Stream.[53] By 1885 the borough council was occupied in removing willows from the banks of the stream in the Botanical Road and Boundary Road (Tremaine Avenue) area, enabling it to more easily discharge into Awapuni Lagoon and thence into the Manawatū River.[54] Clearing and deepening of the lagoon from the river to Tremaine Avenue was contemplated in order to further reduce flood problems and help drain the land.

In May 1885, former mayor George Snelson threatened legal action if the council continued work on the culvert across Rangitikei Street, which, he claimed, would bring floodwater from Mangaone Stream onto his land.[55] Snelson's real concern, however, was Kawau Stream: he had spent £10 cleaning it where it ran through his own property. But until it was 'cleared of debris' from 'Foxton road [Pioneer Highway] up to the Rangitikei

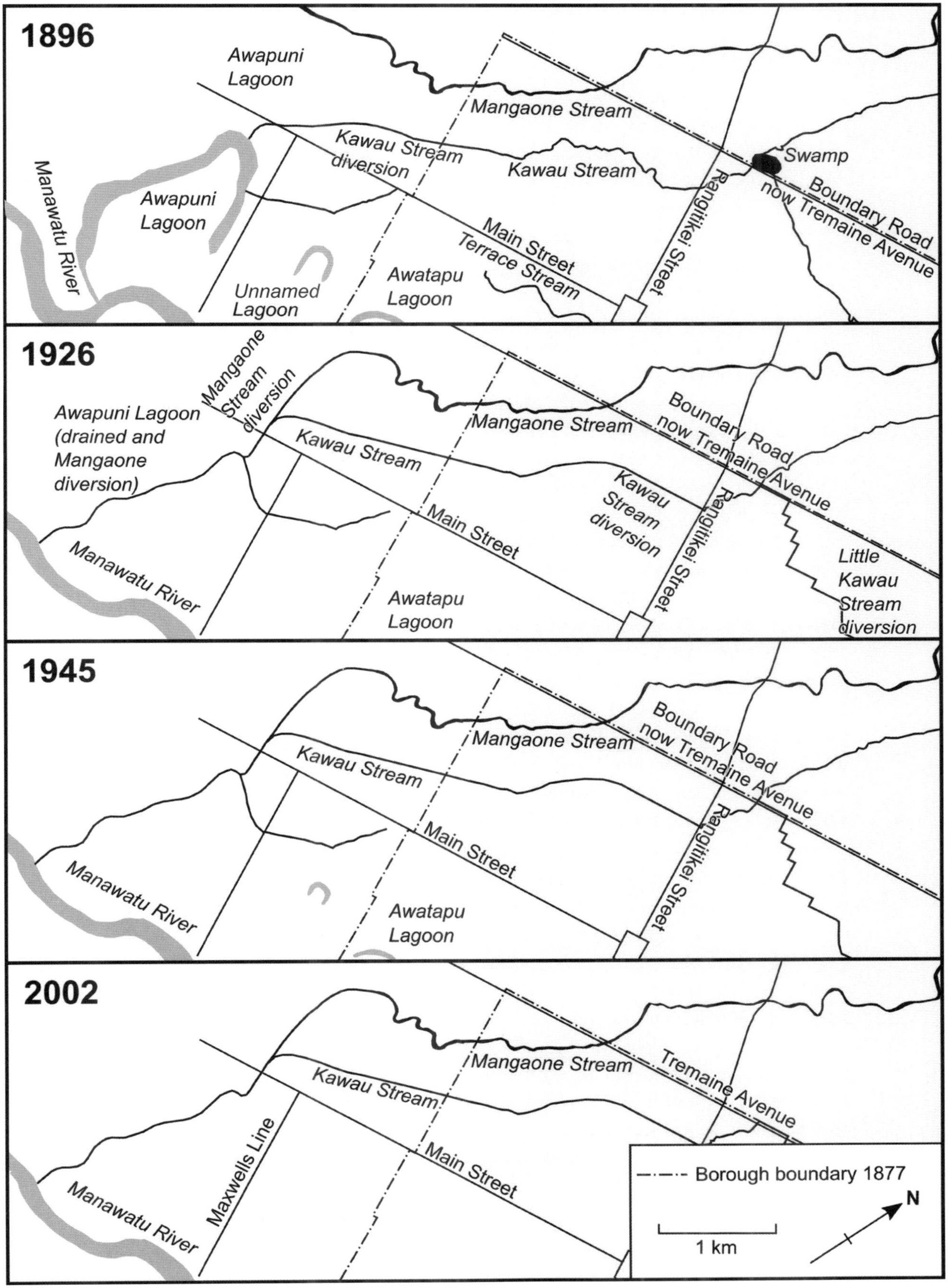

1896
Awapuni Lagoon
Mangaone Stream
Kawau Stream diversion
Kawau Stream
Swamp
Manawatu River
Awapuni Lagoon
Rangitikei Street
Boundary Road now Tremaine Avenue
Main Street
Terrace Stream
Unnamed Lagoon
Awatapu Lagoon
1926
Mangaone Stream diversion
Awapuni Lagoon (drained and Mangaone diversion)
Mangaone Stream
Boundary Road now Tremaine Avenue
Kawau Stream
Kawau Stream diversion
Main Street
Rangitikei Street
Little Kawau Stream diversion
Manawatu River
Awatapu Lagoon
1945
Mangaone Stream
Boundary Road now Tremaine Avenue
Kawau Stream
Main Street
Rangitikei Street
Manawatu River
Awatapu Lagoon
2002
Mangaone Stream
Tremaine Avenue
Kawau Stream
Maxwells Line
Main Street
Manawatu River
Borough boundary 1877
1 km
N

Line no outlet exists for water in that channel. And further, the Kawau creek[56] in itself has no real outlet excepting that made by the Railway Works Department through Jamieson and Week's section to the Awapuni lagoon', he wrote.[57] Councillors insisted that the Kawau was the proper outlet for 'overflow from that locality', while the mayor observed that the water actually came from a district 'the body of which Mr Snelson is chairman'.[58]

The Kawau returned to the council table in 1886 when Joseph Milverton sought compensation of £80 for grass seed and potatoes lost in flooding by the Kawau and Mangaone streams.[59] Milverton threatened to sue the council. Snelson, again a borough councillor, was now inclined to see the stream flooding Milverton's land as 'an act of providence'.[60] At the following meeting a report from a committee of councillors was received. This proposed clearing Kawau Stream from Featherston Street to Tremaine Avenue, raising stopbanks along the stream by Tremaine Avenue, increasing the size of the culvert under Rangitikei Street to 12 inches (30 centimetres), and improving the drainage of low-lying land adjacent to where the stream crossed Tremaine Avenue by cutting a drain to the Kawau, as well as placing a floodgate on Mangaone Stream. Its limited success saw Milverton take the council to court in 1888, claiming £500 damages.[61]

The Kawau was being transformed from stream to stormwater drain. In 1906 the borough council set aside £500 for 'stream improvement' on the section of the Kawau north of Rangitikei Street, and £1200 on that between Rangitikei Street and Kairanga Road.[62] This included straightening, widening and deepening the channel. Three days of rain in August 1909 still resulted in localised flooding. The Kawau overflowed into Featherston Street near Ruahine Street and filled a disused gravel pit, with lesser flooding in Roy Street, North Street and Florence Avenue.[63] Over the next decades a system of stopbanks and floodgates was installed. In 1905 borough engineer Samuel Jickell reported on the Kawau from the bridge at Tremaine Avenue to the junction with the Mangaone at Awapuni, noting that some landowners had lowered stopbanks to allow stock access to the stream, while at other places tall grass clogged the channel.[64]

In 1927 heavy rain caused the sewerage connections of houses in Argyle Avenue and Beresford Street to overflow. In a vibrant debate Councillor Fitzherbert attributed this to the Kawau Stream, although others dissented.[65] Councillor William Milverton proposed diverting the stream to prevent flooding in the Takarō area. This idea was referred to the works committee, although the subsequent report appending that of the drainage board engineer and the district engineer of the Public Works Department was held over for the incoming borough council to consider.[66]

This joint report proposed a larger £5000 flood-protection scheme involving the Manawatū River and Mangaone and Kawau streams. When the Manawatū flooded above Bunnythorpe, some of the water ended up in the Mangaone, which was unable to carry the additional volume (calculated at 3200 cu ft/sec, or 90.6 cu m/sec), particularly in the reach between Setters Line and Pioneer Highway. Floodwaters overflowing from the east bank of the Mangaone tended to end up in Kawau Stream, particularly around Rangitikei Line. Two proposals were put forward for the Kawau. The more expensive option involved cutting a 64-chain (1280-metre) channel through private property alongside Tremaine Avenue from North Street to about Wood Street. The less expensive alternative was connecting the Kawau with the Mangaone where the streams were close together at Rangitikei Line, but this would have to wait until the Mangaone work was completed.

In 1935, after flooding at Takarō Park and Matipo Street, the Takaro Progressive Association approached the council over the state of the floodgates and stopbanks along Kawau Stream, asking for the cattle-crossing to be removed and the banks raised.[67] The association persisted. In 1939, after further flooding, they again drew attention to 'defects in the banking of the Kawau Drain'.[68] The city engineer's report claimed that the stream would carry city floodwater as long as the Mangaone did not overspill its banks and flow into the Kawau. The main problem, however, related back to the earlier protection efforts, for:

> the stop banks are placed immediately on the edge of the drain, when the natural banks become saturated, the superimposed weight of the banks causes the former to slide . . . It was obviously a mistake to construct the banks in that position; had they been built say half a chain [10 metres] clear of the edge of the drain greater flood capacity would also have been provided.[69]

Progress now depended on co-operation between the Palmerston North City Council, which had responsibility for the Kawau only within its limits, Kairanga County Council and the Manawatu Drainage Board. Further joint engineering reports were prepared, which still envisaged the Kawau being re-channelled and diverted into the Mangaone.[70] During the Second World War the project was left in abeyance. Complaints continued after flooding in Takarō in July 1943. By late 1944, Takarō residents had had enough, and 111 residents petitioned the council for action to prevent the constant flooding of the two streams.[71] Only when a larger Mangaone flood-control scheme was completed around 1945 was flooding of Kawau Stream brought largely under 'control'.

In 1972 the Kawau drain attracted attention from a new quarter, when Manawatu Ecology Action members organised a clean-up of 800 metres of the stream on both sides of Rangitikei Street, and removed three large loads of rubbish, including oil drums and a car body.[72] Later that same year residents in the Highbury Avenue, Brentwood Avenue, Botanical Road and Brighton Crescent area protested at the foul-smelling and brightly coloured Kawau Steam.[73] The Manawatu Catchment Board now pursued polluters, and the city council insisted, for instance, that New Zealand Railways prevent further discharges of diesel into the stream.[74]

Since the 1990s, the condition of the stream has improved, partly because of the manner in which it has been incorporated into the city walkway system, but in 2007 there were

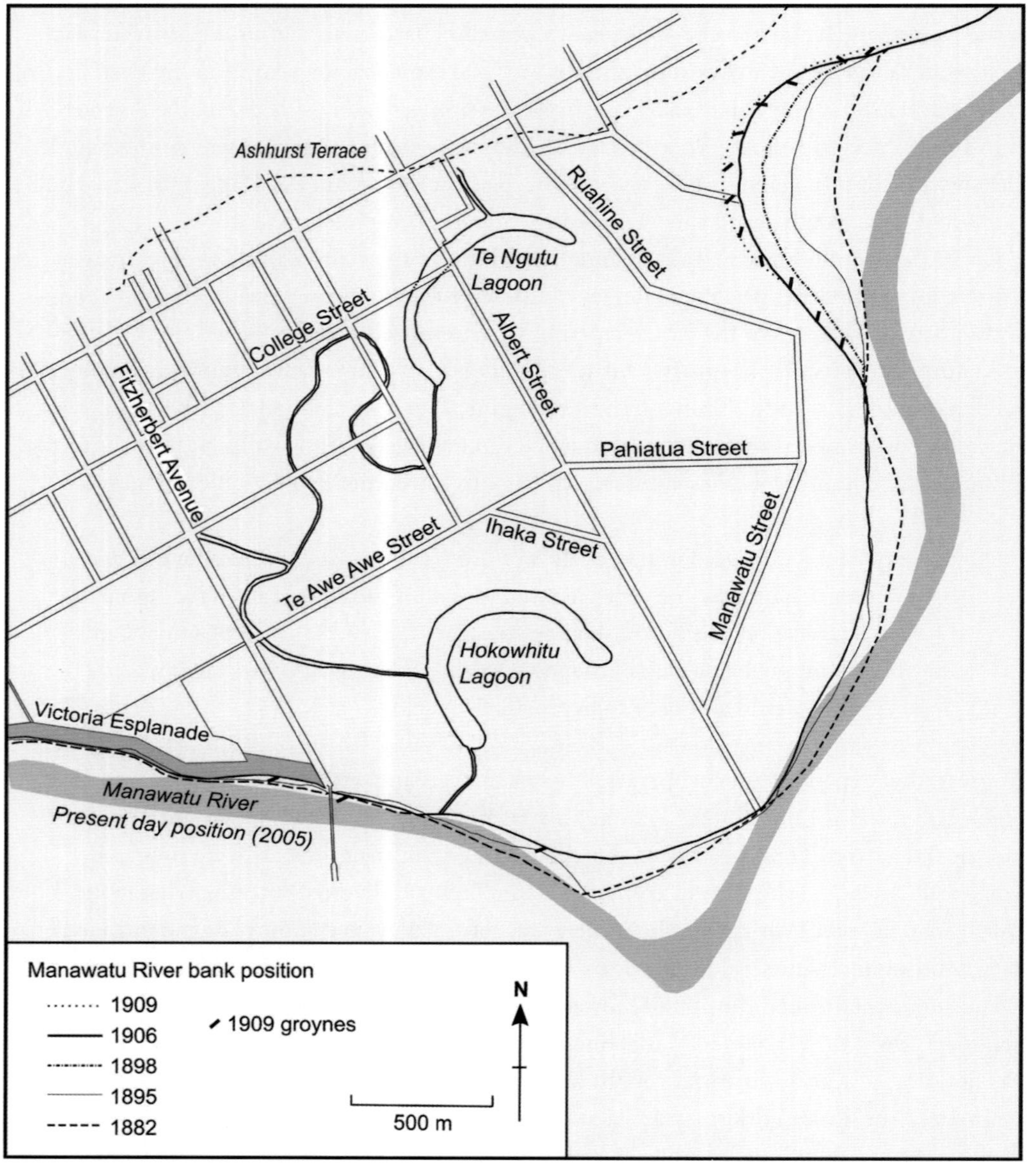

The Hokowhitu Lagoon and riverbank erosion. The suburb of Hokowhitu contained a number of old meander loops, former beds of the Manawatū River. These lagoons became a source of anxiety for the borough as a potential new channel for the river in the event of large floods, and because they were part of the stormwater system. They were also an obstacle to the development of the suburb. Today only Hokowhitu Lagoon remains, although the former channels are still evident, for instance along Awatea Crescent. Based on Upper Hokowhitu Lagoon Drainage, Palmerston North City Council C/24; Correspondence Reserves — Hokowhitu Lagoon, PNCC 1/5/3 : 17: H/3, IMCA four spills of contaminant into the stream, killing fish and eels.[75] Engineering work continued over 2006–09, lining the stream's banks, and making them more channel-like. Stopbanking from Roy Street to Heretaunga Street was intended to ensure the stream had the capacity to handle the water levels during heavy rainfall without overflowing onto private property.[76]

The gravels underneath the town site were sought-after as a source of roading material and railway ballast. From 1873, the town gradually became pockmarked by nearly two dozen gravel pits, the earlier ones being council-operated and the later ones private operations.[77] The first pits were located centrally, but by the 1890s the larger ones were situated in Terrace End. The main publicly operated pits and some of their characteristics are summarised in the table overleaf.

The original Rangitikei Street pit was used for metalling Rangitikei Street; that on Main Street West for railway ballast for the Palmerston North-to-Foxton line; that on Terrace Street (Ruahine Street) for surfacing Main Street; while the large New Zealand Railways pit at Terrace End supplied ballast for the Palmerston North-to-Feilding line, also selling small quantities

In July 1926 after 48 hours of steady rain, the largest flood for 20 years inundated many parts of the borough. The residents of Chelwood Street were among those flooded out, and nearby Takarō Park was also under muddy water. From the 1930s the Takaro Progressive Association had made repeated representations to the council about flooding and stormwater prior to the completion of flood-protection works as part of a larger Mangaone Stream flood-protection scheme finished after the Second World War. Photograph: G. F. Framjee, Manawatū Heritage 2011P_FI77_004561

GRAVEL PITS OF PALMERSTON NORTH

LOCATION	IN USE	OWNERS	KEY EVENTS
Rangitikei Street	1873–79	Wellington Provincial Government transferred to Borough Council	1879 waterlogged pit gradually filled by Borough Council to 1909. Becomes part of Palmerston North Boys' High School site in 1901
Main Street West	1875–79	Borough Council?	Waterlogged in 1879 — Railways Department fill pit when railyards moved to Main Street in 1901
Terrace Street [Ruahine Street]	Early 1870s to 1879	Wellington Provincial Government transferred to Borough Council	
Main Street East	1878–1940s	Manawatu County Council to Railways Department 1888	Transferred to City Council in 1939
Grey Street	1878–87	Borough Council	Open pit until 1927, thereafter successively filled in and subdivided; completed by 1964
Terrace Street [Ruahine Street]	1887–1900	Borough Council	Transferred to Wanganui Education Board
Scandia Street [Albert Street]	1890–1930	Borough Council	Subsequently site of council river-metal crushing plant. Palmerston North City Council depot and storage area
Scandia Street	1900–05	Borough Council?	Partly filled and transferred to Wanganui Education Board

Based on Garry O'Neill, *Terrace End: The Story of Palmerston North's First Suburb* (Palmerston North: self-published, 2009), 2.

to Kairanga County. The Grey Street pit provided material for the adjacent Grey Street and Broad Street (now Broadway Avenue). The local use of the shingle is unsurprising, but the wider regional redistribution of this material as far as Foxton and Feilding is more unexpected. It makes a point that the town's physical as well as economic footprint reached beyond the boundaries of the borough and later the city.

The gravel pits characteristically remained for longer than their working lives as features of the Palmerston North landscape — indeed, as blots on the landscape in the opinions of some. One disgruntled citizen complained to the *Manawatu Evening Standard* in 1917 that 'we have just seven pits all within a stone's throw of each other. There is no sane resident in this locality that is not filled with righteous indignation and holy wrath that this unsightly thing is permitted in a residential situation such as this.'[78] The writer then complained about the impact on property values, and the pits as eyesores and dumping grounds.

With the advent of motor vehicles, shingle could be economically transported further afield. After the 1940s, shingle for borough needs was sourced from beyond the town. But the disused pits remained waterlogged features that were both unsightly and hazardous, and the question of their future beautification and alternative use became a matter of interest to community groups and the council.

Today several of the old pits have long been filled in and built on. Others have been reused: for instance, the Terrace End Bowling Club is on the private Summerhays Street pit. Some are still recognisable — the Matariki Rudolf Steiner School on Ruahine Street, for instance, nestling in the old Terrace Street pit.[79] The Main Street pits in Terrace End were the largest of the gravel pits in the city. When worked out, they were too big to be easily filled in, and so were instead developed as a recreation ground, initially known as Fitzroy Park after the adjacent street. The original steep sides and pit-like features remain even though it has been landscaped to form today's Memorial Park.

The 21-acre (8-hectare) Main Street gravel pit, long labelled an eyesore, was targeted by the Terrace End Progressive Association in 1935, when it pressed for its acquisition by the council and its 'beautification' through a programme of tree-planting. Initially the council declined on the grounds of New Zealand Railways' unrealistic purchase conditions. Undeterred, the association maintained the pressure, arguing that the pit 'offered splendid possibilities for transformation and beautification'.[80] In his capacity as president of the association, J. A. (Jimmy) Nash, former mayor and MP, was emphatic that the pit 'certainly needed planting to hide the eyesore it created'.[81]

Initial work began with the planting of screens around the perimeter of the pit. In 1937 a council delegation to Wellington, assisted by local MP and borough councillor Joseph Hodgens, secured acceptable purchase terms.[82] A development plan had already been drawn up by the curator of reserves, Peter Black, and for 12 months over 1937 and 1938 the council had 35 men working on the project via a contract with the Employment Board. Broom and gorse were cut out, soil and ash removed from the pit, and the bottom

The gravel pits of Roslyn in 1965: Freyberg High School is on the mid-right-hand side of this aerial photograph, which is dominated by the quarry that was eventually redeveloped as Skoglund Park. The search for gravel, and to a lesser extent sources of clay, for roading and brick-making was an important activity in the late nineteenth and early twentieth centuries. Too large to be filled in, some of the bigger pits were redeveloped as sports and recreation grounds. Manawatū Heritage 2012P_Pn17_006549

flattened.[83] The pit walls were given a 'pleasing slope or batter', trees were planted around the rim and on the floor of the pit. Five acres (2 hectares) of grass were planted, with paths winding through the area. A concrete retaining wall was built, with an open-air swimming pool under construction. A lake at the Fitzroy Street end was completed.[84] Future plans included planting creepers on the pit walls.

The newest park in the city was opened as Fitzroy Park on Arbor Day in 1938. The ceremony was led by Mayor Augustus (Gus) Mansford, with children from Terrace End and Hokowhitu schools and members of the public in attendance. The Terrace End Progressive Association chair, Mr E. Anderson, drew a comparison with the Esplanade, noting that he had been present at its opening in 1897, and stating that he saw no reason why Fitzroy Park should not 'reach the same stage of beautification'.[85]

Planned development of the remaining 9-acre (3.6-hectare) northern portion of the pit as a sports stadium was delayed during the Second World War by a lack of finance.[86] By 1951 the grounds committee had developed a plan for the construction of a sound shell and the formation of a grass oval and cycling track. The plan included new memorial gates as well as a shrine of remembrance. The entire project was costed at the considerable sum of £29,000 (later raised to £34,200 with a banked cycling track).[87] Local fundraising began for the memorial.[88]

In early 1952 the city council let a detailed contract for the erection of a war memorial. A tender of £1476 was accepted from Terrazzo Trading Limited in Petone.[89] The contract called for concrete steps supporting an inscribed column, all faced with terrazzo, a composite material comprised of marble and other chips set in concrete.

The memorial, now elevated to a 'shrine', was unveiled on Sunday, 19 October 1952. Rain marred the ceremony, which was nevertheless attended by 3000, waiting in 'proper deference'.[90] Major General Sir Howard Kippenberger unveiled the obelisk, observing that the men had died for a just cause, and that 'it was fitting and right that in the city which was their focal centre this should be remembered'.[91] Local MP Blair Tennent read the lesson, Rev. Keith Elliott VC, a former assistant curate at All Saints' Church, led the singing of a hymn.

The *Manawatu Evening Standard* reporter emotively captured the scene: 'The monument was unveiled, its wet dun colour a striking contrast to the rain washed white Maltese cross set in vivid green grass and the base impressive in its simplicity, the memorial was more symbolic against the drabness of the day.'[92]

A decade on, the 'shrine' was unexpectedly showing signs of deterioration. Its builders had effected repairs on three occasions, and in 1963 the superintendent of reserves even advised the council to consider its removal and replacement.[93] In 1968, Brian Elwood (later city councillor and mayor) and the Public Relations Organisation drew the council's attention to the memorial. The marble plates covering the obelisk had continued to sheer off, and he described the memorial and its surroundings as 'shabby, unkempt, in bad condition and totally without dignity'.[94]

After inspection by the director of reserves and Councillor Julia Wallace, its removal was recommended.[95] However, after protests from the Public Relations Organisation, the council was persuaded to make a further round of repairs.[96] The director of reserves was, however, concerned that Terrazzo Limited's plans amounted effectively to rebuilding the monument, for which insufficient money was available in that financial year.[97] Work stalled — captured by the local *Tribune* newspaper under the poignant headline of 'the war memorial nobody remembers'.[98]

The memorial was finally dismantled in 1983. It had never become a public sacred space, and the main Anzac Day services continued to be held at the Cenotaph in The Square. A second round of memorialisation occurred in 2011 when a Unions Manawatu monument was located at the Fitzroy Street entrance to the park dedicated to those who had died in the workplace.[99]

In the early twentieth century, the town expanded across several cut-off meander loops, previous channels of the Manawatū River. These were Te Ngutu Lagoon, Hokowhitu Lagoon, Awatapu Lagoon and Awapuni Lagoon, along with another at the corner of College Street and Kent Terrace.[100] The outlet to Hokowhitu Lagoon had been straightened by Māori as a place for setting eel traps.[101] Later, Europeans saw the lagoon as something of an untouched wilderness, apprehending neither its earlier importance as a food basket nor the modifications that had taken place.[102] In the twentieth century some lagoons served as game reserves, part of the stormwater system, or as recreation reserves, while others were filled or drained and subdivided for housing.

Hokowhitu Lagoon was gazetted in 1902 as a general game reserve, and English mallard ducks and swans were introduced almost immediately by the Wellington Acclimatisation Society. However, flooding was soon of greater concern.[103]

In 1897 a significant flood covered large areas of lower Ruahine and Albert (Scandia) streets and Victoria Avenue (Alexandra Street). A pattern of the river overflowing at Fitzroy Bend and

Unveiling the war memorial at Memorial Park in 1952. In 1951 Fitzroy Park was designated the city's Second World War memorial park. Planning began for a suitable memorial, and the subsequent obelisk was unveiled by Major General Sir Howard Kippenberger in October 1952. From the first, the memorial weathered badly and required ongoing repairs. The obelisk, intended as the centrepiece of a sacred space, was dismantled in 1983. Manawatū Heritage 2008P_Mo17a_WHF_1972

exiting via the lagoons near the bridge was repeated in the larger flood of 1902.[104] Drainage was the immediate solution: in 1904 Samuel Jickell, newly arrived as borough engineer, initially took the view that this could be achieved by controlled use of the old lagoons to channel water into Hokowhitu Lagoon and thence back into the Manawatū River.[105]

After further flooding in 1907, there was mounting public concern that the riverbank erosion at Fitzroy Bend would divert the river back along the course of the former channels occupied by the old lagoons before flowing back into the river by the Esplanade.[106] A major council effort now went into constructing stopbanks and groynes at Fitzroy Bend, and later into cutting a new channel to realign the river. In the flood of 1916, Hokowhitu Lagoon was completely filled up with water, and parts of the adjacent golf course were inundated.[107]

After the First World War, various engineering solutions for improving drainage in the area were proposed. These included cutting an outlet from the end of Hokowhitu Lagoon to connect with another drain to the river, which was only 3 chains (60 metres) away.[108] Complications arose with a neighbouring landowner objecting to the council digging a drain through his property, claiming that another landowner, Jack Strang — a later owner of today's Caccia Birch House, which he called Woodhey — had refused to allow the council to divert stormwater into Hokowhitu Lagoon, and that ponding stagnant waters posed a public health hazard.[109]

A new engineering plan was put forward in 1920, whereby the outlet from Hokowhitu Lagoon would be enlarged and in part piped to avoid private property.[110] But after a survey of all of the lagoon gradients, borough engineer John Hughes concluded in 1923 that it was impractical to drain them because of the uneven shape of their bottoms, the depth and cost of pipe drains, the added difficulties of having to work around private properties, and the rise in the bed of the watercourse from Jickell Street.[111] In Hughes's opinion, the only solution was to gradually fill the lagoons with spoil. Hokowhitu ratepayers in Ruahine and Scandia streets meantime pressed the council for action over water flowing into the nearby Te Ngutu Lagoon.

By December Hughes had devised a different but more expensive plan, which involved the use of a gravitation sewer to be constructed from the river to the depression on Collingwood Street, along with a deepened and enlarged sewer from Collingwood Street to Victoria Avenue into which water would be pumped from the main lagoon.[112] Hughes sounded a note of caution, however, in remarking that 'this lagoon is a natural storage reservoir for the storm water draining the locality, [so] it may from time to time be called into use'.[113] Renewed public health concerns now prompted the council's health committee to recommend investigation of draining Te Ngutu Lagoon via a pipeline into Hokowhitu Lagoon.[114] This latter work was completed by August of 1925.[115]

Real stormwater issues remained for Hokowhitu Lagoon after the Second World War, but to these were added new efforts to beautify the lagoon and increase its amenity value, each of which attracted a good deal of not always supportive public attention. The latter began in 1940 when Hokowhitu Lagoon was renamed Centennial Lagoon (although it never completely ousted the name Hokowhitu Lagoon), after the new Centennial Drive was constructed as part of the hundredth-anniversary celebration of the signing of the Treaty of Waitangi.

In 1946 the council set aside £800 for what was termed 'development' work. This fundamentally changed the lagoon, which was deepened by dredging, eventually to an average depth of 6 feet (1.8 metres), and given a defined shoreline. Approximately 70 old willow stumps were removed.[116] Old kahikatea and tōtara stumps protruding from the lagoon were also slated for removal. A weir was to be installed at the lagoon outlet in order to control the water level and to protect against the risk of flooding. The intention was to use artesian water to raise the water level in the lagoon back to its 1908 level. The council's development work did not go unremarked. The adjacent Manawatu Golf Club expressed concern that raising the lagoon level might lead to flooding of portions of the course.[117] Stormwater discharge and lagoon water levels remained, however, a management issue.

A second long-term management issue related to the appearance and use of the lagoon. Weed growth posed problems for the use of the lagoon for boating from the mid-1950s. Although the council had obtained an import permit to purchase an American weed-cutting machine, the preferred course of action was to spray.[118] In 1961 there were two applications of Penite 8, a sodium arsenite herbicide imported from the United States. Centennial Drive was closed, and, although residents were assured that vegetation and birdlife would not be affected, pets were not to drink from the lagoon, nor were children to play in the area, and under no circumstance was lagoon water to be used for household purposes.[119] Some 400 imperial gallons (1818 litres) of herbicide were sprayed onto the lagoon.[120] Herbicides were the modern treatments of the day, and their use was a sign that the city was being progressive and up-to-date in embracing new technologies over old (weed-cutting equipment).[121]

The superintendent of reserves explained that 'the city had no other natural waterways and the lagoon would be available for a variety of uses'.[122] The uses suggested were canoeing, water carnivals and aquatic sports. Removing the weed would improve the appearance of the lagoon and help its development as a 'unique area of the city'.[123] In December 1962 additional weed-killer was siphoned into the lagoon, residents being reassured that it would not harm the introduced fish.[124] However, by 1964 it was recognised that spraying was only effective when lagoon water was warmest during the summer months.[125]

By 1969 residents at the north-eastern end of the lagoon were complaining that 'Centennial Lake' was 'in a deplorable condition'.[126] Montgomery Terrace residents backing onto the lagoon requested the council remove the raupō, then clean and deepen the lagoon, as well as manage the water level to prevent stormwater discharge into the lagoon from damaging their plantings and banks. The deputy city engineer offered a blunt assessment: 'a static lake level could only be ensured by constructing a large capacity outlet to the river

Construction of Centennial Drive alongside Hokowhitu Lagoon. In 1940 the development of the lagoon area was taken up by the city council as an official 1840–1940 anniversary project in celebration of the hundredth anniversary of the signing of the Treaty of Waitangi. A new road, Centennial Drive, was created alongside the lagoon, linking Albert Street and Fitzherbert Avenue. The lagoon became known as Centennial Lagoon, or sometimes Centennial Lake, although these names never prevailed. Redevelopment work in the lagoon area gathered momentum only after 1946. The area remained, however, in a naturalistic state until the 1970s, when a Rotary Club development project galvanised public opinion against the 'Disneyland' development of the lagoon, but by 2000 elements reminiscent of 1970s development projects had come to dominate the landscape. Photograph: K. H. Shea 1941, Manawatū Heritage 2014N_Ro35_007890 and a pumping station which would function when the outlet was backed up'.[127] He also reminded the town clerk that the lagoon west of the Chalet was largely the result of human efforts, and that to deepen the portion to the north-east would require a considerable amount of dredging and other earthworks.[128]

The council was nevertheless responsive to the residents' request, and in 1970 plans were developed to deepen the remainder of the lagoon to 5–6 feet (1.5–1.8 metres) and replace the 'open drain' running 300 feet (90 metres) from the end of the lagoon to the Manawatū River with a pipeline. A new weir would regulate the water level.[129] Dredging began in May 1970.[130] However, new problems arose during the drought of 1972, with lagoon levels dropping to expose dead vegetation and foul-smelling mud at the north-eastern end.[131] This raised protests from the Canoe Club and neighbouring Teachers' Training College.

New algae problems emerged by the 1980s with *Spirogyra* and *Oedogonium* flourishing in the summer months, triggered by nutrients in the water from duck droppings. Some councillors pressed for the algae to be chemically treated. Advice from the council chemist was that copper sulphate, the usual treatment, would be toxic to the fish population in the lagoon, and that it was preferable to scoop the algae up or just wait for it to die back as nutrient levels in the water declined.[132] One possibility previously set aside was to install a new bore at the Albert Street end to raise the water level.[133]

Natural events have continued to make the management of the water level challenging. Weeks after a 6.2-magnitude earthquake on 20 January 2014, centred on Eketāhuna, the water level in the lagoon began to fall, causing problems for the national canoe polo championships. By the end of May, water was leaking out at a rate of 50,000 litres per day. Further to this, the inflow from the artesian bore had also dropped and was not expected to return to pre-earthquake levels.[134] By October 2014, the city council was committed to topping up water levels in the lagoon.[135] Regional council advice was to wait and see in case the cracks opened by the quake in the bottom of the lagoon sealed themselves.[136] In December 2014 a non-toxic dye, which nevertheless turned the water blue, was introduced into the lagoon to help locate the leaks, but did not produce any clear-cut results.[137]

In the 1970s various schemes for enhancing the amenity value of Hokowhitu Lagoon had emerged, including constructing a jetty and providing seating.[138] In 1975 Terrace End Rotary Club developed a community service project centred on the lagoon.[139] The plan involved lining the banks with timber piles, providing access to an existing island in the lagoon, expanding the rowing, sailing and model-boat opportunities, creating carparks, forming a new island, adding walking paths and landscaping the site.[140]

Nearby Clifton Terrace resident Rosemary Baragwanath and four others immediately wrote to the council, concerned about the 'Disneyland treatment of the Centennial lagoon'.[141] Along with Glenys Robertson, Helen Duder and Prue Anderson, Rosemary Baragwanath circulated a petition to halt the proposed development at the lagoon, garnering 493 signatures. Innovatively, the council decided on a postal survey of 200

Esplanade bushwalk, 1910. The Esplanade attracted interest as a subject for postcards during the postcard boom of the 1900s and 1910s. Features such as the band rotunda, the pergola or the formal gardens were selected; others favoured the tree-lined vista, but for many professional photographers it was the remnant bush area that attracted their attention. From 1916 into the early 1920s, curator of reserves Peter Black planted the adjoining area in indigenous trees. Private collection

randomly selected households to gauge public opinion.[142] Public meetings organised by the council attracted considerable numbers, and generated heated criticism of the lagoon development proposals. Public opinion was further mobilised in a 14,000-signature petition, supported by a letter from the Massey University Students' Association, regarding the future of the lagoon.[143] The council then withdrew support for the scheme, leaving Terrace End Rotary Club a little bewildered by the response to its plans.[144] Their amenity proposals may have been well-meant, but they triggered an embryonic environmentalist reaction.[145]

Another area to attract attention — and the wish to transform it from 'Wilderness into a veritable Garden of Eden'[146] — was the land backing onto Park Road that borders the river between present-day Fitzherbert Avenue and the vicinity of today's Botanical Road. Originally, it was demarcated as borough reserve when in 1877, after the dissolution of the provinces, the borough was given responsibility for 361 acres (146 hectares) 'to be held in trust for a public park and recreation ground and botanical garden for the inhabitants of Palmerston North and its vicinity'.[147] In 1890 a Palmerston North Reserves Act partitioned the 361 acres into an esplanade of 39 acres (16 hectares), a racecourse of 86 acres (34 hectares) and a recreation ground of 22 acres (9 hectares), with the remainder being leased as farmland to provide a source of revenue for the 'improvement' of the reserve.[148]

In 1897 the Esplanade was fenced and named the Victoria Esplanade to mark the monarch's diamond jubilee.[149] The band rotunda previously in The Square was relocated to the Esplanade in 1907, and a tea kiosk built in 1909. In 1917 Victoria Drive was formed and the Fitzherbert Avenue boundary was fenced. Other features of the Esplanade appeared in subsequent decades, including the duck pond in 1925, the flowering cherries, which were planted as early as 1921 (but along the Park Road entrance in 1930), the paddling pool and 'palm avenue' (phoenix palms) in 1937, and the large flower beds in 1940.[150]

By the 1920s the appearance of the Esplanade was much altered from the 1870s, when native forest had covered the area. Indeed, until around 1890 the site remained bush-

covered. By the 1920s formal gardens, lawns and plantings of various ornamental tree species with pathways, viewing spots and vistas characterised the Esplanade.[151] These efforts at shaping and controlling nature were played out in towns and cities across New Zealand.[152]

The first curator of reserves, Walter Thurston, was replaced in 1907 by the highly regarded W. W. (William) Smith, who, however, resigned in 1908 after a matter of months, when Mayor Richard Essex labelled him a mere 'common cabbage gardener'.[153] Smith was replaced by Peter Black, who served as curator of reserves until his retirement in 1946, and exerted a considerable influence over the formative development of the Esplanade. Black had been an apprentice gardener at Johnston Lodge in Laurencekirk, Scotland. Once qualified, he worked in England at Castle Howard — more familiarly known to TV viewers as Evelyn Waugh's 'Brideshead' from the 1981 *Brideshead Revisited* television series, and the 2008 film remake — then at the royal residence of Sandringham House, and later in the nurseries of Thomas Methven and Sons in Edinburgh. He arrived in New Zealand in around 1904, via India and Australia, to work on John Harding's Mount Vernon Estate in Hawke's Bay. His qualifications included a certificate from the Royal Horticultural Society of England.[154]

From as early as 1910, Black was credited with having 'a far-seeing eye for effects' and patient endeavour in the creation of a landscape by pruning as well as planting.[155] The initiative for some features of the Esplanade, however, came from elsewhere; a sizable 52 by 16 foot (16 by 5 metre) trout-raising pond was opened in 1911 at the behest of the Wellington Acclimatisation Society, for example.[156]

Black had established a plant nursery at the Esplanade, and the planting out of native shrubs, with name-tags giving their botanical names, was under way by 1913.[157] That same year Black received approval for his plan for laying out further gardens and paths.[158] The 'carriageway' linking Fitzherbert Avenue to Cook Street was 'tastefully planted with choice native trees'. Shelter trees (*Cupressus macrocarpa*) on the other side of the road were ultimately to be removed to make way for rhododendrons, adding 'a charming dash of colour when abloom and lend[ing] another picturesque feature to this pleasant spot'.[159]

By 1916, Black had established 'three plantations' of native trees, some 15 chains (300 metres) in length and protected by a *Pinus radiata* hedge. Careful weeding over the first three years was crucial for their survival. In response to a newspaper reporter's question, 'You seem to be doing away with the foreigners here and replacing them with native trees?', Black replied, 'That is about what is happening.'[160]

Black did not, however, neglect formal flower gardens and exotic species.[161] The major task over the winter of 1916 was the removal, by hand, of three rows of blue gums, and the erection of a 100-yard- (90-metre-) long pergola constructed from tree trunks and planted with a variety of creepers.[162] A public appeal raised money for seating, while flower gardens and shrubs were planted out on both sides of the pergola, which was described as a 'handsome and picturesque archway'.[163] The *Manawatu Times* waxed lyrical about the

> stretches of trimmed grass, soft to tread, with a hint of hay scent rising from new-mown fragments, and mingling with the scent of early summer roses. Festoons of wisteria drape the tea kiosk abundantly, as newly greened trees meet overhead, across the paths. Roses, red and white and pink are blooming in sheltered corners.[164]

The sealing of the driveway (Victoria Drive), from Fitzherbert Avenue to Cook Street, commenced in 1918, and the following year those with motor vehicles could drive through the Esplanade.[165] The *Manawatu Evening Standard* in the spring of 1919 noted the 'original native bush' that had been preserved for the purpose of flanking Victoria Drive, but concentrated more on the rhododendrons, the colourful flower beds and in particular the creepers on the pergola. The blending of the 'sombre hues' of native shrubs with the colourful flowers and the 'verdant green' grass drew praise.[166]

Black added new specimens, including a rare Japanese lily and a prized Sydney pink boronia in 1922.[167] Having put considerable time and effort into the gardens in The Square, the council decided in that same year to focus more attention on the Esplanade (and other reserves at Terrace End in North Street and Takarō Park). Black's efforts at creating landscapes were now widely appreciated. The visual spectacle after leaving the motor vehicle was described in detail in the *Manawatu Evening Standard*:

> This is a delightful walk — traversing the picturesque journey along the path over which is formed a natural archway of dense native foliage. Here and there where the foliage is not so dense, the sun streams in, revealing many side tracks leading to other beautiful spots off the main highway. Seats are found at intervals along the glade and occasionally a clearing is reached indicating an ideal picnic spot. Almost every species of New Zealand shrubs abounds in abundance. Suddenly the nature of the scenery changes and the walker finds himself gazing at the lazily flowing waters of the Manawatu. On rounding the next corner a remarkable transformation is witnessed. The path widens and finally evolves into many others, which lead in every direction. On the one hand a straight avenue bordered with stout trees[,] on the other a magnificent rustic archway.[168]

Civic pride shows through in these comments, founded on Black's efforts in making the remnant native bush attractive in terms of British landscape gardening canons, and his reassembling of the exotic and indigenous vegetation to form a picturesque scene. Maintaining the Esplanade so that it remained 'scenic' involved a longer-term

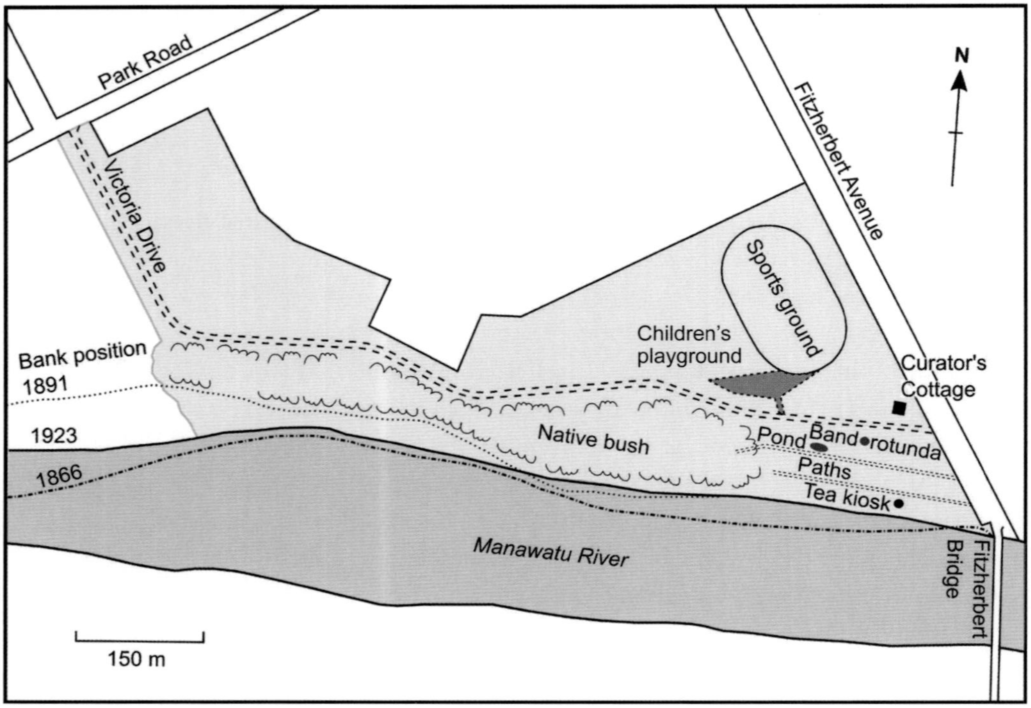

By 1924 the Esplanade included formal gardens with parallel paths and vistas from the Fitzherbert Avenue entrance, along with a road for motor vehicles exiting onto Park Road. This was backed by a remnant of indigenous bush. Based on H. R. Farquhar, Map of the Borough of Palmerston North from 1924. Manawatū Heritage 2007M_PNCC7-6-3-18-M-10_MAP_0546

vision partnered with ongoing intervention, so that in 1926, for example, a windbreak of macrocarpa and native lacebarks were removed because they were 'ragged compared with the picturesque surrounding shrubbery'.[169]

In 1926 Black proposed establishing a botanical garden in the Esplanade with flora from different parts of the world all laid out by species and genus, and all identified by their scientific names. His scheme, approved by council, called for setting aside 6.5 acres (2.6 hectares) in the Esplanade for this purpose. He saw this as a long-term asset for the city, where 'time rather than money was required to establish a representative collection of exotic and native flora'.[170] Initial work took the form of fencing and the planting of shelterbelts. Lack of funds curtailed efforts, but in 1927 the council used eight unemployed labourers to form paths, lawns and borders. Black explained that 'it will be laid out in lawns and collections of shrubs, arranged as far as possible in their botanical orders, and each plant will be named'.[171] In the future he envisaged a hot-house for tropical plants.[172] The botanical gardens never eventuated, although a hot-house — initially for begonias, but later including other tropical plants and now known as the Peter Black Conservatory — was eventually erected in 1940.[173]

By 1925 the tallest trees in Black's 1915 native plantation had reached a height of 25–30 feet (7.5–9 metres) and were praised as 'a good example of the ease with which many native plants may be arranged to assume the appearance of nature's handiwork'.[174] He used shrub species such as lancewood, lacebark, panax, myrsine, myrtle, coprosma, pittosporum and rangiora, rather than the slower-growing larger forest trees such as tōtara, rimu and kahikatea. In 1928, Dr Arthur Hill, director of the Royal Botanical Gardens at Kew, visited the Esplanade. In his diary he recorded: '[an] interesting piece of native bush with Macropiper [kawakawa] in quantities and saw [a] few Adiantim formosum [giant maidenhair fern] found only here and near Auckland (also in Victoria) growing in shade under shrubs'.[175] The long-term architecture of the Esplanade was also laid during Black's time as curator of reserves.

The Palmerston North town site was rapidly refashioned, driven by goals of progress and improvement, confidently espoused but not always easily implemented by nineteenth-century settlers. The forests were rapidly felled, and the physical fabric of the town site was modified, the streams and lagoons becoming stormwater drains. Remnant bush areas, notably in the Esplanade, were incorporated into the civilised landscape of the borough reserves. Simultaneously the town was re-clothed in familiar British ornamental and garden plants, including lawns and avenues of trees, with some 'attractive' and tamed indigenous species. Five periods of human engagement with 'nature' after Palmerston North was established are discernible.

- 1866–90 — 'nature's impress': Initially the physical environment was still very important in terms of influencing the alignment of the streets and as a bundle of natural resources of the economic development of the town.
- 1890–1930 — 'nature's challenges overcome': Engineering work on the river and streams, as well as drainage, was undertaken, which was characterised by the apparent 'overcoming' of some of nature's challenges, particularly in terms of flood damage and riverbank erosion, although the Manawatū River remained into the twenty-first century 'a river with a city problem'.176
- 1930–60 — 'nature reconfigured': For several decades in the mid-twentieth century, modernisation and accompanying ideas of progress and improvement underpinned the development of Palmerston North. Confident reshaping of the face of the landscape with regional-scale river engineering works occurred, as well as the further development of public parks and reserves in the city guided by European landscape canons.
- 1960–90 — 'nature overwhelmed': As the city grew, the built environment rather

The tamed environment: cherry blossoms were first planted on the Victoria Esplanade in the 1920s, attracting hundreds of visitors when in flower, some coming on special trains from Wellington. This photograph is from 1944. Manawatū Heritage 2007N_P38_RES_0145

overwhelmed the 'natural' features of the site on which the city was established. But in this triumph of modernity there were also some of the first signs of resistance — in concerns about the development of Hokowhitu Lagoon and the state of some of the streams in the city.

- 1990–present — 'nature accommodated': The 1990s to the present represent a more complex phase, where a range of older-style conquering nature-type projects have co-existed with more ecologically sensitive development options.

In each period the impact of human engagement has not been uniform across the city. Nor are these entirely discrete periods, with some of the 'conquering nature' approaches having persisted across time. The environmental history of the city is not at an end point; incremental change continues, sometimes with flushes of more rapid alteration driven by external forces, such as the impact of the 2014 earthquake on Hokowhitu Lagoon. The city has expanded and developed over time, and in so doing has moulded the underlying landscape. Nevertheless, at the same time the land is not merely an inert platform on which urban development has taken place.

29.731
29.532

Horticulturalists of Palmerston North[1]

Successive generations of Palmerstonians were quick to plant shelter trees, fruit trees and gardens for utilitarian purposes. Further motivation for planting ornamental trees and flowers was found in a desire to transform the landscape, which was initially described, not especially accurately, as converting 'wilderness into beauty spots'. The public face of this work was represented by the curator of reserves, who also provided trees for the avenues in the borough.

Critical to the efforts of ordinary citizens were the first nurserymen in Palmerston North. Prominent among these were William Just and his sons Arthur and Bruno, Joseph Mayo, Wallace V. Kingsbeer (1892–1937), Arthur J. Shailer (1878–1954) and Alexander Wighton (1880–1927), each of whom specialised in different arrays of plants. Shailer and Kingsbeer were heavily involved in the Palmerston North Nurserymen's Association, the latter also in the national association. Shailer successfully competed in dahlia shows across New Zealand.

William Just (1850–1925), of German descent, arrived in Palmerston North in 1875 and cleared a bush-covered section in College Street West, where he grew and sold vegetables, cut flowers and small fruits. Subsequently he moved into raising fruit trees and shelter plants. Following his death, the business was, from 1926, carried on by his elder son Arthur. Another son, Bruno Just (1878–1945), established his own orchard and nursery, Botanical Nurseries, in 1900. The business shipped tonnes of *Pinus radiata* seed to Australia, England and France. In 1914, Bruno leased 24 acres (9.7 hectares) on which to grow, on contract, *Pinus radiata* seedlings for the government. He also sold native tree species such as kauri, kahikatea and pūriri. This included a shipment of 31 tree ferns to Germany in 1904.

Joseph Mayo (1842–1917) left England for Auckland in 1863, where he established a nursery and orchard. In 1891, Mayo resigned his position as government pomologist and purchased 13 acres (5.2 hectares) for a nursery, glasshouses and an orchard in Palmerston North. In 1905, he was advertising macrocarpa and eucalypts. The Palmerston North property passed to his son Frederick (1869–1948), who traded under the name of Oxford Nurseries.

Palmerston North-born Richmond Harrison (1902–1991) represented a later generation of nurserymen. Specialising in ornamental flowering shrubs, he set up his Albert Street nursery in 1920. Harrison introduced to New Zealand a new strain of Pacific giant delphiniums, hybridised in California. He also devoted considerable efforts to improving polyanthus as border and bedding plants. By the 1950s the firm was importing seeds and plants from as far afield as England, France, Belgium and Holland.

Shailer's Nursery, Albert Street, receives a Vice-Regal visit in 1934. From left: Brian Keiller, Lady and Lord Bledisloe, and Arthur Shailer admiring the dahlias. Shailer was a second-generation nurseryman and breeder of prize-winning dahlias, some referencing local identities. For example, 'Mrs F.J. Nathan' and 'Mrs A.E. Mansford' ('a rich crimson') were so named. Based on Upper Hokowhitu Lagoon Drainage, Palmerston North City Council C/24; Correspondence Reserves — Hokowhitu Lagoon, PNCC 1/5/3 : 17 : H/3, IMCA

C.M.ROSS

04

BUILDING THE CITY

RUSSELL POOLE

An aerial view of Palmerston North, c.1939. From the railway yards on Main Street West looking eastwards over The Square and along Broadway Avenue, Main Street East and Church Street, the photograph captures the businesses, civic buildings and social and cultural venues of the central business district. Many landmark buildings are shown, including the post office (1906), still with its clock tower, and the Temperance and General Insurance (T&G) Building (1938) in the upper centre. The Grand Hotel (1908) and All Saints' Church (1914) are on the lower right. The four quadrants of the gardens in The Square date back to the early twentieth century. Alexander Turnbull Library Wellington 019622 1/4-F

Palmerstonians like to boast of a city made for 'easy living', or more precisely 'easy driving', where any point can be reached just 10 minutes from home. Equally, many would claim that the city is 'handy' to various popular destinations: Wellington, the Kapiti Coast, Martinborough, Napier, Ruapehu. At a more aspirational level, the current official claim is that this is a municipality with 'small city benefits' and 'big city ambition'. Some explanation of how Palmerston North got to be that way (or at least how these claims could be made) can be found in the history of its layout, infrastructure and communications.

Present-day Palmerston North[1] has grown outwards from a large clearing known as Te Papaiōea. This was the site recommended in 1865 for a future 'inland township' by John Tiffin Stewart, chief district surveyor to the Province of Wellington.[2]

The site was first shown to Stewart by the Rangitāne chief Te Hirawanu Kaimokopuna.[3] Rangitāne would have recognised the potential utility to Pākehā of an area of land that was already cleared and lay in proximity to long-established tracks leading to other important districts, such as Rangitīkei to the west and Hawke's Bay to the east. In equal measure the presence of a Pākehā trading settlement in this location would benefit local Māori enterprises, such as market gardening and mahinga kai more generally up and down the river.[4] The first Pākehā settler was George Snelson, an ironmonger, who arrived in December 1870 to set up a store, followed some months later by his wife, Louisa.

Stewart's survey of 1866 provided for town sections of mostly 1 or 2 acres (0.4 or 0.8 hectares) within Te Papaiōea, or southwards from it towards the Manawatū River. The boundaries of the town were constituted by the river on the south side, and by survey lines on the west (Botanical Road), north (Boundary Road, now Tremaine Avenue) and east (Terrace and Ruahine streets, now consolidated as Ruahine Street). Prominent in Stewart's plan was a square of no less than 17 acres (6.9 hectares), on whose western side the trig station for the survey was placed.[5] Also laid out were two principal lines of road intersecting at right angles at The Square, each designed to link to settlements elsewhere in the lower North Island. Leading onwards to Foxton (Te Awahou) to the west and Hawke's Bay to the east was Main Street. Leading onwards to the Rangitīkei district to the north, and potentially to new farming districts to the south, was the line of road represented by Rangitikei Road (now Street) to the north and Fitzherbert Street (now Avenue) to the south. The lines of some other internal streets were established in this same survey.[6] In his first plan of town sections, Stewart confined himself to the northern side of The Square.[7]

Stewart also fixed the boundaries of the Native Reserve, within Hokowhitu, and the Public Reserve, along the right bank of the Manawatū River westwards from today's Fitzherbert Bridge. Beyond the boundaries of the town proper lay lands that were initially controlled by the Manawatu Road Board and later, from 1902, by Kairanga County.[8] Here, Stewart laid out sections ranging from about 30 to 300 acres (12 to 121.4 hectares) to comprise the suburban and rural portion of the township. These were mostly intended for small farms. Stewart's survey established the line of the tramway (later railway) that would link Palmerston North to Foxton and give access to some of the small farms, as well as enabling timber to be transported to the port.

The township came into official existence on 3 October 1866, with a proclamation from Dr Isaac Featherston, Superintendent of Wellington Province. Sales of land ensued within the month, but proved slow. The rural sections, although advertised as the 'cream' of New Zealand's potential farmland, had to be further subdivided for purchase, as prospective settlers had little ready money and wondered when and if government would provide access to this land.[9] Certainly small farms had considerable public support, as contrasted with the vast stations or runs of early Pākehā settlement. On the other hand, whereas run-holders had been responsible for their own infrastructure, small farm development placed the burden of expenditure on roads and drainage on the public purse — an awkward reality that government seemed reluctant to acknowledge.[10] A leading article in the *Manawatu Times* of 11 July 1877 bluntly stated: 'It is now required to make the bush lands accessible',[11] but in reality government mostly expected the small farmers to provide their own access.[12]

Scandinavian immigrants arriving in 1871 were allocated land near Whakarongo and in Awapuni, on the understanding that they would fell the bush along the survey lines and contribute to road formation, for instance by carting metal. By the 1880s they were doing precisely that, as well as building their own houses, with significant support from tangata whenua who had villages and mahinga kai in the area.[13] Longburn was described in 1887 as 'quite a little settlement of importance'. Fitzherbert was declared a district in 1888. A journalist visiting in 1891 reported that 'small settlers . . . are the backbone of Palmerston, the secret of its prosperity. It would never have been what it is today were it not surrounded by magnificent land which is principally owned and occupied by a sturdy, independent industrious class of small farmers.'[14] While the element of boosterism in this account is unmistakable, there is probably also an element of truth, and if not that, then prescience at least.

In the town the first areas to be built up — consistent with the survey and taking full advantage of the pre-existing cleared land — were around the northern and western sides of The Square and along the future railway, leading to the eastern edge of the Te Papaiōea clearing and Terrace End. This suburb, whose economic base was sawmilling, and which was therefore located at the 'timber face', began contemporaneously with Palmerston North itself in 1870. An editorialist stated: 'Were it not that there is likely to be an uninterrupted line of houses all along Main-street, one would be led to imagine that Terrace End was a little independent township or suburb to Palmerston.'[15]

Also part of the economic unit was the pre-existing Māori village of Ruāhine, by the river at the south end of Ruahine Street within the Native Reserve. The alignment of the railway on an east–west axis down the middle of the township conveniently provided for a suburban service to Terrace End and Awapuni, the latter providing for the Māori communities in this area as well as the newly settled Scandinavians. The following decades saw the construction of a series of sidings and spur lines from Main Street and the Foxton Line (later Pioneer Highway) to give access to a variety of businesses and amenities, including the racecourse.[16]

The development of the town's layout over the first five decades, in the absence of detailed planning by government,[17] relied on a few basic principles. One was to safeguard public health, as then understood, by sequestering potentially unhygienic functions. Notably, rubbish disposal and sewage outfall were placed downstream from the Esplanade in today's West End. From the first stages of reticulation, policy was to keep sewage and stormwater separate — and here Palmerston North was in advance of most New Zealand municipalities. Councils did, however, sometimes relax standards to placate businesses that might otherwise move to a competitor settlement, such as Feilding.

Stock sales in various yards on and near Rangitikei Street were a regular fixture during the first 35 years of the borough, with drovers herding large numbers of cattle and other livestock through the streets, until eventually pressure from the Health Department and the public shut them down.[18] Such a step can be seen as a significant assertion of an urban space, albeit a tricky one given the town's economic dependence on its hinterland.[19]

Building regulations were initially loose, but steadily over the years environmental pressures, local body by-laws and the quest for commercial prestige prompted upgrades in standards. In the absence of a local source of stone, the early structures were usually made from wood and corrugated iron. Bricks became the rule in the centre of town after a series of fires in the late nineteenth century.[20] The great storm of 1936 — which caused extensive damage, including the partial destruction of all three of Palmerston North's grandstands — served as a reminder of the need for robust roofing in a high-wind area.

After the Napier and Masterton earthquakes of 1931 and 1942 respectively, towers, chimneys, parapets and other architectural embellishments were stripped from buildings, including the post office, whose clock tower was removed in the latter year. A swarm of

ABOVE Cattle being driven past Palmerston North Technical High School (now part of UCOL) on Duke Street (now Princess Street) to the sale yards in Rangitikei and Grey streets, c.1912. This photograph would have been taken before the sale yards were moved to Boundary Road (now Tremaine Avenue), outside the borough, and stock movements within the borough became prohibited. Thousands of cattle could be sold on a single day at the Palmerston North sale yards. Frederick Radcliffe, Manawatū Heritage 2007N_Scs74_SCH_0440

BELOW The storm-damaged main stand at Awapuni Racecourse, 1936. The seating and lower parts of the building survived comparatively unscathed. The storm crossed the North Island on 2 February 1936; Palmerston North was one of the hardest-hit municipalities. Manawatū Heritage 2014N_Stm13_009081 earthquakes in the South Island and Cook Strait areas starting in 2010 has forced the closure of some significant local buildings. Expensive rehabilitation is proposed for some, but others may be demolished.

Patterns of movement and communications within the urban space were governed by a complex interplay between the policies of council, the planning of borough engineers, and the decisions of individual property-holders and businesses. In the dynamics of 'location, location, location', gravitating towards the centre optimised access and opportunities for businesses. Operations that required rail access — such as Cook's Mill, the Palmerston North Sash, Door and Timber Co., and the gasworks — lined up alongside or close to Main Street. Farm supply businesses gravitated towards Main and Rangitikei streets, where their rural customers could conveniently reach them via the road network. Accordingly, the borough grew concentrically outward from the meeting point of the two lines of road at The Square,[21] a pattern which possibly militated against the ribbon development seen in many other New Zealand towns, and also against the development of any 'Golden Mile'. Terrace End was the main exception, but it lost much of its independent impetus once timber extraction was completed.

Over the decades the central business district became home to a compact cluster of standard urban facilities: courthouse, police station, banks, insurance offices, post office, railway station, fire station, hotels, department stores, picture theatres, library, opera house, halls, churches and so forth. Not until much later, in the 1960s, did more than a tiny number of these structures venture above three storeys. Verandahs were constructed to shelter the footpaths, in the recognised urban style of Australasia.[22] Inner-city infill developments, such as Linton and Fitchett streets, were touted as being only a few minutes' walk from The Square. Also convenient for people on foot or on their bicycles was the placement of working-class residences in the neighbourhood of small factories, as on Joseph Street and in the Campbell Street area. Under the Workers' Dwelling Act 1905, 17 working-class houses were built handy to the Terrace End railway station.[23] Conversely, and against this trend, middle-class housing straggled along Church, Fitzherbert and other streets a little further from the centre, while some affluent householders built large residences south of Ferguson Street (Caccia Birch being a fine extant example), on the terrace above Terrace End or at Fitzherbert.[24]

In spite of its attractive gardens, The Square itself resisted full domestication. Its size might originally have been calculated to impress prospective settlers, but in practice The Square was all too often sodden, windswept and inhospitable, and sometimes the scene of petty crime.[25] Similarly intractable was the long stretch of Main Street, which, with its railway line, marshalling yards and sidings, cut the city in two. Palmerston North presented itself as a true railway town, to an extent hard to imagine nowadays. Upwards of 65 trains a day passed through, not to mention shunting and loading. Traffic disruption, accidents, noise and pollution were the downside of that. It would be difficult to think of any other

sizable town in the entire country with a main artery like Main Street East, flanked by major commercial and civic facilities on either side and the railway running unfenced and unbridged down the middle — a positive invitation to pedestrians to make risky crossings. Locomotive crews on occasion deliberately triggered clouds of smoke as trains entered the city,[26] and occupants of older houses near Main Street tell of finding thick layers of soot above their ceilings.[27] Countering this, the smell of the railway was the smell of money. Businesses resolutely defended it, and any curtailments of services drew protests.[28]

As early as 1920 the government resolved to divert the railway; partly because of its disruptive effect on the town, and partly because greater space was required for a new railway station and marshalling yards than was available on the current site.[29] Fortunately for Palmerston North, a rival proposal for a Levin–Greatford deviation — which would have bypassed the borough completely and removed its main trunk status — was rejected.[30] The new route instead took the line along the northern side of Boundary Road, thus just outside town. In the sequel, the business interests that opposed the 'Milson deviation' must have been gratified by its slow progress: commenced in 1926, construction of the deviation halted with the Depression in 1929, recommenced in 1938, halted with the Second World War in 1940, and finally recommenced in 1947.[31]

'Woodhey', Te Awe Awe Street, c.1903. Built for Jacob Nannestad, a sawmiller, the house, now known as Caccia Birch, stands on the north bank of the Hokowhitu Lagoon. This photograph is taken from the south bank of the lagoon. The house was bought by John Henderson Pollock Strang in 1903 and served briefly as the vice-regal residence after the great fire at Parliament Buildings in 1907. William Caccia Birch acquired the house in 1921 and it was gifted by his family to the government in 1941. Whalley and Co., Crown Studios, Palmerston North, Manawatū Heritage 2009N_Br25_003047

SEWING MACHINES
PETROL

The railway yards on Main Street West, 1937. The view is eastwards along Main Street towards The Square. Conspicuous on the far side of The Square is the post office clock tower, which was removed as an earthquake risk in 1942. The curve in the railway lines seen to right of the picture was created in 1925, after heated debate, so that the Cenotaph could be placed at the intersection point between Main Street (running east–west) and Rangitikei Street and Fitzherbert Avenue (running north–south), close to the geometrical centre of The Square. The station is out of view at bottom left.
Manawatū Heritage 2014N_St95_009036

For a time the designated railway land at Milson was used as a nine-hole golf course by the Palmerston North Golf Club; sleepers were taken up not once, but twice, for use in the Hutt Valley.[32]

Not until 1963 — 43 years after planning began — was rail traffic entirely removed from the middle of town. By then, inevitably, suburban expansion had straddled the new route to the north and east, meaning the railway still divided the city (although not its centre), but subsequent electrification of the main trunk line through Palmerston North has reduced pollution. The first stage in the suburban expansion, ironically, was the Milson railway settlement, built around 1926. Although part of Kairanga County until 1950, it functioned as a working-class district for Palmerston North. Some railway houses, built by prefabrication, can still be seen on Milson Line.[33]

Initiatives towards a more formal extension of the borough began in the early 1920s, quixotically, it would seem, at a time when large areas within the existing boundaries had not yet been built up.[34] The western end of College Street, for instance,

A family shown crossing the railway lines on Main Street East, just east of the post office, c.1936. The tower of All Saints' Church appears to the right of the Public Trust Office, the imposing building at the left. The photograph was published at a time of heightened concern about the hazard created by the unfenced railway lines, following two serious accidents in 1936, one of them fatal. Auckland Libraries Heritage Collections AWNS-19361007-48-4

was leasehold land principally occupied by nurseries, orchards and market gardens, including the well-known firms that gave their names to today's Just and Nairn places. A long stretch of Rangitikei Street remained under-utilised after the removal of the sale yards in 1912.

In 1926 the average population density of the borough stood at only 3.9 persons per acre (0.4 hectares).[35] The resulting diseconomies of scale for reticulation and public transport were significant.[36] Notwithstanding, Mayor J. A. ('Jimmy') Nash argued in 1923 that extension would make the borough 'the Christchurch of the North Island',[37] while for the individual citizen a decision to build on new cheap land in the outer city made sense, both logistically (with the wider use of the motor car) and financially. The most substantial reward of expansion, however, was that it magically increased the population of the municipality to 20,000 — the minimum needed for coveted city status, eventually achieved in 1930.[38] This was a replay of the sleight of hand used to secure borough status some 50 years earlier.[39]

As development moved further from the centre, a break was made from the traditional grid pattern, with its vista of telegraph poles receding into the distance, in favour of a more curvilinear street design, featuring crescents and cul-de-sacs. As well as being visually less monotonous, this design added to amenity by

introducing a distinction between arterial and local streets, the latter being designed to discourage through-traffic. It was first adopted locally in 1925 for subdivisions at Palm Avenue and Carlton Avenue, the latter of which features a small park. The state housing precinct at Savage Crescent — built between 1938 and 1945, and the first such development outside the main centres — takes the design a step further, with curving internal streets and a generously sized internal park.[40] All this was in accord with the 'garden city' movement, whose key ideas had been widely canvassed in New Zealand from the 1910s onwards; very few garden city plans had in fact been executed at this early stage, but for a working example Palmerston North could look to Whanganui's celebrated Durie Hill suburb, dating from 1920.[41]

Although this phase in the city's development coincided with the passing of the Town-planning Act in 1926, the new legislation had little impact in Palmerston North, thanks partly to the city's tendency to 'localism'.[42] Planning lapsed in any case during the Depression and the Second World War. With the end of the war an influx of new arrivals plunged the city into a housing crisis; many families found themselves reduced to living in tents and car packing cases at the Esplanade Motor Camp. In the first social housing initiative to be undertaken by the city, Mayor Augustus ('Gus') Mansford set up the Hokowhitu transit camp, which continued in occupation until 1959.[43]

FOLLOWING PAGES Aerial view of Palmerston North showing the Savage Crescent state housing precinct, which was under construction from 1937 to 1940. College Street runs east–west down the middle of the photo, with the future Pitama Road running at right angles to it at the bottom of the picture. Just above Pitama Road is the former oxbow of the Manawatū River, subsequently developed as Wikiriwhi Crescent. To the left of the oxbow the extensive nurseries owned by the Nairn family can be seen. Manawatū Heritage 2010P_IMCA-DigitalLibrary_004389

Government, however, remained the major provider of publicly financed housing.[44] It increased the local stock of permanent working-class accommodation, supplementing Savage Crescent, through its development of the Ross Block (now known as Roslyn) to the east of Ruahine Street. Here, as elsewhere in the city, a characteristic 'pepper-potting' policy was adopted in the distribution of state housing and privately built dwellings. Complementarily, the 1950s through to the 1970s saw the development of Hokowhitu and Riverdale (part of Awapuni), taking advantage of new stopbanks along the Manawatū River.[45] Noticeably, although these suburbs are considered more middle-class, the dwellings as originally constructed were on a comparatively modest scale thanks to restrictions on loan money.[46]

In 1950 expansion of the city entered a new phase with the annexation of Milson and Kelvin Grove from Kairanga County. The passing of the Town and Country Planning Act 1953 led in due course to Palmerston North's adoption of a district planning scheme in 1959; on this basis the city went to the Local Body Boundary Commission in 1964, seeking sufficient land to allow 25 years' forward planning. The commission made some land available to the west of Monrad Street and near the airport, but withheld good farmland in the vicinity of Gillespies Line, instead pointing the city towards Aokautere, an area less suited to farming. The city had already had its bid for expansion into fertile land extending towards Longburn declined by Kairanga County.[47]

Expansion into Aokautere represented a new departure. It meant accepting the division of the city by the Manawatū River, with the attendant possibility that one day additional bridges would be required. Council also correctly foresaw that the unstable, deeply dissected Aokautere terrain would be expensive to develop.[48] From having been an urban space that predominantly developed along arterial gridlines, filling up blocks of land (including wetlands) as it went (like Levin), Palmerston North now faced the unwelcome prospect of suburban development in the style of Whanganui or New Plymouth, where the built-up areas are interrupted by undevelopable land, resulting in suburban enclaves and traffic bottlenecks. Accordingly, the council kept Aokautere on a rural zoning until the late 1980s, and residential development was not launched until the 1990s.

Influential in this acceptance of expansion into Aokautere was the *Manawatū Urban Growth Strategy Study* prepared by the Ministry of Works and Development and the Palmerston North City Council under city planner Ken Tremaine (1976–89). Extensive and costly reshaping of the landscape proved necessary from the outset, and is seen at its most far-reaching in the terracing of Anzac Cliffs to accommodate a new subdivision at Vaucluse Heights, completed in 2018.[49] Concomitantly, the housing stock in Aokautere — and nearby lifestyle developments, such as Moonshine Valley and Ngahere Park — has been constructed to conspicuously higher specifications than that to be seen in Roslyn, Milson and Cloverlea, although that does not exempt it from the consequences of failures in building standards in the 1990s and 2000s.

The culmination of the series of expansions came with the Local Government Reform Act 1989, which vastly increased Palmerston North's land area from 4302 hectares to 32,594 hectares, belying a population of less than 67,000.[50] Merged into the city at this time were Ashhurst, Turitea and Linton; Longburn and Bunnythorpe followed in 2012. Suburban development to the east, in the direction of Ashhurst, remained the council's preferred trajectory, starting in 2013 with the area between James Line and Stoney Creek Road,[51] but further infill to the west, by the racecourse and onwards to Shirriffs Road, is also projected. These initiatives return the city to its traditional linear mode of development across reclaimed wetlands.

To complement this residential consolidation and expansion, a programme of industrial zoning was initiated in the 1960s, principally on the northern side of the city. Distinguished civil servant W. B. Sutch produced a detailed and optimistic report on the future of manufacturing in Palmerston North in 1971,[52] but well into the 1970s, true to the vision of a century earlier, the city was

A view of the Vaucluse Heights and Edenmor Crescent development in Aokautere, looking southwards towards the Tararua Ranges. The sloping area to the left of the photograph results from the terracing of the bluffs, whose original contours are represented by the extant bluff shown at left above the terraced area. Steps shown to the bottom left form part of the Arapiki a Tāne walkway, which was created in association with the development. Russell Poole, 2019

This photograph was taken from a crane in The Square. Prominent in the foreground is The Plaza complex, surrounding St Andrew's Presbyterian Church. The new Farmers department store stands on the site of the old Opera House. The scale of the complex, marked by dotted lines, reflects the ambition of retailers to cater for the entire Manawatū region and beyond. To the right, Fitzherbert Avenue runs down to the city's sole vehicular bridge across the Manawatū River. Manawatū Heritage 2019P_IMCA-DigitalArchive_026395

still dominated by agricultural servicing[53] and local commerce. Only gradually did warehousing, distribution and other light-industrial operations start lining up near the railway along Bennett Street, Tremaine Avenue, Keith Street and Napier Road, followed in the early 2000s by similar development along Railway Road.

Meanwhile completion of the Milson deviation had opened up possibilities for revamping the heart of the city. In 1965, Christchurch architects Miles Warren and Peter Beaven drew up a bold proposal to integrate the former railway land and The Square, by constructing a town hall and new council offices that straddled the two areas. While aptly symbolic of the city's ambitions, this was too bold for many. In the end, however, Warren and Beaven's concept prevailed and was used by Auckland town planner and architect Ian Reynolds as the basis for a comprehensive plan, released in 1969. The Civic Administration Building formed the focus of the redevelopment, but the Reynolds plan also influenced the selection of sites for the convention centre, art gallery, museum and theatre.[54] Redevelopment of other areas of the original railway lands has been comparatively fitful, and attended by a great deal of controversy.

The private sector was also active in and near the centre, sometimes sidestepping the planners. The Plaza complex stands as its principal achievement. Designed to appeal to out-of-town shoppers — and mindful that with modern roads Palmerston North lies within convenient shopping distance of the Horowhenua, Rangitīkei, Tararua, lower Hawke's Bay and upper Wairarapa districts[55] — it encouraged a shift of the retail centre of gravity to the Church Street side of The Square. Retail developments also spread further east on Broadway and Main Street, merging with the original Terrace End shopping centre. True to its longstanding policy of support for a strong central business district, the municipality intervened in this economic dynamic by resuscitating George Street.[56] Work is currently under way towards a more far-reaching revivification of the area west of The Square to connect it to Central Energy Trust Arena (the former Showgrounds).

Growing in tandem with suburban development and inner-city infill was traffic congestion. In 1964, *The Proposed Transportation Plan for Palmerston North* was put forward as a solution. The first of its kind in New Zealand, it was comparatively modest in scope and limited by the policy of using existing streets. However, the Ministry of Works rejected it in favour of a much more ambitious and invasive plan, which, true to the spirit of the motorway era, called for dedicated vehicle-only through-roads, overpasses at major intersections, and even a flyover leading to a new bridge across the river. Termed the 'Eastern Distributor', it succumbed in the face of ratepayer protests. In 1978 a more modest inner-city ring-road, the 'Traffic Box', was completed as a partial substitute. A third component of the plan was a one-way system around The Square; this was instituted in 1966, only to be rescinded in 1970. Thus the traffic inefficiencies were not really resolved, and in subsequent years heavy vehicle traffic on the city's streets has greatly increased; construction of an outer-city regional freight ring-road is under consideration.[57]

Where urban infrastructure was concerned, the new township of the 1870s had everything to accomplish with virtually nothing by way of capital. It is true that the small farms would become a source of wealth, attracting private enterprise such as Glaxo and public institutions such as Massey Agricultural College, but that lay in the future.[58] In the meantime the timber resource was largely squandered by burning, payable mineral resources remained elusive, there was no possibility of a river port (unlike Whanganui), the town had no defence or military role in its early years (again, unlike Whanganui), and large-scale manufacturing lacked viability in terms of either raw materials or markets.[59] The rates base alone, in such a thinly populated centre, would never suffice to finance the necessary capital works. Exacerbating the problem was keen competition from other municipalities, some much longer established, and all aiming to attract settlers who expected to find urban life and amenities in their adoptive country.[60] Thanks to these pressures, some questionable decisions were made and, as elsewhere in

New Zealand, only belatedly did the true costs of development — financial, environmental and human — begin to be appreciated.

To assist municipalities, government passed legislation in 1876 enabling them to seek ratepayer approval for loans. Having strategically acquired borough status in 1877, Palmerston North sought to gain traction from this legislation. Shortly after his election as mayor in 1885, James Linton stated: 'People who come to this colony will have been accustomed to see civilization. Let them see that we have civilization around us, and it will be a great inducement to settlement. We must have sanitary and other improvements, well-formed streets, good water, and good drainage.' The editor of the *Manawatu Times* was an inveterate campaigner for development: 'It is decidedly better to take time by the forelock and set about improving our town at once, and so attract a population here which will aid in developing the splendid resources of the district.'[61]

From outside the district, the *Wairarapa Daily Times* — based in Masterton, another small farm settlement — acknowledged that 'Palmerston North has gone the right way to work to secure the progress of the town.' Although pointing out that the borough had 'a less population, fewer houses, and a smaller income from rates [than Masterton]', it concluded that 'when the next statistical return is published it will be found that Palmerston has taken the lead and stands first in importance among the inland towns of the North Island'. In the 1901 census, indeed, Palmerston North, at a count of 6534 persons, was far ahead of Masterton (3949), although still behind Whanganui (7329).[62]

In the polls that followed, Palmerston North ratepayers proved to be not so easily swayed by boosterism from politicians and journalists. They rejected loan proposals more often than not, and those that won approval often failed to find investors. The prevailing economic depression did not help. A loan of £10,000 authorised in 1878 was not fully subscribed until 1883; the sole investors were local small-time lenders and debenture-holders. An overseas loan of £50,000, approved in a poll of 1885, was not fully subscribed until 1889.[63] Even so, these loans enabled substantial progress towards Mayor Linton's appurtenances of 'civilization'. Their history is complicated, and only a brief sketch can be given here.

Municipalities depend on provision for the 'three waters': drinking water, stormwater and waste water. All were urgent tasks for Palmerston North. The absence of a pure and copious water supply compromised the essential viability of the town. Wells sat side by side with cesspits on people's properties, and the press was quick to raise public health concerns. Fire-fighting was a futile endeavour for the lack of adequate water pressure, leading to threats from the insurers to withdraw cover. The potential for an uncontaminated gravitational supply was gained in 1884, when the council successfully petitioned the government for a water reserve on Turitea Stream; but financial constraints, government vacillation and objections from Fitzherbert landowner Sir James Prendergast prevented water being taken, until finally a dam was built in 1899. Embarrassingly, Whanganui had gained a comparable supply as early as 1876.[64] Meanwhile, to appease the insurance companies, artesian bores had been drilled to feed fire-plugs in The Square.

Although the dam underwent repeated upgrades, notably in 1907 and 1913, persistent controversy as to the merits of artesian versus gravitational supply retarded progress,[65] and it was not until 1957 that a completely new 30-metre dam on the Turitea was completed. Additional artesian bores continue to be drilled, and the satellite communities remain reliant on them. Water restrictions are customarily imposed during dry periods, amid increasing recognition that the resource is finite.[66]

Reticulating stormwater was another priority, given the largely flat terrain and high water table. In the early years, pedestrians used to walk along the railway line to avoid the ponding on Main Street.[67] Natural drainage was provided by Mangaone Stream, its tributary Kawau Stream, and various old river meanders, but they were all prone to overflowing, and additional outlets to lagoons and the river needed to be created. On the basis of plans drawn up in 1885, an additional major outlet, designed to drain the central city area, was constructed parallel to Kawau Stream along the line of Pioneer Highway.[68] Although the borough thus gained some reticulation, it also relied on a substantial proportion of the stormwater being soaked up by the extensive unimproved areas.[69] This sufficed for many years, but by the 1960s the soakage capacity had been greatly reduced and a wholesale overhaul of the drainage system was taken in hand.[70] Since that time, discussion has returned to the possible institution in new subdivisions of a modern soakage system, with swales and catch-basins, as seen in the Pit Park area and proposed for Aokautere, but it faces the difficulty that 90 per cent or more of typical residential properties consist of impermeable surfaces.

Waste water was the last of the 'three waters' to be attended to. As noted above, disposal of human waste was initially a matter of individual property-owners digging cesspits. Even when a borough cesspit became available, many residents preferred to stay independent, creating work for successive inspectors of nuisances. The press waged a protracted campaign against unhygienic disposal, pointing to the prevalence of typhoid in Sydney during the 1880s, and praising the modern sewerage systems being inaugurated in progressive British cities.

Spurred on in this way, the borough completed its first plant in 1890. The challenge and cost posed by reticulation was formidable; for instance, the swamps to be traversed were in places over 4 metres deep, and the massive 18-inch (0.46-metre) pipes had to be laid on ferro-concrete supports. Council economised by discharging the sewage into the river in its raw form, having obtained opinion that to do so was legal. This deleterious expedient sparked outrage from neighbouring local bodies.[71] After long delays, a new, improved scheme — based on septic tanks and shingle filter-beds, and claimed to be 'the largest out of Britain' — was implemented in 1905 under the direction of Samuel Jickell. It remained in place, albeit not without sporadic serious breaches, until a completely new

Samuel Jickell (1856–1939), Palmerston North's first professional borough engineer

Palmerston North Borough Council staff cross Turitea Stream in a trap, c.1907. Samuel Jickell is at centre and Christian Voss, possibly in his capacity as a member of the Manawatu Land Drainage Board or Kairanga County Council, to the right. They are probably on a visit to the construction site of the second dam in the Turitea Water Reserve.
Manawatū Heritage 2014N_W57_009181

Born in England, Samuel Jickell immigrated to New Zealand in about 1883. He worked in Auckland, Melbourne, Nelson and Petone before his appointment by the Palmerston North Borough Council in 1904.

While at Palmerston North Jickell initiated a series of major projects. His farsightedness and thoroughness were often in stark contrast to the vacillations of elected officials and the penny-pinching attitudes of ratepayers. Savage personal attacks were launched on him in 1907 by Mayor Richard Essex in particular, but he enjoyed majority support on council until the late 1910s.

A major achievement, and his first with the borough, was improving the water supply. Having just constructed New Zealand's first concrete dam at Korokoro in 1903, he presented the Palmerston North council with a similar plan for Turitea Stream. The dam was initially built in a scaled-down version, completed in 1907, after ratepayers rejected the original proposal as too expensive; but in 1913 the dam was increased to the height Jickell had originally envisaged.

During the First World War Jickell prepared a comprehensive report on the drainage, sanitation and water supply of Trentham Military Camp, and when he laid out the Rangiotū camp near Palmerston North in 1915 he made sure that the poor conditions at Trentham were not repeated. Some of his innovations were even adopted by the British Army.

Jickell resigned in 1919, apparently after councillors had criticised him for undertaking outside consultancy work. He went on to practise full-time as a consulting engineer, based in Palmerston North. In partnership with W. H. K. Gilmour he oversaw the widening of the road through the Manawatū Gorge in 1920. He retired in 1931.

For some years he was stage manager for the Palmerston North Operatic and Dramatic Society.

Jickell was the foundation president of the Institute of Local Government Engineers of New Zealand. In Palmerston North he is commemorated by Jickell Street. A notable article about him is Donald G. Irvine's 'Samuel Jickell: An Engineer for the Future', *Manawatū Journal of History* 9 (2013): 58–66.

Samuel Jickell as shown by a cartoonist in *NZ Truth*, 10 March 1917. The original caption reads as follows:

Sam Jickell (Borough Engineer, Palmerston N.).
He knows what makes the wheels go round,
And helps to make them go;
On lots of other things he's sound
That engineers should know.
And what he knows he uses well,
That Palmerston may claim
'Mong landward towns to 'bear the bell',
And an unsullied name.

Workmen laying sewerage pipes on a ferro-concrete base, c.1905. Photographer: Samuel Jickell, Borough Engineer. Manawatū Heritage 2007N_Se3_WOR_0125

treatment plant was opened in 1968. The outlying communities of Ashhurst, Longburn and Bunnythorpe continued to discharge less adequately treated effluent direct to the river until connected to the city treatment plant in 2013–14.[72]

Rubbish disposal was a long-term embarrassment. A collection service was inaugurated in 1879, but the tip, situated on the banks of the Manawatū River near West End School, was smelly, rat-infested and a source of pollution. Calls for the building of a municipal 'destructor' (the contemporary term for an incinerator) mounted, but the project was delayed by ratepayer opposition to loans, high prices during the First World War, and wrangles over where to locate the facility. During the 1918 Spanish influenza pandemic, a smaller-scale experimental incinerator was set up. At the eventual opening of the destructor in 1923, Mayor Nash noted that only four other towns in New Zealand possessed this technology, with Whanganui on its way to doing so. An additional up-to-date touch was the use of electric trucks for rubbish collection. The destructor's subsequent history was less happy: its own destruction by fire was narrowly averted in 1930, and the building was reported as in poor condition in 1945.[73]

A landfill at Awapuni, at the south end of Maxwells Line on the banks of the Manawatū River, was developed as the next disposal facility, and cumulatively gained altitude to become today's waggishly entitled Mount Cleese.[74] Planning for a regional landfill site at Hiwinui, near Ashhurst, begun in 1990, was dropped in the face of opposition from local residents, and following the closure of Awapuni to the public in 1998 two transfer stations were established to accept household waste. Paper recycling commenced in 1991, and by the late 1990s a broader range of materials had begun to be accepted.[75]

Public health considerations also called for the provision of an abattoir. The replacement of the existing private slaughter yards with a public facility was being mooted as early as 1877, but objections to its proposed location upstream from the public reserve impeded further action until council's hand was forced by the passing of the Slaughtering and Inspection Act 1900. In a fine example of localism, councillors rejected the proposition of a regional facility. They would have compromised by accepting an offer from the Longburn freezing works had not Councillor Frederick Pirani, Member for Palmerston North, intervened, swinging opinion towards a fully independent ratepayer-owned facility. Opened in 1906, with its own electricity-generating plant, the abattoir was initially operated by the Manawatu Meat Company, before becoming a principally council-owned facility in 1917. The wheel of policy finally came full circle in 1969 when the city agreed to use the regional abattoir at Feilding.[76]

An essential resource for the borough was energy for heating and lighting. Coal gas manufacture was investigated as early as 1879, mains were laid between 1885 and 1889, and the first gasworks, on a site at the corner of Cook and Main streets, was brought into operation in February 1889. In 1890 gas street lighting was inaugurated. Initially the gasworks was owned by the company that built it, but in response to concerns about high prices the council took it over in 1915. A new gasworks with modern technology and much greater capacity was opened in 1923 on Napier Road. In 1960 the plant was updated, but the operation, which had long been subsidised from electricity sales, terminated in 1970, when the pipeline from the Kapuni gas field reached Palmerston North.[77]

Increasingly, an electricity supply was emerging as a must in the competition between municipalities. An initial proposal to generate hydroelectric power using a local stream did not find favour with ratepayers, and in 1910 Samuel Jickell proposed the more distant Mangahao Stream. His scheme was widely felt to be feasible, but once again action was deferred because of difficult economic times. At this point the government weighed in on two fronts. In a first step, it called for supply to be consolidated under regional boards,

rather than boroughs each setting up their own independent generating stations. The Manawatu–Oroua Electric Power Board was set up on this basis in 1921, incorporating Feilding Borough Council, Oroua County and Manawatu County. Palmerston North, along with Kairanga County, was urged to join but declined. Then the government took over Samuel Jickell's scheme for the Mangahao hydroelectric dam, and did so with such success that from 1924 it was supplying the entire Manawatū district except Palmerston North.[78]

Continuing in its independent course, Palmerston North completed its gas-powered generating station earlier that year. Determined to justify this investment, the council embarked on an energetic marketing campaign, even triggering retailer indignation by trespassing into the sale of electrical appliances. Street lighting was made all-electric by 1927. Unsurprisingly, uptake soon exceeded

The Palmerston North abattoir, situated on Maxwells Line, Awapuni, c.1907, shortly after construction. The two men in bowler hats are the managers of the Manawatu Meat Company: A. J. Rawstrom (left) and C. F. Carter (right). The buildings were demolished in 1969, and the site is now occupied by the Carter Crescent development. Manawatū Heritage 2009N_Bm111_BUI_2676

Palmerston North Electric Power Station, Keith Street, 2011. Situated at Terrace End, and originally with a railway siding for the supply of coal, the power station commenced operations in May 1924. Photograph: Lesley Courtney, Manawatū Heritage 2011BD_IMCA-DigitalMaster_006158

the capacity of the station, at which point the council resorted to stand-over tactics to obtain additional supply from the board. In 1936, upgrades to the station restored the city to self-sufficiency, which proved particularly useful during the national post-war power shortages. Eventually, however, the North Island grid took over as the main provider.[79]

Public transport was comparatively slow in coming to Palmerston North. Interest was whetted by the installation of electric trams in the main centres, followed by Whanganui in 1908. Samuel Jickell produced a plan of a possible network, but projected significant losses, at least initially, and successive ratepayer polls rejected the proposal. Eventually in 1920 a petrol-driven bus service was instituted instead, after consultation with New Plymouth, which had successfully trialled this type of vehicle. The initial fleet was greatly augmented over succeeding decades, with the policy of providing a basic service to all new suburbs irrespective of the losses incurred.[80]

From the time of its initial survey, as we have seen, Palmerston North was conceived of as a communications and transportation node.[81] A public notice over the signature of William Fitzherbert, Commissioner of Crown Lands, dated 17 September 1866, notes that the 'main lines of road now in progress of formation, leading to the navigable part of the river, the Forty Mile Bush, and Rangitik[e]i, concentrate on the town of Palmerston'; in other words, would meet there. Almost immediately the settlement became the beneficiary of the switch from coastal and river transportation to road and rail, instigated by Premier Julius Vogel in the 1870s. Thus the plan for river communication between Palmerston North and Foxton was modified so as to provide for a road running the whole distance between the towns.

The second line of road was to travel eastwards from Palmerston North through the Manawatū Gorge into what became the Tararua district, and thence to Hawke's Bay, a line of communication that could only be opened up thanks to the new focus on overland connections. The road through the gorge was used for nearly 150 years, with successive upgrades to widen and straighten the road. It was ultimately to prove unviable, however, for geotechnical reasons. But the importance of the route, per se, was never in doubt where regional commerce was concerned, and, along with the railway, it has also proved invaluable for regional resilience, a notable example being the mass evacuation of earthquake survivors from Napier to Palmerston North in February 1931.[82] The third line of road led more straightforwardly, without need for public works heroics, towards the established farming district of Rangitīkei.[83]

Missing from this planning was direct access by road to Wellington. That was because a coastal route from Wellington to Whanganui, running through Foxton, already existed; by 1882, however, it had been abandoned in favour of an inland route which took in Palmerston North. Meanwhile another line of road — also designed to link Palmerston North to Wellington, but much further inland, skirting the western flank of the Tararua Range — was being advocated for its potential to open up new farmland.[84] Development of this highway, which proceeded fitfully over many years, presupposed a bridge over the Manawatū River at Palmerston North, and the establishment and continued maintenance of this crossing was to become one of the city's major sagas. Government grudgingly paid for the bridge, opened in 1877, but the structure and its approaches proved scarcely adequate to withstand the ravages of a wild river. The replacement bridge, built in 1935, although much more solid, within a few decades also proved unable to handle the increasing volumes of traffic, and the stability of its piers was in question. When it was replaced in 1987, planning once again fell short of actual requirements, and two extra lanes had to be squeezed in as an afterthought. As noted above, Palmerston North still has no second road bridge across the river.[85]

Plans for rail links, like those for roads, saw Palmerston North as a nodal location. Robert Pharazyn and A. W. F. Halcombe, reporting to the Minister of Public Works in

The second Fitzherbert Bridge across the Manawatū River, with its characteristic 'bowstring' arches, completed in 1935, shown c.1950.
Photograph: R. M. Greenwood, Manawatū Heritage 2007N_Br81_BRW_0569

1870, foresaw that the main trunk railway would run through the township. The construction of a tramway from Palmerston North to Ngāwhakarau ('Half-crown') — a location near Ōpiki that marked the limit of practicable navigation upriver from Foxton — commenced in 1871. In the same year, the right bank of the Manawatū Gorge was being surveyed for a railway that eventually opened in 1891. This route, along with the road connection through the gorge, effectively captured the Hawke's Bay region, whose direct southwards communications with Wellington were problematic. As early as 1877 the claim could be made that 'from its central position and the command it has of the railway routes Palmerston seems destined to become in the interior what Wellington is on the seaboard — "the great distributing port"'.

This claim was reinforced in 1886 by the completion of a Wellington–Manawatū railway terminating in Palmerston North. Its incorporation into the North Island main trunk in 1908 effectively sidelined the Foxton-to-Palmerston North railway, which finally closed in 1964.[86] Palmerston North's ambitions as a transportation hub continue with proposals for the creation of an inland port at Longburn;[87] realisation of this venture would represent a synergy of rail and road networks beyond the dreams of politicians and engineers 150 years ago.

The inauguration of Union Airways commercial service at Milson Aerodrome, 1936. The runway, like the rest of the airport, was grassed. The airline opted for the DH86, a four-engine passenger aircraft, of which three are seen in the photograph. It could carry between 10 and 12 passengers, depending on the precise model. The DH86 took to the limit the possibilities of traditional 'plywood and canvas' aircraft construction. Manawatū Heritage 2007N_Av26_A-E_0296

Air transport announced itself in the 1920s. Stimulated by visits from Charles Kingsford Smith and other celebrity pilots, the city, along with neighbouring local bodies, considered acquiring land for an aerodrome, only to reject the idea as too far ahead of its time. The city was, after all, comparatively well served by ground transportation, and its leaders could hardly have foreseen that by the 1950s New Zealand would have become one of the most 'air-minded' countries in the world. However, other centres had already gone ahead, and private enterprise, in the shape of the Milson Aerodrome Society, was quick to seize the initiative locally. Opened in 1931, the airfield was chosen in 1936 by Union Airways of NZ Ltd (later National Airways Corporation) as headquarters of their inter-island service, bypassing Wellington because of the inadequate infrastructure at Rongotai. This gave Palmerston North the nodal status in air transportation that it already enjoyed for road and rail; indeed its excellent onward connections by rail to both Wellington and Auckland became the justification for what seems an extraordinary decision on the part of Union Airways not to extend the inter-island service to either of these main centres. Similarly, no provision was made for flights to Christchurch, on the basis that that city enjoyed good linkage with Wellington via the Lyttelton ferry. Competition with rail and ferry services was considered unwise.

In 1937 the council felt safe in purchasing a majority interest in the aerodrome society. But, unlike the other modes of transportation, air transport presupposed that the municipality would meet the costs of ground infrastructure. This it was reluctant to do; passenger facilities remained primitive and the grass runway, so far from being sealed, was not even properly drained. Impetus was lost, and in 1953, following a major fire, NAC moved its engineering headquarters to Christchurch. The airport also lost its main trunk status, although the 1960s and 1990s saw progressive improvements, and for a brief period from 1996 it hosted international flights.[88]

In sum, Palmerston North is sustained by its status as a servicing centre for a hinterland of small farms, and as a nodal point for transportation and communications. Although the colonial founders of inland towns often had only a vague notion of the function these communities would fulfil, in the case of Palmerston North their vision has to that extent proved accurate. The essential initial decision was to place the settlement at a crossing of major lower North Island routes; no other local settlement (for example, Foxton, Feilding or Ashhurst) could rival this strategic location. Augmented by the creation of the inland route to Wellington and the opening of the Pohangina Valley, it remains a strength for the city.

Also part of the early planning, the provision for a substantial public reserve, along with The Square, signalled the settlement's ambitions. The tenacity of its early settlers, particularly the Scandinavians, in effecting access and creating farmland, and the goodwill of tangata whenua in supporting them, put the township on a sound footing. Decisive steps towards an urban character were taken in the 1880s, 1890s and early 1900s, with the provision of key infrastructure and the acquisition of banks, a courthouse, schools, a broad spectrum of churches, an opera house and other typical urban facilities and amenities. This was redoubled in the late 1910s and the 1920s with the provision of utilities and amenities, such as the gasworks, an electricity generating station, a destructor, a bus fleet, a library and swimming baths.

Injections of government finance helped to bring Massey Agricultural College in the late 1920s, and bolstered the city's working-class suburbs in the late 1930s and 1940s. A crucial step, finally achieved in the 1960s and 1970s, was the removal of the railway from the centre and its supplantation with a cluster of civic buildings that avowedly expressed the community's ambitions. Periods of vacillation, controversy, loss of impetus, stagnation and even decline are inevitably also part of the history. The city's layout, infrastructure and communications as we see them nowadays can be read as the product of two mutually countervailing forces: ambitions towards expansion, modernity, prosperity and regional domination on the one hand, and a limited ability to attract investment and anxieties about financial over-commitment on the other.

05
A CITY AT WORK

MARGARET TENNANT & SIMON JOHNSON

The Manawatu Knitting Mills is one of Palmerston North's oldest businesses, and an important employer of women. It was known as the Manawatu Hosiery Factory when this photograph was taken, probably in the early 1920s. Sisters often worked alongside each other, since recruitment was often via friends and family members already on the staff. Manawatū Heritage 2011N-P137_006066

Te Papaiōea and its surroundings have always provided sites where people laboured on a seasonal or more permanent basis. As noted in earlier chapters, the adjoining forest was a bountiful source of sustenance for Māori, and the Hokowhitu, Te Ngutu, Awatapu and Awapuni lagoons were rich sources of eels. Kūmara gardens were cultivated on the Manawatū River flats south of where the Fitzherbert Bridge is located. By the 1850s Māori living further south had extensive gardens along the fertile banks of the Manawatū, producing maize, kūmara, wheat and potatoes for a Wellington market heavily dependent on their industry.[1]

Flax was also traded at Foxton, Māori supplying fibre dressed by traditional methods, which was regarded as superior to that from European-owned mills.[2] In 1865 Foxton resident Amos Burr was appointed overseer of Māori labourers in the Manawatū, an early indication of the spaces designated for Māori in a settler-dominated future.[3] A transition to waged labour features in the story of tangata whenua, but whānau-based work continued, even within supposedly 'modern' workplaces.

The first Europeans to arrive collectively in Palmerston North were specifically recruited because of their work skills: Scandinavians, who were experienced in forestry. Some were also experienced in railway work, having been engaged in cutting sleepers and laying railway lines in their home countries, which made them attractive as labourers on public works schemes. The Norwegians who arrived in 1871 provided an employer's template for the ideal worker, then and since: mostly aged 21–36 years old, they were described as 'of robust constitution, used to hard work and still harder fare, sober and industrious and of cheerful disposition and easily contented'.[4] But they were not to remain employees, for it was intended that they would become farmers on their own holdings, soon joining the ranks of the self-employed.

The Norwegian wives were approvingly described as having employed themselves in spinning and weaving, all of the men's clothing being 'entirely of home manufacturing'.[5] It was a reminder of women's centrality to the family economy through their unpaid work: they represented the 'colonial helpmeets' described by Raewyn Dalziel and others, settler women whose support and labour anchored the male transition into life in a new country.[6] The 15 children among the first Scandinavian group were described as very young, but they, too, were potential workers, and not only when they reached maturity.

Work was paid and unpaid, took place in multiple contexts, and involved men, women and children. Its arrangement, status and categorisation have challenged New Zealand historians. Quantitative sources, such as the census, only partially help us to understand employment patterns, since occupational descriptors changed, and, in the nineteenth century especially, census respondents themselves supplied ambiguous occupational labels — a reflection of their own complex and changing relationship with the world of work.[7] For example, individuals often had more than one occupation, at the same time, seasonally, and over a lifetime — and some still do. There are varied lenses onto work, which provided sustenance, status, companionship and, for more fortunate participants, personal satisfaction; it could also be tedious, dangerous, exploitative and conflict-ridden.

Palmerston North as a city at work can be usefully divided into two periods of time. Over the late nineteenth century, Palmerston North represented a version of settler colonialism, work initially involving forestry — the area's main extractive industry — and primary production. Waged labour of diverse kinds provided an aspirational pathway to self-sufficiency based on property and business ownership. Work for many was physical, the individual body an engine of toil. Family enterprises were common. Urban occupational patterns had already started to emerge by 1900, the growth of the town itself generating an internal service sector alongside workplaces catering to the needs of Palmerston North's rural hinterland.

Between 1850 and 2000, 'work and workers changed so fundamentally as to constitute a complete social transformation in New Zealand'.[8] Palmerston North participated in these changes, which saw the rise of white-collar occupations, the professionalisation of many areas of work, and an expansion of government employment, alongside a decline in the proportion of the workforce that was self-employed. The acceleration of women's entry into paid work was a feature of the late twentieth century, while Māori increasingly moved from being a largely rural labour force to one actively recruited for urban employment from the 1960s. The service sector was an especially important generator of employment in Palmerston North.

In the 1870s the bushman may have been 'king',[9] but the following decade was already characterised by change. The timber town was in the process of becoming a rural service centre offering a widening range of employment opportunities, as evidenced in the census-night population of Palmerston North rising from 880 in 1878, to 2606 in 1888, and 6534 in 1901.[10] Occupations were no more fixed in the new settlement than elsewhere in New Zealand — historians have commented on the 'jack-of-all-trades' and the need for workers to be adaptable.[11] But some settlers were already making the shift from waged labouring to ownership of small, increasingly self-sufficient family farms that also began to produce surpluses for an expanding local market. There were wider prospects on the horizon for them and for associated businesses as dairy exports expanded and a local freezing industry developed from 1890. While family labour often sustained farms and other workplaces, Palmerstonians also became employers of labour, with new workplace divisions starting to emerge, some more marked than others.

Much of the work was still physically demanding, and it increasingly included the construction of infrastructure and utilities. With nationwide economic depression by the 1880s, there were cutbacks in the public works, which had provided an important employment backstop for families 'breaking in' their own farms. Work opportunities on the railway south continued under private investment, however, and construction of the railway east to Hawke's Bay was resumed after considerable protest, eventually opening in 1891.

The Palmerston North Borough Council had begun a substantial investment in infrastructure, which may have cushioned some of the effects of recession locally. This was enabled by the £10,000 loan sought in 1878, and the extraordinarily large £50,000 loan raised between 1885 and 1889 (at a time of national recession), which underwrote work on water supply and sewage disposal, along with further improvements to streets and stormwater drainage.[12]

Amidst the figures it is easy to forget that most of this work involved hard physical toil with pick and shovel. While many of the larger projects involved contractors, the council's foreman of works supervised a small number of 'day men' employed directly by the council in levelling, metalling and maintaining roads and footpaths. Reports to council carefully detailed expenditure, but also give a sense of the laborious nature of the work:

> In North Street [in mid-1884], 23 chains of Metalling, 8 ft wide and 6in thick, had taken the Horse, Cart, and Man 26½ days at a cost of £15 18s, and one man stripping and spreading gravel 26½ days £9 5s 6d — being in all at the rate of 2s 2 1/4d per yard.[13]

Across the Wellington province, general labourers could earn 7–8 shillings a day, without keep; artisans such as carpenters 10 shillings a day. 'Stonebreakers' were paid according to productivity: 3s 6d per cubic yard was the going rate in the mid-1880s.[14]

In the 1870s and 1880s the forests and sawmills of the district provided work for axemen, for the bullockies and horse-tram drivers who carted the logs between the felling site and the mill, for cooks and other support workers, and for the mill hands. Local historian George Petersen gives a figure of 23 steam-driven mills in the Upper Manawatū in 1879: at least five operated within the present boundaries of Palmerston North over the 1870s and 1880s, opening and closing as the forest retreated, shifting to new sites and,

sometimes, burning down.[15] There were signs of diversification from the timber work, with a flour mill adjacent to the Richter Nannestad and Co. timber operation on the corner of Scandia (now Albert) Street and Broad Street, and the emergence of sash and door and building companies.

In his recollections of the 1880s, Michael Rosanowski remembered the mill workers who received 4–6 shillings a day and 'could live well on the wages received' — when, and if they were received. For he also recalled:

> When the bush and mill hands went to get their month's pay the firm said, 'We cannot pay you as we have no money'. But they gave them an order on the grocer (and) they took out in groceries and clothing to the amount of the order. This went on for months until the firm got their money in for timber sold.[16]

This anecdote is a reminder of the precariousness of work at the time, and of networks of support, for the grocer was part of

The Palmerston North Sash, Door and Timber Co. Ltd yard, c.1900. Sawmills often generated joinery companies and other forms of productivity, including the flour mill erected by Richter, Nannestad and Co. Ltd in 1878 (the three-storey white building in the middle distance, which stood on the north side of what is now Broadway near Albert Street, currently the site of a supermarket). Note the special rail siding running from Main Street to the flour mill. Manawatū Heritage 2007N_Ti42_WOR_0130 the exchange and probably also waited for payment. The fragility of the various enterprises in which the town's early residents engaged is reflected in the many reports of bankruptcies in local newspapers, and even prominence and popularity did not provide protection from the vagaries of colonial life. George Snelson was often referred to as the 'father' of Palmerston North, and was its first mayor and a leading member of multiple community and local bodies. His work identities were, like many New Zealanders' at the time, multiple. He most often appears as an auctioneer and valuer, but was also at various times an ironmonger, a storekeeper and, in his last decade, the local coroner, making him a government functionary, part-time, at least. Yet even he experienced financial difficulties following ill health in the 1890s, which saw him give up his business. He was forced to seek rates relief in 1898, and left behind an impoverished widow on his death in 1901.[17]

For those reliant on manual labour, illness and injury could be devastating. There are numerous reports of accidents in Palmerston North newspapers of the time, as workers were caught under falling trees, buried by rockfalls and earthworks, crushed by out-of-control logging trams, and injured in various ways by panicked and bolting horses.

Among the various institutions which emerged to mitigate the effects of accident and illness were friendly societies, which offered welfare and funeral benefits to breadwinners and their dependents. The Ancient Order of Foresters had a particularly strong hold in the area, having its own hall by 1876, and 10 years later a membership of more than 200. Men also joined up with the Oddfellows, Druids and Rechabites, all of which had a presence by the mid-1880s.[18] Lauded as 'the backbone of the working man's freedom and independence', the benefit societies were also seen as encouraging worker respectability; even, a *Manawatu Times* editorial optimistically suggested, having 'a salutary effect upon men in their domestic and social relations', making them better husbands, more thoughtful fathers, and more principled masters and servants.[19]

Unions were another form of worker solidarity, and early signs of concern about work conditions and wages are shown in the formation of a Palmerston North branch of the Railway Employees' Union in 1889, and of the Carpenters' and Joiners' Union and the Knights of Labour in 1890.[20] Like the friendly societies, unions resulted from external recruitment, visiting canvassers linking Palmerston North workers to a national — and in the case of the Knights of Labour, international — labour cause.

Referencing the flax industry to the south of Palmerston North, Erik Olssen suggests that pioneering society was 'strongly egalitarian' and based on informality, versatility and shared physical labour. It was in Palmerston North township that social divisions emerged, initially 'between the stable residents and the footloose transients who patronised the boarding houses, bars and brothels that sprang up along the railway tracks in the centre of Palmerston North'.[21] There were signs of this divide in the 1870s and 1880s, with single men being regarded as less likely than their married counterparts to settle and become solid community members. The borough, and then the city, would always have its wayfarers, those passing through, but they would be less visibly transient — and *un*settled — than the labouring men of the nineteenth century.

Status divisions became more entrenched, Olssen suggests, once the borough developed further into a rural service town.[22] One sign was the 1884 formation of an exclusive gentlemen's club, the Manawatu Club, by a number of local businessmen, lawyers, doctors and other professionals — those 'in trade' being unacceptable as members.[23] In 1889, Palmerston North working men formed their own club, from 1927 known as the Cosmopolitan Club, but its membership was always more varied.

Women's work is less visible than men's in the historical record, and was to become even more hidden once women (along with children) were classified as 'dependants' in the 1896 and subsequent censuses. In 1886, 70 per cent of Palmerston North females aged over 15 were married or widowed (compared with 50 per cent of adult males),[24] and most of their work would have been domestic and unpaid, but nonetheless vitally significant to household standards of living and cleanliness. As Stevan Eldred-Grigg has pointed out: 'Kitchens, laundries and outhouses were

The Palmerston North Friendly Societies Council in the early 1900s. The Foresters, Hibernians, Oddfellows, Rechabites and Druids were represented, their members and families estimated to make up a quarter of the city's population by 1912. This was enough to justify the opening of a Friendly Societies Dispensary (chemist shop) in Cuba Street in 1914. Manawatū Heritage 2007N_Pg51_GRO_1100

busy workshops, places where people constantly cooked and baked, bottled and brewed, knitted and sewed, mended and made . . . Work of this sort boosted the real wealth of the individual household and the whole economy.'[25]

In the late-nineteenth-century borough where there was still much of the rural, with undeveloped sections and wandering stock, women's contribution to the family economy could also involve keeping poultry, overseeing the orchard, milking cows and churning butter. Some, at least, sold their butter for 6d per pound to the Ready Money Store.[26]

Nationally, about half of the paid female workforce was in domestic service during the 1880s, and there were ongoing complaints about the 'servant shortage'.[27] Servants were in demand in Palmerston North as families acquired sufficient wealth to employ them, and household space in which to put them — so much so that a Mrs Morley found it worthwhile in 1883 to combine a servants' registry office with her work as a milliner and ladies' outfitter and her feather cleaning and dyeing service. (Workforce versatility obviously was not the prerogative of men.)

In 1883 and 1884 Mrs Morley's advertisements appeared regularly in the *Manawatu Times*: 'Situations wanted by General Servants, Housemaids, Married Couple and Lads for Farm. Engagements required by music teacher and Monthly Nurse. Mrs Morley, Registry Office next Ready Money Store, The Square.'[28] Women seeking domestic servants also

Businesses soon spread after Palmerston North's establishment, the borough council having to resist pressures to further subdivide The Square for commerce. Looking from Main Street east towards Church Street, this image shows the Ready Money Store with Mrs Morley's Millinery shop next to it. The sign above the verandah also advertises her servants' registry office. The Club Hotel is on the opposite side of the Church Street corner.
Manawatū Heritage 2014N_Sq49_008579

advertised directly: 'A Strong Woman as General Servant, in a family where there are three young children, references required, good wages.'[29] Advertisements also appeared seeking apprentices for the dressmaking departments of drapery and clothing stores, dressmaking being a more general mainstay for women who needed to earn a living.[30] Lydia Burr, the estranged wife of Amos Burr (who appears earlier in this chapter as overseer of Māori labourers), worked first as a dressmaker from her Foxton home before becoming head of the dressmaking department of Leopold Simmons' Palmerston North drapery store.[31]

Women's efforts could boost the family income in even more entrepreneurial ways. One of Palmerston North's oldest factories, Manawatu Knitting Mills, originated from the mechanised sock-knitting efforts of a married woman, Mary Alice Stubbs, in 1884. Operating as a cottage industry — first from a railway cottage at Aorangi, and later from a Kairanga farm — the business was established as a factory shop in Main Street, Palmerston North, in 1889.[32] Other women assisted in existing family businesses.

Widowed in her seventies before the advent of old-age pensions, Emma Belk appears in street directories in the early 1890s as a 'grocer', helping to run her son's shop in Main Street.[33] But the largest single descriptor for women householders in the post office directories of the late nineteenth century was 'boarding house keeper', an activity compatible with childcare and requiring little initial capital.[34] It was closely followed by 'nurse' (which did not necessarily mean a woman with formal hospital training).

Even the first mayoress, Louisa Snelson, provides an example of women's diverse use of their skills. During her early years in the settlement she took in boarders, and provided a letter-writing service at 6d a letter to Scandinavians who could not write in English. In her penurious widowhood she boosted her income through giving art lessons and selling flower paintings. And throughout her time in Palmerston North she was a mainstay of another form of women's work: a leader in many voluntary and fundraising efforts of the kinds noted in Chapter 9.[35]

Not all forms of women's work in Palmerston North were reassuringly respectable and family-focused. A more illicit form of female work was exemplified by Louisa Cullen, who was charged in May 1885 with keeping a disorderly house (the alternative term for a brothel) in Taonui Street. A neighbour, cook Henry Hopkins, deposed that he frequently saw drunken and sober men go to the house at all hours, often coming to his own house by mistake and waking up his wife. The language used 'was not fit to be repeated'. Louisa Cullen was eventually convicted by magistrates Snelson and Waldegrave, fined £5 and costs, and 'cleared out during the next day or two without paying up'.[36] As Catherine Bishop notes in her history of colonial businesswomen, female brothel keepers and prostitutes who worked independently had 'a niche role in the colonial economy, making money by catering for a ready demand for sex', but undertaking such work often resulted from desperation and limited alternatives.[37] Unless neighbours complained, as they did about Louisa Cullen, discreet activity on this front was usually tolerated. But in 1894 it was reported that Palmerston North police were making strenuous efforts to 'close the houses of ill-fame in the town, the evil having increased considerably over the past year'.[38]

What of child workers? Nationally some 9300 children under the age of 15 were classified as 'breadwinners' in the 1891 census, the first to give a detailed age breakdown.[39] The number in Palmerston North is unknown, but the many advertisements for 'a good strong lad' in local newspapers during the 1880s show that young, cheap labour was in demand. But even children classified as 'dependants' played their part in the family economy, with the tension between schooling and family demands shown in the high levels of absenteeism at the Palmerston North (and other) schools, as noted in Chapter 7. The exemptions from schooling allowed in the 1877 Education Act acknowledged the importance of child labour to families (especially those in rural and semi-rural areas), and it would be some decades before schooling was embedded as the proper 'work' of those aged 14 and under.

The 1902 *Wise's Post Office Directory* suggests that the largest single occupational

The butchering of animals linked Palmerston North to its rural hinterland. Individuals had the skill to process a whole beast in small slaughterhouses at the time this photo was taken at the turn of the century. The job was increasingly deskilled once the chain system was introduced at large meat works such as Longburn. Manawatū Heritage 2011N_Mt3_005676 category in Palmerston North at the beginning of the twentieth century was still 'farmer' or 'settler', followed by 'labourer'. However, there was a widening range of occupations, from builders, storekeepers, blacksmiths, brewers, butchers and bakers; government employees such as the constables, teachers and postmaster; to self-employed professionals such as architects and solicitors.[40] Labour Department reports showed that the number of factories was increasing, from 61 in 1897 to 115 in 1902, and 206 in 1905 (employing 1052 males and 223 females). Most were effectively small workshops, the Longburn freezing works being the largest plant (70 men in 1898).[41] A handful of these entrepreneurial small businesses remained in some form into the twenty-first century — Robêrt Embroideries, Martin Engineering and the Manawatu Knitting Mills, for example.

As the number of non-manual occupations increased and bosses moved off the shop floor, work started to intersect with status and other forms of identity. Palmerston North's relatively late settlement and small-scale industry meant that employment was never mirrored by residential segregation to the degree found in larger, older and more industrialised settlements such as Dunedin.

A history of Palmerston North business might linger on the entrepreneurship of the early twentieth century and the many firms captured in the 1937 diamond jubilee publication, *From Swamp to City*. But by 2000 the majority of these established businesses, employers large and small, had closed down or transformed. More significantly, the nature of employment altered considerably in the last decades of the century as Palmerston North participated in global changes. The world of work was much more complex and specialised than in the foundation years, and workers' experience can get lost under the mass of statistics and studies on the one hand,[42] and institutional histories foregrounding founders on the other.[43]

Inspired by the 1968 National Development Conference, Palmerston North's town planners oversaw a clutch of work-related studies from the late 1960s. The labour force as a whole had become something to be studied, planned for, and directed into areas that would enhance the productivity 'and hence the economic and social wellbeing of the community'[44] — it was significant that among this cluster there was a report on vocational guidance, which brought together the individual and strategic significance of work choices.[45]

This and other research suggested that national employment trends were being replicated in Palmerston North, including the steady increase in part-time workers, mostly linked to a significant rise in the number of married women in the labour force; and a continued decline in members of the workforce who were employers and self-employed. (In 1996, 11.6 per cent of males and 3.8 per cent of females, compared with 23.5 per cent and 12.8 per cent, respectively, in 1916, the year that the census data first gave detailed information on urban areas.)[46]

Palmerston North City Council treasury staff at work in what is now the Square Edge building, 1958. White-collar clerical work became more common over the twentieth century, and these council staff show a range of tasks undertaken manually in a pre-computer age. Rear table, from left: Bryan Weston (stores and vehicle transfers), Bill Dick (voucher payments), Colin McVicar (stores). Centre table: Arthur Matthews (salaries). Front table: Bert Newth and Bill Potbury (wages). Manawatū Heritage 2010N_Cc29_3263

Industries data from the 1970s and 1980s showed that Palmerston North's workforce approximated that of the country as a whole, but with some differences. A very small proportion was now in agriculture and forestry, and an insignificant number in mining and quarrying locally; and proportionately fewer than the national average were in manufacturing (around 20 per cent compared with 23–24 per cent nationally by 1981). There was a significantly higher proportion in community, social and personal services than national averages (some 36 per cent of the employed by 1981, compared with 26 per cent nationally).[47] The overall importance of the service sector, compared with national averages, had been boosted in the 1960s by the expansion of advanced educational facilities, most especially Massey University, and by the nearby research institutes. They were not only employers, but development sites, and collaborators in business innovation.

From the late 1960s city leaders and planners fixated on industry, concerned that the city's rate of growth in manufacturing was below the national average. There were proportionately fewer workers per Palmerston North factory than nationally, and the number of employers in the sector was declining.[48] Planners believed that 'the establishment of secondary industry is . . . a movement towards maturity in the development of a town',[49] and economist W. B. Sutch was commissioned to write a detailed report on Palmerston North's potential for industrial growth.[50] Large amounts of land were zoned for industry in the Kelvin Grove area, and long-term city planner Ken Tremaine later remembered being horrified at the 'humungous' amounts involved when he first arrived in 1976. He supposed the development was based on an assumption that 'if you zoned it, it would happen', but any aspirations that Palmerston North might have had to be 'the Ruhr of the South Pacific' were soon curtailed by external forces.[51]

By the late 1960s the New Zealand government was already reducing tariffs and restrictions on imports, and the neo-liberal reforms of the 1980s and 1990s further opened markets up to global competition. Between 1986 and 2012 industrial employment declined from 20 per cent of total city employment to around 6 per cent.[52] Prominent firms that closed down or substantially changed their function included Glaxo, Sanitarium, Sunbeam/Ralta, Lane Walker Rudkin's 'Libertyland', the Bridewell's and Boniface bread-manufacturing plants, and the freezing works at Longburn. These developments showed the vulnerability of the city's workforce to external forces, and most came with a human cost.

The public sector also experienced huge changes. The public service presence in Palmerston North at the end of the nineteenth century had largely consisted of the postmaster and his eight or nine staff, the sergeant major of police and his handful of subordinates, some 30 railways staff (plus others 'along the line'), and 25 public school teachers.[53] Palmerston North later benefited from the boom in the role of the state between the late 1940s and the early 1970s. By 1981 the largest 'core' government departments were the Post Office (1092 staff), Railways (800), the district engineer's department (370), Defence (670) and Agriculture and Fisheries (246). Combined with the many other government functions represented in the city — from police, audit, government printing, and forestry to health and welfare — the public service provided jobs for nearly 5000 Palmerstonians. If other public sector institutions were added — such as Massey University, with 2800 employees, the public hospital (1263), the Palmerston North City Corporation (680) and the DSIR (286) — government-related employment involved 10,502 persons, or 37 per cent of Palmerston North's labour force in 1981.[54] In relation to the size of the workforce, government sector investment was greater than in any other centre in New Zealand.[55]

This dominance meant that government sector restructuring had a significant impact on Palmerston North, especially in the 1990s. Prior to this, some of the effects were masked by the return of troops from Singapore to the Linton Camp, but over 1990–91 the number of full-time-equivalent government sector positions in Palmerston North dropped by 8.4 per cent. While the decline had stabilised by 2000 and the public sector remained important to the city, it was now represented by state-owned enterprises and commercial and non-commercial government entities, as well as the more standard education, welfare, health and community organisations. Employment numbers were not the whole story, for the

While the public service rented buildings throughout the city, the solidity of the large government building on the corner of George and Cuba streets symbolised the huge importance of government to the city. It was demolished in 1992, at a time when public sector restructuring was having an impact on the city. Manawatū Heritage 2009P_Bg16b_BUI_2750

Businesses that were part of the Palmerston North landscape for many years included (from top) the Glaxo pharmaceuticals factory and laboratory on Botanical Road, Libertyland underwear factory on Tremaine Avenue, the Sanitarium cereals and health food factory at Longburn (famed for its gardens), and the Hodder and Tolley 'Tui' building on Rangitikei Street. Hodder and Tolley began as a seed and stock food business, and its founders, staunch Methodists Rayner Hodder and Harry Tolley, would not have foreseen the current use of their 1926 building as home to another form of women's work.

Glaxo: Elmar Studios, Manawatū Heritage 2008N_Bc94_BUI_1804; Libertyland: photograph: A. Taylor, Manawatū Heritage 2007N_Bc148_BUI_0180; Sanitarium: MS, Manawatū Heritage 2009P_Bc197_BUI_2611; Hodder and Tolley: photograph: Val Burr public sector shared in a transformation that affected the workforce as a whole: a deference to business models and a retreat from the notions of a lifetime career, full-time work and steady progression through the ranks of a workplace.

This was apparent at the public hospital, for example. As well as health-related staff, the hospital employed over the years a range of household, outdoor and other workers — the engineers, firemen and stokers, motor mechanics, cooks, porters, storemen, gardeners and clerks who knew all about the metaphorical bones and sinews of the hospital's inner and outer workings. Some stayed for decades, the hospital's history noting a number of staff in the 1966–79 period whose record extended over more than 40 years. This became less common, or possible, as an increasing number of the hospital's functions were contracted out to the private sector in the 1990s. As 'MidCentral Health', the hospital lost its old triumvirate of chief medical officer, chief nurse and chief executive (earlier, the board secretary) which was replaced in 1989 by a general manager. Although the business ethos had softened by the early 2000s, and the leadership of care returned more directly to those with aligned skills, staff continued to work within a framework of efficiency, accountability and reporting that would have been alien to earlier generations. More positively, with these changes came greater attention to cultural awareness and patients' rights, along with a still-expanding but more ethnically diverse workforce. The hospital and its wider services were at the sharp end of wider workplace changes in the late twentieth century.

TOP 10 INDUSTRY SECTORS IN TERMS OF EARNINGS, 2018
(JOBS AS AT FEBRUARY 2018; EARNINGS, YEAR ENDED MARCH 2018)

INDUSTRY	JOBS	EARNINGS ($M)
Health care and social assistance	7200	404
Public safety and administration	5700	350
Education and training	6200	338
Logistics	5250	333
Retail sector	7900	288
Professional, scientific, tech services	2700	240
Construction	3750	239
Manufacturing	3250	211
Other services	1850	92
Admin and support services	2550	85
Other sectors	3665	280
Total	50,015	2860

Report to Economic Development Committee, Palmerston North City Council, March 2020, http://palmerstonnorth.infocouncil.biz/Open/2020/03/ECO_20200311_AGN_9845_AT_WEB.htm

Consumer meets retail: Mrs Betty Evans became the exemplar of the mid-twentieth-century housewife in national publicity materials produced in 1947. She was shown shopping at the Manawatu Co-operative's shop on the corner of Cook and College streets. The home-based worker/housewife of the later twentieth century was increasingly likely to be purchasing foodstuffs and other goods rather than making them in her own home. Manawatū Heritage 2010__A175-67-1_004206

With a declining birth rate and cutbacks in education, the health and care sector had surpassed education as the largest source of earnings in the city by 2018. The public administration and safety sector became the city's second largest in terms of earnings, reflecting the presence of government departments, state-owned enterprises and the Linton army camp. Retail provided the largest number of jobs in the city, but its proportionately large share of part-time and casual jobs made it less important in terms of total earnings.

Measurement of work in terms of earnings was more common in city council publications as economic contribution became the key indicator of the value of work to the city, and as part-time and casual work made job counts complex. Casualisation of the workforce was a change from the mid-twentieth century, when work was more usually full-time, often in the same workplace until retirement, and dominated by assumptions about male breadwinning.

From the 1970s there was a growing recognition of the resource inherent in women's paid work, and the profound social shift around married women earning in their own right, rather than being secondary beneficiaries of the male workforce. Women constituted approximately one-third of Palmerston North's workforce in 1971: by 2013 the proportion was just under one-half.[56] The importance of the service sector locally meant that female representation in the workforce was higher than the national average, although women continued to be more heavily represented in part-time work than male employees.[57]

Māori were another significant group to gain separate mention in labour force studies. Although their work was vitally important to the early settlement, it became less visible in subsequent decades, with Māori mostly residing in the surrounding rural areas. In the 1960s the potential of the Māori labour force was highlighted locally and nationally. A 1971 city planning report lamented that 'young and gifted Maori men and women' from the Manawatū and East Coast regions bypassed the city to work in the Wellington–Hutt region when they could be contributing to Palmerston North's growth — and, it was implied, to greater social diversity.[58] By 2006, largely as a result of migration to the city, there were 4770 Māori workers from a number of iwi, around 13 per cent of the total city labour force. Māori were especially heavily represented in some sections of the workforce,

avoid waste
save coupons
MEAT
29
35
Butter
SAVE FOOD FOR BRITAIN
EVEREADY

For some, such as trainee nurses, single male railway workers and Longburn freezing workers, the workplace provided a home. In 1952 railway worker and Dutch immigrant Andre Zentveld posed outside a hut near the railway yards provided as accommodation for single men. Manawatū Heritage 2014N_R63_007827

including at Linton military camp, where they made up 30 per cent of employees by 2016.[59] However, the overall Māori unemployment rate was also higher than the city average (but lower than the national average).[60]

As the Māori, Pasifika and Asian populations of Palmerston North increased more rapidly than the New Zealand average, so, too, did the diversity of the workforce over the first two decades of the twenty-first century. Some groups were more highly represented than others in unemployment and under-employment, including recent refugee arrivals, for whom there could be a lengthy transition to work in a vastly different environment.[61] As always, some benefited more fully than others from participation in the world of work.

The geographical location of different kinds of work shifted over time.[62] The more noxious activities associated with the city's rural connections were gradually moved or eliminated: small slaughter yards had largely disappeared by the First World War; the Rangitikei Street stock sale yards were shifted beyond the borough boundaries in 1912, eventually closing in 1926; and the abattoir in Maxwells Line was closed in 1969. The shift of the railway line had a major impact: industries located near the old railway line in Main Street, some with their own rail sidings, gravitated towards Tremaine Avenue and Rangitikei Line after the opening of the Milson railway deviation in the early 1960s. Market gardens and commercial orchards were pushed out of the city by suburban expansion.

The grand inner-city department stores came and went; although, at the other end of retail, a number of small suburban dairy-groceries still survive using family labour.[63] By the 2000s retail activities and associated employment were being reshaped by the location of large national 'big box' retailers such as Mitre 10 and The Warehouse, and by the location of the city's main mall, The Plaza. The Plaza drew shoppers towards the Church Street side of The Square, employing large numbers of casual, part-time workers (boosted by the student population). High levels of motor vehicle ownership assisted these developments, but were also reflected in another twentieth-century phenomenon: the expansion of the commuter workforce. A 1970 survey estimated that nearly 6 per cent of the city's workforce commuted from beyond the city boundaries, the majority travelling by private motor vehicle. Although the city's boundaries had extended, the 2013 census showed the proportion of commuters had increased to 20 per cent.[64]

Individual workplaces provide a more finely grained picture of work in the city. The fate of three of the city's longer-term businesses show how significant workplaces have altered over time. Each had its own character, and their workers had their own interactions with change as these firms grew, thrived and eventually closed down.[65]

Longburn freezing works: The large, unionised workplace

The Longburn freezing works provided a rich sensory experience: New Zealand meat works were often smelt before they were seen. Within, there was the aroma of blood and faeces, intensified in the rendering department by heat and steam from the cookers; the combination of sulphuric acid and lime in the fellmongery; and the whiff of cigarettes in the days when smoking was tolerated on the chain. There was the chill of the boning room, where a temperature drop of 4 degrees could make the difference between controlling a knife and having it slip into one's arm or wrist, or even losing a finger. Elsewhere there were temperatures that could reach 40 degrees or more in the height of summer.

There was the sting of a piece of intestine deftly flicked at one's cheek, the heavier thump of a piece of chilled carcass accidentally — or deliberately — making contact with the unwary. There was industrial noise, interspersed with jokes and song, and the occasional bellow of a frantic beast after a failed kill. From outside, the works appeared as a descendant of the nineteenth century's dark satanic mills, but, within, the innovative new mutton board of the 1970s seemed the epitome of hygienic modernity, at least before the start of the killing day. And that brought its own sights, union leader Roger Middlemass remembering its paradoxical beauty:

> Before the kill started . . . all you could see was grey concrete. Within twenty minutes there was not a bit of grey concrete to be seen anywhere around you — it was just *crimson* . . . and the blood was everywhere — it was really beautiful in its way. Around two o'clock in the afternoon on a good day the sun would come round from the sheep yards . . . there is nothing more crimson than blood and the sunlight on that blood was really something.[66]

A rich variety of workers shared in this 'world of noise, heat and smell', including student Laurie McCallum, who in 1969 found himself working alongside distinctive characters 'who had not been homogenised by education, television and global culture'.[67] Amidst the grimness, Longburn was a place of camaraderie. Workers shared in sporting events, picnics and parties, and kinship ties were strong, successive generations following one another into the works.[68]

In the 1970s Māori constituted around 40–50 per cent of New Zealand's freezing industry workforce, and they were heavily represented at Longburn. Sonny Rata was just one who remembered leaving school at 16 against his parents' wishes to be with his mates on the Longburn chain: 'The freezing works in those days meant big money. You did not need any education and all my mates were there.' At Longburn the workers' sense of solidarity was underpinned by what has been termed 'workplace whānau', kin and those who effectively became kin through close association.[69]

Workers on the number one chain were an elite among the Longburn manual workers, although the job was increasingly pressured and monotonous. Some slaughtermen followed the killing season down the country from Northland to Ocean Beach in the south, living in the 'tough' single men's quarters while at Longburn.[70] Among those on the chain were tradesmen who could earn far more there than as carpenters and plumbers and electricians, but who often returned to their trade in the off-season. The high-paying freezing works employed another category of seasonal workers: around 100 students from November to March in the 1970s. Longburn exposed them to the realities of a working-class environment. As the 'lowest of the low', student workers soon learned to be vigilant, and to avoid smart remarks. John Muirhead, an alumnus of the Longburn boning room (and also an experienced brain scooper in the small-goods room), soon learned not to turn his back on co-workers lest a chunk of chilled meat be lobbed at his head: the younger labourers 'regarded us as natural enemies' he recalled.[71] The Longburn narrative has been captured by the meat-workers' story, but there were others without whom 'the works' could not have functioned. They included the veterinarians and meat inspectors, who were government rather than company employees, and who occupied an ambiguous role at Longburn (as elsewhere), especially once hygiene regulations tightened. There were office staff, carpenters, electricians and engineers, such as the talented chief engineer Bill Freeman. Freeman worked with Massey University's Dick Earle on new innovations in freezing technology,

ABOVE A Longburn worker processing sheep intestines, 1940s. Most of the cleaned intestines went to the adjacent Kiwi Bacon Factory for casing sausages. Photograph: Elmar Studios, Manawatū Heritage 2011G_Elmar-2-B14_005323

BELOW Workers and supporters protest in March 1980 about the lay-off of 60 beef slaughtermen and ancillary staff after a killing season of only three months. *Manawatu Evening Standard*, Manawatū Heritage 2008N_De2_A-E_1447 including a double-deck freezing tunnel, the design of which was later adopted nationally and internationally.[72] And there was 'management', vilified by union advocates as the agents of uncaring international investors.

Overseas ownership dated back to 1939, but killing at Longburn started in 1890 when the meat works was established by a co-operative, mostly comprising Manawatū farmers. Its location was justified by the presence of the railway line at Longburn, and by its centrality in a growing area of pastoral farming. More than 57,000 animals were slaughtered in the first season (in its best season, nearly 100 years later, 1.5 million).[73]

In 1895 the co-operative was wound up and its principal creditor, the National Mortgage and Agency Company of New Zealand (NMA), took over operations after the business failed to sell at auction — instability and over-capacity for stock on offer were part of Longburn's foundation history. The NMA sold the works to the Co-operative Wholesale Society of Britain (CWS) in 1939, but not before overseeing an important change in its operations, when the solo butchers, who could each process 100 or more lambs per day, were replaced by the chain system in 1931.[74] The associated breakdown of tasks into a 'dis-assembly' line of specialised cuts and operations allowed tasks to be taught to new workers in shorter and shorter timeframes.[75]

The Longburn works had been unionised since at least 1907, but the 1970s and 1980s saw a high point of open confrontation against a background of the 'informal resistance' which characterised the industry as a whole — including wildcat strikes, absenteeism, pilfering and sabotage.[76] In a militant industry, the Longburn site was one of the most cohesively resistant to new pressures, as management, faced with international competition, sought to reduce costs and speed up production. In the 1970s there were major changes within the Longburn works, including the introduction of halal slaughtering, the employment of women and, most significantly for the culture of the works, the extension of new hygiene regulations. Many practices which had made the grisly and monotonous nature of employment bearable for workers were no longer tolerated.

Industrial relations at Longburn were overlain by interpersonal dynamics involving Roger Middlemass, 'an official of the modern school' adept at communication and publicity, and Tom Hastie, manager from 1951 until the mid-1970s. Hastie was described by a local newspaper as 'highly efficient, kindly, and at times, ruthless', but was presented by union representatives as paternalistic and dogmatic.[77] Subsequent managers gained no more co-operation, nor appreciation of their role in managing a complex and difficult operation in changing times.

After a change of ownership to Borthwicks CWS, Longburn succumbed to a downturn in export markets, a reduction in farmer subsidies and the over-supply of facilities for a declining number of stock. Despite its having a relatively new, state-of-the-art mutton-processing board, Longburn's reputation for strikes did not aid survival. It closed in 1986, a lockout eventually becoming permanent, and more than 800 workers lost their jobs.

Like many of the other large urban freezing works, it was replaced by smaller plants with a similar output based largely on shiftwork and a further deskilling of tasks.

Although located outside the city's boundaries, Longburn had been one of its largest employers, the most militant in its history; an enterprise which linked management, workers and whānau from Palmerston North to Rangiotū to Foxton with global processes.

Collinson and Cunninghame: Genteel retail

Customer memories of Broadway's Collinson and Cunninghame department store include the ever-popular magic cave in the basement, the bronze horse near the front of the shop, the elegant tearooms, and the quality products sold in its various departments. Staff likewise remember these trappings of 'the grand old lady',[78] but they also recall a particular style of retail and of employment relationship, both largely associated with a bygone era.

Internationally, the 1920s to the 1960s constituted the heyday of the department store, the multi-level 'cathedral to consumption' that offered a number of services alongside the sale of a wide range of merchandise.[79] Palmerston North had its two large rival stores, Collinson and Cunninghame and C. M. Ross and Co. ('Rosco's'), later joined by the Premier Drapery Company (PDC). None survived the century.

Collinson and Cunninghame staff regarded their firm as the elite of Palmerston North's retail hierarchy. The store opened in 1904 as a drapery, a joint venture between the horse-loving Leo Collinson and staunch Methodist John Cunninghame.[80] Despite their lifestyle differences, the partnership prospered and 'C&C's' became one of Palmerston North's establishment businesses, eventually employing more than 100 staff.

C&C's local, family basis was important to the character of the business, and to employees' perception of it — as in other workplaces of the time, the notion of 'family' was extended to employees, and many showed great steadfastness in embracing it. Indeed, as a 1910 store booklet emphasised: 'Loyalty to the Store is a qualification very much desired in every Assistant, for without it no business can succeed. Those who co-operate in promoting success are valued members of the Staff, those who do not, are a drag on others.'[81] This ethos continued until the store's sale in 1983, former staff enthusing about the experience of working for Collinson and Cunninghame. They fondly remember the annual bonuses, the Christmas gift of a cup and saucer (value calibrated according to staff seniority), the gold watch after 21 years of service, and the personal touches, such as 'Mr Keith' Collinson's annual gift of his homegrown orchids to office staffer Helen Mullinger. The reciprocities of trust and regard were reinforced by picnics and other social occasions in which the store's owners fully participated, and by the existence of men's and women's sports teams, which competed against other businesses in the city. But not all bought into this culture, with former fabric buyer Bryan Gaskin remembering one or two who 'had their hand in the till' and were quietly dismissed.[82]

Bryan Gaskin's memories also acknowledge the combination of integrity and business acumen of the store's owners, the second generation by the time he joined the staff in 1961. He was employed upon his third application to join the firm, his persistence seeing him appointed 'number 13' in the fabric department; he eventually became its 'buyer', or manager. His starting wage was £12 per week, rather less than the £60 he had been earning at Feilding's freezing works (white-collar work often bestowed status rather than generous remuneration). Persistently clocking in three minutes late because his Feilding bus arrived at 9 a.m., Bryan was called into 'Mr Horace's office and alerted to the large loss of productivity which would ensue if all 100-plus staff were persistently three minutes late over a whole year'. (Bryan consequently bought a car for his commute.) Later, as a fabric buyer, Bryan appreciated the astuteness of Horace Cunninghame and Keith and Eric Collinson and their predecessors in gaining import licences for a range of products, mostly from the United Kingdom, which boosted the firm's reputation for quality and exclusiveness. Advertisements show that 'Britishness' was heavily promoted.

Those working at Collinson and Cunninghame were not only counter staff. There were employees in the office, typing, checking on credit and processing the dockets from the many customers with monthly accounts. Dockets and cash were delivered to the office by the Lamson pneumatic chute in the days before cash registers — an unwise employee who caused chaos by putting a mouse in the canister was fired. The second-floor tearooms helped entice customers further into the store, and required kitchen staff as well as waitresses and a laundress who kept the tablecloths beautifully white. At various times there were dressmaking and millinery rooms, a tailoring department and shoe repairs, an events booking office and even a bedding and upholstery factory.

Most emblematic of the department store as a shopping experience were the display staff, charged with making the store as alluring as possible, inside and out, to the predominantly female customers. Window dressing was presented as 'high art', and Collinson and Cunninghame won the coveted Australasian window-dressing championships at least twice in the 1930s.[83] Claude Dixon, the chief dresser from 1912 to 1955, studied at the Koester School for window dressing in Chicago, while Joan Klee was one of the first female display artists employed in New Zealand.[84] Dixon and his team created spectacular window displays, their seasonal unveiling much promoted and anticipated. Special events such as fashion parades were carefully choreographed; a 1926 'Fashion Parade with Pictures' directed by Claude Dixon showed 'almost every garment worn by a modern woman'. Modernity was reinforced by the other item in the double-bill, a movie titled *Daughters of Today* — 'A startling story of life as lived by the modern flapper — in whose hand the cigarette has taken the place of the knitting needle' and for whom 'common sense and restraint [are] in the discard'.[85]

By the 1970s C&C's was no longer the epitome of modernity, as references to the 'grand old lady' attest. Its primacy had been increasingly challenged by boutiques and specialist shops on the one hand, and malls and retail chains on the other. In 1983 it was bought by

ABOVE Collinson and Cunninghame was a family business in which family members participated through and across generations. Myrtle Cunninghame, the daughter of the firm's co-founder, John Cunninghame, is shown with an assistant in the firm's office, with heavy ledger books behind her. Te Manawa Museum

BELOW Collinson and Cunninghame display staff pose with store mannequins in the 1940s: at back left, Brian Thompson and Joan Klee; at front left, Claude Dixon and Eileen Revere Wright, right. Manawatū Heritage 2014_IMCA-DigitalMaster_008467

one of these chains, Farmers Trading. Many of its existing staff decided at this point to retire or, like Bryan Gaskin, to set up business on their own account.

In the first two decades of the twenty-first century retail employed the largest number of workers in Palmerston North, but their terms of engagement had become very different from those of the Collinson and Cunninghame staff. Casual and part-time employment became common, with one of the largest employers, Ezibuy, involved primarily in mail-order. Long-term employer–employee relationships on the C&C familial model, with formalised customer interactions, were increasingly a relic of the past. And shopping is now more likely to link Palmerston North with China than with the supposed exclusiveness of 'British'-originated goods.

Berry Engineering: The skilled trades sector

The Berry Engineering collection in the Ian Matheson Community Archive contains envelope after envelope of photographs, not of people, but of pieces of machinery. Unlabelled and mysterious to the uninitiated, the images include the stainless-steel tanks for which Berry Engineering gained national and international renown; and possibly its pasteurisers and surface coolers for ice-cream manufacture; its dye vats and bolt washing machines for textile and woollen mills; or other plant for soapworks, cordial factories and chemical works — a visitor to the factory in 1960 found the range of work being done bewilderingly impressive.[86]

But the significance of the objects lies less in what they were, than in the fact that they were photographed and the images retained, for it is said that a snapshot was taken of just about every piece of equipment Berry's ever made.[87] The practice may have had a protective function, since the firm's founder had an early invention plagiarised in the absence of patent protection, but the images are emblematic of worker pride in skill and inventiveness. A 1958 *Dominion* feature on 'Manawatu Makes It' identified 51 metal engineering works in Palmerston North, by far heading the list of factory types (with 28 furniture firms following). Berry Engineering, with its ace welders of stainless steel, had a particularly proud reputation.[88]

Australian-born and -trained, engineer Edwin Daniel Berry was engaged by the New Zealand Farmers' Dairy Union to work in Palmerston North in 1895, setting up his own business repairing dairy equipment in 1907. Much of his subsequent success was attributed to a love of machinery at the aesthetic and creative level: 'To him the sweetest music in the world was, and always has been, the rattle and clatter and whirr of the engineering workshop and to his eyes there is no finer or more heart-touching picture than that of a smooth-running machine in action'.[89] Even allowing for hyperbole, the description is one of a man for whom his business was also his hobby and a platform for inventiveness.

By the late 1920s Berry held more than a dozen patents, especially for freezing componentry, and his firm was soon to become a New Zealand pioneer in stainless-steel sheet-metal work. 'Innovation' may have become a Palmerton North business slogan in the late twentieth century, but Berry Engineering was acknowledged for experimentation and innovation long before that. In 1977 Berry's could claim that 'the only thing they don't make in the dairy industry is the cow and the milk bottle'.[90]

Building on a one-man operation, the number of employees at Berry Engineering rose to 26 by 1926, and stood at 70 in 1960, and around 80 by 1977.[91] Like Collinson and Cunninghame, Berry Engineering remained a family business for decades, with Edwin Berry's three sons joining him in the factory. Describing the workplace as 'a very happy environment', former employee Norm Goodwin noted that: 'The family was not scared to get their hands dirty — they were always part of the team. They knew that if it wasn't for "the boys" the firm wouldn't make money.'[92]

Berry Engineering's highly skilled and specialised workers knew their worth, and stayed with the firm for decades. At a 1977 event, three workers were each presented with the traditional gold watch, now supplemented by a colour television set, for their more than 40 years of service; a gold watch went to others for 27 to 37 years with the firm. (Wives were praised for the support they had given their husbands over the years and presented with bouquets of flowers.) The longest-serving employee was actually a woman, the firm's accountant Myra Hickin, 'the Ruler Supreme of the girls in the office', according to an anniversary publication.[93] Other women had been depicted in news photographs assembling refrigeration components at least 17 years earlier.[94]

As a family business, Berry Engineering reflected its founder's strong religious principles. An employee who started in 1942 remembered every workday starting with a prayer, and that printed forms such as timesheets included biblical quotes. Edwin Berry did not like to accept work from businesses connected with alcohol, a problem when breweries wanted the firm's highly regarded tanks: the client's name and the equipment were therefore disguised in the paperwork.[95]

Edwin Berry resigned as chairman of directors in 1952, handing over to his sons, but the firm's later trajectory followed one familiar to Palmerston North manufacturing plants. Around 1960 the business was bought out by an Australian company, Mauri Bros. and Thomson, although until 1977 the name stayed the same.[96] There was a period of productive collaboration with bodies such as the Dairy Research Institute, making components for mechanised cheese production, for example. But Berry staffer Brian Crews considered that in the long run 'the Australians ruined the flavour'.[97]

Mauri and Thomson was itself bought out in 1982, and the Palmerston North business became 'Protech', relocating to Railway Road. The old Berry buildings on the corner of Ashley and Ferguson streets were demolished in 1985 to make way for a Foodtown supermarket. In 1986 the collapse of Protech Engineering 'came as a bombshell' to the 87 staff who lost their jobs, although 57 were eventually employed by John McOviney's Steelfort company.[98] Such closures and industry reconfigurations were an all-too-common scenario across New Zealand in the 1980s and 1990s, as longstanding family firms with a reputation for quality and inventiveness lost out to global forces.

Palmerston North was a provincial centre in which a distinctive assemblage of work opportunities had emerged by the end of the twentieth century. There was a significant human-to-human service sector, larger than the national average. Part of this involved tertiary education, including a full university and a college of education, the first outside the four main centres. There were the research institutes, which, alongside Massey University, came into collaborative alignment with Palmerston North industries and the rural hinterland. There was the military presence, which, like other forms of public sector employment, generated spending, and purchasing of services and construction. And there was the centrality of the city, which produced jobs associated with the movement of goods, at first via its strategically important railway line; then, with the deregulation of road transport from the 1980s, via a truck-dominated transport 'hub'.

Historically, the notion of the workplace as 'family' is evident in many of the city's oldest establishments; it is a concept less obvious today. Work could be a place of danger and of conflict, as well as solidarity; sometimes all at once, as shown by the Longburn freezing works and the railways. The public sector workplace, an important employer of women locally, could be an instrument of government policy, as shown in the post-1984 state sector reforms.

For individual workers there was pride in skill, be it the handling of a knife and presentation of a finely dressed carcass, the nursing of a patient through the crisis of a fever, the creation of an alluring shop display, or the promulgation of an internationally significant piece of research. Hierarchies prevailed, their effects mitigated by the shared possibility of advancement over time.

Employed individuals might spend more waking time at work than with their families, but workplaces also connected them with global forces. Berry Engineering was working up an export trade in Australia by 1926, and soon sold products as far afield as the United Kingdom and South Africa: it was eventually taken over by an Australian company. Collinson and Cunninghame long had representatives in London seeking out the latest fashions; Longburn works sent carcasses to, and was eventually owned from, the other side of the world. Large workplaces like Massey University and the public hospital recruited expertise on a global marketplace and thereby added to the diversity of the city.

At the same time, there were always individuals whose engagement with the world of work was more marginal than for others. The Palmerston North Council's nineteenth-century 'day labourers' were the predecessors of those in today's casualised workforce.

Berry Engineering's skilled workers manufactured tanks to high specifications for a number of industries, some so large that they provided a challenge for removal to their final destination.
Image supplied by Brian Crews

This watercolour by John Hamilton Tetley from the 1940s captures the steam, dust and grime of the Palmerston North railway yards. Manawatū Heritage 2009Ps_TETLEY_2908

Tragedy in the shunting yards, 1925

On 4 August 1925, 30-year-old Palmerston North shunter Thomas Carmichael, father of three, was heard by his workmates to scream out 'I am done, boys!' He was discovered terribly injured, caught between a wire rope and a wagon in the Palmerston North railway shunting yards. Carried to hospital (not very expeditiously, for the railways stretcher did not fit in the ambulance that arrived), he died in the evening from shock and haemorrhage following a compound fracture of the thigh.[1]

This incident had been preceded two months earlier by the even more grisly death of Denis Murphy, 29, who was killed crossing a set of rails just after midnight, having coupled an engine to a special goods train. Unable to see or hear properly because of the steam being 'blown off' by a stationary engine in the congested, poorly lit Palmerston North yard, he was run over by a set of 13 sheep wagons being pushed from behind by another engine. 'Frightfully mangled', he died on the scene half an hour later. [2]

These were but two among a number of deaths in New Zealand's railway yards in the 1920s, the frequency of accidents prompting a national inquiry over the latter months of 1925. The death of Shunter Carmichael gained particular attention, especially from the Labour Party, for he indicated on the way to hospital that his wife had always feared him losing his life at work because of the way he was pressured by his superiors. The Palmerston North shunting yards became the subject of a special, and separate, inquiry over July and September 1925. The 67 pages of evidence given to the investigation by 42 witnesses, including shunters, firemen, engine drivers, signalmen, train examiners, porters, foremen and the stationmaster, give a telling insight into workplace relations in the Palmerston North yards, and the yards' strategic importance but perilous under-capacity.[3]

Behind Palmerston North's much-vaunted reputation as 'one of the great railway centres of New Zealand'[4] were congestion and danger. Strategically important, it was a distribution point for rail traffic from Wellington, Wairarapa, Hawke's Bay, New Plymouth, Foxton and the main trunk lines. More than 100 trains passed through The Square daily, but the number of wagons handled by the shunters per day could reach as many as 1600. As the advocate for the Amalgamated Society of Railway Servants pointed out, this was not the full story, for congestion required multiple handling of wagons — as many as four to five times each.

There was standing room in the yards for only 591 wagons. Shunting operations were much more complex than at a terminating station, with very few trains arriving in marshalling order: it was not uncommon, said Shunter Cyril Pepperill, to get a train of 40 wagons with no more than two grouped together for any one destination. The poor marshalling of trains at previous yards made Palmerston North the 'dump' of the North Island rail system, he concluded. To compound the workers' difficulties, shunting needed to continue throughout the night in poorly lit and sometimes waterlogged conditions.

The inquiry into the yards also highlighted workplace relations in an unusually public way. Shunter Carmichael, most witnesses agreed, was the victim of what was even then deemed workplace harassment, and in trying to speed up his work to meet requirements, he made the mistake that cost him his life. If left alone he worked well, the inquiry was told, but one foreman, in particular, would follow him around, criticising and interfering. The foreman was at one stage called '"the Ghost" because he was always haunting the men like a shadow': 'He nags, grizzles, and grumbles from the beginning to the end of the shift', picking on small details and 'harping on little jobs' that the shunters felt they had under control. Another foreman was aggressive and unpredictable in his behaviour towards the men, and was also disliked.

There were said to be 'undercurrents' of feeling dating back to the national strike of April 1924, when the foremen stayed loyal to the Railways Department and the shunters supported the strike. For the most part, the foremen and shunters got on well enough, but the inquiry concluded that 'troubles' would continue in the yard unless the two problematic supervisors were replaced. It also recommended that shunting gangs be kept up to strength in Palmerston North, and that the practice of transferring senior men to other centres and replacing them with inexperienced workers should be reviewed for such a busy and complex location.

The board of inquiry made other recommendations about improvements to lighting and drainage, but also noted that new shunting yards were being built in Milson — meaning expenditure on temporary improvements to the cramped city yards was clearly not a priority. Unfortunately, the Milson deviation was delayed by depression and war, and it was not until the early 1960s that the yards were moved to their new location. Shunter Carmichael was by no means the last to be killed or severely maimed in this busy, but dangerous, inner-city workplace.[5]

06 TOWARDS A POLITICAL BIOGRAPHY

ELIZABETH WARD & GEOFF WATSON

James Nash and his wife, Elizabeth, sitting behind him to the right, gave considerable service to Palmerston North in multiple capacities. Elizabeth Nash was awarded an MBE for her war service to the community. James not only served as mayor (1908–23) and MP (1918–35), he also sat on the Harbour Board and the Power Board for many years. Manawatū Heritage 2011N_N5_005713

The political history of Palmerston North provides another lens onto its characteristics as a settlement, borough, and then city. A useful overview of local government can be gained by focusing on six identities with particular claims to historical significance: George Snelson, James 'Jimmy' Nash, A. E. 'Gus' Mansford, Brian Elwood, Paul Rieger and Jill White. Moving beyond the local, Palmerston North holds a special place in national politics, notably as it has emerged as a swing seat, thereby reflecting, and sometimes anticipating, changing political trends in New Zealand.

George Snelson (mayor 1877–79, 1883–84, 1889–92, 1901): Bringing the 'progress industry' to Palmerston North

George Snelson (1837–1901) was Palmerston North's first mayor, and is widely regarded as the city's founding father.[1] When he first arrived in Palmerston North — reportedly on 31 December 1870, to open its first ironmongery and general store — the settlement's environs were literally being hewn out of the bush. When he died in office in October 1901, its population numbered 6534 and it was a regional hub connecting the settlements in the central North Island.[2]

Snelson was elected mayor unopposed when Palmerston North became a borough in 1877, a testament to the community work in which he was already involved. He held the office of mayor in four separate terms (mayoral elections were held annually between 1877 and 1915) — more than any other mayor. He was a councillor for much of the 1880s, and stood for Parliament twice. Writing in 1903, Lindsay Buick aptly described him as a 'general-utility man' in early Palmerston North.[3] He had been the founding chairman of the Manawatu Highway Board[4] and its successor the Manawatu Road Board.[5] The first church services were conducted in his home, he was chairman of the first school committee, a foundation member of the Manawatu and West Coast Agricultural and Pastoral Association and, with his wife, at the forefront of the campaign for a public hospital.[6]

Palmerston North's development under Snelson epitomised what James Belich has called the 'progress industry', by which he means the utilisation of public works and immigration to stimulate new settlements.[7] As discussed in Chapter 4, public works and Scandinavian settlers

were central to the initial development of Palmerston North, and public works by local government complemented similar initiatives from central government.

The new borough needed considerable investment in roading, drainage and sewerage.[8] During his first term as mayor, Snelson led the effort to raise a loan of £10,000 towards the work. But, as George Petersen notes, he had some difficulty obtaining a loan, suggesting that those outside the town did not share his optimism in the future of Palmerston North.[9] In 1879 Snelson chose not to stand, and James Linton was returned unopposed.[10] Also in the 1879 general election, Snelson stood as a 'liberal' candidate for Manawatū, seeking a fair share of the government's overall public works expenditure for Palmerston North, and to secure the inland route for the proposed west coast railway, so it would pass through Palmerston North rather than Foxton.[11] Although he was not elected, his actions showed his commitment to promoting Palmerston North at a national level.

Snelson returned to the council in 1881, and served a further

George and Louisa Snelson pictured at their Fitzherbert Avenue home, c.1890, with three boarders. Louisa and other Palmerston North women often supplemented the family income by taking in boarders, usually single men. When not occupied in domestic duties, Louisa took a lead in social issues, and was one of some 520 Palmerston North women who signed the 1893 petition which led to women gaining the vote. Manawatū Heritage 2013P_Pi496_006600 term as mayor between 1883 and 1884.[12] By 1884, however, Palmerston North was feeling the effects of the so-called 'Long Depression'. Despite the economic downturn, Snelson and his fellow councillors remained committed to raising loans, which they saw as essential for Palmerston North's continued progress. Snelson did not seek re-election in the 1884 mayoral election, but his successor James Linton shared his commitment to raising loans. In April 1885 Palmerstonians voted in favour of a £50,000 loan, suggesting their continued faith in the town's progress.[13]

His next terms as mayor, between 1889 and 1892, saw the opening of the railway through the Manawatū Gorge in 1892. With the privately financed railway between Wellington and Palmerston North having been completed in 1886, this critical connection linked the east coast railway line with the west coast and made Palmerston North a significant railway junction, securing the advancement of the town Snelson had worked so hard for.[14]

Snelson was last elected mayor in May 1901, beating two former mayors, Henry Haydon and William Park, and sitting councillor Andrew Guy.[15] Sadly he died in office on 31 October that year, reportedly from a heart condition.[16] When Snelson began as mayor the main concerns had been constructing roads, whereas during his last term the borough was grappling with how to maintain an adequate sewerage system for the settlement's expanding population, which is illustrative of how much it had developed.[17]

Snelson's funeral was a major municipal event that reflected his foundation role, not only in the political life of Palmerston North, but also in a life of service in multiple voluntary associations, from the Music Union to the Palmerston North Rifles; and from the first school committee to All Saints' Church. Flags were flown at half-mast, shops closed and special transport was arranged from Feilding for the occasion. Local Māori also paid tribute to Snelson, many attending his funeral. A letter to the *Manawatu Times* entitled 'A Maori Lament' acknowledged his close connection to Rangitāne, referring to 'your tribe, your people the great Tane-nui-arangi'.[18] And yet, while others profited from the local 'progress industry' Snelson did so much to advance, he did not: he 'lacked that capacity for adding to this world's goods', and died leaving his widow Louisa in a 'parlous' financial state.[19]

James 'Jimmy' Nash (mayor 1908–23): Leading the transition from town to city

James Nash (1871–1952) was so strongly identified with Palmerston North that *NZ Truth* took to calling the borough 'Nashville', claiming that 'If Jimmy Nash's brain-pan had its lid taken off . . . you would find its corrugations wriggling out the magic sign: "Palmerston North!"'[20] Raised in the borough, James Nash became mayor in 1908 after a turbulent era in Palmerston North's local politics, and ushered in a lengthy era of stable leadership and continued progress. He oversaw a significant expansion of Palmerston North's infrastructure, laying the foundation for its subsequent transition to city status.

In 1907 Nash, owner of a number of local businesses, had stood for council, and, despite it being his first attempt, he placed third in the poll.[21] This was probably because he was already well known in Palmerston North due to involvement in many of the town's organisations, not least the Chamber of Commerce and a ginger group advocating for the beautification of The Square.[22] The next year, 1908, he successfully stood for mayor against the incumbent, Richard Essex, whose criticisms of public works officials had so incensed councillors that they set up a public works subcommittee to bypass him.[23] Nash won 10 successive elections, although only half were contested.[24]

It might be argued that he benefited from generally positive media coverage. His brother, Norman ('Harry') Nash, was owner and editor of the local *Manawatu Evening Standard* from 1903, and Jimmy Nash owned a share in the paper.[25] The newspaper, which had previously supported the Liberals under its previous owners Frederick and David Pirani, changed to supporting the Reform Party, which James Nash represented.[26] Nash's popular appeal, however, was genuinely broad-based. He was very much a 'man of the people' who had a deep concern for his community.[27] That community had grown significantly in the first decade of the twentieth century, with the population almost doubling between 1900 and 1910, and growing another 50 per cent during Nash's term as mayor.[28]

The First World War dominated the middle section of Nash's mayoralty. Nash, with his wife, Elizabeth, led Palmerston North's war effort, co-ordinating the fundraising efforts of the Manawatu Patriotic Committee and its successor the Patriotic Society.[29] About 10 per cent of New Zealand's fighting force was trained in the Manawatū,[30] and Nash, as chairman of the Patriotic Society, played a key role in securing money for building a soldiers' club (later the RSA) on the corner of Cuba and George streets. Built on a site donated by wealthy landowner Percy McHardy, the 'Anzac Club' provided a place for soldiers on leave to stay and socialise.[31] The personal touch Nash brought to his various roles was exemplified by his handing out hot tea and coffee to troops passing through Palmerston North railway station.[32]

During Nash's mayoralty the borough council grew to become one of the largest employers in the town.[33] The provision of roads, sewerage and water to cater for the expanding population remained core work of the borough council, and several loans were obtained for this purpose during Nash's tenure.[34] The council also began to investigate the provision of public transport, obtaining several loans to construct an electric tram service. Rising costs during the war made the idea of a tram uneconomical,[35] and in 1920 the borough bus service began.[36]

However, the idea of electric trams was tied to the provision of electrical lighting for the town. In 1915 Nash led the move to purchase the privately owned gasworks with the idea of the borough providing electrical generation.[37] After the war another loan was obtained to further this,[38] but, while the borough generator was being planned and built, the Manawatu–Oroua Electric Power Board was established in 1921, with Nash elected

Local politicians from the 1920s and 1930s caricatured by J. S. ('Jack') Monro. Clockwise from top left: Archie Graham, mayor 1927–31; Jimmy Nash, mayor 1908–23 and Member of Parliament 1918–35; Gus Mansford, councillor 1927–31 and mayor 1931–47; Joe Hodgens, councillor 1919–21, 1923–44; Member of Parliament 1935–46. From J. S. Monro, *Round the Square Again* (1929); *Just for Fun: Personalities at Par* (1934)

as chair in 1922. This organisation distributed the power generated from the station at Mangahao, near Shannon, which opened in 1924.[39]

In 1923 Nash announced that he would not be standing for the mayoralty at that year's elections. He had been elected on a Reform Party ticket as Member of Parliament (MP) for Palmerston in 1918, and was no longer able to devote his full attention to both jobs.[40] Although no longer mayor, Nash remained involved in local body politics, serving on both the Palmerston North Hospital Board and the Foxton Harbour Board for over 40 years,[41] and the Manawatu–Oroua Electric Power Board for 30.[42] In his reminiscences he stated that securing a much-upgraded road through the Manawatū Gorge and the provision of significant facilities for the hospital board were two achievements in which he took particular satisfaction.[43] This pattern of long-term service to local bodies was characteristic of a number of Palmerston North mayors.

Augustus 'Gus' Mansford (mayor 1931–47): A wise head in difficult times

Accountant Augustus 'Gus' Mansford (c.1886–1962) became a city councillor in 1927 and was elected mayor in 1931. He held the mayoral chains until 1947, making him Palmerston North's longest-serving incumbent. He was mayor during two of the twentieth century's more difficult periods: the Depression of the 1930s and the Second World War.[44] Another popular mayor, in all he faced six elections, three of them uncontested.[45]

The year Mansford became mayor, New Zealand was facing a deepening economic depression. This was reflected in the mayoral election campaign, during which candidates were questioned about whether they supported wage cuts for council employees and how council might assist the unemployed.[46] Although in national politics Mansford's political sympathies had been with the Reform Party, he was endorsed by the local Labour Party as the mayoral candidate with 'the most kindly heart' and being 'easy of approach even by the humblest in the city'.[47] Mansford displayed these qualities in his dealings with those affected by the Depression. In January 1934 a delegation of unemployed, marching from Gisborne to Wellington, passed through Palmerston North; Mansford met with them, allowed them to collect money on the streets and helped them to find accommodation.[48]

Gus Mansford was Palmerston North's longest-serving mayor (1931–47). He is pictured here in his mayoral robes and chain with Governor-General Lord Galway, who was on his farewell tour of New Zealand, in 1940. Mansford was mayor during the Depression and the Second World War, and is remembered for his compassion towards the unemployed. After the war he campaigned for Palmerston North to have more state houses to alleviate the post-war shortage.
Manawatū Heritage 2008N_O58_A-E_1299

In May 1934 the Unemployment Board announced that both single and married unemployed men in Palmerston North would be drafted into the workforce, planting pines in Kāingaroa, which sparked a series of protests led by the Unemployed Workers' Movement.[49] The largest occurred on 22 May, when a protest group formed outside the Grand Hotel, where Prime Minister George Forbes and Minister for Unemployment Adam Hamilton were staying with a visiting government party. Forbes appeared on the balcony to speak to the crowd, and, in justifying the government decision, asked what the people of Palmerston North were doing to help the unemployed of the city. Mansford, who had been on the edge of the crowd listening, then appeared on the balcony, at which point the crowd gave him a rousing cheer. Mansford defended his council's record and told Forbes he was not in favour of compulsory camps. He then followed up by using his position to broker a meeting between the protesters and Forbes, thereby defusing the situation.[50]

Mansford retained the mayoralty in 1935 and 1938, and was leading the city

when the Second World War broke out in 1939. Like Nash in the First World War, Mansford led the local Patriotic Committee.[51] These committees were centrally organised, and Mansford represented Zone D of the Wellington Provincial Patriotic Council, which ranged from Palmerston North to Shannon and out to the coast.[52] As mayor, Mansford headed the Palmerston North Emergency Precautions Scheme (E.P.S.), which took on the responsibilities for home defence during the war, in addition to its existing role as a response unit for national disasters.[53] In this capacity, Mansford and the council were responsible for providing air-raid sirens, preparing for blackouts, ensuring emergency electricity generation and building air-raid shelters.[54]

Mansford stood unopposed for mayor in 1944. His last term was marked by the end of the war, and the council planning a large programme of development to make up for work that had been deferred due to the Depression and the war, including expanding the city boundaries.[55] He decided not to stand for re-election in 1947, and his deputy, Geoffrey Tremaine, was elected unopposed.

Brian Elwood (mayor 1971–85): The moderniser

In May 1965, a delegation of about two hundred Hokowhitu residents appeared before the Palmerston North City Council to protest a new roading proposal that would cut through the suburb. They were led by a young lawyer and resident of Hokowhitu, Brian Elwood (1933–). It was this experience that led Elwood to stand for council in 1968, and then for mayor in 1971.[56] The sitting mayor, Des Black, was not seeking re-election, and Elwood won the three-way mayoralty race with almost twice as many votes as the next candidate.[57] A skilled communicator, as reflected in his previous association with Palmerston North's Public Relations Organisation, in his campaign he echoed his mayoral predecessor George Snelson as he promised to lift 'Palmerston North to greater achievements'.[58]

Elwood led the city during a period of considerable change, both for the city and the council.[59] Palmerston North had experienced significant population growth after the Second World War, and it had acquired a teachers' college and a full university by the time Elwood became mayor. The completion of the Milson railway deviation had left a large piece of vacant land in the centre of the city. The enlarged population meant that the city needed to provide new community amenities.

City historian Ian Matheson noted that the council elections of 1968 and 1971 saw a 'younger, more visionary group of councillors elected, replacing the older, conservative group'.[60] Joyce Dunmore was among the new councillors elected in 1968, although she found little support for her proposals on social housing, which may have been too progressive for council.[61] Elwood was part of this shift, and as mayor he tried to diversify the council further by encouraging more skilled professionals to stand for election. But it was Elwood's own management style and vision for the city[62] that made his mayoralty arguably the most influential of the twentieth century.[63]

When Elwood took office there were already plans for a new council building to occupy the vacant railway land. Showing that he planned to be a mayor who made decisions, he committed to the project, believing that it would create confidence and reinvigorate the western end of the city.[64] The planned new seven-storey council building was plagued with problems, including a large cost overrun and attempts by a group of citizens to stop the building through court action.[65] It became known, somewhat unfairly, as 'Elwood's battleship'. However, its completion in 1979 allowed all of the council staff to be housed on the same site for the first time in many years, something Elwood believed would alleviate the 'silo' effect of departments being housed in different buildings. Although the building was a controversial part of Elwood's term, he believed that the complex was one the city could be proud of.[66]

Another feature of his mayoralty was the change in the way city councillors and employees interacted. Prior to Elwood's term, many councillors played a hands-on role in day-to-day administration, which led to council employees feeling that councillors were telling them how to do their jobs.[67] Elwood

Mayor Brian Elwood greets Queen Elizabeth during a royal stopover on 26 February 1977. Elwood set out to transform Palmerston North from a rural service centre to a modern city. During his time as mayor, he became frustrated that Palmerston North's development was being hindered by the small local bodies surrounding the city. A second bridge across the river was blocked by the Kairanga County Council. John Cleland Studio, Manawatū Heritage 2008P_O44_A-E_1311

Ken Tremaine variously served as city planner (1976–89), director of planning and development (1989–93) and city development manager (1993–94). During the Elwood mayoralty, senior council staff such as Tremaine were given greater autonomy in their roles, with elected councillors transferring their focus to higher-level governance issues rather than day-to-day management. Tremaine also played an important role in a number of heritage projects, including the restoration of Caccia Birch, and the purchase and restoration of the Regent Theatre.
Manawatū Heritage 2019P_2017-20_026382

changed this through his strong leadership style.[68] During his mayoralty the council became more focused on governance issues and the overall management of the city. This then provided a cohesive direction to the professionals employed by the council, something that Elwood felt had been lacking before he became mayor.[69] Elwood's approach to the mayoralty paved the way for the appointment of a chief executive officer for the city, who would focus on operational matters while the mayor and council focused on governance.[70] Elwood resigned from the mayoralty in 1985, having been appointed chair of the new Local Government Commission. In that capacity he would oversee a radical overhaul of local government in New Zealand.

Paul Rieger (mayor 1985–98): Presiding over an expanding electorate

Brian Elwood's resignation from the mayoralty triggered a by-election in which five candidates emerged. One of these was the deputy (then acting) mayor Paul Rieger (1934–), a former lawyer and sharebroker who had been a councillor since 1971.[71] He ran on a platform of fiscal responsibility with modest rates rises.[72] Moreover, he emphasised that the city was about to go through a period of potentially significant change, as the decisions of the Local Government Commission became more clear.[73] The *Manawatu Standard* backed Rieger, pointing out that of the five candidates he had the most experience, particularly as the economic prospects of Palmerston North needed to be promoted.[74] Rieger won in a landslide, obtaining almost four times as many votes as the next candidate.[75]

Over the next seven years Rieger's position as mayor remained secure, and he was elected unopposed in both the 1986 and the 1989 local body elections. This provided stability during the local body reorganisation, in which the city boundaries expanded significantly. The total area of Palmerston North grew from 4302 hectares to 32,594 hectares,[76] much of the increase resulting from the territory of the largely rural Kairanga County Council becoming part of the city. This was not an easy process, with the rural population voicing concerns that their rates would 'sky-rocket' and their unique needs would be ignored, since urban voters comprised the vast majority of the reconfigured city's electorate.[77] To allay these concerns, a ward system was created which lasted until 2013, and Ashhurst was given a local board, to ensure that all areas of the city were evenly represented.[78]

It was not only local body government that was changing. Rieger's mayoralty coincided with a fundamental transition in central government, beginning with the economic reforms of the Fourth Labour Government (1984–1990), which were continued by the National-led governments between 1990 and 1999. Having come to the council with a strong voluntary sector background, Rieger paid particular attention to community groups that sought to assist people to adapt to these changes, as well as strengthening relationships with Massey University and local iwi.[79]

Notwithstanding the disruption occasioned by the economic and political reforms of the era, it was the prosaic issue of widening Fitzherbert Avenue that created widely publicised protest during his mayoralty. Traffic congestion between Fitzherbert Avenue and Massey University was becoming an increasing problem by the mid-1980s. Shortly after Rieger took office, a new bridge was opened in 1987, replacing the previous one which had been built in 1936. However, at the time of opening the new bridge had only two lanes, like its predecessor, so did little to ease congestion.[80] While the new bridge did have the ability to take more lanes, obtaining them required widening the roads on both sides of the river and removing the trees which lined Fitzherbert Avenue, the northern approach to the bridge.[81] These proposals sparked vigorous protest.[82]

In 1992 Rieger faced his first contest as mayor; one of the issues at this election was the possibility of building a second bridge, rather than widening the existing one.[83] Government funding for a second bridge, however, was contingent on widening the existing bridge.[84] The council became tied up in court battles launched by a group called Save the Avenue, which wanted to retain the existing trees.[85] This became the main issue of the 1995

Mark Bell-Booth, right, mayor from 2001 to 2004, came to public attention through his leadership of Save the Avenue, a group that opposed the removal of the trees that lined Fitzherbert Avenue. It became clear in early January 1997 that legal attempts to prevent the felling of the trees had failed. In response, Save the Avenue began direct action. Ultimately the protests were unsuccessful, and the protesters were removed from the trees by the police. Manawatū Heritage 2019P_IMCADigitalMaster_026905

election,[86] where Rieger faced two opponents. He won convincingly, with almost 10,000 more votes than the next-highest-polling candidate.[87]

The council was granted permission to fell the trees in 1996, but opposition remained fierce.[88] In early January 1997, members of Save the Avenue organised a protest that involved around three hundred people 'occupying' the trees, either by huddling around the trunks or in some cases climbing up into the branches.[89] The protests attracted national attention. The images of protesters being dragged out of trees by police made for graphic television viewing, particularly as early January can be a slow time for news. Rieger admitted that he was surprised by the depth of feeling around the removal of the trees. He also believed, however, that the majority of Palmerston North residents wanted a wider Fitzherbert Avenue, a view borne out by the outcome of the 1995 mayoral election.[90]

The council also embarked on two significant projects that enhanced the cultural life of Palmerston North. In 1992 the council bought the former Rosco/DIC building for the purpose of housing a new central library. Ian Athfield, a leading Wellington architect, was contracted to convert the building, which opened as the library in 1996. The building was situated on the western side of The Square near Coleman Mall, and the renovation helped to fulfil Brian Elwood's vision of revitalising the area. In 1993 the council purchased the historic Regent on Broadway theatre. This was the culmination of a campaign, begun in 1988, to save the building from demolition.[91] The Regent was reopened in a two-week-long gala festival in May 1998.[92]

In 1998 Rieger announced that he would not be seeking re-election as mayor. Having been on the council since 1971 and mayor since 1985, Rieger had given a considerable portion of his life in service of the city. However, his time in local government had not finished. He was elected to the Manawatū–Wanganui Regional Council (subsequently reconfigured as Horizons Regional Council) in 1998, and served for 21 years on that body before standing down in 2019.

CAR

Taken in 2015, this photograph shows six recent mayors of Palmerston North, representing four decades of leadership. From left: Jill White, Palmerston North's first female mayor, elected in 1998; Mark Bell-Booth, White's successor from 2001 to 2004; Paul Rieger, mayor from 1985 until 1998; current mayor Grant Smith (2015–); Sir Brian Elwood, mayor between 1971 and 1985; and Heather Tanguay, who served as mayor from 2004 to 2007. Smith described the collective noun for the group of mayors as a 'chain'. MS, 29 May 2015

Jill White (mayor 1998–2001): A pioneering female politician

Jill White (1941–) made history in the city when she became the first woman to be elected Mayor of Palmerston North, in 1998. Her success was the third act of a trilogy of pioneering female political achievements, as she had been the first woman elected to the Manawatū–Wanganui Regional Council in 1989, and, when she won the seat for Labour in 1993, the first woman elected as MP for Manawatū. She remained in Parliament as a list MP after the Manawatū seat was disestablished in 1996, resigning to contest the Palmerston North mayoralty in 1998.

White came to politics after a career as a public health nurse, and her political philosophy was also shaped by her Methodist upbringing, which instilled in her a sense of responsibility towards others.[93] These views were reflected in her policy platforms, her vision of Palmerston North being 'a city with pizazz, full employment, ethnic and cultural diversity, excellence in performing arts, education and science and supportive of its frail and vulnerable'.[94] She secured a decisive victory, being more than 2000 votes ahead of the second-placed candidate John Hornblow.[95]

Unfortunately, her mayoralty was affected by two significant challenges. The first was what the *Standard* characterised as an ongoing 'cancer of divisiveness' within council, noting that a number of sitting councillors had contested the mayoralty after Rieger's long incumbency.[96] White found it difficult to get majority support for the positions she advocated. This was graphically illustrated early in her mayoralty when three of her nominations for committee chairpersons were rejected by council.[97]

The second challenge, which persisted throughout her mayoralty, was the fallout from the unsuccessful attempt by the city council to sell its civic administration building. The sale was advocated by council staff, who believed the building had outlived its usefulness because, owing to the increasing use of independent contractors, the number of personnel employed by the city council had declined from 700 full-time-equivalent staff in 1989 to 551 in 1995.[98] Accordingly, council voted to sell the building to a developer and lease another building then tenanted by Inland Revenue on the corner of Ashley and Ferguson streets.[99] The sale fell through, however, and by the time of the 2001 mayoral elections the council had two buildings, including the untenanted premises at the Inland Revenue Building, costing ratepayers $52,916 per month. Public dissatisfaction with this is widely credited as a significant factor in White losing her mayoralty, even though she had opposed the sale.[100] She was succeeded by Mark Bell-Booth, who ran on his experience as a councillor and businessman and won by just over 900 votes, securing 10,975 votes to White's 10,058.[101] He was the first mayor with an ancestral link to Rangitāne.[102]

There were nonetheless significant long-term achievements during White's mayoralty. She successfully oversaw the sale of its majority shareholding in CentralPower, which earned the council $70 million in 2000.[103] She also initiated redevelopment of The Square, a project which after many iterations has resulted in a much more vibrant and user-friendly central space for Palmerstonians.[104]

Palmerston North and national politics

There is some justification for regarding Palmerston North as a 'bellwether' seat in national politics. Historically, the political party that became government has also tended to hold Palmerston North. From the beginning of the party era in 1890 to the end of the 'first past the post' era of New Zealand politics in 1996, when the House of Representatives consisted solely of electorate seats, the MP who represented Palmerston North was in government for 74 years (70 per cent) and in opposition for 32 years (30 per cent). At four elections — those of 1935, 1949, 1960 and 1975 — a change in MP in Palmerston North has accompanied a change of government.

Voter behaviour in Palmerston North reflects its transition from a largely rural centre to a provincial city with a large well-educated urban population. Palmerston North was formally incorporated into national politics in 1870, when the Manawatū district was granted representation in the Wellington Provincial Council and the House of Representatives.[105] Initially the Manawatu electorate spanned much of the west coast of the lower North Island, from Paraparaumu in the south to settlements in the Ruāhine

Fred Pirani (seated), photographed with his brother, David, was the MP for Palmerston North from 1893 until 1902. His election marked a shift in the electorate away from MPs who were large landowners to men who were urban workers. Fred and David owned the *Manawatu Evening Standard*, and Fred had begun his working life as a printer with John Ballance's *Wanganui Herald*. The Pirani brothers' Jewish heritage is something they had in common with Palmerston North mayors Solomon Abrahams, Maurice Cohen and Fred Nathan. Manawatū Heritage 2007P_Pi585_PEO_0394

Ranges north of Feilding.[106] The main settlement within that electorate was Foxton, the designated county town, and as such its interests commanded the attention of candidates.[107] The growth of Palmerston North led to the creation of the new seat of Palmerston (later changed to Palmerston North, in 1937) in the 1890 electorate boundary changes.[108] However, it was more of a renaming than a reshaping, as the new seat took in much of the old Manawatu electorate.

It was not until the 1892 boundary changes that Palmerston North became the centre of the Palmerston electorate, while the lower west coast towns became part of the Ōtaki electorate.[109] The effect of this was seen at the 1893 election when Frederick Pirani was elected MP for Palmerston. Pirani was the owner of the *Manawatu Evening Standard*, a well-known supporter of the Liberals, who are widely regarded as New Zealand's first political party.[110] Pirani endorsed their policies on breaking up large estates into small farms, and was an advocate for the 'working man'.[111] (It is fitting that the present restaurant of Palmerston North's Cosmopolitan Club, which began life as the Workingmen's Club, should bear his name.)[112] Pirani's involvement in the Knights of Labour, a largely working-class organisation, and his occupation as a journalist were in direct contrast to the previous MP, James Wilson, who owned and farmed a large amount of land near Bulls and became a leading figure in the Farmers' Union (now Federated Farmers).[113] Pirani's occupation and interests typified the growing urban identification of the citizens of Palmerston North. Pirani won in 1896 and 1899, despite falling out with Premier Richard Seddon before the election and consequently facing an 'official' Liberal Party candidate.[114]

In 1902 Pirani stood in the Hutt electorate, leaving the way clear for Seddon's preferred candidate, William Wood, who won the Palmerston seat. Like Pirani, Wood had a strong identification with urban interests. A blacksmith by profession, he had served the town, both in council (he was mayor when elected MP) and as a dedicated member of All Saints' Church. One theme that emerges across many of the MPs who represented Palmerston North is that they had a strong record of service to the community. It seems that voters

valued a representative who had proved themselves in the community.

Although Wood successfully defended his seat in the 1905 election, there were wider changes affecting Palmerston North and New Zealand electoral politics in general. The Liberal Party was in decline and were facing a far more organised opposition. Moreover, the New Zealand economy was becoming increasingly reliant on the export of primary products, leading towns that had previously aligned themselves with urban ideals to perceive their future as being more in accord with rural interests.[115] The Palmerston electorate contained a core urban area, but also covered the fertile farmland surrounding the town, making it susceptible to rural influences.

In 1908 Wood was successfully challenged by David Buick, who farmed on the outskirts of Palmerston North and had considerable involvement in the Manawatu and West Coast Agricultural and Pastoral Association and the Farmers' Union. Buick's victory was illustrative of growing support for the newly organised Reform Party in the lower North Island.[116] Indeed, Palmerston North has a plausible claim to being the de facto birthplace of the Reform Party. In 1908 the party's national organiser, Richard Martin, was based in Palmerston North, and in February 1909 William Massey announced at a rally in town that the party would be formally known as the Reform Party.[117]

James Nash became the official Reform candidate for the 1918 by-election when, sadly, Buick fell victim to the influenza pandemic. There was a tight three-way contest, which Nash won by 315 votes. Nash strengthened his hold on the Palmerston seat during the 1920s — his majority was over 3000 in the 1925 election. He was aided by a strong local party organisation, headed by local businessman Arthur Bennett, which Nash credited with playing a vital role in changing the political allegiance of Palmerstonians from the Liberals towards the Reform Party.[118]

During the 1920s the Palmerston electorate shrank in size as the town grew, and by the time of the 1927 redistribution much of the rural surrounds of Palmerston North were in the Manawatu electorate.[119] This change may well have helped Nash retain his seat in the 1931 general election, albeit with a reduced majority, with his strong local support offsetting the pre-election turmoil when Reform entered a coalition with the rump of the Liberal Party. In all, Reform won nine straight elections in the Palmerston seat, a testament to the strength of the party in Palmerston North during the first half of the twentieth century.

By the 1935 election, however, the mood of the electorate had changed, and Palmerston elected its first Labour MP, Joe Hodgens. During the inter-war period the Labour Party became the second party in Palmerston North, even though it was troubled by splits.[120] Hodgens, a carpenter and building contractor by trade, had been involved in the Palmerston North Labour Party since the First World War and was known as a moderate.[121] Moreover, he had a record of long service on the city council, the Palmerston North Hospital Board and as an active member of St Patrick's Catholic Church.

Crowds gathered in The Square outside the *Manawatu Evening Standard* building to watch the results of the 1938 general election. Interest in general elections in Palmerston North has always been strong, particularly in the period after the Second World War when the seat was marginal. By contrast, interest in local body elections waned after the Second World War, with turnout reaching a low of 37 per cent in 1977. The introduction of postal voting in 1983 gave local body elections a considerable boost, with 70 per cent of the roll voting. This proved to be short-lived, however, with the turnout dropping at subsequent elections.
Manawatū Heritage 2007P_El3_A-E_0305

Joseph Hodgens was elected MP for Palmerston North in 1935, becoming its first Labour Member of Parliament. Before his election, Hodgens had an impressive record of community service. He had been a city councillor since 1923 and deputy mayor since 1931. He also sat on the Manawatu–Oroua Power Board, the Manawatu River Board and the Hospital Board. Hodgens held the Palmerston North seat until 1946, when he retired. In 1951 he stood for Parliament again, but was beaten by sitting MP Blair Tennent. Manawatū Heritage 2007N_Pi25_PNCC_1021

His victory was partly due to the strong nationwide vote for Labour, and also because a split had opened within the Reform ranks. Mayor Gus Mansford, who had been a Reform supporter, stood against the incumbent Nash.[122] This split enabled Hodgens to win by 115 votes. Hodgens held the seat until 1946, when he retired due to the ill health of his wife. He was a strong advocate of state housing, and played a leading role in the Savage Crescent housing precinct, the first state housing area built outside the four main centres.[123]

Hodgens was succeeded as a Labour MP by Ormond Wilson, a farmer who lived at Mt Lees (between Bulls and Sanson), and had represented the Rangitīkei electorate between 1935 and 1938.[124] To some degree, Wilson's success was attributable to the National Party (which was formed in 1936, and comprised largely of former members of the Reform, United and Democratic parties) not standing a candidate in Palmerston North in 1946, with Gus Mansford standing as an independent.[125]

By 1949, however, National had consolidated, and had selected a strong candidate, Blair Tennent. A dentist by profession, Tennent was another with a long record of community service, including an eight-year term on the city council, over 15 years on the Wanganui Education Board, and leadership roles at St Andrew's Presbyterian Church.[126] He used this to his advantage in his campaign, especially as Wilson was not considered a local because he lived at Mt Lees, near Bulls, and not in Palmerston North.[127] Wilson's perceived deficiencies in promoting Palmerston North's interests, particularly the long-awaited railway deviation, may also have worked against him.[128] Tennent won the election on the back of a nationwide swing to National. His hold on the seat was tenuous, however, as was shown in the 1951 election when Hodgens returned to political life as the Labour candidate, leading the poll on election night by two votes.[129] The final result returned Tennent with a majority of 200, but, in an election that had strongly favoured National, this signalled that Palmerston North had become a marginal seat.

This trend continued throughout the 1950s and 1960s. In 1954 Labour stood Philip Skoglund, a well-known figure in the community, who was a city councillor, an

Being seen in the local community was important for both local body and national politicians. Blair Tennent, pictured here, presented the prizes at the Tokomaru School Lamb and Calf Day in 1958. He is presenting a cup to Heather Watson, who won the senior care and rearing prize. Manawatū Heritage 2017N_2017-20_015001

accomplished bowls player and a popular teacher at Palmerston North Boys' High School.[130] The election saw a swing to Labour and, given that Tennent had a small majority, it was not surprising that Skoglund scraped a win with a majority of 364, which he significantly increased in 1957 on the back of a strong swing towards Labour.

In 1960, however, Palmerston North again changed hands. National candidate Bill Brown had been a city councillor and had long periods of service on the Hospital Board and Wanganui Education Board.[131] Brown's campaign may have been boosted by Keith Holyoake promising at his Palmerston North rally that a National government would suport the formation of a veterinary school, a long-promised initiative which had been delayed under the Labour government.[132] Skoglund led the voting on election night, but Brown was subsequently declared the winner by 133 votes. Palmerston North remained a marginal seat, Brown's margin being 772 votes in 1963 and 259 in 1966.

In 1966 Brown had faced a strong Labour candidate in Joe Walding, a three-term city councillor well known to the public through his business activities, which included managing the Smith and Walding Catering Business and Prepared

The opening of Awapuni School in 1958 brought together Palmerston North's politicians, and illustrates the varied roles they played within the community. The speaker is Phil Skoglund, MP for Palmerston North. Seated to his left is Blair Tennent, Skoglund's predecessor as MP, here in his role as mayor. Second from Skoglund's right is William Brown, who attended as chair of the Wanganui Education Board. Brown stood against Skoglund in the 1960 general election and won, remaining the MP until 1967. Manawatū Heritage 2017N_2017-20_015004

Foods, a food-exporting business. He was also president of the local Jaycees, an organisation for young professionals that was extensively involved in fundraising for community activities.[133] In 1967 Brown died suddenly, triggering a by-election, which Walding won by 592 votes. The marginal nature of Palmerston North meant that this margin was much reduced in 1969, although the swing to Labour in 1972 gave him a majority of 1766, at the time the largest post-war majority of any Palmerston North MP.

The changeable nature of the Palmerston North electorate reasserted itself over the next two elections. In 1975, there was a strong nationwide swing to National, and in a surprise result Walding lost to National candidate John Lithgow. Lithgow, a field manager for Imperial Chemical Industries (ICI), differed from previous Palmerston North MPs in that he did not have a record of community service. However, he ran an effective door-knocking campaign, which helped him to become better known in the electorate.[134] Moreover, there was a housing shortage in Palmerston North, and Walding, who was a Cabinet minister, was thought to have neglected his constituency.[135] Undaunted, Walding regained the seat in 1978 with a resounding majority of 2736 votes. Prime Minister Robert Muldoon's combative personality — a factor in his 1975 victory — had by 1978 alienated much of the electorate, and he was severely heckled at his Palmerston North rally.[136] This

may well have affected Lithgow, who was perceived as very much a 'Muldoon man'.[137]

Walding retired prior to the 1981 election due to ill health, but the seat was retained by Labour. Their candidate, the colourful lawyer Trevor de Cleene, was extremely well known in Palmerston North, and the first MP to be born in the city. He had been a city councillor since 1962, and had stood for mayor in 1974.[138] He enjoyed large majorities in the 1980s, standing down before the 1990 election. Indeed, the size of his win in 1981 led the *Manawatu Evening Standard* to declare that Palmerston North was no longer marginal.[139] Even in 1990, when there was a strong swing towards National, the party managed to hold the seat. Labour's new candidate, Steve Maharey, a one-term city councillor, won by a much-reduced majority of 349.

The introduction of the mixed member proportional (MMP) system in 1996 changed the political dynamics, with the party vote being the key determinant of election results. During Steve Maharey's terms as MP he maintained a healthy majority, but the party vote in the electorate was more volatile. In 1996 National had a narrow lead, but this was reversed in 1999, and Labour increased

Steve Maharey, in the centre with the microphone, is pictured here campaigning for re-election in 1999. His wife, Liz McKay, is standing second from right. Maharey was the MP for Palmerston North between 1990 and 2008. He won six elections and represented Palmerston North for 18 years, becoming the seat's longest-serving MP. After retiring from politics in 2008, Maharey went on to serve as Vice-Chancellor of Massey University between 2008 and 2016. MS, 22 November 1999, 4

As MP for Palmerston North (1981–90), Trevor de Cleene gained notoriety for announcing in Parliament that he slept with a loaded gun under his bed, and that any intruder would get both barrels. De Cleene had a colourful career as a lawyer and a city councillor (1962–66, 1968–71, 1974–76), as well as MP. During his tenure, Palmerston North became a safe Labour seat, reversing a trend of it having been a marginal electorate since 1945. MS, 3 March 2001, 13

its share in 2002 and 2005. Maharey retired before the 2008 election, and Iain Lees-Galloway, who had a background in student and union politics, was selected as the Labour candidate and won the seat, which, leading into the 2020 elections, he had held for four terms. However, in 2008 Labour and National received an almost equal number of party votes, and in 2011 and in 2014 National won the party vote. This was reversed in 2017, but only to the point that Labour and National were virtually equal again. Palmerston North remains a seat indicative of the national mood.

As Palmerston North grew between the 1950s and early 1970s, the urban area began to stretch outside of the Palmerston North electorate boundaries. From the mid-1950s this began to affect the composition of the neighbouring Manawatu electorate, which encircled the city. In 1957 former Palmerston North MP Blair Tennent was elected, replacing retiring National MP Matthew Oram. Tennent was the first MP to represent Manawatu who was not a farmer, although his successor as National MP in 1966 was Colyton farmer Les Gandar. Manawatu began to resemble the Palmerston electorate of the early twentieth century, with an increasing number of urban voters diluting the more rural composition of the electorate. This is best illustrated by the 1978 election, when National stood Michael Cox, a local accountant, and Labour stood Trevor de Cleene, a lawyer, both men being firmly aligned with urban interests. Although de Cleene was unsuccessful, he made a considerable dent in the National majority. The increasingly changeable nature of the seat was further reflected in the election of Labour MP David Robinson in 1987, and its first female MP, Jill White, who won the seat for Labour in the 1993 election.

Political characteristics of Palmerston North

What sorts of people have Palmerstonians elected to represent them? As a generalisation, the electorate has tended to support self-made people who have complemented proven commercial or professional acumen with a demonstrated commitment to public service. Commitment to public service could be through either a leadership role in organisations such as the Agricultural and Pastoral Association or involvement in the church. As an electorate, Palmerston North has tended towards giving MPs, mayors and councillors at least two terms in office; few office-holders have failed to win re-election after only one term. Reflecting on his political career, Steve Maharey described the Palmerston North electorate as 'very supportive' and 'very understanding' of the demands of being an MP. Moreover, he noted, 'once you are elected, you have to earn it, but the people are quite loyal to you'.[140]

Successful mayors and councillors have had a broad-based appeal which transcends party politics or single-issue campaigns. The single transferable vote (STV) system, first adopted for Palmerston North local body elections in 2013, has reinforced this characteristic. This system, in which voters can rank as many candidates for mayor and council as they like in descending order, means successful candidates need to appeal to a wide cross-section of the electorate. For example, Grant Smith, elected as mayor in 2015, ran on the slogan 'A head for business, a heart for community, a passion for Palmerston North'. This slogan alluded to his successful career in business and extensive community involvement, particularly in sport. The latter included a lengthy involvement in squash, and he also chaired the successful 'Save the Turbos' campaign in 2009, which kept the Manawatu Turbos in the top tier of New Zealand's domestic rugby.[141]

Historically, Palmerstonians, and, as Marianne Tremaine has suggested, New Zealanders more broadly, have been wary of mixing party politics and local government.[142] In the 1984 contest for the Palmerston North seat, for example, Trevor de Cleene easily held off five-time mayor Brian Elwood. De Cleene's campaign slogan 'Elwood for Mayor, de Cleene for Parliament' neatly summarised the distinction he and the electorate saw between the roles.[143] There have been instances of councillors aligning themselves with political parties — Pat Kelliher, Ken Wynks and Sam Mīhaere formed a Labour grouping in the 1970s — but Elwood believed party political divisions became less marked during his mayoralty.[144]

In the 2016 and 2019 council elections, however, party politics became more prominent.

Mayoresses and consorts of Palmerston North

Karen and Jono Naylor represent a twenty-first-century mayor and mayoress. Jono Naylor served as mayor between 2007 and 2014. After the general election in 2014, he was a list MP until 2017. Interviewed by the *Manawatu Standard,* he noted he found the role 'a little bit like going to work each day in someone else's clothes. They might have fitted and looked OK, but they were not mine.' He has subsequently served on the Horizons Regional Council since 2018, when a by-election was held owing to the death of sitting councillor Pat Kelly. Karen Naylor was elected to the MidCentral District Health Board in 2010, and in 2016 she was elected as a city councillor. She has continued the role of the mayoresses serving the city, but she has done so in both elected and voluntary positions. Warwick Smith, *MS*, 9 October 2010

Spouses of mayors have made a significant contribution to the community, particularly in periods when women's political participation was marginal. The first mayoress, Louisa Snelson, was an excellent example of a female community leader. She was a committed Christian in whose home the first Anglican services were held, and she laid the foundation stone for the first All Saints' Church in 1875. Active in the campaign to have land set aside for a school, she also led the fundraising effort for a public hospital, opened in 1893.[1] Snelson engaged in political matters, signing the women's suffrage petition in 1893, and organising women to vote for her husband in his 1901 mayoral campaign. She continued her community service well into her seventies, when in 1915 she organised a collection of clothing and other goods for Belgian refugees.[2] In her obituary she was referred to as the 'mother of Palmerston' for her hospitality towards others and her contribution towards the development of the growing town.[3]

Elizabeth Nash, mayoress from 1908 to 1923, was well known for her dedication to the Palmerston North community. She was a member of the committee that established the Plunket Society in Palmerston North,[4] and organised fundraising for groups such as the Old Men's Home,[5] a new hospital ward for women suffering from tuberculosis,[6] and new high-school classrooms.[7] It was during the First World War that her ability to organise within the community really came to the fore. She headed the Mayoress's Patriotic Committee, a group of women who co-ordinated the collection and packaging of clothes, food and other comforts to soldiers.[8] They then distributed these through the Red Cross and contributed to the Lady Liverpool Fund, which sent parcels containing clothing and other goods to New Zealand soldiers. During the 1918 influenza pandemic Nash was praised for her work with the victims, organising the distribution of food and clothing.[9] In 1921 she was made an MBE for her community and war work.

After the Second World War, changing patterns around women in paid employment, including a greater acceptance of married women working, meant that in some instances the role of mayoress changed.[10] This is exemplified in the election of Palmerston North's first female mayor, Jill White. Her husband, Bruce Wilson, who also served on the city council from 2007 to 2013, became the city's first male consort. Karen Naylor, mayoress from 2007 to 2014, demonstrated both the tradition of community service and the way in which the role of mayoress has been reshaped. As mayoress she acted as patron for the local National Council of Women and the Plunket Society.[11] However, Naylor, a nurse, was elected to the Mid-Central District Health Board in 2010 and has been re-elected twice. She then went on to stand for council, and was successful in the 2016 and 2019 local body elections. She continues to serve the community. As a trustee of the Pascal Street Community Trust she was one of the main fundraisers for the Junior Road Safety Park, which was installed in the Esplanade in 2017.[12]

In 2016, four candidates — Lorna Johnson, Zulfiqar Butt, David Chisholm and Sheryl Hoera — stood as Labour Party-endorsed candidates, and Brent Barrett stood with Green Party backing.[145] The strategy had mixed results. Brent Barrett was among the highest-polling councillors, becoming the first Green Party candidate elected to the Palmerston North City Council. Lorna Johnson was, however, the only successful candidate on the Labour Party platform.

In 2019, however, all four council candidates endorsed by political parties — Zulfiqar Butt and Lorna Johnson as Labour-endorsed candidates, and Brent Barrett and Renee Dingwall as Green Party-endorsed candidates — were elected. It is difficult to ascertain the exact degree to which their endorsement by political parties influenced voters' opinions, but Dingwall and Butt were the fourteenth and fifteenth elected candidates in terms of polling order, so it might be argued that the organisational backing and advice provided by political parties aided their success.[146] Although flyers for party-endorsed candidates in the 2019 election included party branding, their content was not explicitly party-aligned, but focused on local issues and the personal attributes of the respective candidates. Incumbent Mayor Grant Smith, who had earlier expressed his wariness of party politics in local government, acknowledged that the elected councillors would 'bring their values, but I ask them to leave their party colours at the door'.[147]

The 2019 council maintained the gender diversity of its predecessor — seven of the 15 councillors were female and eight male — and extended its ethnic diversity. Zulfiqar Butt is Palmerston North's first Muslim councillor, and he and Dingwall are the first councillors to identify as having Asian ancestry; Dingwall is also Palmerston North's first councillor of Samoan ancestry.[148] The gender diversity of the council has increased markedly in the past four decades, with 27 of the 29 female councillors in Palmerston North having been elected since 1980, a reflection of the wider impact of second-wave feminism, including organisations such as the Women's Electoral Lobby.[149]

One interesting feature of local politics in Palmerston North is the connection between politics and religion. Historically, the New Zealand electorate has resisted appeals to vote on religious lines, but there is circumstantial evidence that a leadership position within a religious body has helped candidates achieve name recognition and credibility in local body elections. Many mayors and councillors have been closely connected with religious organisations, particularly local churches, although religious involvement has tended to be presented as part of a wider portfolio of commitment to community.[150] George Snelson and his wife were prominent members of All Saints' Church, as was William Wood (mayor 1895–1901, 1903–05) and A. E. Mansford.[151] James Nash was a long-serving member of St Andrew's Presbyterian Church;[152] Henry Haydon (mayor 1899–1901) was a Methodist; Joe Hodgens was a Catholic; and Jono Naylor (mayor 2007–14) openly acknowledged his Christian faith.[153] Solomon Abraham (mayor 1887–89) was Jewish, as were Maurice Cohen (mayor 1905–07) and Frederick Nathan (mayor 1923–27).[154]

While religious adherence has declined significantly — 42 per cent of New Zealanders identified as Christian in 2013 compared with 95 per cent in 1878, and only 14 per cent of Palmerstonians regularly attended church in 2009 — a significant number of councillors have continued to have connections with local churches, even if they did not explicitly run as Christian candidates. Voter turnout in the local body elections between 2010 and 2019 averaged 39 per cent, suggesting that if a candidate could attract support from a particular section of the community it may well have helped them garner sufficient votes overall to gain election. In 2009, Deputy Mayor John Hornblow, himself a priest at All Saints' Church, noted six of the then council were practising Christians, although he emphasised that they did not vote as a bloc and that local churches had a wide variety of political perspectives.[155]

The citizens of Palmerston North have, for the most part, been well served by their elected representatives. Under their stewardship the city has developed in a progressive and orderly manner. Despite appeals to frugality, the electorate, by virtue of their responses to polls and as demonstrated in voting patterns in elections, have supported significant expenditure on infrastructure, through approving the raising of loans and the funding of public projects. Like New Zealanders more broadly, Palmerstonians have tended to elect mayors and councillors with a demonstrable record of career success and public-spiritedness.

Arguably, they expect the same characteristics of their parliamentarians, alongside a commitment to championing the city's interests to the government of the day. At a national level, Palmerston North can lay claim to representing that often alluded to, yet seldom identified, constituency known as 'middle New Zealand', which historically determines political power in New Zealand. Politically speaking, in both local and national government, Palmerston North is very much a city at the centre of the New Zealand electorate.

Julia Wallace and the many facets of politics

Julia Wallace became Palmerston North's first female city councillor when she was elected in 1962. She is pictured here at the opening of the Manawatu Museum in 1971. Other dignitaries on the stage include, second from left, Manawatu MP Les Gandar (obscured), mayor Des Black, mayoress Lorna Black and Joe Walding, MP for Palmerston North. Wallace played an important role in the formation of the museum as the chair of the council's parks and reserves committee.
Manawatū Heritage 2011N_Mu4_005670

Julia Nannie Wallace was Palmerston North's most prominent woman citizen of the post-war years, her personal standing achieved without any existing attachment to a male dignitary. It was recognised by the awarding of an OBE in 1968, a Massey University Medal in 1991, and by the posthumous tribute of a retirement village being named after her — thereby linking her to such luminaries as Malvina Major, Sir Edmund Hillary and Rita Angus (the last-named an early student of the school at which Julia Wallace was 'lady principal' for some 22 years). Wallace's reputation was based first on her long tenure as a highly esteemed head of Palmerston North Girls' High School from 1948 to 1969; second, on her election in 1962 as Palmerston North's first woman city councillor; and third, on her involvement in multiple community and professional organisations. She was intellectually versatile, graduating from Victoria University of Wellington with a Master of Arts in 1919 and a Bachelor of Commerce in 1943. These qualities were to stand her in good stead as a city councillor.[1]

In the 1962 local body elections, four women candidates stood for the Palmerston North City Council. There had been none in 1959, and earlier female nominees, such as Zillah Gill, the first woman to stand for the council, in 1918, had found the territorial authority a much tougher electoral barrier than the hospital board, on which Gill served for many years. Times were changing by the 1960s, and at least one letter to the *Standard*, from a Mrs Margaret Blane, urged all women to rally around the female candidates, for 'we women represent about 50 per cent of the citizens, but we have no say whatever in the affairs of the city'.[2] Of the four candidates, only Julia Wallace was elected, her standing as a respected school principal giving her the public profile for success.

The *Standard* noted that 'two precedents' were set in the 1962 election, for not only was Miss Wallace the first woman on the council, but Māori welfare officer Sam Mīhaere became 'the first of his race' to sit on that body.[3] Wallace later indicated that she was 'not keen on people making a big deal of her being the first woman to join the ranks of men', insisting that her gender made no difference. She served two terms on the council, her 'greatest joys' being the chairing of the parks and reserves committee and planning for a new art gallery and museum.[4]

After losing her council seat in the 1968 election, Wallace became first chair of the Manawatu Museum Society, just one of a suite of voluntary activities, national and local, undertaken over her lifetime, including leadership roles in the YMCA and the National Council of Women. She was a member of the 1959 Dalgleish Committee for the Implementation of Equal Pay, and, after serving on the Post Primary Teachers' Association national executive for many years, she became its first elected female president in 1961. Because she had contracted poliomyelitis as a child and had ongoing physical consequences from it, her work for the Crippled Children's Society was especially close to her heart.[5]

Although Julia Wallace is remembered as the first woman to be elected to the city council in Palmerston North, these other activities are even more significant. Feminist historians have written of women's ways of 'doing politics' historically, which were not only via male-dominated electoral processes and party politics.[6] Women, including Palmerston North women, have long used their organisations as formal and informal pressure groups, petitioning, writing submissions and using social contacts to promote their agendas. Far beyond her two terms on the council, Julia Wallace was active in these other modes of engagement. Although she resisted being depicted as a 'trail-blazer for the women's movement' and claimed 'I've never been terribly feministic',[7] she was a long-term advocate of equal pay for women, and of equal opportunities more generally.[8]

07 EDUCATING THE CITY

MARGARET TENNANT

Pupils lined up in caps and panama hats for the official opening of Palmerston North Intermediate School on 12 February 1941. It was 'another milestone in the forward march of Palmerston North', proclaimed the school's first committee chairman W. G. Black. Auckland Libraries Heritage Collections AWNS 19410219_38_4(1)

By the mid-1990s, more than 40 per cent of Palmerston North's population attended or worked at an educational institution in the city.[1] The 'Knowledge City' slogan that this figure generated was one of the city's more sustained attempts at marketing itself. It has residues in the past, not least in mayoral claims that Palmerston North would become the 'Cambridge of New Zealand' with the development of Massey Agricultural College in 1927.[2] 'Knowledge City' invariably referenced the tertiary and research institutions in Palmerston North, plugging their economic benefits to the city and its businesses.

Past promotional materials were as likely to emphasise the range and number of schools, which were seen as a vector for individual betterment and social mobility. Assisting the children of workers to access white-collar jobs, they also inculcated values of citizenship and work discipline. While the range of tertiary institutions has made Palmerston North distinctive among provincial cities, as we shall see its schools have impinged on the lives of many more of its residents. As places where virtually all compulsorily spend their formative years, schools are a key part of the city's memory landscape. Our educational institutions have written histories aplenty, from the weighty tome to the commemorative booklet: What do they mean in total for the history of Palmerston North?[3]

In 1879 the *Manawatu Herald* colourfully compared the houses of the district to beehives from which an ever-increasing 'junior portion of humanity' swarmed daily. Their destination was the schools of Palmerston North and surrounding settlements.[4] By that time, the Palmerston school, built in 1872, was already overcrowded, even though fewer than 60 per cent of the borough's children aged five to 15 were enrolled there, and even fewer attended consistently.[5]

Palmerston North was settled at a significant time for education in New Zealand. The establishment of the primary school, and the settlement's first public secondary school some 30 years later, linked Palmerston North with a wider climate of debate about access to education and the state's responsibility for it. This was manifest in two key pieces of national legislation passed in close proximity to these local 'firsts': the 1877 Education Act, which provided for 'free, compulsory and secular' primary education; and then the 1903 Secondary Schools Act, which greatly extended the free-place scheme for entry to secondary schools. Both were signs of a pre-existing settler investment in education.

Historian Rollo Arnold has written about a 'great leap forward' in New Zealand education between 1871 and 1877, with a marked increase in children attending 'common schools' financed mostly from rates and taxes, and beyond the jurisdiction of the churches.[6] Arnold argues that the second phase of Pākehā settlement in New Zealand, marked by the opening up of new communities in the North Island bush, brought with it a rejection of earlier patterns of educational provision, especially church schools, in favour of public provision.[7] In settlements such as Palmerston North, a mixing of 'blood, ideas and customs drawn from all parts of Britain, with not uncommonly a Continental element as well',[8] meant that the main trajectory of education in the 1870s was firmly in the direction of schools funded from central government revenues, open to all and 'entirely of a secular character'.[9]

Many of the settlement's Scandinavian migrants came from Norway and Denmark, where schooling had long been universal. Palmerston North's first school was very much part of this pressure for universal elementary education — it appeared soon after the first permanent Pākehā presence in Te Papaiōea, when the settlement was barely a village. It followed representations made to the Wellington Provincial Council by Louisa Snelson for a land grant, and was underwritten by public subscriptions for a building. Anticipating the community role of modern school buildings, this simple, windowless structure was formally opened in October 1872 for religious and other gatherings, and appears to have been first used for teaching in March 1873.[10] The foundation principal was Robert Keeling, later to become the borough's first town clerk. Located on the corner of the present-day Princess and Main streets (more recently the site of the Empire Hotel), 'Central School', as it became known, moved in 1890 to Campbell Street, and then to Featherston Street in 1922.

In April 1884 Terrace End became the next part of Palmerston North to gain a public school, preceded days earlier by the first Catholic school, on Broad Street, near St Patrick's Church. College Street School opened in 1893: it, Terrace End and Central School are regarded as the borough's 'pioneering' public schools, although there were country schools, now within the city boundaries, that date back to the nineteenth century — among them Ashhurst, Linton, Karere (Longburn), Tiritea (Turitea), Stoney Creek (Whakarongo) and Aokautere. In 1917 a deputation to the Minister of Education claimed that there were 90 schools within a 25-mile (40-kilometre) radius of Palmerston North.[11]

The city's early schools had many of the dynamics of a settler society inscribed on them. There was initially a multi-lingual element, historian George Petersen suggesting that as many as half of the children may have come from Scandinavian homes where no English was spoken.[12] Fire was a scourge of bush settlements such as Palmerston North, and an unverified tradition has the first schoolhouse joining the ranks of its razed buildings.[13]

Newspaper reports confirm that the house of Terrace End schoolmaster, Irish-born and -educated David Guthrie, was destroyed by fire in 1886, his family barely escaping with their lives.[14] Guthrie was no stranger to tragedy, having experienced the loss of his infant daughter Isabella six years earlier. Like fire, accidental death frequently accompanied colonial life, and little Isabella's 'melancholy' (and nationally reported) death was caused by sucking on phosphorus matches.[15] More positively, Guthrie's career also exemplifies the upward mobility of colonials able to benefit from education. Forced out of teaching through ill health, he first went farming, served time on the Wanganui Education Board, and followed his father-in-law, former cabinet Minister John Bryce, into politics, eventually becoming Reform government Minister of Lands in 1918.[16]

The exigencies of life in a settler community meant that endorsement of education did not always translate into regular school attendance. Recognising this, the 1877 Act pragmatically required Pākehā children with access to a school to attend only half the time it was open, and for Māori the requirements were even looser. The early minutes of the Palmerston North School Committee show high absentee rates, a matter of concern for its schools and their staff since funding was linked to pupils' attendance. In 1891, for example, Central School had a roll of 599. Daily attendance over the previous year had averaged 433, and was never more than 500. The Terrace End School had 302 pupils enrolled, an average attendance of 191, and a lowest attendance of 138.[17]

Simply getting to school was a challenge, especially in bad weather. Country schools usually had a pony paddock, but even those in the borough were accustomed to children arriving on horseback, their mounts tethered in the already overcrowded school grounds. College Street School, for one, had to ban horses from the playground in 1907.[18] Some of the children's journeys seem heroic by today's standards. The Ashhurst school's history records the four hours spent daily on horseback in the 1920s by children of its Tararua 'riding party', who trekked bareback, often in freezing, wind-blasted weather, across gullies, tracks and surrounding farmlands, and past what is now the site of the wind farm.[19] (In contrast, during zoning disputes of the 1980s a ruling by Justice Ongley deemed it unreasonable to expect a pupil to cycle 5–6 kilometres across Palmerston North's flat terrain.)[20]

If weather did not get in the way of nineteenth-century school attendance, sickness often did, and excerpts from school logbooks record frequent outbreaks of measles, mumps, scarlet fever and influenza, cross-infection doubtless assisted by overcrowding. School closures due to royal commemorations, military victories (especially during the South African War) and visits by dignitaries seem to abound, while more frivolous counter-attractions, such as race days, circuses and picnics, also slashed attendances and led to schools closing early.

ABOVE Children at Palmerston North's first state school, 23 November 1881. The quirky range of expressions on the faces of children posed for school photographs remains a constant in the many class photographs which survive. Manawatū Heritage 2007N_Sc142_SCH_0424

BELOW Terrace End School cadets at the showgrounds, 1905, after winning a trophy. School cadets did not become compulsory until the Defence Act of 1909, but rifle skills had long been regarded as an asset in the colonial environment, for hunting as much as defence. School cadets were part of wider training in citizenship and service to Empire. Manawatū Heritage 2014N_Sc62_007928

Some children were kept home by parents, their assistance needed within the family economy. The presence of hop gardens around Ashhurst saw a seasonal drop in attendance when children went hop-picking; and again in May when some withdrew to collect edible fungus. The Palmerston North School Committee noted in 1893 that 'considerable friction was caused by parents sending impertinent notes to teachers, and also by others sending their children late and asking for them to be let out early to go to . . . music or dancing or some other distraction'.[21]

On the other hand, absenteeism could relieve the unpleasantly overcrowded schools, as the Central School headmaster feelingly wrote in the school logbook on 13 June 1888: 'Attendances getting smaller and *beautifully* less owing to sickness.'[22] The Wanganui Education Board appointed a truancy officer in 1892, and within 10 years he was bringing cases against more than 100 sets of Palmerston North parents annually.[23] Although sickness could still decimate school attendances, both enrolment and attendance had markedly increased by the 1920s, and the 'battle of compulsory attendance' was largely won, in Palmerston North, as elsewhere. By then, persistent truancy was seen as a sign of family problems rather than a tolerable inevitability, although Palmerston North probably retained a share of the 'milking children', whose early starts in the cowshed affected their ability to stay awake at school.[24]

Many of the city's school principals were characterised by long tenures and contributions to the community. The Central School's F. E. (Francis) Watson was known to his later pupils as 'old Pa' Watson, his leadership of the school spanning a remarkable 39 years from 1879. Watson was nothing if not versatile: he was a president of many local sports associations, first president of the Manawatu Arts Society, an All Saints' churchwarden, steward for the A & P Association, member of the town's choral societies, and at one stage president of the New Zealand Dairy Cattle Breeders' Association.[25] Also a dog breeder, he was remembered as doing his school rounds accompanied by an impressively fat, surly-looking white bulldog.[26] Fred Fairbrother stayed at the Terrace End School for nearly 30 years after his appointment in 1893, and David Low at College Street for 20 years, after which he served as a city councillor.[27] Many of their successors were similarly long-serving and influential.

By the First World War the pioneering period in education was over, and, as Palmerston North's suburbs expanded, new primary schools were opened on land reserved for the purpose: West End in 1913, Hokowhitu in 1924, Milson (partly for the children of railway workers) in 1928, Russell Street in 1929. The opening of a new school relieved overcrowding in other schools, and each was viewed as a core amenity of its developing area.

A cluster of five new schools opened in the 1950s, three in the new suburbs to the west of the city, but also in Roslyn, to the east. School memories of post-war baby boomers often included the smell of new paint and the sound of drills and hammers as their new school expanded around them, and, more generally, classes held in asbestos-clad 'prefabs'. The establishment of new primary schools slowed after the 1970s as the birth rate declined, with most new developments having a special purpose, usually religious or reflecting the new consciousness about Māori language and culture.

Extending the state primary school network from the mid-century were the intermediates, the first of which, now Palmerston North Intermediate Normal, opened in 1941 (followed by Ross Intermediate in 1958 and Monrad in 1963). While the intermediates usefully relieved some of the post-war baby-boom pressure on existing primary schools, they were touted as having a special purpose, being the embodiment of the age's 'expansive, realistic and socially integrative education', in the words of Prime Minister Peter Fraser.[28] In 1941 idealism gave way to military exigency, with Palmerston North's shiny new 27-classroom intermediate being handed over to the military for use as a hospital.

When the school was returned to educational use in April 1943, it retained the idealistic principles on which it was founded. In 1947 its principal, the energetic, sandy-haired John Whibley — famed for riding his bicycle around the long school corridors, ringing its bell in warning before cornering — linked his school to the optimism and internationalism of the post-war years. There was, he said, a need for an informed and independent-thinking citizenry inspired by an ethos of community service: 'higher living standards carry with them higher responsibilities . . . we must deserve and show our appreciation of these better living conditions by adequate service in return'.[29] On a more practical plane, the intermediates offered 'manual' education (sewing and cooking for girls; woodwork and metalwork for boys) in specialised facilities, as well as providing science laboratories.

Superimposed on the state school system from an early period were more targeted schools, with religion the main driver. An Adventist School, established in 1917, represented the Protestant wing of this activity, but the Catholic network was the most extensive. In February 1884 local priest Father McManus

> vigorously denounced the godless character of the State School system and read portions of Bishop Redwood's Pastoral Letter on the subject. He urged that the time had come when the Catholics of Palmerston North ought to do something to provide a school of their own, and avoid the loss of faith which was the result of children being sent to purely secular institutions.[30]

The first Catholic school was opened in part of the Broad Street church in March 1884. Twenty years later the Sisters of Mercy opened a girls' secondary school, St Joseph's, in 1904, but it was some time before the Marist Brothers' school opened in 1939 (both merging into St Peter's in 1974). Not unexpectedly, Catholic primary schools, like those in the state system, showed the effects of the post-war baby boom, with Our Lady of Lourdes

Teacher Ira Charles posed in front of a West End School class as part of a series of government publicity photographs taken in 1947. Although the school opened in 1913, many of its students later came from the newly developed Savage Crescent state housing subdivision. Classrooms of the mid-century were brighter, better ventilated and consequently healthier than their nineteenth-century predecessors. Manawatū Heritage 2010N_A175-67-1_004214

and St Mary's opening in 1950, and St James' in 1958.[31]

The Catholic schools had built doctrinal instruction, prayers and ritual into the school day, intended to ensure that students would remain immersed in the tenets of their faith. To more universal memories of school days — the smell of stale sandwiches in leather schoolbags, chalk and blackboards, friendships made, unmade and remade, the strap, the 'murder house' (dental clinic) — were added First Communion, the Catechism, holy days, visits from priests, and, in the days when nuns wore wimples, speculation about the sisters' hair.[32]

Despite the chants directed at Catholic students by state school counterparts ('Catholic dogs jump like frogs, don't eat meat on Fridays'), and their initial staffing by religious sisters and brothers, the Catholic schools' sense of separateness had diminished by the 1970s, when they were staffed increasingly by lay teachers. Already teaching to the state curriculum and subject to state inspection, but under financial stress, Palmerston North's Catholic schools, like others throughout the county, were gradually integrated into the state system from 1977.

'The spaces between'

As he often did, on Wednesday, 8 September 1915, 11-year-old Lionel Thomson went with three other boys to play at being 'railway men' in the Terrace End gravel pit (now Memorial Park). One of the boys released the brake on an empty ballast truck and Lionel was caught between it and another truck. He suffered internal injuries and died almost immediately. It was a high price to pay for an innocent game at what was essentially an industrial site, and the coroner recommended that all such trucks should have the wheels chained while standing in places where children had access. But there was no curtailment of that access.[1]

Young learners were ideally in school or at home, but there were also the zones in between where a different kind of education occurred. Getting to and from school long provided opportunities to linger and play away from adult supervision. Each suburb had large vacant sections and wilderness spaces, while the banks of the Manawatū River and many of the parks were less tamed than they are today.

The riverbank, littered and weedy, with rusting car bodies and fallen trees, was, as Jill White has pointed out, 'an ideal adventure park'. 'River kids' like Jack Register engaged in mud fights and hunted rats at the old Dittmer Drive rubbish tip. In the 1960s Simon Johnson and friends headed to the Albert Street end of the river, fascinated by the various pieces of machinery for crushing and sifting metal, while other boys tested homemade slingshots with the endless supply of finely graded stones. The land which is now the Chilton Grove area was also a wasteland. Here Simon practised his 'bomb-making' techniques, tamarillo bombs being the most effective around Guy Fawkes time: tight skins, soft pulp, 'double-happy' firecracker inserted, and 'best lobbed into porches and carports' before the pulp soaked into the cracker! 'Mighty cannons' offered an opportunity to blow up the neighbour's potatoes, using a long fuse so as to be safely home before the explosion occurred.[2]

Girls seemed to feature less among the wild children of Palmerston North, but, growing up in McGiffert Street, Val Mills spent a lot of time playing in the central-city railway yards, visiting the man in the signal box, and playing in old carriages abandoned on side lines.[3] Tina White's favourite stamping ground in the 1950s was the overgrown grounds of the former Coombs property ('Hillcrest') in Featherston Street, then divided into flats for assisted immigrants from Britain. Here girls as well as boys explored, played hide-and-seek, kicked the damp autumn leaves and smelt the blossoms in spring, and suffered the inevitable scraped knees and scratches and falls from the tall oak trees.[4]

Filled in during 1975, Gardner's Pool in Roslyn was originally part of the Kawau Stream and a popular meeting point for young people in the 1950s and 1960s. It features in Mervyn Dykes' memories as the place where he and his brother Ray almost drowned while swimming unsupervised:

On private property in Karina Terrace, Gardner's Pool was originally part of Kawau Stream. It was used by as many as 200 children in its heyday. During 1975 it was filled in. This photograph was taken c.1945–50. Manawatū Heritage 2011P_IMCA-DigitalMaster_004779

'One moment you can be playing and the next you are fighting for your life,' he remembers.[5] In those days, Mervyn also notes, 'the bicycle was king' and girls and boys of the mid-century experienced the liberation of being able to roam far afield, often cycling vast distances on single-geared bicycles to Foxton, Whanganui, and even beyond.

The bicycle also provided an opportunity to explore Palmerston North itself, etching the bounds of the city and its distinctive spaces on childhood memory. In the 1930s Merv Hancock, who lived in the semi-rural Rata Street (where his father then 'milked a cow and ran 100 chooks'), emphasised his local knowledge: 'Oh yes, I knew every street in the city, I could name them . . . and there was even an activity in the Scouts for which you could get a badge — knowledge of the city.'[6] When not catching eels in the Mangaone Stream on 'boats' made from pieces of wood and corrugated iron, Alan Crews experienced another dimension of children's bicycle-ownership: the opportunity to earn. Alan worked as a delivery boy first for his father's grocery store, and then, when at Boys' High School, as a prescription courier for a local pharmacy. The bicycle brought independence of many kinds.[7]

In each era of Palmerston North's development, a children's map of the city might differ from those used for official purposes. Education took many forms, some of it in the adventurous spaces beyond school and home. But as Lionel Thomson's friends sadly learnt, it was not always without cost.

A handful of privately owned and operated schools also functioned in Palmerston North over the late nineteenth and early twentieth centuries. These also need to be factored into the patterning of education, for, although they claimed to teach Christian values, social privilege was a clearer differential. By the 1890s Kenneth Wilson's high school for boys provided an alternative and closer option to boarding schools elsewhere. Carow School, which, although a 'ladies collegiate', also had a few boys on the roll, and Craven School for Girls, also provided post-primary education of a genteel but academically respectable kind.

Most private establishments were short-lived, with only Carncot School, founded in 1903 to provide pre-secondary education, still surviving.[33] Dorothy Pilkington notes that the families of those attending Carncot in its early years were from the 'cream' of Palmerston North society, a high number of pupils the progeny of local lawyers, dentists and doctors, attending alongside the sons and daughters of affluent businessmen and landowners. Names such as Monrad, Keiller, Waldegrave, Fitzherbert and Guy featured among Carncot's pupils, their families having sufficient wealth to choose from the educational alternatives on offer. (It was, however, Craven School which could claim the ultimate coup of enrolling a Governor's daughter, when the Hon. Joyce Plunket briefly boarded there in the 1900s.)[34] Carncot continued in its exclusive role throughout the twentieth century, with demand for places leading to the opening of new buildings in 1999. Carncot's governors had decided not to integrate into the state sector following the 1975 Private Schools Conditional Integration Act, and by the end of the century its pupils were among the 3.3 per cent of New Zealand children being educated in independent schools.[35]

Carncot's expansion in the late twentieth century reflected challenges to a broad consensus about equality and uniformity in state education. From the late 1970s no more state primary or secondary schools were built in Palmerston North, but there were further 'special character' schools. Four of them extended the kōhanga reo or Māori language nest concept, and used a Māori worldview as their reference point: Mana Tamariki (1989 as a kōhanga reo, teaching up to Year 13 from 1995), Te Kura Kaupapa Māori o Manawatū (1990), Tu Toa (2005) and Manukura (2014). Reflecting a counterpoint to the increasingly secular city revealed by the census, another Christian school also emerged in 1987: Cornerstone, which 'uses the Bible as a standard against which to compare and interpret all curriculum material'.[36] The uniformity of mid-twentieth-century education was now seen as an undesirable homogeneity that did not benefit all students, especially Māori, and, in an era of growing demand for educational choice, even some of the state schools were deemed more desirable than others.

City leaders took a close interest in school rolls and locations. The Palmerston North Borough (then City) Council had provided land for education in the past, including the sites of the boys' and girls' high schools, Central School, Massey University and Manawatu Polytechnic.[37] This was more properly the responsibility of the Education Department, which had the role of identifying reserved sites when new suburbs were proposed. Over much of the twentieth century new schools in expanding suburbs helped take pressure off existing ones, but as the birth rate declined, older schools became competitors, extending their catchment areas into new suburbs in order to maintain rolls and funding, and senior positions. By the 1980s the Education Department would not allow new schools to be built without a quarter of classrooms being relocatable, so they could eventually be sent from schools with declining rolls to those which were growing (from West End to Cloverlea, for example). Education reserves were identified for disposal.[38]

Declining rolls had other implications. Just as Palmerston North's first school buildings provided a space for worship, entertainment, tea meetings and polling booths, later schools were also used for more than teaching purposes. Immediate communities were often highly invested in their neighbourhood school: school histories record voluntary effort in constructing school baths, for example, with fathers photographed in their singlets painting or pouring concrete at weekends. By the 1980s, however, this 'community of use' was becoming geographically divorced from schools and their immediate, often ageing, catchments. It was difficult to justify new schools when the existing ones were under-utilised, and school zoning and bussing became subjects of controversy. From the late 1980s came the era of 'Tomorrow's Schools', with associated demands for parental choice, the most vociferous debates around these matters being related to secondary schooling.

William Gray, appointed the first head teacher at Palmerston North's District High School in 1901, later mused upon the differences between his Palmerston North pupils and those he had taught in Otago:

> I was greatly struck by the difference between the Otago boy and girl as I had known them and those at Palmerston North. Was it the wide open spaces? Was it the new pioneering life? Was it the greater freedom from social and religious constraints? I don't know. They were a 'mixed' lot — all shades of opinion among the people, but the children were wonderfully friendly and responsive, at the same time respectful.[39]

If Gray's Palmerston North pupils showed an appreciation of their opportunity for further education, it was not surprising. Many parents had long urged this development, for secondary education was viewed as a gateway to employment in the expanding service sector, most especially to white-collar work. As with the city's first primary school, timing was critical to public investment in the high school. Prior to 1900 many secondary schools were dominated by an elite who 'took steps to ensure that their children did not share in the schooling of the common herd'.[40] They had been established with large land endowments that generated income, and, even where endowments permitted fees to be kept low, they

Palmerston North High School pupils in the assembly hall of the city's first high school, c.1906. The school at this stage was co-educational, and girls can be seen at the far side of the room. Note that school attire had not yet been standardised into uniforms. The school was allegedly burnt down by the notorious fugitive Joseph Pawelka in 1910, a charge he denied. Manawatū Heritage 2007P_Scs83_SCH_0441

were seen as enabling the affluent to educate their children on the cheap.[41]

From the late 1890s the Liberal Government began to extend the number of government-funded places for able students in secondary schools, encouraged by Richard Seddon, the premier, who took over the education portfolio in 1903. A son and also a father of school teachers, Seddon had 'a finely attuned populist antennae', which alerted him to increasing parental demands for education beyond primary level. Between 1901 and 1905 the number of students in secondary schooling rose from 963 to 4273.[42] Palmerston North scholars were among them.

Local MP and long-term member of the Wanganui Education Board, the 'terrier-like' Frederick Pirani also took a special interest in education.[43] He was among those leading the charge for a state secondary school in Palmerston North, preferably one that also had a technical department.[44] Pirani and other members of the board were not satisfied with Education Department suggestions that the privately operated Craven School for Girls and Kenneth Wilson's high school were adequate substitutes.[45]

In the end, the board advanced a temporary expedient more acceptable to the Education Department on economic grounds.[46] College Street was identified as the primary school onto which a district high would be grafted, and William Gray was appointed headmaster of both. Secondary classes were first held in the hall of St Andrew's Presbyterian Church, before a more permanent building was constructed on land provided by the borough council in Featherston Street. Within two years it had become a separate high school under its own board.[47] The expedient had worked, and the number of Palmerston North scholars in secondary education increased from 184 to 395 between 1901 and 1906.[48]

The new high school had a number of significant characteristics. Historians have noted the strong Scottish influence via Otago and Southland appointees in its early years — William Gray was followed by the longer-serving John ('Pa') Vernon, who had been educated in Scotland and then taught at Southland Boys' High School. The first four rectors (the title itself of Scottish origin) came from the south, along with some long-serving and influential assistant masters.

The Palmerston North Boys' High School historian suggests a strong Presbyterian representation among its early board of governors, and an underlying debt to the value placed on education in Scotland.[49] These connections with older high schools may have contributed to a belief that Palmerston North Boys' High School also provided (in the words of a later rector, Eric White) 'a sense of continuity, a firm link with a past which many present parents believe had more positive and unyielding moral standards'.[50] More than any other school in the city, Boys' High assiduously cultivated a sense of tradition, assisted over the years by the presence of long-serving masters and rectors — men with nicknames like 'Snoop' (J. Murray), 'Cooney' (J. A. Colquhoun), 'Crafty' (O. Doel) and 'Coke' (I. Colquhoun).[51]

The Boys' High School may have shared an emphasis on tradition with older boys' schools, but because of its later establishment it lacked the generous land endowments of Otago Boys' High School and Whanganui Collegiate, for example. The co-educational school from which Boys' High originated had to rely mostly on government capitation payments, and there were complaints that it was a poor relation as a consequence.[52] Funding — especially for developments such as hostels to service the surrounding rural constituency — was a difficulty which required complicated negotiations with the Education Department's central and regional offices, the Wanganui Education Board, and, where land was concerned, the Palmerston North City Council.

Another characteristic of the high school which had long-term consequences was its initial emergence as a single, co-educational, multi-course district high school under one board of governors. When the girls moved to their own establishment in 1920, leaving the boys' school to its masculine trajectory, the same board continued to govern both, along with a technical school and, from 1955, a new co-educational school (Freyberg). Palmerston North's single high-school board was later praised by ministers of education as an efficient example of governance able to consider needs on a city-wide basis, but in its last years it was increasingly resented and challenged by Boys' High rectors and parent groups, ambitious to assert their school's distinctive needs and claim on resources.

Initially, there were more girls than boys on the roll of the first co-educational school, but numbers soon moved in favour of the males. Disparity in numbers was paralleled by an apparent disparity in recognition, although Rector John Vernon is said to have done his best to further the girls' interests.[53]

As in most urban primary schools during the early twentieth century, boys' and girls' recreational areas were segregated. At the lower levels, classes were as well, Vernon explaining in 1912 that, having 'tried it both ways', he had come to believe in the separation of boys and girls, and that discipline had been better since he had made the change in forms three and four. At the upper levels there were still mixed classes taught by teachers of both sexes, however.[54]

When a new school was proposed, it was always assumed that the girls would be the ones to move, their presence increasingly cast as a problem. In 1918, when the school was 'absolutely crowded out' with an enrolment of 371 students, a letter to the school magazine, the *Palmerstonian*, pointed out that 'Were the girls to move to a school of their own the boys would have all that much extra room, and the gym, armoury, cooking room and masters' cloak room would revert to their old uses.' In the *Palmerstonian* itself the girls commanded fewer than 30 of its 109 pages, which were mostly dedicated to male sports and exhortations to 'play the game' in life as on the football (rugby) field.[55]

'It will certainly be glorious to have a school of our own', wrote student Catherine McHaffie in the 1918 *Palmerstonian*,[56] although it would be another two years before Palmerston North Girls' High School opened its doors, in September 1920. The borough council had once again come to the party, releasing 6 acres (2.5 hectares) in Fitzherbert Street, rather less than the 10 acres (4 hectares) occupied by the Boys' High School.[57]

Miss Clara Beatrice Mills was the school's first 'lady principal' (a title used by the board, at least, until the 1960s). Highly qualified, with a BSc and a first class masterate in English and French, Mills had previously been senior mistress at the Palmerston North High School with an intervening period of service at Waitaki Girls' High School.[58] She was just one of a number of exceptional women, mostly spinsters, who 'had fought hard for university education themselves [and] encouraged, coaxed and occasionally bullied' the girls into making the best use of what capabilities they possessed.[59] The most remarkable of all was the school's longest-serving principal, Julia Wallace (1948–69), who appears elsewhere in this volume as the city's first woman councillor.

Although the Palmerston North Girls' High School was less focused on female accomplishments than earlier private schools, it commenced at a time when there was a thrust for greater differentiation between boys' and girls' education. Changes to free-place regulations in 1916 and 1917 had made at least some home science compulsory for girls in secondary schools, and the Palmerston North girls' school inevitably offered such courses. Speakers at prizegiving ceremonies spoke approvingly of the certificates given for subjects such as cooking, hygiene and home nursing, linking them to the value that needed to be placed on 'happy home life'.[60]

However, when the *Palmerstonian* and its Girls' High School successor, *Pinnacle*, reported the destinations of former pupils, there was not only mention of marriages and babies, but of 'old girls' employed in banks, insurance companies and offices, while a good number went into teaching (including Catherine McHaffie, who appears with an MSc on the staff of the Girls' High School in 1924).[61] At the end of the 1930s, the largest number of new entrants to Girls' High went into its commercial course.[62] Girls' High parents wanted their daughters to gain skills beyond the domestic.

These young women were part of the 'white blouse' revolution in women's paid work during the early twentieth century. But by this time there was more than one provider of vocational subjects in Palmerston North. Technical education was advanced in New Zealand from the late 1890s, primarily for those who would not pass the proficiency examination as a pathway to high-school education of an academic nature.

In Palmerston North, technical classes in subjects such as drawing, woodcarving, plumbing and tinsmiths' work, and commercial subjects, were initially tacked onto the teaching of the high school. With an enrolment of 241 pupils by 1907, they were sufficiently successful to justify a separate director, Frank D. Opie, and a new building. Located on the corner of King and Duke streets, the technical school benefited from generous public fundraising, and was opened on 29 September 1909.[63] It was 'concerned with the part-time education of artisans, office workers and persons interested in art or domestic pursuits [and] did not aspire to provide full-time post-primary education for pupils to whom the ordinary secondary schools may not appeal'.[64] Many classes were held in the evening. Overseen by the high-schools board, it provided yet another strand in the patterning of education in Palmerston North, but one which always suffered from ambivalent public perceptions.

Three factors undermined the distinctiveness and viability of the technical school long-term. First, the boys' and girls' high schools also taught some vocational subjects — mostly typing and shorthand at the girls' high, bookkeeping and agriculture at the boys'. Then, in response to demand, the technical school, like others across the country, gradually increased the number of 'advanced' subjects on offer, some students qualifying for university entrance even in the 1930s. With the Labour Government's 1936 abolition of the proficiency examination (previously the gateway to free secondary schooling), its extension of compulsory education to the age of 15, and the introduction of a common core of subjects for all secondary students in the 1940s, the technical school's daytime enrolments grew.

The technical school came closer to other secondary schools in its range of offerings, and by the 1950s it was known as the 'Palmerston North Technical High School', becoming

ABOVE Time out of class! Palmerston North Girls' High School pupils at the 1937 Springbok rugby game in Palmerston North. Auckland Libraries Heritage Collections AWNS 19370811_4_5(1)

BELOW Palmerston North Girls' High School pupils arrive for the start of the 1961 school year. Bicycles were an important mode of transport across the city, only the rare student having access to a car at the time. Manawatū Heritage 2017N_2017-20_016078

'Queen Elizabeth College' in 1966.[65] By then it was on a new site in Rangitikei Street, where it remains. 'The Tech', as it was still often called, had transformed in response to the mid-century emphasis on a uniform, egalitarian, multi-course secondary education, but was dogged by public perceptions that it was a technical school for those of lesser ability. Former student Edward Body provides a telling anecdote, suggestive of even wider educational trajectories within the city:

> Toward the end of 1946 pupils in the top class at Palmerston North Intermediate were asked to say which post-primary school they would be attending the following year. The response was constant — Girls' High, Boys' High — until one girl said 'Tech'. There was a gasp from most pupils and a disapproving look from the teacher. When a boy also said 'Tech', the teacher responded, 'Students from this class go to High School. They do not go to a technical school.'[66]

Prejudice lingered. Although Queen Elizabeth's roll reached more than 1100 in the early 1970s, its staff complained about the distribution of students and the more narrow examination focus of other secondary schools. In 1974 Queen Elizabeth's deputy principal claimed that his school was more successful in adding academic subjects than other high schools had been in moving away from their traditional curriculum and providing a rounded education for a range of abilities.[67] Already attracting a significant proportion of Māori students, the college had started offering a Māori language class in 1970, and appears to have been one of the first mainstream secondary schools in the city to do so.[68] Soon the concern would not be the imbalance in student intake, but total numbers, as the school roll had dropped substantially by the end of the century.[69]

The city's schools moved in and out of fashion, and Queen Elizabeth was not the only one to suffer as the birth rate declined. In keeping with educational ideals of the time, Freyberg High School was established in 1955 as a co-educational school, and was situated on the eastern side of the city, catering to expansion in Milson and Roslyn. New and modern, it became the school of choice for those who wanted an alternative to single-sex schooling. However, by 1983 it, too, was in the doldrums, with the newest school, Awatapu, located in the expanding area to the west and claiming the largest number of third-form (year nine) first-choice applications (303; compared with Queen Elizabeth, 291, Boys' High, 232, Girls' High, 192, and Freyberg, 97).[70] Such disparities ensured that enrolments became the subject of bitter contestation and even litigation.

Overlaying local concerns was the advent of a more assertive 'parentocracy' and the assertion of choice in education.[71] National trends took a particular intensity in Palmerston North because of the continued existence of a single high-schools board on which some schools felt outvoted, and because the city had an increasing number of tertiary staff and other professionals who were not backward in expressing their views on education. An

Freyberg High School hosted Te Piringa kapa haka group, shown performing at a Freyberg High School fundraiser in July 2008. Kapa haka groups from local schools regularly compete in local and national kapa haka festivals, symbolising the regeneration of Māori culture and language. Warwick Smith, *MS*, 27 July 2008

early manifestation of this saw Awatapu College gain its own board after it opened in 1976. Parents — some of the more vocal associated with Massey University and the research institutes — persuaded the Minister of Education that a separate board would enhance community participation in the new school.[72] Their success increased pressure from the Boys' High support networks for a similar concession. Coupled with the two boards' attempts to manage rolls so that third-form admissions were shared more equitably among schools, feelings ran high by the 1980s. References abound in board records to 'fractious' meetings, intemperate language and allegedly threatening behaviour.[73]

A 1983 attempt to equalise rolls via a scheme where third-formers gave their preferences in order and then effectively went into a ballot, gained nationwide coverage for its radicalism. One Boys' High master denounced it as 'deporting' students from his school.[74] A challenge was mounted in the courts on behalf of seven third-formers who missed out on their first choice of school, and Justice Ongley ruled that the minister of education had incorrectly

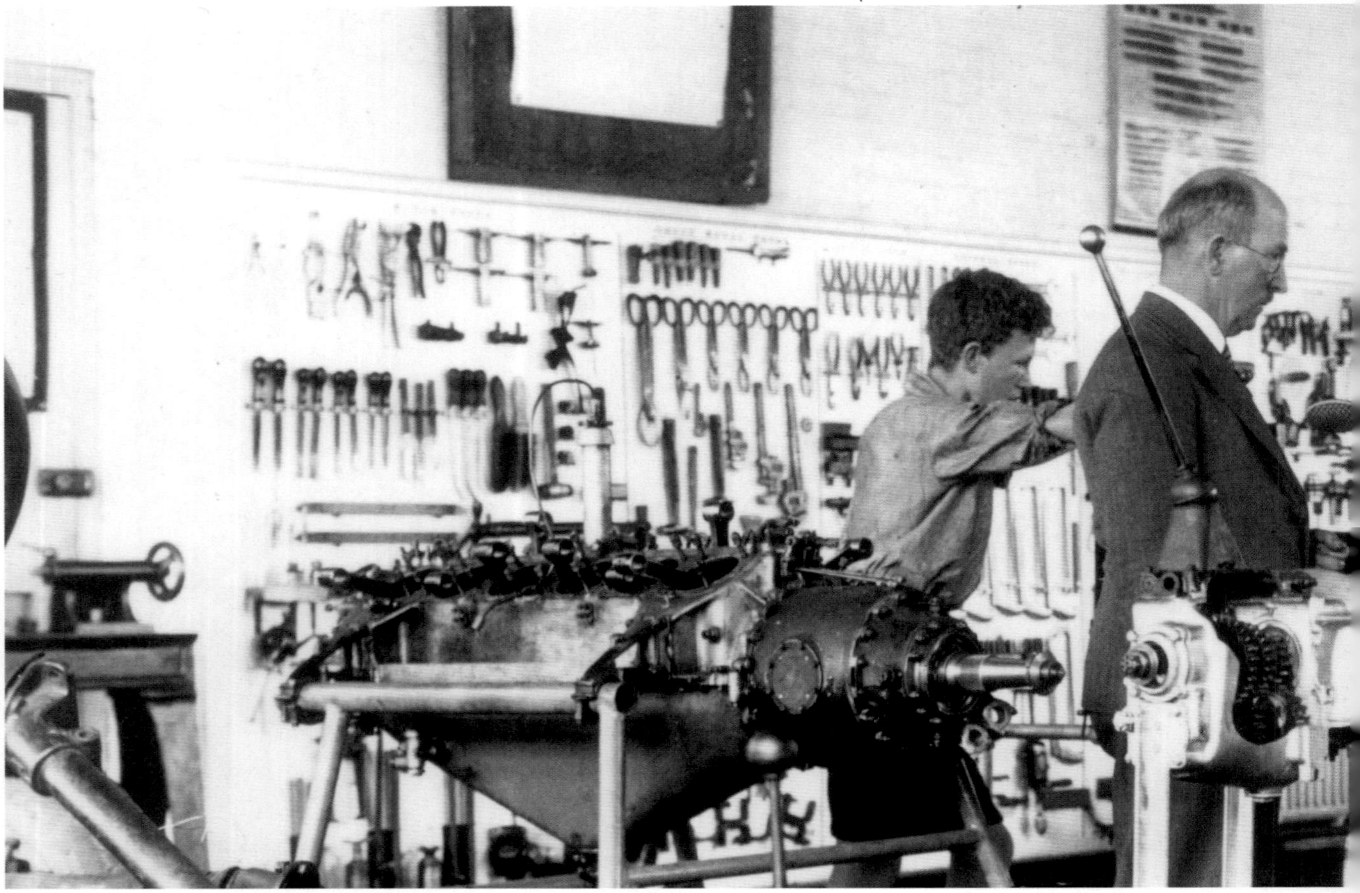

approved the scheme. The basis of the judgment did little to reveal how geography was intersected by human perceptions and prejudices. It came down to what was a 'reasonable' distance for an urban student to be expected to travel for their education, disregarding the availability of buses supplied by the high-schools board. Deciding that the most convenient way of attending school on Palmerston North's flat terrain was by bicycle (an assumption very much embedded in time and place), Justice Ongley gave the example of a student living only 2 kilometres or so from Awatapu being required to attend Freyberg High School at least 6 kilometres away, and determined that this was unreasonable in terms of the Education Act. In the end, the seven students got to attend their school of choice while another scheme was considered.[75]

By the end of the decade 'Tomorrow's Schools' had launched, the high-schools board gave way to individual school boards of trustees, and the mechanisms for distributing students and using existing school plant rationally became subject to changing government policies, with some more than others endorsing market choice. Boards generally had to admit students from their 'home' zone, but were allowed to select from applicants beyond it.[76]

The drawing of boundaries in itself sent socioeconomic messages, with some Palmerston North schools and not others featuring in real estate agents' advertisements. The desirable

Palmerston North Boys' High School zone now extends out several kilometres to the new, more affluent suburbs of Summerhill and Aokautere, but stops east of Botanical Road and Cook Street. (Real estate agent Tim Mordaunt claimed in 2005 that 'single sex education tended to appeal more to higher socio-economic people, who would mostly live inside the [Boys' High] zone'.)[77] Freyberg High, since restored to favour and benefiting from the city's eastward Kelvin Grove expansion, has extended its zone as far as Ashhurst and the Pohangina Valley.

By 2016, 22 per cent of Palmerston North students attended 'out of zone' schools, twice the national average. Single-sex schooling was in favour, but, with only one school for each sex, Palmerston North Boys' drew 50 per cent of its students from beyond its zone, and Palmerston North Girls', 66 per cent.[78] The ruling about it being unreasonable for a student to cycle as much as 6 kilometres has long since been jettisoned as students are driven — or, if family resources permit, drive themselves — to school.

Boys in the Palmerston North Technical School workshop, date unknown. The technical school later became Queen Elizabeth College, with the more applied sections of its education becoming the Technical Institute in 1971, eventually evolving into the degree-granting UCOL. Manawatū Heritage 2017P_IMCA-DigitalMaster_019928

Palmerston North's 'Get in the Know' branding in the 1990s drew on the existence of an unusually wide range of tertiary institutions for a provincial city, alongside the crown research institutes. Leading the pack was Massey University, which, as Massey Agricultural College, had admitted its first students in 1928 and evolved into a full multi-course university in 1964. The Palmerston North Teachers' College was established in 1956, and absorbed into Massey in 1996. Also in the higher-education sector was UCOL, the Universal College of Learning, formerly the Manawatu Polytechnic (a title it was anxious to disown in the rush to degree-granting status during the 1990s).[79] IPU, the Institute of the Pacific United New Zealand, opened in 1990 as the International Pacific College, initially with a focus on Japanese students. Finally, Te Wānanga o Aotearoa has had a campus in the city since 2000, promoting a uniquely Māori learning environment and its distinctiveness from the other labels ('We're not a university or a poly tech. We're a wānanga').[80]

The first two of these bodies have had authoritative histories written about them which focus on internal dynamics, but it is their interaction with the city of Palmerston North that is of interest here.[81] The relationship with Massey University, the largest, has been the most complex, not least because of its position 'across the river' and, originally, in Kairanga County. The Palmerston North Borough Council played a role in securing the location of New Zealand's second agricultural college on the southern side of the Manawatū River.

In making the decision, founding Professors Peren and Riddet favoured the site not only because the land was suitable for a wide variety of agriculture, but because of its location near a town large enough to support the college, one with a railway connection, a well-established agricultural and pastoral show, and a close proximity to freezing works.[82] Urban advantages combined with rural suitability, but the borough council further sweetened the deal (opponents saw it as a bribe) by offering to purchase one of the hilltop sites above the river if the government began building on an adjacent property.[83] The raising of a civic loan of £10,000 for the purchase of the McHardy land was approved by a ratepayer poll in 1926, and, after a hard-fought contest, Palmerston North 'landed the Big Fish' as the disgruntled mayor of Marton, a rival location, put it.[84]

The growth of Massey College extended the city's educational hinterland across the lower North Island, but also gave international linkages via staff recruited from overseas and their research connections. Palmerston North's own relationship with Massey was mixed. The city was represented on the college board of governors, with at least one mayor, Augustus Mansford, serving as an early chancellor. On the other side of the exchange, many Massey staff and their young families lived within the city boundaries, a significant cluster of their leading lights around the Girls' High School, Fitzherbert Avenue and Marne Street area in the 1930s and 1940s. After an initial period when a cohort of British recruits and their families formed a supportive 'community within a community', Massey staff and their wives not only joined local associations, but often played a prominent role within them,[85] and their children attended city schools.

Massey University in 1928, its agricultural emphasis very clear. Massey was to have an uneasy relationship with Palmerston North, but it helped differentiate the town from other provincial centres. Auckland Libraries Heritage Collections AWNS-19281220-43-1

If members of the Massey community were a part of the city, the college itself was apart from it, separated by the Manawatū River, part of another local body, and linked with the surrounding rural community via its farms and rural orientation. Its first principal, Geoffrey Peren, and a majority of students resided on campus. There was initially no bus service, the 1939 college *Calendar* advising visitors from the city to travel to the campus by taxi. (Twenty years later there were four municipal buses daily, with an increasing number of students residing 'in town'.)[86]

As more Palmerstonians gained motor vehicles, a Sunday drive around the Massey campus became a popular way of passing the time, to such an extent that students complained of feeling like exhibits in a zoo.[87] The city seemed proud of 'its' college in its first three decades, but, as an editorial in the student magazine *Bleat* commented in 1939: 'When the people of Palmerston North are proud of this College as an institution rather than as a fine building in an ideal site, then Massey College can claim to have accomplished no mean feat — the appreciation of the University in a provincial centre.' Students mostly impinged upon the city at capping time, when their 'rags' 'should be smiled upon rather than condemned'.[88]

From the outset some Palmerston North residents felt short-changed by a college teaching only agricultural subjects. One grumbled in 1927 that supporters of the ratepayer poll to finance the McHardy purchase had implied it would be possible 'to study all branches of learning at this new university', when in reality very few children of ratepayers would want to attend an agricultural college. (Even more absurd, he added, was the mayoral claim that 'this little agricultural college' would eventually be the Cambridge University of New Zealand!)[89] Parental aspirations were increasingly for educational opportunities to equip their offspring for urban and professional jobs.

Widening options came with the 1956 establishment of the Palmerston North Teachers' Training College, the first teachers' college outside the four main centres. This development was a response to an acute teacher shortage, and the city was chosen because of assumptions about the readily available accommodation and proximity to other tertiary activity. There was also an existing building, the old technical school in Princess Street, which could be economically renovated.[90] The first 160 students were mostly female and from rural areas, their average age between 16 and 17. Their youth, coupled with a dangerous proximity to the predominantly male student body of Massey College, put an onus on college staff to provide moral oversight. (Historian Roger Openshaw suggests that the Fitzherbert Bridge was a 'kind of checkpoint Charlie between the sexes'!) In the days when the Regent Arcade's Nicoberg Coffee Lounge was a 'Mecca' for the young, there was a hotline between its manager and the training college's dean of women that was activated whenever a young student gave cause for anxiety.[91]

An international tide in favour of expanding tertiary education meant that Massey also reached a 'fork in the road' around this time.[92] Between 1945 and 1971 the population

Palmerston North Teachers' Training College end-of-year ceremony, c.1960. The college was located at this time in the brick building on the corner of Princess and King streets, now part of UCOL. The youthfulness and female predominance of the trainees is obvious. Manawatū Heritage 2016N_IMCA-DigitalMaster_013459 in secondary schools trebled, the demands of the workplace became more complex, and the right of access to a university education became a matter of geographical as well as social equity.[93] In Palmerston North, a marginal electorate, a group termed the Council for the Development of University Education in the Manawatu acted as an effective lobby group from 1961. Submissions showed a general consensus that the university should be multidisciplinary, in a single location, and heavily residential — this was seen as a way of attracting students from across the country, given the limited sites and difficulties of tertiary accommodation in the main centres.[94] There was debate as to whether an existing Palmerston North branch of Victoria University of Wellington or Massey College should lead the new development, but the laurel eventually went to Massey, the combined branches of activity becoming 'Massey University of the Manawatu', and then simply 'Massey University'.

Massey thus became the only university in New Zealand without a sense of place incorporated in its title. This was in keeping with the original college intention to provide an agricultural education for students from across New Zealand, and the new university's incorporation of courses and, subsequently, full degrees taught extramurally. It also foreshadowed the university's later expansion into campuses at Albany and Wellington, and the 2012 slogan which branded Massey as the 'University of New Zealand'.

Nevertheless, the university continued to have a significant, if not always easy, relationship with Palmerston North. In the 1970s and 1980s Mayor Brian Elwood and Vice-chancellor Alan Stewart maintained dialogue about how their respective bodies saw the future, particularly in relation to city expansion towards Aokautere. Prior to the 1989 local government restructuring, Massey leaders generally saw their institution as better served by inclusion in the Kairanga County, and were concerned about the effects of urban encroachment on university farms — and marauding urban dogs on their stock![95]

Even before its inclusion in the city boundaries, Massey's huge social, economic and cultural impact on the city was clear. Palmerston North was the smallest urban university centre in New Zealand at the time, and Helen Dollery has suggested that its impact on the city was proportionately greater than universities in the main centres.[96] Internal enrolments at Massey rose from 959 in 1964 to just under 4000 10 years later, with an additional 3300 extramural students, many of whom spent time in the city on courses.[97]

A 1978 study estimated that for every 100 internal students enrolled full- or part-time, 35 staff members and their dependents were added to the city population, 18 housing units were required, 19 jobs were created at the university, six jobs in support industries were created in the city, 0.72 classrooms were required, and $377,075 was added to the regional income from all sources.[98] Two immediate effects may be noted: in 1966 the high-schools board was already concerned about the loss of well-qualified secondary teachers to the university and other tertiary institutions,[99] while by the 1970s there was a clear impact on housing. For example, the central city area comprised a mix of commercial premises and old houses, and was an area of population decline before 1970. Between the 1971 and 1976 censuses, its predominantly elderly population was rapidly overtaken by an influx of young people in the 20–29 age group, the number of residents there growing by almost 100 per cent.[100]

The presence of tertiary and research institutions resulted in a constituency of articulate citizens with high expectations for the governance of the city. They did more than keep the council on its toes: from the 1970s and 1980s some became city councillors themselves. DSIR plant scientist Bernard Forde served on council from 1971 to 1998, and was one of a 'tight group' credited with reshaping the city during this time.[101] Alongside him at various times were economics professor Jim Rowe, sociologist Robyn Leeming, counsellor Merv Hancock, Massey assistant registrar Vern Chettleburgh, and Steve Maharey, another sociologist, and a 'local boy' who was later to become an MP and then a vice-chancellor of the university. Hancock, for one, was concerned about emerging conflicts between students and other low-income groups over access to housing, pushing the city council towards greater social investment and economic development.[102] The residues of this thrust remain, with the Palmerston North City Council being one of only four in New Zealand still investing in social housing by 2019.[103]

The sector also contributed to the cultural life of Palmerston North. The newer tertiary staff of the 1950s and 1960s, and the well-educated 'staff wives' who accompanied male appointees, did their best to transform what some perceived as a cultural backwater. There was already a strong musical scene of various kinds, and this was strengthened by families associated with Massey, the Palmerston North Teachers' College and the Department of Scientific and Industrial Research (DSIR), who provided participants in local activities and a 'culture-hungry' audience for local and national performances.[104] There are memories of Keith Thomson, Massey's dean of social sciences, who was 'into everything' cultural. An experienced actor and director, he held 'soirées' at the historic Caccia Birch House during the early 1960s, established Saturday-morning drama classes, contributed to theatre productions within and beyond Massey, and was also a stalwart of the Manawatu Art Gallery Society and the Manawatu Museum Society.[105] Formed in 1959, the Art Gallery Society was heavily populated by individuals associated with the tertiary and research institutions, as was the Chamber Music Society, whose gatherings 'were like seeing a Massey common room some nights'.[106]

As tertiary staff aged and retired, other community organisations showed a similar influx of now-greying academic heads, with greater time to participate and contribute: although not unique to Palmerston North and other tertiary centres, bodies such as the Royal Society and the University of the Third Age benefited from a ready supply of lecturers and researchers to maintain their speaking programmes.

On a less-elevated front, the student body became more visible within the city from 1964, and not always in a good way. Pubs like 'the Fitz', student flats and capping stunts brought media attention. The once-a-year student 'rags' from a relatively conservative

NO U TURN
You Fought HITLER, OPPOSE NIXON
N.Z. TROOPS
CONDEMN RAPE of
WAR IS

Massey University students drenched with pigs' blood follow behind the 1971 Procesh to protest the Vietnam War. This departure from Massey students' usual satirical but humorous stance did not go down well with many citizens of Palmerston North. MS, 22 April 1971, Massey University Archives

agricultural college had been tolerated in a rural town, and the annual 'procesh' generated donations to charity. But when they involved stunts of an increasingly challenging kind, a wider range of students and a political edge, tolerance declined and the licence conceded for student transgressions waned.

Some capping stunts were memorable, even witty; some were simply destructive; a handful saw students appear in court. Among the more notable was the 1965 letter to Hokowhitu residents, ostensibly from the Health Department, seeking samples of pet-bird droppings and human urine to combat an alleged outbreak of *Salmonella*: 'a number of samples were received', but some, unfortunately, had burst in the mail. The 1972 appearance of a nappy on the revolving kiwi above the PDC store prompted amusement. But when students 'borrowed' a truck from Linton army camp (which did not notice its absence until informed by the local press) and left it in the central city, they were charged with vehicle theft.[107] Over time the bounds of good taste and tolerance were tested, and capping events restricted. In more recent years, activity has been limited to the official university graduation rituals, largely without input from the current undergraduates.

Whatever their misdeeds and occasional

The presence of international students had become more noticeable in Palmerston North by the end of the 1990s, with secondary schools as well as tertiary institutions vying for international student fees. The associated cultural enrichment was symbolised by the Institute of the Pacific United's Sakura Festival. Students are shown among the cherry blossoms before the 2009 festival. Warwick Smith, MS, 16 September 2009 disfavour, students brought money into the city. Estimates of their spending have ranged from $10.6 million in 1977–78 to between $205 million and $278 million for the city and region in 2011.[108] A 2003 study suggested that the total direct and indirect economic impact of the tertiary education sector in Palmerston North from both institutional and student spending amounted to more than $1022.8 million, contributing 4033 full-time-equivalent jobs to the city.[109] Other benefits include contributions to research and development, an increasingly diverse international population, a more youthful age structure for the city, and (more diffusely) city 'vibrancy'. A 2014 headline proudly declared that 'Palmy folk are a brainy bunch', since Palmerston North had a higher proportion of doctoral degrees per head of population than any other place in New Zealand. Some, including a later mayor, Grant Smith, rightly felt this was a rather limited indicator of the citizenry's smartness.[110]

With more than 40 per cent of Palmerston North's population directly experiencing, delivering or supporting education, it was not surprising that Palmerston North's promoters seized upon the 'Knowledge City' concept in 1993.[111] Although this has been overtaken by subsequent branding exercises, including the more recent 'Defence City' slogan, education continues to be socially, economically and symbolically vital to Palmerston North. The historical patterning of education in Palmerston North largely followed national trends, and it was the existence of a strong tertiary sector with a teachers' college and then a full university which came to distinguish Palmerston North from most other provincial cities. Education remains as important to the contemporary residents of the city as it was to the first citizens who pressed for the simple schoolhouse built in 1872. All have experienced the sector; many continue to see it as the gateway to a better future for their children; a significant number make their living from it.

Educating downwards

In Palmerston North, as elsewhere, formal education has absorbed an increasing proportion of childhood and early adulthood. Many remain within the education system well into their twenties, and some rely on it for additional training in later life stages. But there was also a movement downwards into the pre-primary years, and by 2012 nearly 99 per cent of primary-school entrants in the city had already experienced early childhood education services (ECE), a higher proportion than the national average (95 per cent).[1]

The churches were early to recognise the plasticity of young minds, opening their Sunday schools to preschoolers as well as older children. In England, Sunday schools had already played an important role in advancing literacy in the interests of Bible study. In Palmerston North the Wesleyans appear to have been the first denomination to run a Sunday school, initially in the public school, before building their Broad Street church in 1875. Eventually the church had a 'cradle roll' as well as a 'beginners' department'.[2]

An intriguing appropriation of the Sunday school concept was the 'Socialist Sunday School' opened in Palmerston

Te Āwhina Kōhanga Reo, the first to be established in Palmerston North, celebrated its thirtieth anniversary in 2013. Rolland Simmonds (kaitiaki) helps tamariki in the sandpit. *MS, 18 September 2013*

North by Social Democratic stalwart Rod Ross in 1920. Promoting love and universal brotherhood, the school was one of three in the country at the time.[3] While the primary-school children learned about evolution and practised the Esperanto language, the preschool 'Sunbeams' modelled in plasticine and engaged in crafts. All had 'the glorious gospel of Socialism explained to them'. When locals complained about the children's singing of the 'Red Flag', they retaliated by sending 'Good Thoughts' to 'these backward neighbours'.[4] Denounced throughout the country for its corruption of young minds, the Socialist Sunday School's fate is unknown beyond the mid-1920s, but it was a parallel, if radical, expression of the churches' thrust to engage children in early learning of a doctrinal kind.

More mainstream ECE took four forms, involving the Play Centre movement, kindergartens and early childcare, with kōhanga reo feeding demand for further Māori language education from the 1980s. The Palmerston North Playcentres Association was the third in the country when it was formed with the encouragement of Mayor Mansford in 1943. It benefited from proximity to the Feilding Community Centre, and its co-ordinator, preschool guru Gwen Somerset. Play Centre fostered an ethos of parental (effectively mothers') involvement in Play Centre sessions, and in oversight of the organisation. The kindergarten movement was established in Palmerston North in 1949, by which time it came under the umbrella of the Department of Education. This meant kindergartens received funding from the department and used kindergarten-trained teachers.

From the 1960s demand for childcare for the offspring of working mothers led to a third strand of provision, with licensed full-time childcare centres emerging in larger workplaces such as Massey University.[5] Not all approved: when Palmerston North Women's Liberation urged quality childcare in 1972, a *Standard* editorial made a disapproving distinction between mothers who 'needed' to work and the mother who 'dumped' her children in daycare in order to earn extra money for 'wall-to-wall carpet or a second deep freeze'.[6] By 2010 childcare services, hours and employment were growing more rapidly than other parts of the sector, with enrolments of children aged under one year showing the most significant increase.[7]

Te kōhanga reo comprised the fourth strand of modern preschool education. In Palmerston North, Te Āwhina Kōhanga Reo was one of the first in the country following funding through the Tu Tangata programme in the late 1970s. It opened in February 1983 with an enrolment of 10 tamariki, its initial site at 41 Fitchett Street loaned at a peppercorn rental by generous whānau. Te reo Māori was to be spoken from 8 a.m. to 5 p.m., and children of 'any race, colour or creed' were welcome.[8] Other kōhanga followed, the number in the city ranging from 11 in 2009 to seven in 2017, as some merged over time.[9] Whānau-based, their success fed into the development of the city's kura kaupapa Māori, and ultimately into a generation of young people confident in Māori language and culture.

LETCHER
MARATHON
Rotorua
New Zealand 1981
Finisher

08

SPORT AND LEISURE

GEOFF WATSON

Women's running groups were part of the diversification of sport and leisure opportunities since 1945. This picture was taken in 1982, one year before Palmerston North hosted its inaugural half-marathon. The Manawatu Striders now runs a very popular 'Super Sevens' series in January and February, which attracts several thousand people who have the option of running or walking 3 or 7 kilometres. Manawatū Heritage 2014N_Sp55_008536

Sport and leisure have been an integral feature of life for successive generations of Palmerstonians. Historically, they have shaped community identities at local, regional and national levels, connecting Palmerston North with its surrounding settlements and the wider world. Leisure activities are perhaps less visible in narratives of identity formation, but the ways in which people choose to utilise their spare time, and indeed whether they have spare time available, tells us much about a society.

Moreover, sport and leisure have particular rituals, which generate a sense of place. Leisure rituals vary between generations and peer groups, but activities such as going to the A & P Show, consuming a fish burger at Golden Takeaways and travelling on the miniature railway in the Esplanade take on particular meanings for people as rites of passage, and reinforce a sense of what is distinct about being a Palmerstonian.

The development of sport and leisure in Palmerston North can be seen as going through three broad historical phases. The period prior to 1914 saw an extensive variety of sport and leisure organisations formed, with the era between 1914 and 1945 being one of consolidation, seeing a significant expansion of sport and leisure options as Palmerston North transitioned from a town into a city.[1] Since 1945 a pattern of diversification is evident. Mainstream forms of sport and leisure have remained important, but ethnic diversity has become more evident, and both local and central government have become more directly involved.

Between 1870 and 1914, Palmerston North developed a sophisticated culture of sport and leisure. By the 1880s, just a decade after being 'founded' as a settlement, Palmerston North had an active leisure culture, with a number of sports established or in the process of being established, and leisure activities such as arts and musical societies also in existence. Accompanying the establishment of formalised 'respectable' sport and leisure activities was an equally visible disreputable element, characterised by excessive consumption of alcohol, and much less celebrated in official accounts.

Although ostensibly recreational, leisure, both reputable and disreputable, sent signals about the standing of a community. The presence of leisure activities reassured participants

Music was an important source of entertainment for Palmerstonians from the earliest stages of settlement. The Palmerston North Brass Band, founded in 1881, was among the earliest musical groups in the city. This photograph is from 1903. Manawatū Heritage 2007N_Mus13_EPN_0275

that, although recently established and among New Zealand's more isolated settlements, Palmerston North had the trappings of a civilised society; disreputable pursuits underlined the precariousness of this status. The *Manawatu Herald* of 15 April 1879 commented: 'the town of Ashhurst appears to be growing rapidly. One of the latest signs of civilisation is the formation of a Football Club.'[2] Many nineteenth-century settlements had a short and precarious existence in New Zealand, and the ongoing presence of sport and leisure activities provided reassurance, however illusory in practice, that a settlement had passed its formative stages and was progressing to a permanent and enduring stage.[3]

Sport and leisure, featuring introduced European activities, were evident from the outset in Palmerston North. The European population was small but increasing, numbering 193 in 1874, 880 in 1878, and 1366 in 1881.[4] As occurred in many parts of New Zealand, racing and athletic sports were among the earliest sporting events. Racing was held from at least as early as 1871 on a 'roughly marked out track along Rangitikei, Featherston and Taonui Streets'.[5]

Organised sporting competitions tended to be infrequent in the early years of settlement, as the population was small and fully involved in establishing housing and employment, so sports events tended to be concentrated around public holidays. Such events were common in the early years of many New Zealand settlements, and for many represented a link to their Anglo-Saxon heritage.[6] A sports event advertised on 15 December 1877, located in paddocks adjacent to the Princess Family Hotel in Terrace End, for example, included events such as races for boys and girls, 'throwing heavy hammer', throwing a cricket ball, a 'Maori Women Race', and climbing a greasy pole, alongside 'Dancing on the Green; Music provided' and 'Numerous Old English Games'.[7] On Easter Monday 1879, a 'good number' of local citizens enjoyed 'merry-go-rounds, swings and other amusements for children; and quoits, skittles and tilting-in-the-ring for grown-up persons'.[8] The wider significance of these occasions was that in re-creating scenes of British life in New Zealand, they hinted at both an emerging sense of community and continuity with British customs.

Music and drama were also important forms of recreation, connecting residents of British, Scandinavian and Māori ancestry. Singing familiar songs from home, learning new ones and listening to 'popular airs' of the day were variously a means of reconnecting with one's homeland, learning to assimilate and keeping up with the times.[9]

The importance of music is underscored in the famous tale of Bishop Ditlev Monrad having a table-grand piano transported up the river by local Māori in 1867.[10] For colonial New Zealanders, Dorothy Pilkington suggested:

> the piano was as essential [in New Zealand] as it was in the drawing room of successful families in England and Europe. Becoming a competent performer on the piano or some other musical instrument was important for the upwardly mobile in society in order to take one's place as an accepted member of the desirable genteel social circle.[11]

Music, however, was not solely for the well-to-do. It had a cross-class constituency. Pilkington observes that many early European settlers in Palmerston North came from agricultural labouring classes and brought instruments with them, and a number may have played in brass bands formed in factory towns.

The construction of the Foresters' Hall in 1875 (later altered and renamed the Theatre Royal in 1884) — a sizable venue which extended from its frontage on Coleman Place through to Cuba Street — provided an important venue for early concerts. An advertisement for a concert in 1877 included English songs 'Royal Windsor Gallop', performed by a band; a solo rendition of 'Old Sexton'; and 'To the Memory of a Friend' and 'Light as a Bird' by a Scandinavian quartet.[12] The Manawatu Dramatic Club gave a number of performances in the same venue that year.[13] The Palmerston North Orchestral Society was founded in 1894, apparently the first orchestral society to be formed outside of Wellington, Christchurch and Dunedin.[14]

Nor were performances confined to locals. Palmerston North soon became part of the touring circuit for the many overseas acts that toured New Zealand, such as the Georgia Minstrels in 1879, a troupe of African-American performers endorsed by the *Manawatu Times* as 'worthy of the most liberal patronage'.[15] Movies also came to Palmerston North in this period, Palmerston North's first public screening taking place in 1896, and by 1915 there were four dedicated movie theatres, with the Opera House also screening films.[16]

During the 1880s, sporting and musical groups were placed on a more organised footing. The Manawatu Racing Club was formally established on 23 October 1880; the Palmerston North Brass Band in 1881; the Manawatu Rugby Union in 1886; the Manawatu and West Coast Agricultural and Pastoral Association (A & P Association) in 1886; the Palmerston North Bowling Club in 1889.[17]

From a promotional perspective, the annual show run by the A & P Association was perhaps the most significant event, because it boosted Palmerston North's credentials as a centre of national importance in an industry central to New Zealand's economy and national identity. The first show was held on 19 November 1886,

The Showgrounds, established by the Agricultural and Pastoral Association in 1886, the year they held their first show, remains Palmerston North's premier sporting facility.
Manawatū Heritage 2009P_Bm74_BUI_2719

and was reportedly a 'splendid success' with more than 2000 people attending, which meant the association realised a profit of £100 (approximately $20,000 in 2019).[18] By 1903, upwards of 20,000 attended the annual show, and the Showgrounds were the principal venue for sport and public entertainment in Palmerston North, a status it retains to this day.[19] By 1900 the A & P Association had over 800 members and its income was £8124 (approximately $1.5 million in 2019), underscoring the significance of the pastoral sector in community development.[20]

Sport developed unevenly in Palmerston North. After the earliest rugby and cricket matches were played in the 1870s, the 1890s saw a falling-off in interest in organised sport. The Manawatu Rugby Union went into recess between 1899 and 1902 (although lower-grade and junior rugby continued to be played), and there was only limited interest in cricket. An attempt to establish a private sports ground in Palmerston North in 1894 was unsuccessful because the Manawatu Sports Association could not attract sufficient custom to cover its costs, and experienced difficulties extracting payments from those who did use their facilities.[21] The council's acquisition of the facility in 1900 seemed to have a positive effect on sport, with hockey clubs being formed and the cricket competition also expanding in the following two years.

Golf and polo, possibly because they catered for a wealthier constituency, were on a more stable footing. The Manawatu Golf Club was founded in 1895 on land then owned by the Manawatu Athletic Park Company, located in its present premises near the lagoon. The adjoining land was used for polo, and also included a rifle range.[22]

By 1914 sport and leisure activities were well established in Palmerston North, whose population now numbered 12,042. There were four rugby teams in the senior competition and three grades; four men's teams in the Saturday cricket competition, and a number of school cricket teams, including High School, Campbell Street and College Street; men's and women's hockey; a men's soccer competition; and netball (known as basketball until the name was changed in 1970) was introduced into Palmerston North Girls' High School in 1914. The participation of Manawatū teams in inter-provincial matches, particularly rugby union, generated an enduring symbol of regional identity, with the green-and-white uniform being adopted by the Manawatu Rugby Union in 1896.[23]

The development of sport and leisure was both a 'bottom-up' and 'top-down' process. On the one hand, it was driven by dedicated individuals, a number of whom had come to Palmerston North from overseas. The Fraser sisters, who came to Palmerston North via Ireland and established the private Craven School for Girls, were important pioneers.[24] Craven School's hockey teams enjoyed considerable success in the early 1900s. They won a national inter-club tournament in Wellington on three successive occasions between 1902 and 1904.[25] Surviving photos show the school playing hockey on the Showgrounds, an important symbolic acknowledgement of women's sport in Palmerston North at a time when the notion of the female athlete was still arousing considerable public debate.

The Craven Girls' School hockey team, photographed in 1903, won the women's national inter-club hockey tournament in 1902, 1903 and 1904. Women played in long skirts and wore hats and ties to maintain 'respectability'. Annie Dalrymple Album, IMCA

The Regent Theatre, built in 1930, has served Palmerston North in many capacities, including as a picture theatre and a graduation venue, and for hosting a variety of performers, from touring international acts to school concerts. When it ceased to function as a movie theatre, heritage advocates saved it from demolition. It was purchased by the Palmerston North City Council in 1993 and is run by the Regent Theatre Trust Board, supported by the council. Manawatū Heritage 2018P_2018-54_025401

Community groups, notably churches, also played an important part in organising sport and leisure activities. Jessica McLean has noted that the Catholic Church in Palmerston North organised a tremendous range of activities, including a church choir, an annual sport picnic on St Patrick's Day and a literary and debating society.[26]

While individual and community initiatives were undeniably significant, local and central government also played a vital role in the development of sport and leisure. Recreation was very much part of the planning for Palmerston North, indeed the facilities developed in this time remain the city's major recreation spaces. A Crown grant of 9 acres and 2 roods (3.8 hectares) was allocated to the West Coast Agricultural and Pastoral Association in June 1886 'as a site for a showground'.[27] The Palmerston North Reserves Act of 1890 set aside 361 acres (146 hectares) as reserves, of which 39 acres (16 hectares) were allocated for an esplanade on the riverbank, 86 acres (34 hectares) for a racecourse at Awapuni, and 22 acres (9 hectares) for a recreation ground on Park Road.[28]

The development of an esplanade was given impetus in 1897 when it was fenced and a gravel path laid, and it was named the Victoria Esplanade in recognition of Queen Victoria's diamond jubilee. After a prolonged gestation, the Municipal Baths opened on 1 December 1917. Located on Ashley Street, at 100 feet long and 35 feet wide it was substantially larger than the existing facility (a private baths owned by Mr Edwards at the intersection of Princess and Main streets), although the fact they remained unheated for some time remained a constant source of criticism.[29]

Council involvement also extended to the arts. The Palmerston North Opera House, located on the corner of Church and Ashley streets and formally opened on 12 July 1905, represented a significant investment. In response to public petitions, the council sought, and received, public approval for a loan of £10,000 to build the two-storeyed facility, which, at 204 feet in length and 70 feet wide, could accommodate 1300 people and included both a stage and seating downstairs, as well as a municipal hall upstairs for public lectures. Speaking at the opening of the building, Mayor Hurley stated 'the time was fast approaching when it would be recognised that the progress and culture of a people depended upon its diversions as well as its occupations'.[30]

The provision of such amenities was a farsighted decision by the council, as the population of Palmerston North was 6534 in 1901, and it reflected the expectation of continued growth characteristic of the era.[31] The subsequent demolition of the Opera House in 1996 reflected changing patterns in entertainment — moviegoers now went to the recently created Downtown Cinema complex — and the Regent Theatre, built in 1930, had superseded the Opera House as Palmerston North's premier entertainment venue. By 1991, however, the Regent Theatre was itself under threat as declining patronage forced its closure.

Faced with the prospect of Palmerston North having no major performance venue, the Palmerston North City Council again became a major actor in the arts, purchasing the

Regent Theatre in October 1993 and contributing $10 million towards its restoration. It is presently administered by the Regent Theatre Trust Board.[32]

John Tiffin Stewart established the central feature of Palmerstonians' recreation when he set aside 17 acres (6.88 hectares) for a reserve, which became known as 'The Square', in his original plans for the settlement.[33] The Square soon became a focal point where both reputable and disreputable forms of recreation were practised. In the formative years of Palmerston North, The Square reportedly became a temporary residence for inebriates, who would sleep off their excesses underneath the macrocarpa trees.[34] Lindsay Buick records that publicans seeking to induce patrons to vacate their premises at closing time would carry alcohol into The Square so revellers could continue their activities until sated.[35]

By the 1890s, however, The Square was more orderly in appearance and began to be developed for more respectable forms of recreation. A rotunda was erected, providing a platform for musicians and speeches. Assisted by a beautification society, a lakelet was created in 1909, becoming home to exotic species including donated black swans.[36] The Square has remained a focal point for Palmerstonians at leisure, with the practice of promenading around its perimeter being a time-honoured recreation for citizens. When automobiles became a standard feature of life, promenading assumed a vehicular form, with citizens circumnavigating The Square and hailing fellow residents with varied salutations. Prominent among these were 'boy racers', whose perceived excesses prompted the formation of Citizens Against Rowdy Motoring (CARM) in 2002.[37]

Records of Māori engagement in sport and recreation, particularly in Manawatū, are incomplete, but Māori did participate in a variety of activities. Studies of recreational activities prior to European contact suggest that physical activity was incorporated into everyday life, rather than being a discrete activity.[38] Māori did have a symbolic presence in the centre of the city. After consulting with Mātene Te Whiwhi of Ngāti Raukawa, Te Peeti Te Aweawe and Hoani Meihana suggested to Mayor George Snelson the name Te Marae o Hine — The Courtyard of the Daughter of Peace — as a name for The Square.[39]

Unfortunately this name soon dropped out of popular usage, as society became more Europeanised, but with a number of different tribes coming to Palmerston North to attend the Native Land Court, The Square became on occasion a site for Māori recreation. An 1878 report on the aftermath of a Native Land Court hearing on the Awahuri Block recorded a feast in The Square provisioned with 'two hogsheads of beer, a five-gallon keg of brandy, cases of wine and Old Tom together with two dozen tins of assorted biscuits and four-dozen boxes of sardines'. Proceedings wound up with a ball in the Foresters' Hall.[40] Māori also participated in wider community gatherings. A 1904 report on a concert at Palmerston North's Lyceum noted a poi dance performed by young Māori from Awapuni, after which 'three times they were recalled'.[41]

While most Māori lived in settlements outside the boundaries of Palmerston North, there were particular occasions when Māori came to the town and made it a Māori space.[42]

Palmerston North hosted the Māori Tennis Championships in 1910 and 1911. Teams at this competition competed for the Marumaru Cup, donated by Taraua Utiku Marumaru, who lived at Pārewanui (near the town of Bulls). The Māori tennis tournament was initiated for the purposes of encouraging greater unity among Māori, and was a forerunner of the Māori Lawn Tennis Association tournament which began in 1926.[43] Played at the grounds of the Palmerston North Tennis Club, the leading club in Palmerston North, the event symbolised a wider Māori resurgence, and the 1910 tournament was attended by Mayor James Nash and Sir James Carroll; E. D. Hoben, editor of the *Manawatu Times,* presided over the 1911 tournament. In addition to supporting tennis, Marumaru was very successful in horseracing as both a breeder and a jockey.[44]

The inter-war period saw a significant expansion of sport and leisure amenities in Palmerston North. Between 1919 and 1939 the number of teams participating in local team sports — rugby, cricket, hockey, netball, basketball and table tennis — increased from at least 37 teams in 1919 to at least 152 teams in 1939. Not only were more people participating in sport, the range of sports in which people participated also increased. In 1919, adult team sports were limited to rugby, cricket and men's and women's hockey. By 1939, men's soccer had been re-established; netball had become the dominant team sport for women, with a total of 28 teams; there were men's and women's indoor basketball competitions; and a mixed table-tennis competition.[45] To some degree the increase in sporting participation can be explained by service personnel returning from the First World War, and an increase in the population of Palmerston North from 14,866 in 1919 to 25,300 in 1939. Yet the fourfold increase in the number of teams entered in local competitions greatly exceeded the 70 per cent increase in population, so other factors were clearly at play.[46]

Local government was important in the expansion of sport and leisure opportunities. In 1919 the Palmerston North Borough Council owned approximately 400 acres (162 hectares) of reserves. By 1939 it owned 1125 acres (455 hectares). Many of these reserves were developed in suburban areas for sport and leisure. Papaioea Park, in Terrace End, which included sports grounds and a playground, was opened in 1922, and a children's playground was built at Milverton Park, Hokowhitu, after land was gifted to the council by William Milverton in 1925.

Bowls was a major beneficiary of council involvement in sport. Between 1918 and 1939 three bowling clubs — the Manawatu Bowling Club, which opened its premises on the corner of Fitzherbert Avenue and Park Road in 1918; the Takaro Bowling Club (subsequently the Takaro Bowling and Tennis Club), which was established in 1922; and the Hokowhitu Bowling Club — were formed, all on council-owned land. A fourth club, the Terrace End Bowling Club, was sold to the council in 1937. These clubs joined existing

BAR

Racing has been a feature of Palmerston North life since at least the 1870s. Awapuni Racecourse, pictured here in 1950, moved to its present location in 1903. At one point a railway line connected the racecourse to the main trunk line, so horses could be more easily transported to events.
Manawatū Heritage 2014P_Ra13_007590

bowling clubs — the Northern Bowling Club and the Palmerston North Bowling Club — to give Palmerston North six bowling clubs by 1939.

Reserve land adjacent to Hokowhitu School was developed as the Hokowhitu Domain, and by 1939 it was being used for the men's hockey association competition, and also by the Hokowhitu Bowling Club, which opened in 1937.[47] In addition to bowls, in 1930 the council opened a golf course on the corner of Botanical and Park roads, the site presently occupied by Awatapu College.[48] The council charged the bowling and croquet clubs a peppercorn rental (£1 per year) for the use of these facilities, which suggests a conscious effort to democratise sport, particularly golf and bowls, making them available for all citizens.[49]

In addition to sporting facilities, the city council developed new play areas and public spaces and further improved existing playgrounds. Play areas were developed in North Street and the Esplanade, and a 13-acre (5-hectare) gravel pit in Terrace End was developed as Fitzroy Park (now called Memorial Park). The Esplanade was also extensively redeveloped, transitioning from a planned wilderness to a playground for the people. The road through the Esplanade from Fitzherbert Avenue to Park Road was completed in 1919. The flowering cherry trees and phoenix palms characteristic of today's Esplanade were planted in the 1920s and 1930s, respectively. The paddling pool was erected by the Returned Soldiers Association in 1937, and the Peter Black Conservatory in 1940.[50] The camping ground was developed in 1925, in recognition of the growing number of motor cars in New Zealand and the hope that a camp would attract tourists to the city.[51]

Local government support for recreation was not confined to the provision of facilities. The municipal bus network, established in 1920, was attracting 587,763 users per year by 1939.[52] This service may well have assisted the increasing participation of suburban teams in local sports competitions, and also made leisure amenities more accessible.

Historically there is a strong correlation between the expansion of education and the expansion of sport and leisure activities, and by 1939 more than 20 per cent of young Palmerstonians were engaged in some form of education as either pupils or staff.[53] If local government provided the infrastructure, and sports organisations the adult players and administrators, the expanding education sector was equally significant to sport and leisure, introducing children to sport via school teams and physical education, and ensuring an ongoing supply to local clubs of young adults inculcated with sporting values. Moreover, many sports clubs in New Zealand began their life as an old boys' or old girls' team of a particular school or institution. In the inter-war period, secondary education became a fact of life for many New Zealand school children, and in Palmerston North a growing number of people were attending the Technical College, Palmerston North Boys' and Girls' High Schools (the latter established as a separate school in 1920), and Massey Agricultural College (later Massey University), which opened in 1927. All of these institutions entered teams in local competitions.

Motor vehicles, in the form of speedway, provided a new form of entertainment for Palmerstonians in the inter-war era, linking Palmerston North into an international network in the process. Speedway came to Palmerston North on Boxing Day 1930, just one year after the sport was introduced into New Zealand, when an international contingent of riders, including Australian Herb 'Daredevil' Durkin, competed alongside domestic riders at the Showgrounds. With the assistance of unemployed residents and local contractors, the outer perimeter of the Showgrounds was transformed into a race track; a configuration which remains today.[54] Palmerston North's newest form of recreation soon became integrated with one of its oldest — the A & P Show — with racing and stunts complementing more established activities. In 1936, American Putt Mossman thrilled spectators with a combination of racing and stunts, and a New Zealand team won a motorcycle test match against the United States.[55]

Tours by Asian and African-American teams were another international connection in the inter-war period. The Showgrounds hosted the Indian Army Hockey Team in 1926, All-India in 1935 and the Prince of Manavadar's Team in 1938.[56] The Chinese Universities

Soccer Team, touring New Zealand in 1924, also played at the Showgrounds, and left a lasting legacy in the form of a trophy presented to the Manawatu Football Association.[57] The Chinese Cup is presently played as a pre-season tournament.[58] An African-American debating team from Le Moyne College, Tennessee, debated against Massey University during their 1938 tour of New Zealand.[59]

In addition to their sporting dimension, these tours had an ambassadorial element, with the management of the teams presenting lectures on their history and culture to local societies. They were also an opportunity for local Indian and Chinese communities to meet people from their ancestral homelands. The Manawatū Chinese community hosted the Chinese Universities team at a function in the local municipal hall. Over 300 people attended, reportedly including 'over one hundred Chinese' — the bulk of the Chinese population then living in the region.[60]

Movies were another example of the growing influence of America in the cultural lives of Palmerstonians, and New Zealanders more broadly. Pauline Knuckey's research has shown that between 1919 and 1945 at least 80 per cent of the feature films shown in Palmerston North were made in the United States.[61] Palmerstonians' tastes in movies were also similar to those of people in Britain and the United States, with drama and comedy being the most popular genres.[62] Movies were an affordable and accessible means of recreation. In 1943 moviegoing reached its peak popularity: New Zealanders on average attended the movies 23 times per year.[63]

If moviegoing was the leading source of entertainment outside the home, listening to the radio became a leading form of at-home entertainment. Between 1927 and 1934 the number of radio licences in the greater Palmerston North area increased from 239 to 2694.[64] Radio 2ZA, a staple feature of Palmerston North life, began in 1938.

Since 1945 there has been a marked diversification in the range of sport and leisure activities available to Palmerstonians. Traditional sports, such as rugby union, cricket and netball, remain important, but they have been complemented by other sports such as softball and touch. In addition to team sports, individual sports have increased significantly in popularity. The river and its environs, hitherto a place for largely informal recreation, has become integrated into wider leisure networks. The growing number of motor vehicles in private ownership also extended the effective bounds of the city for recreational purposes, bringing the beach settlements of Himatangi, Tangimoana and Foxton more readily into the wider orbit of recreational options.[65]

The development of sport and leisure was further facilitated by the relatively prosperous economic climate in New Zealand in the two decades after the Second World War. Not only were New Zealanders better off, there were many more of them. New Zealand experienced a 'baby boom' between 1945 and 1961, when the national population increased from 1,747,679 to 2,417,543, creating additional demand for community facilities, particularly in the many newly formed suburbs.[66] Ian Matheson notes that between 1945 and 1971 the population of Palmerston North increased at an annual rate of 7.4 per cent, compared with an average of 2.7 per cent for New Zealand as a whole.[67]

The impact of this soon became evident in sporting participation in Palmerston North. In 1951, when Palmerston North had a population of 32,908, there were at least 71 adult and children's rugby teams and 22 secondary-school rugby teams (more than twice the equivalent figure for 1939), 24 men's soccer teams, 21 men's hockey teams and at least 13 women's hockey teams, at least 55 adult and secondary-school netball teams, 24 men's basketball teams and 29 women's basketball teams, 58 table-tennis teams, 23 men's cricket teams, 11 men's tennis teams, three cycling clubs, two athletics clubs and four rifle shooting clubs.[68] Not including children's teams, there were at least 350 sports teams in Palmerston North in 1951, which suggests most people played at least one sporting code. Compared to 1939, the number of sports teams in Palmerston North had more than doubled while the population had increased by approximately 30 per cent. By 1969 there were at least 550 voluntary organisations in Palmerston North, including 214 sports clubs and 53 social clubs, with 18,000 competing in winter sports and 14,000 in summer sports.[69]

Squash was one sport in which Palmerston North was particularly prominent. In 1949 Palmerston North became the headquarters of the New Zealand Squash Rackets Association (NZSRA); two years later, in 1951, it hosted the New Zealand squash championships for the fourth time, this event including the first women's national squash championship. Roy Haddon, from the Palmerston North Squash Club, played a significant role in the development of squash in New Zealand, serving as secretary of the NZSRA between 1953 and 1971. In 1956 the squash club amalgamated with the Palmerston North Lawn Tennis Club and opened new premises on Princess Street, which remain in use to this day.[70]

Increasing participation in sport and recreation saw the council under pressure to provide more and better facilities. Netball was one sport to benefit. Catherine Vautier and Nona Craig, president and vice-president respectively of the Manawatu Netball Association, wrote to the city council in 1961 asking for a new facility, and noting that the association had expanded from 68 teams in 1950 to 142 in 1961, and now had 1300 players. Council subsequently agreed to support a new facility, which was opened in 1964 in what had been a disused metal pit opposite the hospital, with funding from the council, Manawatu Netball and a £3500 Golden Kiwi lottery grant.[71]

The 1960s saw a significant investment in sport and leisure facilities, many of which remain central to Palmerston North today. In 1965 a new city library opened on the corner of Main Street and The Square, providing an 'increase of almost 100% in floor space and book holding capacity'. (It held 40,000 books on the shelves, and had space for 30,000 in the basement.) The mobile library began in 1967.[72] Facilities such as the Lido Swimming

ABOVE Chess was one of the more sedentary forms of recreation practised by Palmerstonians. Members of the Scandia Chess Club were photographed playing an inter-city match against Waitemata in 1969, Michael Kopytko relaying the moves by telephone. Ian Whitson is in the foreground, and Les Morris beside him. Manawatū Heritage 2020P_2020-3_028648

LEFT Palmerston North has a distinguished association with squash. The Palmerston North Squash Club, established in 1936, was among New Zealand's earliest squash clubs, and Palmerston North was the administrative centre of the game in New Zealand during the 1950s and 1960s. This photograph was taken in 1961. Manawatū Heritage 2017N_2017-20_016344

Pool in 1966 and the Chalet building on the lagoon were developed, and there was also extensive redevelopment of many parks, including Memorial Park and the Esplanade, where the Dugald MacKenzie Rose Garden was opened in 1968 and the miniature railway in 1969. The pronouncements accompanying these developments suggested a confidence in Palmerston North as the leading city in the Central North Island. Mayor Gilbert Rennie proclaimed the Lido pool 'the largest of its type in New Zealand', signalling the ambition of Palmerston North to be a centre of national, rather than simply regional, significance.[73]

This ambition has been realised to no small degree in motorsport. The Showgrounds, which came under council control in 1973, have provided a venue for stockcar racing.[74] A reported 12,000 spectators attended the first stockcar opening night on 23 February 1963, and on 2–3 February 2019 Palmerston North hosted the Robertson Holden International, which filled the 14,500-person venue to capacity.[75] Palmerston North remains one of the few venues where the major sporting venue includes both a motor-racing track and a sports ground. Whereas motor racing has faced concerns over noise levels elsewhere, notably in Auckland, there has been very little public opposition to motorsport in Palmerston North.

The Showgrounds were also the venue where the Manawatū rugby team defended the Ranfurly Shield between 1976 and 1978. Under the coaching of Graham Hamer, Manawatū teams featuring All Blacks Gary Knight, Frank Oliver, Mark Shaw, Geoff Old and Doug Rollerson had considerable success, winning the National Provincial Championship Division One Title in 1980. In 1981 the Pascal Street Sports Stadium was opened on the site, which has proved an extremely useful addition to Palmerston North's sporting facilities, hosting many community sport competitions in codes such as volleyball, indoor hockey and basketball, as well as many age-group and school tournaments.

Women's sport also developed considerably in this period, with the football codes, previously largely closed to women, becoming an option. Palmerston North can claim the distinction of hosting the first inter-provincial women's rugby match in New Zealand, in 1980. It was also a leading centre for women's running. By the early 1980s there were three running clubs for women in Palmerston North, including the Manawatu Marathon Clinic (a forerunner of the Manawatu Striders) which held its first half-marathon in 1983.[76]

The expansion of recreational facilities was complemented by the growth of the cultural sector. A council survey in 1969 identified 97 cultural groups in the city involving 8000 people.[77] The Palmerston North City Art Gallery was opened in 1959, and the Manawatu Museum in 1971. Centrepoint, one of the very few provincial professional theatres in New Zealand, opened in 1974, and has remained part of the artistic scene since. The Palmerston North Rugby Museum, which opened in 1969 at the initiative of John Sinclair, who accompanied the 1967 All Blacks on their tour of North America and Europe, was another enduring contribution from this era.[78] The following year, at the instigation of the Manawatu Rugby Union, a monument recognising Charles Monro, a former Palmerston North resident credited with introducing rugby union to New Zealand,

ABOVE The Esplanade has been a playground for many generations of Palmerstonians since it was formally opened in 1897. The rocket ship was part of children's experience of growing up in Palmerston North during the 1960s and 1970s. Manawatū Heritage 2016N_PNCC5-6-1_013009

BELOW Sport and the arts combine as the Ranfurly Shield is welcomed to Palmerston North in 1976 after Manawatū defeated Auckland 12–10 to claim the coveted trophy for the first, and so far only, time. Victorious captain Duncan Hales is accompanied by Vivienna Ayers and Janice Walker, two cast members of the Manawatu Theatre Society's production of *Orpheus in the Underworld*. Manawatū Heritage 2014P_Sp32_008772 was opened at Massey University, near the site of Monro's former residence.[79]

The growing number of museums, memorials and cultural facilities was indicative of a growing awareness that Palmerston North — and indeed New Zealand — had a history worth recording. The desirability of a museum had been acknowledged at least as early as 1901, when the *Manawatu Times* noted that 'although Palmerston North likes to be considered a progressive town', it lacked 'anything pertaining to a public collection of rare and curious articles, which are usually found within the walls of a museum'.[80] The Manawatu Philosophical Society, founded in 1904, took the initiative in setting up a museum, which opened in 1906 in the library building on Main Street East.[81] The Manawatu Philosophical Society, which was struggling to maintain its membership during the 1920s, asked the council to take ownership of the collection in 1926. The council agreed to do so. The Manawatu Museum Society, founded in 1967, renewed calls for a museum, and one was eventually opened in 1971 on Amesbury Street. It featured maps of The Square and displays of Māori culture alongside historical items relating to the development of the dairy industry and the natural landscape.[82]

The development of the Palmerston North Museum and Rugby Museum may have been aided by the centenaries of the first game of rugby union in New Zealand in 1970 and Palmerston North's centennial celebrations of 1971. The relocation of 'Totaranui' — one of Palmerston North's oldest houses — and a replica of George Snelson's store to Main Street in 1970 symbolised a city placing its history at its heart.

This sense of a distinct local history was encapsulated in *The Birth of Palmerston North*, a 100-page supplement published by the *Evening Standard* in 1971 to coincide with the centennial celebrations. City archivist Ian Matheson's text incorporated the standard celebratory themes, demonstrating the steady progress of the city in terms of population and infrastructure growth, and the development of pastoral and commercial sectors; but it was not uncritically hagiographical. Matheson's text was determinedly bicultural, devoting considerable coverage to the role of Māori, a subject in which he had a strong personal interest. The bicultural theme is further reflected in the cover image, a commissioned painting by Frank Davis — a senior lecturer in art at Palmerston North Teachers' College whose work featured historical scenes of Māori–Pākehā relations — depicting an early European settler showing a Māori his vision for the future.[83]

The heightened visibility of history and heritage in Palmerston North reflected the existence of a Manawatū-centred literary and artistic culture. Māori artists and lecturers Cliff Whiting and John Bevan Ford produced a significant body of work in the 1970s and 1980s, reflecting a wider Māori revival.[84] Palmerston North's museums and galleries exhibited this diversifying creative culture. In 1981, by which time the museum had moved to Church Street near the Grand Hotel, Manawatu Museum Society President John Owens — a lecturer in history at Massey University — reported that 25,000 people had visited the museum, including 11,000 students.[85]

In 1990 the museum shifted to the corner of Pitt and Church streets, and subsequently extended to open onto Main Street. This new facility, called the Science Centre and Manawatu Museum, opened in 1994. Renamed Te Manawa in 2002, the premises now include the New Zealand Rugby Museum, which relocated from its Cuba Street premises outside the Showgrounds in 2011. The New Zealand Rugby Museum attracts approximately 10,000 visitors per year, and Te Manawa approximately 100,000.[86] The centennial histories of Palmerston North and the Manawatu District Council by George Petersen and Monte Holcroft, respectively, further underlined the wider interest in the city's past.[87]

Music has remained a prominent presence in Palmerston North's cultural scene. The Choral Society, founded in 1923, has been of a consistently high standard, ably led by conductors such as John Holmes Runnicles (1923–33, 1945–55), Clarence Hopwood (1961–66), Guy Donaldson (1980–87), Graham Parsons (1999–2003) and Alison Stewart (2003–).[88] The Manawatu Sinfonia and Palmerston North Youth Orchestra also have a lengthy history, the Schwabe family being prominently involved in both organisations. During the 1980s, Palmerston North bands such as the Skeptics, Three Leaning Men and Harry Death were part of a wider independent New Zealand music movement, in which Dunedin's Flying Nun records was perhaps the most publicly visible. Meltdown Records issued a compilation LP of Palmerston North music in 1987, and The Stomach, founded as a community studio in 1988, has been a breeding ground for many local musicians.

Despite (or possibly because of) its reputation as a 'boring' place for young adults, many comedians have emerged from Palmerston North, including John Clarke (better known to many New Zealanders as Fred Dagg), Jeremy Corbett (host of the television comedy show *Seven Days*) and Jon Bridges (producer of *Seven Days*). Laura Daniel — whose 2017 song 'Palmy North' brilliantly celebrated and satirised the city ('It's a great place to raise a family/that's why there's so much teenage pregnancy') — has become one of New Zealand's most prominent comedians and was also a finalist in the 2019 series of *Dancing with the Stars*.[89]

Since 1945, Palmerston North's physical environment has been significantly transformed for recreational purposes, most notably on its riverbanks and surrounding environs. Despite the proximity of the Esplanade to the Manawatū River, the river remained under-utilised as a recreational resource for many years. It was an informal venue for swimming for early Māori and European residents, although in the 1890s some raised concern over public decency.[90] Nevertheless, in contrast to settlements such as Whanganui and Hamilton, the river did not become a central recreational feature. One possible explanation is a wariness of the river owing to flooding, and the fact that the clearing of Te Papaiōea, where Palmerston North was originally sited, was several kilometres from the river. Moreover, because of the early development of the railway between Palmerston North and Foxton, there was never any attempt to construct jetties or port facilities in the settlement.

Two Palmerston North icons, Centrepoint Theatre and the stockcars, met in *Stockcars: The Musical*. Robertson Motors, long-time sponsors of the Palmerston North speedway series, also gave support to the musical. The production clearly resonated with Palmerston North audiences, achieving 36 performances in 2013, and a return season in 2014. Centrepoint Theatre

Nevertheless, following the Second World War, the river, and aquatic activities more generally, have featured more prominently in recreation. The Palmerston North Boating Club was formed at least as early as the late 1940s. The two-day boat race between Palmerston North and Foxton was a popular event, as was a race between Ballance Bridge and the Fitzherbert Bridge. Raft races were particularly popular in the 1970s and 1980s. The advent of jet boats from the 1960s significantly lessened the travelling distance between Palmerston North and Foxton, but the noise generated by the vessels disrupted the ambience of riverside picnicking for some, and there were also concerns about their impact on fish and wildlife.[91]

It was not only the river which developed as a place for water-based recreation: the lagoon, made more accessible by the construction of Centennial Drive in 1940, also became a focal point. The Palmerston North Canoe Club, under the direction of Davey Dilks, made extensive use of the lagoon, hosting racing events and hiring canoes to the public.[92] The club was very successful in national competitions, club representatives being the K1500 and K2 1000 New Zealand Canoeing Champions every year between 1955 and 1971, and winning the K1500 and K1 1000 events on 16 and 15 occasions, respectively, in the same period.[93]

During the 1960s the riverbank itself started to be developed as a walkway, when in 1963 the Manawatu Pony Club asked the city council for permission to create a track along the river where they could walk their horses, a request which reflected the increasingly busy city streets. Colloquially known as the 'bridle track', this opened up the river for a greater range of users, although it remained relatively undeveloped until the early 2000s. The development of the bridle path was the beginning of the end of the riverbank as a wilderness for youthful exploration, although it retained something of its overgrown character throughout the 1970s and 1980s.

Since 2000 the riverbank has undergone a marked transformation which is still continuing. The hitherto unsealed track has been asphalted from Te Matai Road to Dittmer Drive. It is now used for a wide variety of recreational purposes, from individual activities such as dog-walking and biking to more organised events such as the Manawatu Striders marathon and half-marathon. Since 2013 the majority of the course for this event has been situated along the riverbank. In 2014 Manawatu Striders initiated an Ashhurst-to-Esplanade run, utilising, in part, the newly developed riverbank pathways.

Centrepoint Theatre presents
STOCKCARS: THE MUSICAL
WRITTEN BY: JOHN LEPPER AND SIMON FERRY
MUSIC AND LYRICS BY: DEAN PARKINSON
2 NOVEMBER – 14 DECEMBER
show sponsors:
Stewarts ELECTRICAL SUPPLIES
ROBERTSON HOLDEN
HOLDEN
linkup paints
36
THE FUNNIEST MUSICAL ABOUT STOCKCARS YOU WILL EVER SEE!
tickets from $18 to $38
book now on (06) 354 5740 or www.centrepoint.co.nz
show times:
tuesday 6.30 pm
wednesday 6.30 pm
thursday – saturday 8 pm
sunday 5 pm
280 church street, palmerston north
centrepoint THEATRE
principal co-sponsors:
FitzherbertRowe
Property Brokers

Since 2016 the council has further developed the riverbanks, clearing the willow trees at Awapuni and opening up the riverbank there, the repurposed space being named Ahimate Reserve. In 2017 work began on a bridge for cyclists and pedestrians across the river, located near the Esplanade camping ground. This culminated with the opening of He Ara Kotahi on 7 June 2019. Extending 194 metres in length, the bridge connects to pathways to Massey University and Linton. Its design is inspired by the karaka, which is strongly linked to local iwi Rangitāne's history.[94] More than 12,000 people traversed the pathway on its opening weekend, taking advantage of the hitherto unprecedented pathways on both sides of the river.[95]

Since the 1960s, the council has extended its role from being a provider of recreational facilities to becoming actively involved in organising and promoting events. This was evident during the 1950s and 1960s when the city's public relations office ran particular events, including hula-hooping in The Square and a carnival of the lake in the Hokowhitu Lagoon.[96] Palmerston North's central location and plentiful sports grounds make it an attractive location for school and representative tournaments, something the city council is intent on promoting.

Sport and leisure have been used to promote wider objectives of community harmony. The council has hosted a festival of cultures since 1993. Typically held in March, this event sees different ethnicities and organisations allocated tents and stalls, in which a variety of foods are sold, and a stage is provided for cultural performances. The 2019 events attracted 25,000 people and over 60 ethnic groups participated.[97] The 'Ethkick' soccer tournament, a five-a-side soccer tournament for ethnic-based teams, co-ordinated by the council and the police, is another such initiative. The intention of the tournament, which was fully subscribed with 40 entries in 2018, is to encourage friendly interaction between the police and new migrants, a number of whom have come from places where the police forces are seen as corrupt and not to be trusted.[98] The council is also one of the partners in the New Zealand Rural Games, which have been hosted in The Square since 2017. With competitions such as dog trials, wood-chopping and coal shovelling, the Rural Games echo the A & P Shows of yesteryear, bringing the country into the city. It has proven a popular addition to the calendar, with more than 30,000 attending in 2018.[99]

The prominent role of the council as a provider of sport and recreation is reflected in its expenditure. In the 2019/20 budget, sport, parks and recreation were the single largest category of expenditure, at 15.83 per cent. Leisure facilities were also well-supported, with libraries and arts, and culture and heritage comprising 9.33 per cent and 6.58 per cent, respectively. Budgeted expenditure in these categories was on a par with, or ahead of, what some might deem 'core' council activities. Transport, wastewater facilities and rubbish and recycling accounted for 14.81 per cent, 9.67 per cent and 7.61 per cent, respectively.[100] Despite comprising nearly one-third of the council expenditure, sport and leisure funding has seldom been a controversial issue in elections. This may be because most of the

ABOVE The Festival of Cultures, organised by the city council, has become a showcase for the multicultural diversity of Palmerston North. The event features tents, a lantern parade and, pictured, a fashion show that displays traditional dress. Photograph: Rob Edwards, 2018, Manawatū Heritage COMM 1535061144

LEFT The lantern parade forms part of Palmerston North's Festival of Cultures, 2018. Photograph: Jenny Gutry, Manawatū Heritage COMM 1523823770

The Pascal Street stadium, pictured here in 1981 hosting a women's basketball match in its opening year, has rendered valuable service as a venue for community sports, school and age-group tournaments and international matches, including hosting the Silver Ferns on several occasions.
Manawatū Heritage 2014N_Sp68_008540

expenditure is targeted towards community facilities, rather than high-performance centres, and accordingly is seen as being for the benefit of the wider public. Indeed, a 2013 council proposal to sell 15 parks and reserves was abandoned after more than 300 opposing submissions. Long-serving *Manawatu Standard* reporter Janine Rankin concluded: 'if there's one thing certain to get Palmerston North residents wound up, it is an attack on their green spaces'.[101]

The sport and recreation sector has become notably more ethnically diverse since 1945. A Manawatu Indians sports club was in existence at least as early as 1947, becoming Central Districts Indian Sports Club (CDISC) in 1982. CDISC has made a significant contribution to Indian sport, hosting the national Indian sports tournament, the Queen's Birthday tournament, on three occasions (most recently in 2017), and winning the Dhyan Chand Trophy in 2009.

Manawatū has hosted some significant events in Indian sport, notably the first game by a New Zealand Indians hockey team, which occurred in Feilding in 1955, and Palmerston North was the venue for the 1966 meeting where the New Zealand Indian Sports Association adopted its present name. The venue for that meeting

was the Māori Battalion Hall, which was opened in 1964.[102]

Māori urbanisation post-1945 saw Māori teams and athletes become much more visible in community sport and recreation. Debi Marshall-Lobb, who grew up in Palmerston North, noted the importance of kapa haka and sport to Māori in the 1960s and 1970s.[103] The establishment of Te Wānanga o Aotearoa and two schools with a strong sporting character, Tu Toa and Manukura, both of which have a focus on Māori educational philosophies, has provided a pathway for students to combine education and sport. The council has also become more actively involved in interlinking Palmerston North's pre-European Māori history with its riverside development and recreation programmes. The riverbank now features a number of installations and signs discussing the Māori history of the city and its surrounding regions. For the Christmas holidays of 2017–18, the 'Passport to Palmy' initiative, in which entrants are tasked with visiting particular places and making a pencil rubbing of a marking at each site, focused on sites of significance to Rangitāne.

Sport and leisure are an important part of the experience of being a Palmerstonian. Historically, Palmerston North has prided itself on being a place that provides a wide variety of sporting, leisure and cultural pursuits for its citizens. The achievements of its past and present citizens in sporting and cultural pursuits have been a source of considerable pride for city residents, reinforcing a belief that an upbringing in the city is a legitimate pathway to the highest levels. Successes at the elite level are complemented by historically high levels of participation. This, in turn, has been facilitated by the ready accessibility of parks and recreational facilities for most of its citizens, which has reinforced a narrative that Palmerston North is 'a good place to bring up kids'. As the city has progressively expanded, the easy access of sport and leisure facilities has become, for many residents, an important point of difference between Palmerston North and other main centres.

The Square has been a centre for many sport and leisure activities, both formal and informal. The 2019 Rural Games continue the tradition of the A & P Show in bringing the country into the town.
Raphael Cardoso , Manawatū Heritage 2019BD_IMCA-DigitalArchive_026414

09 AN ORGANISED CITY

HELEN DOLLERY

Jaycees delivering wood to 93-year-old pensioners, Mr and Mrs J. Brooks, of Church Street, 1963. Care for the aged was an important part of service clubs' mandate at a time when their numbers were high and members had spare time for such activities as delivering and stacking wood.
Manawatū Heritage 2017N_2017-20_017642

Community, in all of its diversity of age, gender, ethnicity, purpose and culture, is the intangible substance to which residents of a place cleave for common ends — or which cleaves them apart, as different factions take sides on civic issues. The mix of these encounters, and the consequent industry of active citizenship, is one vital dimension of Palmerston North's interwoven stories. Over time many voices have clamoured for attention, or have drawn together those with common interests: voices quiet and loud, playful and purposeful, powerful and powerless, heard and unheard. Whether for work or play, Palmerstonians have a history of collectively organising themselves.

Alongside sport and leisure groups sit community groups, especially those with a civic purpose. Growth and change in the city's formal associational life can be usefully looked at as falling into four periods. The first — from Palmerston North's emergence as a township to the end of the First World War — illustrates pre-existing threads of settler identity that endured alongside mutual aid networks and growing civic pride. From the 1920s to the 1950s — when the initial establishment was completed, and the city had settled into its sense of a collective self — existing groups expanded to provide a wider range of clubs and societies. Organised responses to significant world events were required as a widespread depression and another world war demanded active responses. The post-war years showed a purposeful rebuilding of communities of interest, reflecting a stronger emphasis on family life and stability after the preceding period of upheaval. The third period, from the 1960s to the 1980s, saw considerable social and demographic change and the city's organised responses to it. Many longlived groups endured, yet others developed to meet new circumstances. The city council's fostering of social service groups financially and through mentoring was significant. The last period, from the 1990s until the 2010s, saw organisations, as well as cultural festivals and displays, that wove new threads into the city's identity. Throughout Palmerston North's history residents' collective engagement has involved some organisations with remarkably long life cycles, and others that were a response to a particular moment or issue.

Around 11 a.m. on 27 November 1877 fire totally destroyed a new store in Main Street owned by Halford Snelson, the recently arrived brother of the township's mayor. The adjoining property of solicitor C. Elliot Warburton was charred and partially gutted, but was saved by a bucket-chain of men who poured water from its roof. Community effort came together in an emergency, and was followed by a meeting in the Foresters' Hall to form a fire brigade. It took a while for this informal effort to coalesce into a more permanent voluntary brigade from 1883, which it did following a borough council grant for fire-fighting equipment. Here was an early example of the council underwriting community effort, but also of the kinds of pressing need that drew people together as the town grew. Fire brigades became a key resource in communities where buildings were wooden, interspersed among empty grass-filled sections, and — as in Palmerston North — surrounded by spectacular and unpredictable rural fires during the burn-off season.[1]

Associational life in Palmerston North's early years was based on the need for such mutual supports, but was further flavoured by patterns of shared identity and belief. In keeping with larger and longer-established colonial centres, Palmerston North's immigrant settlers placed a 'high emphasis . . . on constructing civil society' — no sooner had the first residents arrived and set about building lives, homes and businesses than they also gathered together with like minds.[2] But as Pākehā organisations developed in parallel with the new township's physical expansion, land loss and growing settler ascendancy undermined the inherent collectivism of tangata whenua.

From the 1870s, newly arrived Scandinavian families helped the new settlement socially as well as practically. Scandinavians became influential members of the town's civic and social domains, with the Norwegian timber miller Frits Jenssen serving as mayor over 1882–83 and as borough treasurer between 1877 and 1885, for example.[3]

Mutual support preceded more formal associations: a Scandinavian group whose membership spanned five countries of origin was active in 1884 for social gatherings; yet it foreshadowed a pattern whereby groups established and then lapsed as internal or external circumstances dictated. Chairman Lars Langkjær's death in 1885 may have led to the club's hiatus, until it was reconstituted just before war broke out in 1914.[4] The club was no longer evident in local papers after 1917. It may have been subsumed into the wider patriotic efforts in which its members already participated, choosing to blend in during a time of global conflict — a time of anti-German sentiment, where Scandinavian street names that sounded too 'Germanic' were changed. And yet there were subsequent iterations of the club between 1939 and the late 1950s, and from 1979 onwards, as those of Scandinavian descent embraced their cultural inheritance.[5]

Religion provided another important basis for association. The example of early shared church services held in saw yards and survey offices illustrates a wider colonial willingness to adapt to 'a simple and makeshift religion, important to people who felt far from home and civilisation'. Peter Lineham considers that there was an 'unusually ecumenical' religious foundation to Palmerston North, the mix including a remarkably strong representation of Lutherans and Methodists as well as Anglicans, Presbyterians and Catholics. There was also a pragmatically co-operative rotation of services by visiting clergy as well as by lay preachers.[6]

This dissipated slightly as local denominations built their own churches and congregations in the mid-1870s and 1880s under resident clergy: the Methodists in 1875, followed by the Anglicans in the same year, the Presbyterians in 1877, the Catholics in 1878, and the Emmaus congregation's Lutheran church in 1882.[7] For Palmerston North's nineteenth-century residents, as for church people elsewhere, 'the church' — whichever denomination it was — provided membership of faith communities that reflected religious and cultural heritage, and also a range of associated social activities. As Lineham notes:

> For each little church — its architecture at least in the front expressing its praise of God and its statement of its authority to the community — gave meaning to people's lives. Churches had their internal wrangles, they struggled with debts from over-ambitious buildings, but the struggles were part of what made people's lives significant. One should also remember that in towns churches often came to create meaningful sub-units of community, especially for the young and the old, the lonely and the needy. Some of these functions seem . . . incredibly secular. Sunday schools may have an obvious religious function, but parish picnics . . . may seem rather social in intent. Similarly denominational Bible Classes and the youth-led Bible Class Union . . . played a crucial role far beyond religious formation. Churches became deeply involved in campaigns to reform the community standards of the city, including Prohibition and Bible in Schools, and church-based clubs were popular in a day when there were few other public buildings.[8]

By early 1872, when there were 23 dwellings in the township itself (as well as more in surrounding areas) and the first shops and a post office were operating, the new schoolhouse became another early community gathering place for civic, social and church affairs that appropriately accommodated men, women and children — when public houses could not.[9] In prioritising the schoolhouse over other communal buildings, residents affirmed their civic aspirations for improvement, stability and order at a time when men outnumbered women.[10] Within a year, a *Wellington Independent* commentator (possibly its former editor Arthur Halcombe) opined that order was imposed in ways that showed the transition from a bush township and its attendant male-dominated disorder to a community whose 'social life has now become as decently humdrum as any colonial Mrs Grundy could desire'.[11] For the Mr and Mrs Grundys of early Palmerston North, public facilities like lodge halls, hotels, the survey office and courthouse, schools and churches provided sites for community

The fire brigade was an early, and necessary, form of community activity for men in wooden townships such as Palmerston North. Manawatū Heritage 2008N_F8_WOR_1420

The Foresters' Hall was built by the Ancient Order of Foresters on the western side of The Square in 1876. It rapidly became a community hub that hosted a range of activities, from Sunday-school instruction to amateur dramatics. The hall later became the Theatre Royal, and was rebuilt after a fire, when its multiple uses continued. In this photograph the interior, shown c.1900, is set up for a flower show. T. Billens and Co., Manawatū Heritage 2014N_T6_009091

gatherings before a designated town hall was purchased in 1878.

As new churches, lodge premises and a public hall mushroomed in the next decade, community organisations multiplied. Formal groups for men appeared before those for women and children, reflecting men's greater ability to engage and publicly express their masculine identities.[12] As noted in Chapter 5, working men's lodges such as the Foresters, Druids and Rechabites provided mutual health and financial aid in a period when the state was little involved in welfare provision, alongside fellowship and networking.

Established in 1884, the Manawatu Club delivered a different mix of social, civic and business connections for the town's leading businessmen and others 'of substance'. Company directors Richard Abraham and his brother Lionel were members of a local elite who featured among the early leaders of the club (and of many other voluntary and public bodies), with doctors, lawyers and bank managers also appearing in the list of early presidents.[13] Many of the club's members also became prominent in the Manawatu and West Coast Agricultural and Pastoral Society (later Association), which was established in 1886.

The Workingmen's Club, established in 1889, and later

renamed the Cosmopolitan Club, comprised a mix of member occupations. These ranged from labourers, bushmen and butchers to a fair sprinkling of small businessmen and professionals, and at least one architect (and later mayor), the Danish-born Ludolph Georg West. Inveterate 'joiner' and later Palmerston MP Frederick Pirani was among its first life members.[14] All three of these organisations have endured as networks of local industry and identity.

For women, opportunities to form gendered groups came later. Demarcations between women's domestic work and leisure were blurred; and in a period when women's suffrage was politically 'hot' and public facilities for women were scarce, more meetings were held in private homes than in the township's centre. It is almost certain that connections were made and issues canvassed, but such informal beginnings were not necessarily recorded.

The Women's Christian Temperance Union (WCTU) led the women's suffrage campaign nationally, and Awahuri-based Learmonth Dalrymple locally.[15] She organised Palmerston North and Feilding women's door-knocking, canvassers having to traverse not only the physical barriers and rudimentary walking paths of their communities, but also the restrictive social norms about women's public engagement.[16] While the WCTU seems to have had more of an organisational presence in Feilding than in Palmerston North during the campaign, there was sufficient support for Palmerston North to host the union's national convention in 1895, and a branch of some 36 members was in existence by 1897.[17] In 1920 the WCTU opened the Willard Home in Russell Street 'for orphans and indigent children', named in honour of the American temperance heroine Frances Willard.[18]

Although over 520 Palmerston North women signed the petition for women's suffrage in 1893, community work of the Willard Home variety was more acceptable than political activism for women. They were highly involved in 'caring', whether in direct family contexts, charitable board memberships or as churchgoers. Churches' ladies' guilds and fellowships contributed to congregational affairs, church social events and fundraising for new buildings.[19]

Palmerston North had relied largely on informal community aid in its infancy, and the town's growth paralleled the state's increasing role in welfare through significant, but not necessarily sufficient, welfare legislation.[20] Avenues for communal charity existed through church-based welfare, neighbourly care, lodges' benevolence to members and their families, or the more formal disbursements through the borough council to 'deserving' cases — as, for example, in the accounts for the year ending 31 March 1880, when the 'other charges' expenditure section includes lighting, deposits returned and charitable aid.[21]

In contrast with the four main centres and many other established communities, a benevolent society was not formed in Palmerston North in this period, despite council discussions about the need for such a body. A particular sticking point was whether a benevolent society should be privately philanthropic or supported by local government.[22] Legislation passed in 1885 charged 'hospital and charitable aid boards' with the distribution

Mrs W. T. (Ellen) Wood was wife of the MP for Palmerston North when this photograph was taken in November 1906. She was involved in multiple forms of philanthropy, including fundraising for the hospital and the Awapuni Old Men's Home. Here, she and William Wood are shown in the company of Kerei Te Panau and his wife, Ereni Te Aweawe. Mrs Wood had just been presented with woven mats in acknowledgement of her role in having the post office clock named after the Rangitāne chief. Auckland Libraries Heritage Collections NZG-19061215-9-3

of public welfare, but the boards could also subsidise voluntary charity. In Palmerston North voluntary groups supplemented hospital board relief and state pensions with local benevolence, but on an intermittent basis.[23]

Other organisations emerged to meet more specific community needs. The St John Ambulance Association formed in Palmerston North in 1900, seeded by the established Wellington centre to teach first-aid classes.[24] The quickly growing branch successfully negotiated with the hospital board for an ambulance service and established a voluntary home nursing guild within five years.[25] Its female nurses included labour activist Zillah Gill, who became the first woman to win a seat on the Palmerston North Hospital Board, in 1915.

Community support and fundraising for the vulnerable also manifested itself in other forms: local branches of the Society for the Prevention of Cruelty to Animals (SPCA) and the Discharged Prisoners' Aid Society were in existence by 1910, and the opening of the Awapuni Home in 1915 resulted from disclosures about the appalling conditions in which some of Manawatū's 'derelict' old men were living.[26] Female fundraising led by former mayoress Ellen Wood was especially important to the home, but all such ventures had their committed champions who determinedly pushed for moral and financial support. However, where leadership faltered or burned out, so, too, could voluntary societies. Neither prisoners' aid work nor the SPCA had an uninterrupted existence, while the Awapuni Home was reliant largely on hospital board funding for its ongoing existence.

Although the first thrust of communal activity was towards the town's physical and social infrastructure for adults, after 1900 there was greater attention to youth welfare and instruction. The churches played an important role, driven by a wider international concern for citizens of the future. The Anglican denomination was the largest in the borough (with 43 per cent of the population in the 1900s), and in 1906 a wider 'child rescue' dynamic meshed with a Palmerston North vicar's unsuccessful attempt to find a home for an orphaned boy. This had led the Rev. C. C. Harper to mobilise his All Saints' congregation and other sympathisers to open a small children's home. The home expanded

over the years to provide some 36 beds for children (the majority not full orphans), and multiple opportunities for voluntary citizen service on its trust board, ladies' committee and fundraising campaigns.[27] In operation until 1964, All Saints' Children's Home, like the WCTU's Willard Home, met local needs in the same way as institutional homes for older residents, when private homes could not.

While life at the children's homes was, for the most part, regimented,[28] James Belich has referred to the colonial 'wild child' who, apart from compulsory primary schooling from 1877 and significant family work within families, had freedom to roam — often in the absence of any organised youth sports or leisure.[29] Early twentieth-century organisations aimed at 'taming' young persons and combatting 'larrikinism' through moral and physical training. A youths' institute was founded in 1897 in response to concerns about boys loitering in town, but it gave way to the Young Men's Christian Association in 1904. By late 1909 two troops of Boy Scouts were active in Palmerston North,[30] their work meeting with widespread approval in an increasingly militaristic social climate. Their female counterparts, Girl Peace Scouts, took slightly longer to establish, given the more restrictive gendered social norms for active girls: a Miss Collins of College Street School formed a group in June 1914, and the girls' services were offered to the local patriotic society when war broke out.[31]

Poster costumes at the All Saints' ladies' guild bazaar in Palmerston North, 1909. Beyond worship, church groups hosted bazaars, concerts and opportunities to dress up and have fun in the name of a good cause. Note the range of goods and businesses advertised. Photographer: E. Denton, Auckland Libraries Heritage Collections NZG-19091208-29-1

With New Zealand still tightly tied to an imperial 'Home', the outbreak of the First World War prompted both national and local responses. These largely supported the dominant political narrative of 'doing our bit', men volunteering for military service before conscription in 1916, while those on the 'home front' supported patriotic societies. These raised funds, morale and crops to feed overseas troops, the country and the empire.

The Manawatu Patriotic Society formed in 1915, following regular press coverage of the Queen Carnival fundraising contest run by its Wellington-based counterpart.[32] As manifestations of community thought and action, umbrella groups like the Patriotic Society followed an existing pattern whereby notable Palmerstonians spearheaded local efforts, while indicating that 'any citizen who feels he can assist the good cause will be welcome to attend'.[33] By June 1915 the committee numbered 45, Mayor Jimmy Nash making it clear that councillors not yet on it should attend the weekly meetings.[34]

Women were pivotal to the war effort; as noted in Chapter 6,

Leaders and joiners

From the 1890s to the 1930s Lionel and Constance Abraham moved easily among the elite of Palmerston North's associational life. They epitomised the web of commercial, sporting and organisational interests sustained by its leading families at a dynamic time in the town's history. Their home, 'Te Ranara Whare', opposite what is now Ongley Park, was one of the settlement's grand houses, and in constant use for charitable fundraising. Many a project was planned around its dinner table.

Lionel Abraham was one of the founders of the seed and grain business Barraud and Abraham, giving him strong links into the surrounding rural community, and, along with his stock-agent brother Richard, he had a life-long interest in the A & P Association. He was also the founder of the Manawatu Golf Club, and its secretary for 35 years; for 46 years he was steward of the Manawatu Racing Club, one of the first members of the Manawatu Club, a past master of the United Manawatu Lodge of Freemasons, and a long-term vestryman, church warden and lay reader of All Saints' Church.

Constance Abraham ('Mrs L. A.') shared many of her husband's sporting interests, and was an accomplished horsewoman and golfer, and a leading light in the associated clubs. Like Lionel, she was heavily involved in activities at All Saints', where she no doubt gained standing from her father's service back 'Home' as a chaplain to Queen Victoria. First president of the All Saints' Ladies' Guild, she helped Canon Harper found the All Saints' Children's Home and served as its secretary for 25 years. During the First World War she was heavily involved in fundraising, especially through the patriotic shop, and she organised the publication of a patriotic cookbook (she never cooked herself — her astonishing level of activity was smoothed by the existence of domestic staff at Te Ranara to service her growing family). Towards the end of the war 'Mrs L. A.' was one of those taking the initiative to form a local YWCA and, later, a Plunket Society. The award of an OBE followed in 1919. When a central relief committee was formed in Palmerston North during the 1930s Depression, Constance Abraham was inevitably to the fore, most especially since she was also an elected member of the Palmerston North Hospital Board from 1921 to 1935.

After Constance Abraham's retirement from public life in 1937, a gathering of more than 18 organisations in which she had been involved honoured her. They included, as well as the bodies mentioned, the Manawatu Women's Club, the Mothers' Union, the District Nursing Guild, the Red Cross and the Women's Division of the Farmers' Union.[1]

Most places have their 'joiners', people whose names appear in multiple contexts. As Palmerston North moved beyond its foundation period, it provided a niche for those who, like Lionel and Constance Abraham, came with personal abilities, social capital and a degree of affluence, to play a foundation role in many different kinds of civic organisations.

"MRS. LIONEL"

"L.A."

LEFT Constance Abraham, caricatured in *Just for Fun: Personalities at Par* (Palmerston North PAT Studios, 1934).

RIGHT Lionel Abraham caricatured, probably during the First World War. From David Abraham, *Abraham and His Seed Forever*, 96

Mayoress Elizabeth Nash led the Patriotic Society's highly effective fundraising committee. Participation in local wartime fundraising efforts was not only invited, but expected, activities including troop recruitment drives, contributions towards a military hospital ship, and the Sick and Wounded Fund. Local papers published lists of individual and group donations supporting these efforts; such lists combined public acknowledgement with an incentive for others to follow suit. Simon Johnson's colourful account shows how even in the final year of war a wide range of Palmerston North groups were able to come together and raise more than £12,000 in two months via a highly organised pseudo-military campaign called 'The Final Battle'.[35]

The demands of war cut across existing associational life, with the war years negatively affecting some groups' memberships, as younger men went overseas and other citizens were diverted into patriotic work. Men's organisations were the hardest hit: the Savage Club, established in 1908 to entertain Palmerstonians, went into recess until 1921, and gendered youth programmes like Scouts and the Boys' Brigade suffered from a deficit of young male leaders.[36]

Yet as some groups struggled, local branches of national organisations gained a foothold in wartime. Reflecting concerns about the welfare of single working women, the Young Women's Christian Association (YWCA) commenced activities in 1917, opening a hostel in Queen Street the following year. The Plunket Society was represented in Palmerston North by Nurse Parlane, who held a clinic two days a week from December 1918, the financial side of her work overseen by the District Nursing Guild. Palmerston North formed an independent branch of Plunket in October 1921.[37]

In the decades from the 1920s to the 1950s, some groups re-formed while others extended existing opportunities for social involvement. Organisations continued to be dependent on individuals as leaders, as advocates, as networkers and as gatherers of like minds, and a new generation of joiners and influencers emerged. Again, the regular pattern of associational life was intersected by periods of crisis — the Depression, another war. These required a recalibration of effort, sometimes distracting from core activities. Important new developments saw the emergence of a category of international men's service clubs, the expansion of women's organisations beyond the umbrella of the churches, and growing evidence of suburban identities within Palmerston North.

The Palmerston North Rotary Club, established in 1924 under the presidency of Mayor Fred Nathan, represented a particular trend in men's organisations. It was international, not only in its origin, but in its ongoing links to a worldwide body and its governance charter. Whereas the friendly societies mostly had their roots in British equivalents, Rotary — like many of the other service clubs that followed (for example, Jaycees and Lions) — looked outward to the United States. Rotary's pattern of weekly lunch or tea meetings, worthy projects, 'fines' administered by a sergeant-at-arms, and a membership based on occupational categories, linked Palmerston North with a structure shared by men around the world.[38] Other local clubs followed. At their most expansive between the 1950s and the 1970s, Palmerston North's men's service clubs became more open to female membership once numbers started to decline in the 1980s.[39]

At the same time, women added new, more structured associations to their existing informal networks. Examples were the Hinekoa Rebekah Lodge, founded in 1924[40] as a female branch of the Oddfellows, and the County Club, which from 1928 provided a venue for more affluent women to meet socially, originally in Coleman Mall.[41] In Palmerston North's surrounding rural areas, both the Country Women's Institute and the Women's Division of the Farmers' Union quickly took hold in the 1920s, indicating a thirst for active citizenship that, although primarily focused on 'home and country', provided members with organisational skills, social companionship and community projects. The latter included the Women's Division's 'Kainga Moe' home in Long Melford Road, run from 1939 as a rest home for rural women, and a domestic training centre for girls.[42]

Concerns about the need to promote and support motherhood were also a feature of the early twentieth century. Plunket consolidated its services, and a local branch of the non-denominational League of Mothers emerged in 1927. Formed to uphold the sanctity of marriage and motherhood, it was promoted nationally by vice-regal consort Lady Alice Fergusson, and sustained locally by former matron of the Palmerston North Hospital Mary McLagan, who was its first secretary.[43] Within a decade, the League claimed 418 local members, with an average monthly meeting attendance of 250.[44]

Youth organisations such as Scouting and the Boys' Brigade grew, while new girls' organisations, including Girl Guides, the YWCA's Girl Citizens and church-affiliated youth groups, provided opportunities for wholesome outdoors activity and civics. This was a period when healthy, trained minds and bodies were seen as optimal for future citizens, and when the phenomenon of the 'modern girl' incited some disquiet.[45] Constance Abraham, addressing the high-schools board about an upcoming YWCA Girl Citizens conference in Palmerston North in 1924, reassured 'that there were other young women in the country besides those who thought only of jazzing and silk stockings'.[46] These youth movements were quietly progressive in their outdoor programmes at least a decade before the First Labour Government established a national fitness policy.[47] Scouts and Guides invariably turned out at civic events and parades to represent the shiny, wholesome and active face of young Palmerston North citizenry, and were endorsed as such by councils, mayors and church leaders.

It was not only the young who were encouraged to be civically active — a new kind of organisation promoted suburban identities and community development as the city grew. The Milson Progressive Association formed in 1927, followed by progressive associations in Takarō in 1931, and both Terrace End and West End in 1935. The term 'citizens'

Many youth groups were attached to churches, among them the Girls' Life Brigade, which started in New Zealand in 1928, and which had a presence in Palmerston North by the mid-1930s. The Palmerston North Fourth Girls' Life Brigade junior section was photographed outside St Paul's Methodist church in the 1940s. Loosely uniformed, the girls wear sashes displaying badges that testify to industry, achievement and service. Elmar Studios, Manawatū Heritage 2013G_ELMAR-F250_006998 committee' was also commonly used in Palmerston North, as elsewhere, between the wars. These local committees formed to raise funds, support local entities and organise the city's fiftieth jubilee in 1927.

The jubilee citizens' committee co-ordinated the participation of many groups, including Scottish pipe bands, a ladies' committee making paper decorations for a Queen Carnival, and those marshalling others' garden parties and social events. The home of Alice and William Wilson in College Street became the Starlight Cabaret, where evening dancing on the lawns proved popular; while the friendly societies held a 'friendly-make-you-feel-at-home-sort-of-dance' at the Zealandia Hall.[48] Manifestations of civic pride commemorating 50 years as a borough included a visit from the Duke and Duchess of York, and a procession featuring elected council members, tableaux by youth organisations and other groups, as well as a 36-foot (11-metre) waka on a timber jinker cart, with a Rangitāne crew demonstrating short-paddling.[49] While the local groups noted in this commemoration did not represent the full range of voluntary activity at the time, they indicated how a thriving regional centre depicted itself through organised events.

If the 1920s provided a relatively settled environment for organisations, the Depression and the Second World War again generated new associational threads but weakened others. Local clubs and societies often struggled to maintain members when Depression job losses cut discretionary spending and men moved for work.[50] Palmerston North Rotary's history records bankruptcies and a decline in numbers as members were unable to meet their Rotary dues.[51] Youth organisations were similarly constrained.

By June 1931, recognising that many local bodies had relief schemes for the unemployed to supplement meagre state provision, the Palmerston North Hospital Board proposed a central co-ordinating agency. Again with mayoral and council leadership, the city's volunteers from many churches, friendly societies, the RSA, Red Cross, Rotary, women's organisations such as Plunket and the Rebekah Lodge, and the YMCA and YWCA came together to support the vulnerable.[52] Three city depots for food and provisions, firewood and clothing were set up, along with a mayor's relief fund.[53] Up to 1 August 1931 the Central Relief Committee had 'distributed two tons of bread, one-third of a ton of butter, two tons of flour, three tons of meat, one and a half tons of oatmeal, four tons of potatoes, three-quarters of a ton of rice, sago etc, one ton of sugar and a quarter of a ton of tea' to local households.[54] The Depression affected different residents to different degrees: those who maintained their comfortable lifestyle organised and attended fundraisers like charity balls and concerts and jumble sales, or arranged business development schemes to find work for men and boys locally.[55]

By mid-1932, 1100 local men were registered as unemployed, with women's unemployment not officially recorded but undoubtedly exacerbating the need for support. These pressures led to another form of organising, one where Palmerston North's respectables were less obvious. A Palmerston North branch of the Unemployed Workers'

Guardians of Our Freedom

The New Zealand Home Guard Anthem

Dedicated to C. V. Ciochetto Esq., Area Commander 6a Home Guard

Words By A. K. JACQUES
Music By R. H. RADFORD

Price 2/-

Printed by Harry H. Tombs Ltd.

'Anzacs in the Empire's Wars/Pledged to serve the sacred cause/Never hostile foreign yoke/ Shall subdue our Island Folk.' Palmerston North woman Ann Jacques wrote the words of the New Zealand Home Guard anthem, which was dedicated to Charles Ciochetto, Area Commander of Palmerston-based 6a Home Guard. Ciochetto won the Military Cross in the First World War, and at the time of his appointment to the Home Guard, worked as Barraud and Abraham's merchandising manager. He was active in Rotary and a member of the Citizens' Lunch Club, while Ann Jacques was prominent in many causes, including the SPCA and the Polish League — multiple community affiliations and service were common at the time. Manawatū Heritage 2018Pa_PolishArmyLeagueS6F1_024637

Union, led by Himatangi farmer and national Communist Party organiser Leo Sim, was formed in January 1931, and was subsequently active in protesting against the despatch of married men to work camps (which Sim deemed 'slave camps') away from the city.[56]

The First Labour Government's national social security scheme, introduced in the later 1930s, stabilised the situation, without obviating the need for aid agencies, and in Palmerston North specialised voluntary organisations supplemented public welfare. Recurrent poliomyelitis epidemics had affected many children's health, and in 1935 a Manawatu–Oroua branch of the Crippled Children's Society (CCS) formed to support families and to lobby for resources.[57] Here, and elsewhere, Rotary championed the cause and immediately gained support from the council and professional agencies. The RSA, supporting disabled veterans, also endorsed it.

The Second World War presented local groups with new forms of civically oriented activities. A Chinese Club was established in 1937 following Japan's invasion of China, and the Scandinavian Club was re-established in 1939. These groups asserted their cultural identities when faced with threats to ancestral homelands, while contributing to mainstream fundraising. The war effort once more diverted collective energy from existing causes. From 1940 the Home Guard paraded in anticipation of defending the city against invasion, while organisations like the Red Cross, the Palmerston North Women's War Service Auxiliary (an umbrella group for 30 organisations) and the Manawatu Land Service Club supported both troops and national food production.[58] Girl Guides wove camouflage nets, the RSA assisted servicemen and their families, and the Polish Army League gathered and packed overseas parcels on behalf of many contributing groups.[59]

The Māori Battalion's presence in the city invited local support for the troops in training at the Showgrounds, and a district Māori committee provided manākitanga for the camp.[60]

New Zealand in wartime was a much-uniformed community, even beyond the armed forces. Women as well as men aspired to don a uniform and share in patriotic service. Local members of the voluntary Women's Land Service are shown here in dress uniform, and in large events, such as this Victory Parade of August 1945, they marched alongside the women's branches of the armed forces, the Women's War Service Auxiliary, and the Red Cross Voluntary Detachments and St John Ambulance. High-school girls, Girl Guides, and Girls' Life Brigade joined in, all proudly and immaculately uniformed as an expression of civic solidarity. Manawatū Heritage 2011G_ELMAR-2-B11_005267

The battalion's members also entertained the city's residents through a ball and other events, and were actively involved in local centennial commemorations.[61]

Patterns of voluntary war work in the Second World War generally followed those of 1914–18, although patriotic fundraising came under greater government control via a national patriotic board, and there was a tempering of the socially coercive expectations around participation that had been evident earlier. Men and women of means and influence once again fronted organisations, aided by other residents, many in youth groups and churches. One such leader was Charlotte Warburton, whose private means underwrote an immense and decades-long voluntary presence in Palmerston North Guiding, the National Party, the Order of St John and the Palmerston North Business and Professional Women's Club. She chaired the local branch of the Women's War Service Auxiliary, and in 1946 was awarded an MBE for meritorious service during the war.[62]

FOXTON 24
NAPIER 186
WANGANUI 48
OMAKEA

One outgrowth of war was the Overseas Ladies' Club for 'war brides', formed in 1947. Started by Jill Cook, a British war bride from the First World War, and the ever-busy Charlotte Warburton, the club had its first meeting in Jill Cook's neo-Georgian house on the corner of College and Cook streets. It provided new arrivals with support and companionship, and initiated them into the idiosyncrasies of New Zealand life — a higher level of sex segregation at social gatherings than many were used to, and what it meant to 'be crook' and to 'bring a plate'. Numbers were augmented by the arrival of Dutch 'overseas ladies' in the 1950s, but fell when more and more members went into paid work in the 1970s.[63]

As well as signalling the influx of post-war British and European immigrants who arrived in Palmerston North through national immigration schemes, the Overseas Ladies' Club represents other themes in post-war associational life. Its members went into home-building mode, but also joined groups according to their stages of life, social interests and emerging needs. With one million babies born in New Zealand in the 20 years following the war's end, the 'baby boom' generated community facilities in new suburbs and organisations that emphasised nuclear-family life.

So the wives and mothers of the Overseas Ladies' Club, the Takaro Ladies' Club, the YWCA-based 'Merry Wives' Club and other groups gathered with like minds for fellowship and community service. Plunket committees and family-oriented groups worked to build rooms in new suburbs (assisted by volunteer labour from husbands and fathers).

At a time when 'the great New Zealand weekend' was a reality, men with leisure time could choose between already existing men's clubs such as the Cosmopolitan Club, lodges or the Savage Club — all revitalised after the war — or be part of the proliferation of Lions, Jaycees and Rotary service clubs.[64] These provided a generation of veterans with social outlets, sustained business networks, and enabled men to use their practical skills in the construction of playgrounds and school swimming pools. (This was an era when many men were all too familiar with the concrete mixer!)[65]

Youth groups burgeoned as children abounded, supported by adult volunteers.[66] The city's Old Folks' Association — formed in 1943 to provide older citizens with fellowship and entertainment — continued to flourish, and enjoyed both commercial and council support.[67]

A purposeful, but perhaps slightly confining, homogeneity was supplemented by new avenues for sporting, political and cultural engagement, but also by the development of advocacy and support groups around health and welfare. Within a widely endorsed and increasingly embedded welfare state, national organisations — including the Cancer Society, the Intellectually Handicapped Children's Society, CCS, and the Hearing Association — expanded locally to supplement or advocate for state provision. Other organisations started to acknowledge families beyond the nuclear-family ideal. Birthright, which formed in Palmerston North in 1959 as a single-parent-focused community organisation, was one such example.

ABOVE Identified only as 'The Vogel Street Sunday School', this 1954 image shows how the children of the post-war baby boom boosted the ranks of many religious and other community groups. Church denominations as well as new schools followed population expansion into the suburbs. Manawatū Heritage 2014N_ELMAR_008111

BELOW Baby shows were popular in the twentieth century, and two bonny winners are shown here at a West End Plunket gala day held in 1960. Plunket was expanding into the city's new suburbs at this time, fostered by the high birth rate and the post-war emphasis on home and family. Manawatū Heritage 2017N_2017-20_015767

Voluntary sector engagement in Palmerston North during this period shows adaptation to local, national and global change alongside conscious community-building. A grounding in child and family groups prepared many women for further community engagement in later life. While many organisations established in this period carried on into the next, as baby-boomer families grew up and out, others did not, having outlived their usefulness or losing out to more recent and attractive alternatives.

From the 1970s and 1980s, The Square and Broadway, previously the domain of celebratory processions and military parades, hosted a new kind of civic presence: there were marches for and against abortion, against the Vietnam War and sporting contacts with apartheid South Africa, and in support of women's right to 'reclaim the night'. These events represented a new thread in associational life; one which involved advocacy and protest as political and social schisms became more apparent within the city and across the country. Groups such as the Society for the Protection of the Unborn Child, the Abortion Law Reform Association and the local branch of Halt All Racist Tours claimed public space in new and sometimes challenging ways, before fading from the headlines.

And yet the more general tenor of organisational life in Palmerston North was civil and benign, showing a fair degree of continuity with the past and overlaps of membership. The city's workplaces — whether private businesses, civil service hubs, the rapidly expanding Massey University or the Longburn freezing works — attracted new residents who negotiated their sometimes tenuous sense of belonging through participation in voluntary groups. Among them were Māori, the city's Māori population almost doubling from 723 to 1376 between the 1961 and 1966 censuses, through births and migration.[68]

A 1969 survey by the city council's planning section found that after the 214 sports clubs and associations (discussed in Chapter 8), Palmerston North had 53 social clubs, societies and associations, which drew in some 13,000 people; 97 cultural equivalents, involving around 8000; 67 concerned with welfare (12,000 persons); and 91 religious clubs, societies and associations (some 4000 people). The report noted that memberships were often token, and that they were also not mutually exclusive.[69]

The report also showed the ambiguities around notions of 'joining', 'membership' and 'belonging', for the bodies with the largest memberships were the Automobile Association (12,000-plus), and the National Council of Women (5000-plus).[70] The former had commenced in 1912 as a motorists' club, but by 1969 most would have joined only to gain access to its roadside breakdown service.[71] The Manawatu Branch of the National Council of Women was an umbrella organisation established in 1934, its membership total drawing on those who belonged to its linked organisations.

The report concluded that while the city had a very rich representation of activities, patronage of this wide range of offerings was low for a city of 52,000[72] — even though

Miss Graine McConnell entertains some bemused-looking members of the Palmerston North Happiness Club with a 'skipping ballet' in 1958. At the same meeting, the Happiness Club dispersed £280 to local charities, the Eventide Home for the Aged gaining £150, the largest share. Organisations like the Happiness Club, a wartime initiative, and the Sunshine Club (formed in the 1920s to 'bring sunshine' into needy lives), had a limited life cycle. Manawatū Heritage 2017N_2017-20_015041 the membership figures given in individual cases seem enviably high from a twenty-first-century perspective (5000 for the National Council of Women; 2000–3000 for the YMCA; 1000–2000 for CCS, for example).

This report was not alone in noting a relatively high turnover of population in the city, linked to the strong element of public sector employment.[73] The resulting 'relatively loose confederation of people' meant that voluntary organisations needed to be nurtured, the report concluded.[74] And this is where the city council started to extend its role further into the 'social' side of city life, encouraged by some of the more progressive councillors and staff. Its relatively early involvement in recognising, seeding and financially supporting community development was a feature of this period, although within council the move was not uncontested.[75] One of the pathways for collaboration was the innovative Community Services Council umbrella group for many 'helping' organisations, founded in 1971.[76] The 'Palmerston North Support Model' involved a per capita grant to the Community Services Council, which Mayor Brian Elwood claimed was unique in New Zealand during the 1980s.[77]

Many of the organisations affiliated to the Community Services Council provided services well beyond their own membership. Despite the welfare state, Merv Hancock later commented that the 'affluent sixties' did not seem quite like that to welfare workers such as himself, aware of stresses on families that included, but went beyond, insufficiency of income.[78] He became involved in organisations such as Marriage Guidance, which gained a presence in Palmerston North from the 1960s, as did the Mothers' Helpers Association (1966), the Manawatu Home Budgeting Service (1962) and the Family Planning Association (1971). They were followed by other welfare organisations in the 1980s, including Tough Love (Kapiti–Manawatu) and Barnardos family services.[79] The Citizens' Advice Bureau (1975) helped people negotiate their way around an increasing number of legal and bureaucratic complexities, while the Samaritans (1967) and Youthline (1970) did much of their work via telephone contacts, often in conjunction with existing church-led or state social services.

Within the associational landscape there was again an interplay of the old and the new, and some recalibration of effort. Many organisations served their purpose and then faded. Groups marching against the Vietnam War or the 1981 Springbok tour (such as MAST, Manawatu Action Against the Springbok Tour) were historically specific in their efforts to bring people together.[80] The Overseas Ladies' Club found it impossible to form a committee once its members started to join the paid workforce or 'became integrated', and so it folded in 1982.[81]

With the advent of the welfare state, many of the original lodges and friendly societies had long placed greater emphasis on their social role than their welfare role. In this period they faced competition from other men's clubs and social activities. Some of the lodges combined resources, their meeting halls sold for other purposes: the beautiful Egyptianstyled Aqaba café on Broadway pays homage to the United Freemasons' Lodge which built it in 1931, but which moved to the Kilwinning Lodge rooms in 1987.[82]

The uniformed youth groups had peaked by the 1970s, and teenagers were looking for more novel activities. Towards the end of the period council-supported youth spaces, and the opening of The Stomach music space by the Creative Sounds Society in 1988, helped provide young Palmerstonians with peer-based outlets for creativity.[83] On the margins, earlier groups of 'milk-bar cowboys' evolved into motorcycle gangs in the 1970s, demonstrating that 'joining' took many forms, not all of which were endorsed by other city residents. The homegrown 'Mothers', whose motorbikes roared their way to the Café de Paris pub from 1971, preferred to be known as a 'motorcycle club'. (The Mothers wound up in 2017, to be replaced by a United States import, Hell's Angels, showing that the reach of globalisation had no bounds!)[84]

The membership of the service clubs, also American in origin, peaked in this period, when members had the time to work on projects and the practical skills to complete them. Women became members of existing clubs, but also developed new, less maternally based alternatives to older women's organisations, especially

Palmerston North hosted the Dominion conference of the Māori Women's Welfare League over 28–30 April 1958. One of its 50 remits complimented Palmerston North hotel owners for their help to delegates, but called upon New Zealand hotels in general to admit Māori guests without discrimination. In December 1960 *Te Ao Hou* reported that the Ngā Pamutana branch of the league covered an area from Palmerston North to Ōtaki. Mrs M. Durie of Aorangi was its patron.
Manawatū Heritage 2017N_2017-20_014731

Akela Collins: West End Scout Group cub pack leader, 1941–54

ABOVE Akela Annie Collins with her Scoutmaster husband, left, and her son Bill, who died fighting in the New Hebrides in 1943. West End Scouts

OPPOSITE Annie Collins at the centre of the West End cub pack, probably in the early 1950s. It was a strong pack, and Akela Collins is pictured with six assistants, allowing for a wide range of activities. Tony Evans Collection, Manawatū Heritage 2010P_IMCA-DigitalMaster_004466

Annie Eliza Jane Collins (née Hudson; 1900–1954), known to many boys simply as 'Akela', was part of the Collins family who were all immersed in Palmerston North Scouting. The 3rd West End Scout Group's Cub Pack was established in 1938 under W. A. (Bill) Collins' leadership as a young man; in 1941, he left the pack in his mother's hands in anticipation of his return from active service overseas. His service as a commando in the New Georgia campaign was mentioned in despatches, and he was awarded the Silver Star (US). Sergeant Collins was killed in July 1943. Akela Collins tended the Cub pack for the rest of her life, building relationships with children and parents locally, despite having opportunities to work at higher levels in the Scouting movement. Losing a much-loved son was hard to bear, and her work with the

West End Cubs was her way of honouring her son's commitment to Scouting and youth work.

Scouting was very popular with local boys, and Akela's pack often numbered 45 Cubs, with a waiting list to join. Mrs Collins had an aptitude for working 'boywise', according to Robert Baden-Powell's principles, combining physical activities with the disciplines of learning new skills and honing juvenile citizenship. West End's suburban development, including the Savage Crescent state housing precinct, provided many potential members, and the Scout group used West End School's facilities for many years. Recognising the need for their own 'den', the Collins family donated a Ferguson Street section, and the group fundraised widely until the new hall — constructed from recycled army huts and named for Sergeant Collins — was opened in 1950.

Akela carefully planned pack activities in the hall, and weekend camps in the surrounding countryside, with the help of assistants and parents for badge work, games and transporting the pack to camps and sporting exchanges. She was skilled at engaging others in the city for the boys' benefit, through wider Scouting contacts with local churches and businesses. Akela Collins modelled active citizenship, and expected the Cubs to follow this — to her pack, DYB/DOB ('Do your best/Do our best') was not just for pack night but an everyday expectation. Her Scouting work continued until her untimely death in 1954, whereupon the Collins legacy was continued by other family members and West End Cub Pack assistants.[1]

from the 1970s. These reflected changing social norms and greater numbers of women in paid work.[85] Soroptimists and Zonta formed Manawatū branches in the 1970s, joining established women's groups such as the National Council of Women and the Federation of Graduate Women. (Formed in 1956, the latter gained an especially strong presence after Massey became a university — gown hire gave it an income as well as visibility.) These women's groups engaged in advocacy on women's issues alongside community support. As with other such clubs, they maintained links city-wide, nationally and internationally. The community focus of service clubs established in the mid-twentieth century has remained a constant in Palmerston North. Yet within these service clubs an ageing membership was becoming apparent by the late 1980s.[86]

Local collectivities still reflected larger social trends. These included second-wave feminism, the emergence of more varied sexual identities, and a growing awareness of the need for physically or mentally disabled people to have a voice in decisions affecting their lives. Palmerston North Women's Liberation was in existence by 1971. Subsets of 'causes' then followed — new organisations such as Women's Refuge (1979), Manline (1981), Rape Crisis (1982) and the Women's Health Collective (1984) linking advocacy and support. The Manawatu Lesbian and Gay Rights Association emerged as New Zealand's first established local LGBT organisation, in 1977.

New health and disability groups also developed when state care facilities 'deinstitutionalised', encouraging a rise in community-based responses. Following the 1981 Year of Disabled Persons, new groups such as the Schizophrenia Fellowship and the Disabled Persons Assembly (1983) formed locally and nationally.[87] An ageing population generated age-related groups such as the Alzheimer's Society (Manawatū) in 1987, and also branches of Age Concern and Grey Power in the 1980s. Supplementing existing 'senior citizens' clubs, these new organisations advocated strongly for age-related policy change, locally and nationally. So, too, did groups addressing 1980s housing and employment problems: the Manawatu Tenants' Union (1983) and the Community Development Forum (1984) acted locally, yet within a national context of shifting social and economic conditions. The list could continue.

Community building, in this period as in others, found physical expression. Community halls and facilities provided groups with places to form and meet, and as new suburbs developed, so too did Plunket rooms, school halls and council-subsidised centres. A 1970 town-planning report noted at least 163 city meeting places and halls, hosting diverse groups of users.[88] Church and school halls remained busy hubs for community participation, often beyond denominational or educational needs, while other groups built their own discrete spaces. Community fundraising underwrote the Chinese Association's new hall, which opened in 1963, and the Māori Battalion Hall, which followed in 1964. Each provided a space for shared identity and socialising beyond its foundation group. New community centres took over from older-style halls in the council's suburban planning:

the Centennial Pavilion was relocated from The Square to the facilities-poor Kelvin Grove in 1980, while the Highbury Whānau Resource Centre opened in 1984 as a hub that engendered a renewal of positive activity and community associations — 'we put the unity in community'.[89] Joined by Te Aroha Noa in 1989, these bodies provided community development activities with the physical and social space to flourish.

The baby-boom generation grew up in the 1960s to 1980s, and the range of organisations in the city partly reflected the maturation and ageing of this large cohort. By the late 1980s, contemporary forms of collective voice were more evident, many centred on support and advocacy for residents struggling to thrive. The council's willingness to work with voluntary agencies through the Community Services Council was a new development, recognising that residents' active civic engagement boosted wellbeing and made the city a more attractive place to live.

The Palmerston North City Council's Community Support Plan 2018–21 included the goal of 'a connected and safe community' that recognised and endorsed the ways Palmerstonians already interacted in groups, and the council's facilitative role in active participation.[90] But whatever the rhetoric, wider forces impinge upon 'connectedness', sometimes enabling, sometimes inhibiting associational life. Three trends were particularly apparent after 1990: the contraction of the welfare state increased demand on service organisations; the city's more complex ethnic mix generated new organisations; and while new groups met new needs, an increasingly individual trend in residents' leisure and community engagement threatened the longevity of other groups.

Nationally, voluntarism was undercut by the expansion of the working week, starting with retail and weekend trading, and also by the entry of a traditional part of its workforce, married women, into paid employment — the Constance Abrahams and Akela Collinses of an earlier era were less readily available.[91] And church congregations were less central to associational life by the twenty-first century, a 2006 figure suggesting that only 14 per cent of Palmerstonians attended church regularly.[92]

There was adaptation to new circumstances. In the 1990s the Savage and Cosmopolitan Clubs still gathered, but many male clubs now welcomed women members to boost falling numbers. As gendered organisations, the YWCA and YMCA also reoriented their community work for contemporary conditions, reflecting changing youth and adult 'markets' for their programmes. 'Seniors' clubs and organisations continued their sometimes vociferous political and health advocacy, while Senior Net (1997) advanced seniors' digital literacy as a complement to existing social connections. Many of the organisations in the city's service directories developed Facebook pages and other forms of digital presence.

St John and Red Cross volunteers maintained their hands-on presence in emergencies and in supporting everyday events, but with greater expectations of training and professionalism. The face of the Red Cross in the mid-twentieth century had been its uniformed voluntary auxiliary detachments and first-aid activities. By the end of the century it had paid managers and its first-aid classes were delivered as a paid service to outside groups and individuals. Its public face was nonetheless dominated by activities where volunteers were still critical: the annual book sale started by manager Heather Tanguay in 1990 (now supplemented by a bookshop) and the usual op shop. Even in the refugee resettlement process, run by the Red Cross under contract to government from 2013, voluntary human-to-human interactions were fundamental.[93]

The 'winding back' of the welfare state had implications for local organisations as well as local government once central government sought to devolve responsibilities. For service organisations especially, government policies significantly shaped local needs and the forms by which they were met. Some organisations already relied on professionals to maintain the quality and consistency of services, and many had to take up government contracts in order to pay salaries. 'With the change from volunteers to paid staff the passion of the organisation has often gone,' claimed local analyst Ian Ritchie in 1996,[94] while the diminishing number of volunteers was faced with increasingly onerous accountabilities and requirements for training.

Foodbanks were one response to re-emerging needs in the 1990s. Following benefit cuts, the Salvation Army and Methodist Social Services were instrumental in developing local foodbanks, combining support with advocacy. ACROSS, an Anglican–Catholic welfare agency (1990), joined them in both voluntary and contractual community work.

A more diverse ethnic presence was evident within associational life during this period. Such faith groups as the Manawatu Muslims Association (1980) and Halafungani (Tongan Methodist community, 1990) emerged, reflecting the cultural identities of a growing number of people who were choosing to make Palmerston North their home. Residents had claimed links to their cultural heritages throughout the city's history, and groups representing Māori, Scandinavian, British and other established populations continued under enthusiastic leaders, but in this period others emerged, too. The Central Districts Indian Association (1999) replaced earlier groups, and in the twenty-first century an annual Diwali festival has drawn together Indian families and international university students with the city's wider population. Similarly, the annual Lantern Parade in The Square, as part of the Festival of Cultures, provides opportunities for cross-cultural goodwill and engagement.

These community-led and council-endorsed festivals now convey something of the city's collective contemporary 'face'. As mayor, Paul Rieger had prompted council staff to provide new residents with greater opportunities for civic participation, and the Ethnic Council was formed in 1993 after wide discussion with constituent organisations and community leaders. Renamed the Manawatu Multicultural Council in 2009, it also seeded another community development agency now known as the Migrant Resource Centre.

Again, new agencies emerged to meet specific needs — whether through the Youth One

ABOVE A '60+' day held in July 2018 at Event Central in the Palmerston North City Library. Local body libraries have become important facilitators of community events, not least for retirees who feature among the volunteers and 'joiners' of the twenty-first century. Lesley Courtney, Manawatū Heritage COMM 1533526205

BELOW Cambodian refugees gathered to learn about health and wellness at Kelvin Grove Community Hall in 1993. Growing diversity was a characteristic of Palmerston North in the 1990s, and various groups formed to aid refugee resettlement. Sivleang Ung, Manawatū Heritage COMM 1482197375

The Scandinavian wall hanging in the Palmerston North Central Library resulted from the combined efforts of two community groups: the Scandinavian Club of the Manawatū and the Manawatū Embroiderers' Guild. Designed by Elizabeth Berkahn and Betty Crawford, it depicts many aspects of the Scandinavians' arrival and settlement. The swan represents the five Scandinavian countries — Sweden, Denmark, Norway, Finland and Iceland. Peter McDermott Photography, Manawatū Heritage COMM 1481877229

Stop Shop in 1994, the Palmerston North Street Van as a voluntary mobile response to public safety the following year, or other welfare and disability resource groups. Some older citizens practised 'active retirement' through groups such as the University of the Third Age (2000), Menzshed (2012), and opportunity shop or hospice volunteering.

Some annual events became well-embedded in the city's calendar and consciousness. Palmerston North woman Faye James led the way in introducing the Cancer Society's Relay for Life to New Zealand in 2001, with more than 85 Palmerston North teams participating in the first event held in Hokowhitu.[95] Environmental groups have had an impact on the landscape, as Forest and Bird was supplemented in 2001 by Green Corridors and its members' native plantings in Summerhill and the Turitea Valley. While the city's most visible expression of youth activism has involved protest about climate change, the voice of youth is represented in many Palmerston North organisations, political, creative and community.

It is tempting to over-emphasise the shift to individual over collective (and informal over formal) engagement in this period, as book clubs and walking groups gain traction over older lodges and incorporated societies; yet the organised city continues to gather

Palmerston North was the first place in New Zealand to host the Relay for Life, which originated in the United States in 1985. It was introduced locally by Faye James, raising $140,000 for the Cancer Society and its offshoots in March 2001. It is an example of an umbrella event that brings together multiple smaller groups, including family and business teams, as well as subsets of the overall cause, such as Canteen. Murray Wilson, *MS*, 12 March 2001, 4

collectively as needed. Council-supported community development through umbrella organisations has expanded residents' sense of who they are culturally, socially and politically, and public displays of associational life have both endorsed and developed a collective identity. The baby-boom generation's influence has continued to show in organisational strength or decline; yet along with age, cultural diversity has become more widely celebrated.

Palmerston North's 'organised' history began early in the city's development, and has been a part of the ongoing process of community building. The people of Palmerston North have grouped themselves through shared intent or interests, and re-grouped to meet changing circumstances. Meetings were attended, minutes diligently typed, discussions engaged in, heatedly or with assent, decisions made, events planned, lectures listened to. International crises — including world wars and depressions — rippled through the lives of city residents, alongside collective responses supporting the locally vulnerable. Not everyone agreed or made an equal contribution, and dissent also drew residents together — cleaving has two meanings here.

Occasions of 'gathering for good', from patriotic committees to Relays for Life, have had an overall purpose, yet have also worked to connect many smaller groups. 'Gathering for goodwill' has also been a recurring thread in the city's fabric. Residents have publicly endorsed (and sometimes challenged) the city's sense of self through nineteenth-century borough status celebrations, twentieth-century jubilee or Anzac Day commemorations, and twenty-first-century multicultural festivals, Mātāriki or youth-led climate change protests.

The electronic age has raised new challenges for local groups. Online communities and identities range vastly beyond the local, with notions of 'gathering' which can undermine face-to-face interactions. But in Palmerston North The Square remains a venue for manifestations of collective identity and action, symbolising the continued importance of city-wide gathering places for groups of all sizes. Community building still needs physical spaces, and local church and school halls, clubrooms and council centres, such as the public library, remain places for social, political, faith and lobby groups' kōrero and companionship.

Merv Hancock, shortly before he was elected a Palmerston North city councillor in 1983. Massey University Archives

Merv Hancock (1926–2016): Sharing time and knowledge

The Methodist Social Service Centre, established in 1963, was a locally innovative community response that drew on a strong history of church pastoral care. It combined with a professional social work model to meet emerging social and family needs in Palmerston North.[1] The bridge between the two approaches was Mervyn (Merv) Wilkinson Hancock, who exerted influence through his various roles as Methodist lay reader, social worker, counsellor, university lecturer and city councillor (from 1983 to 1992). One of the city's most astute and generous community leaders of the late twentieth century, Hancock gave more of time and wisdom than money.

Born in Palmerston North, but with wider experience as a child welfare officer elsewhere, Hancock had the capacity to see short- and long-term needs, and to engage with the city's voluntary, academic, faith, council and business constituencies. He acted in hands-on and governance roles locally and nationally, while 'for some . . . groups, he did not so much lead as encourage and empower others in their mission'.[2] Prior to becoming a city councillor, Hancock was instrumental in the establishment of the Community Services Council, but his hand was also behind such organisations as Birthright, Marriage Guidance, and Men Against Violence. On the city council he played an influential role, not just on its social side, but in chairing the economic development committee. Hancock Community House carries the name of this important son of the city, acknowledging his multiple contributions to community development.[3]

CONCLUSION

MARGARET TENNANT & GEOFF WATSON

John Coley, *Around the Square*, 1999. Coley's painting shows The Square and its surroundings before the changes of the 2000s. There are nevertheless many recognisable elements and continuities. Overlaying them is Coley's childhood memory of The Square and growing up in Palmerston North at a time when the railway ran through it. On the left-hand side of the painting, where the railway line is shown crossing The Square, is a red smudge. As a child of about seven Coley was returning home from College Street School in 1941 and encountered a large crowd at the corner of Main Street and The Square near the old post office. Weaving his way through a sea of legs he saw what the 'red smudge' was. The train had run over a person, and John took *nervous fright*. The image stayed with him all his life, and was incorporated into his memory of The Square.

Palmerston North was founded as one of a second wave of colonial towns, part of a drive to subdue the North Island interior, open up communications and undercut continued Māori resistance to Pākehā settlement. The 'North' in its title is a reminder that at the time the 'north' was secondary to the South Island's primacy. This was soon to change, for the new township signified a process by which New Zealand's centre of gravity shifted away from the southern settlements.

Between 1870 and the early 1900s the trajectory of Palmerston North's future development was established, together with its status as the leading regional centre for the Manawatū and a significant transport hub for the North Island, and its reputation as an orderly place to live. The wilderness that greeted J. T. Stewart had largely been 'tamed', and Māori, who had played a central role in the initial development of the settlement, had become marginalised to its periphery, a trend that has only begun to be reversed in recent decades.

The transformation of the environment was perhaps the most visible change. Early European visitors to the region noted it was almost exclusively covered in dense and beautiful forest. This made Te Papaiōea clearing a logical location for a settlement. Within 30 years, however, the bush had largely disappeared, much of it as a result of the extractive industries, such as the sawmills and gravel pits, which provided the raw material for early housing and railway lines. The surviving remnants of the original vegetation were largely in those areas designated reserves. Extensive reserves, particularly the area around the Esplanade, were already delimited. The river and its associated streams remained the only significant antagonist to this new order, its tendency towards flooding a repeated source of anxiety and alarm for citizens.

For Rangitāne, the tangata whenua, the period between 1870 and 1900 represented another phase in their long residence in Manawatū, which began at least 200 years prior to the arrival of Europeans. Palmerston North would not have been established so readily without Māori support, as early historians such as Lindsay Buick have acknowledged. The manākitanga they extended to its early European settlers enabled these Pākehā to survive the precarious early years. From the outset, Rangitāne formed relationships with key European leaders such as George Snelson.

As the European population of Palmerston North expanded from a few hundred to several thousand, the initially bicultural character of settlement changed. Rangitāne became marginalised politically and economically — although they continued to assert their presence in a number of ways. As a result of these setbacks they found themselves obliged, as a matter of economic survival, to sell their reserves at Hokowhitu. Arguably, in the past two decades Māori have reasserted their centrality; a process that began with the Treaty settlements, and is culminating in a much closer working partnership with the council.

In terms of urban development and the workplace, the key features of Palmerston North were clearly evident by the early 1900s. The Square had become the centrepiece of the city. Suburban life had also become established, with Hokowhitu, Terrace End and West End taking on particular identities. Social distinctions accompanied suburbanisation, with working-class areas developing in Terrace End, a 'social set' building grander residences in a variety of locations, and an intermediary middle class residing in such inner-city neighbourhoods as Broad and Church streets.

Although 'farmer' was the most commonly listed occupation among Palmerston North's residents in 1902, there were also many labourers in both small and larger-scale workplaces, many retailers

The raising of the Rangitāne flag between the New Zealand and Palmerston North flags on Waitangi Day 2020 was seen to symbolise co-operation between the twenty-first-century Māori and Pākehā leaders of the city, mirroring the ties between Rangitāne and the city's Pākehā founders of the nineteenth century. *MS, 7 March 2020*

and a growing number of government employees as the expanding city required more specialised technical and professional skills. The education sector was firmly established by the early 1900s, with a mix of private and state providers. A particularly significant year, 1902 saw the establishment of the public high school and also the commencement of technical education, foreshadowing the later development of the tertiary sector in Palmerston North.

For the most part, Palmerston North had benefited by the 1900s from ambitious leadership at local and national levels. Initially a minor settlement within the Manawatu electorate, it soon became an electorate in its own right. The election of Frederick Pirani as Member of the House of Representatives in 1893 signalled the transition from a rural to an urban settlement, and an accompanying change of outlook among the electorate. Palmerston North epitomised the 'progress industry' that James Belich alluded to in *Making Peoples,* in that its citizens lent a fair degree of support to their leaders in raising large loans for development.[1] Constituents looked for visible evidence of progress from their elected representatives, rewarding those perceived to have delivered for the settlement.

The political and urban development of Palmerston North was accompanied by a corresponding development of civil society. A remarkable variety of voluntary organisations were founded in the 30-odd years between 1870 and 1902, many of which continue today. Prominent among these early community organisations were religious bodies, which provided spiritual support to their adherents as well as a variety of social networks and community services. By the early 1900s Palmerston North's associational life encompassed men's and women's groups across the social spectrum.

The development of sport and leisure organisations was another expression of civil society. By the early 1900s Palmerston North had established local sporting competitions, and was also integrated into national and international sporting networks. The principal sport and leisure venues were the Showgrounds, famous for attracting thousands to the annual A & P Show, and the Esplanade, both core amenities to this day. An emerging cultural community complemented the sporting scene, with organisations such as the Palmerston North Orchestral Society and local brass bands catering to a variety of musical tastes. The council supported sporting and cultural organisations, providing facilities such as the Fitzherbert Avenue Sportsground in 1900 and the Opera House in 1906. The Opera House symbolised the faith of the city leaders in the town's advancement and cultural vigour: a town of some 6500 people built a facility seating 1200.

Chapters in this volume have presented the early to mid-twentieth century as a period of consolidation for Palmerston North. After its early and rapid growth, the borough became comfortably embedded in its role as a rural service centre, gaining city status in 1930. Its increasing primacy over similar-sized urban centres on the west coast of the North Island, such as Whanganui, was due to its importance as a transport node as well as a market town and the centre of a 'fecund mix' of dairy and sheep farming.[2]

Industries processing primary produce were supplemented by agricultural engineering works, which increasingly marketed their specialised wares nationally, or even internationally in the case of a few. Most businesses were still family firms, with their capital sourced locally, but a growing tendency was being detected for local firms to seek outside capital by becoming public companies. Meanwhile the establishment of branches of outside firms was further reducing local autonomy.[3] Seminars and studies on industrial development positioned industry as the city's great hope for future prosperity. Land was zoned accordingly — but optimistically.

Māori remained few in number, but those few continued to assert their presence in the city. For example, Rangi Māwhete played a leading role in the development of the Labour Party's relationship with Rātana, and became a member of the Legislative Council in 1936. Rangitāne continued to participate in local affairs, including the diamond jubilee in 1937. The Māori heritage of the city was also reflected in some of the names for council parks created during the inter-war period, notably Papaioea Park and the Takarō sports ground.

There were other dynamics to this period. It was intersected by war and the Depression, both of which brought global events to this otherwise stable provincial context, protracting such key developments as the Milson railway deviation. And yet even the Depression did not totally reverse the expansionist thrust of earlier decades: at the same time as the council was providing relief works for the unemployed, significant improvements were being made to the bus fleet, the electric power station and the water supply, while later, in 1937, the city purchased the Milson Aerodrome from its private operators.[4]

The inter-war period also saw a significant investment in local amenities, all of which remain in use today. Notably, the council purchased land around the lagoon in 1936, later selecting this venue as the site for the 1940 centennial commemorations. The environment was, however, yet to be fully 'tamed'. Major floods in 1941 and 1953 underscored the 'uneasy relationship' between Palmerston North and the Manawatū River.[5]

There was nothing unique about Palmerston North's patriotic response to the First and Second World Wars, but in each conflict the city became a training ground for distinctive groups of military: the New Zealand Army Medical Corps in the First World War, and the Māori Battalion in the Second. In 1939 Ōhakea became the first of two permanent defence bases, followed by the Linton army camp in 1942.[6] Both would become significant contributors to the local economy by the twenty-first century.

And there was another institution that would have long-term implications for Palmerston North's growth and character. The city council's financial contribution to the establishment of Massey Agricultural College on farmlands across the Manawatū River in 1927 had a generous return when the college later became a full university. The Dairy Research Institute and branches of the Department of Scientific and Industrial Research

(DSIR) also attracted staff from across the world, and added a platform of internationally significant research and scientific innovation to the city's claims.

'Solid' and 'steady' were terms often used to describe Palmerston North in these decades. In a feature on Palmerston North's seventy-fifth anniversary in 1952, the *Manawatu Times* made grand claims to Palmerston North as 'New Zealand's City of Destiny', but more accurately referred to it as 'a City of solid prosperity'. The newly formed Public Relations Committee reassured potential employers in the 1960s that this was 'not a "boom town" where mushroom growth had outstripped facilities', but a place of steady, uninterrupted and, increasingly, planned growth. Centrality was complemented by 'ample room for expansion', and another lure was Palmerston North's status as 'a city of healthy, contented workers with a remarkably low record of absenteeism'.[7] Moderation and contentment were the urban virtues of mid-century Palmerston North, increasingly seen as the exemplar of 'middle New Zealand'. Even in politics 'middleness' prevailed from the late 1940s, with the city being regarded as an electoral bellwether for the rest of the country. (Arguably, this trend continued into the MMP era, at least with regard to the party vote.)

From the 1960s, most of the areas covered in this history were characterised by change, amounting in some contexts to transformation.[8] The most distinctive physical change for the city followed from the removal of the railway to Milson in 1964. After nearly a century of bifurcation by a dirty, dangerous railway line, Palmerston North had to reconfigure its centre, a process that was slow and contested, but which also provided space for new amenities. While the desolation of the 'old railway land' in the 1970s may now be largely forgotten, the imprint of the railway is still seen along Main Street.

Also significant was the dramatic expansion of Palmerston North's boundaries following local government reform in 1989. Ashhurst and the Pohangina Valley were transformed from rural outliers into satellite settlements of Palmerston North. The city's development into Aokautere signalled a new relationship with the Manawatū River, and a more challenging proposition for development than had characterised expansion on the flat land north of the river. Meanwhile, complementing this expansion, further work on the river and its stopbanks meant the 2004 floods had minimal impact on Palmerston North, and that the environs of the river could be extensively developed for recreation. The issue of waste discharge into the river has, however, become increasingly urgent, with the 'Nature Calls' project scheduled to devise a new wastewater treatment plan between 2020 and 2022.[9]

When long-term city planner Ken Tremaine arrived in Palmerston North in 1976, he gained the impression of a council trying to turn 'a provincial rural servicing town into a strong semi-metropolitan city'.[10] Councillors, he felt, were keen to build the city, to provide new amenities, and to spend public money in a way that would attract private sector capital. Much of this activity was initiated under the mayoralty of Brian Elwood (1971–85), and

Town and gown meet at Massey University's annual graduation ceremonies. The procession along Broadway in 1999 was led by Massey marshalls Nigel Long (carrying the mace) and Andrea McIlroy, followed by Vice-Chancellor James McWha; Morva Croxson, the university's first woman Chancellor; and pianist Michael Houston, who had been awarded an honorary doctorate. Massey University Archives L-1-1-4-11-1.4-4 it involved a more strategic and directive approach to the city's governance than had been evident in the mid-century. The Palmerston North City Council, no longer dominated by what Tremaine termed 'a power elite of well-intentioned but narrowly focused men',[11] started to become more varied and more representative of the city — the 1994 council had seven women and nine men, two of the women Māori.

Particularly important in the last three decades of the century was a community development thrust which went beyond the provision of playing fields to give direct council funding to voluntary agencies and to social services. Not all concurred that community support was properly the role of local government (or of the public sector at all), but it remains a significant council budget item, and in 2019 the Palmerston North City Council was one of only four in New Zealand still investing in social housing.[12] By 2018 the wider healthcare and social assistance sector was the largest in the city in terms of earnings, and the second-largest employer.

Another especially important development was the elevation of Massey College into a full university from 1963. Massey was still 'across the bridge' and in Kairanga County until 1989, its leaders wary of urban encroachment. Coupled with the closely aligned DSIR and the presence of the first teachers' college to be established outside the four main centres, the university's expansion nonetheless had a massive impact on the city, economically, culturally and politically.

The public sector had long had a significant presence in Palmerston North, but the combination of educational institutions, the defence sector and the regional hospital meant there was usually one major building development or another under way in the city over the late twentieth century. By the same token, however, the city was always vulnerable to cutbacks by public agencies, notably from the late 1980s. Massey University's move to invest in campuses at Albany and Wellington (from 1989 and 1999, respectively) also sent less than positive signals about growth in the Manawatū, suggesting, as a later commentator put it, that while the university was 'in' the city, Palmerston North was not necessarily a 'university city'.[13]

The 1980s and 1990s also saw the closure or relocation of a number of significant private sector activities, such as the Longburn freezing works, Coachwork International and the Sunbeam electric blanket factory. The 1960s fixation on industrial growth as the prime indicator of progress had come too late for Palmerston North: manufacturing went in the other direction. Agglomeration economics favoured the large main centres over the regions, and, increasingly, global competitors over New Zealand manufacturers. More positively, the city retained a diverse economic base in the first two decades of the twenty-first century, which provided a hedge against decline in any one sector.[14]

In other areas of change, Palmerston North also followed national trends. Māori became much more of a force in the city, their number increasing from the 54 recorded in 1926 to 15,807 in 2018.[15] Through Treaty settlements, joint management of key sites such as

Te Motu o Poutoa and the 2019 invitation to join council committees — with voting rights — Rangitāne gained acknowledgement as tangata whenua in ways that went beyond the largely intermittent and ceremonial recognition of earlier decades. Although Palmerston North's wider ethnic mix was well behind the 'superdiversity' that characterised Auckland in the 2010s, by 2012 its Māori, Pasifika and Asian populations were increasing faster than the New Zealand average.[16]

A richer population mix meant that associational life also became more complex, with new elements of identity politics, advocacy and protest. Forms of sport and recreation were more varied than in the past, council partnering in many community events and providing an increasing range of facilities. Music and the arts also flourished. Centrepoint's survival as the only professional theatre outside the main centres pointed to a population able to sustain significant cultural amenities. And whereas Palmerston North trailed behind places such as Whanganui and Napier in establishing an art gallery and museum before the 1960s, the Art Gallery, Te Manawa and the Rugby Museum soon evolved into institutions of national as well as regional significance.

Many of the chapters in this volume refer to 'Palmerstonians', an all-purpose term that now encompasses a range of relationships

Memorial Park's playground closed on 27 March 2020. The shut-down of most businesses and community facilities during the Covid-19 pandemic was just one indication that Palmerston North was part of a global system, and not just in economic terms. Author's collection

He Ara Kotahi, the walking and cycling bridge across the Manawatū River, completed in 2019, is seen by many as a sign of the city's current vitality alongside the older attributes of 'liveability'.
Manawatū Heritage P1044399

with the city, from urban tangata whenua to the most recent refugee arrivals. Palmerston North has always had its 'wayfarers' as well as those who put down deep roots. From the single male transients of the nineteenth century to those who temporarily, and not always enthusiastically, made it home on their way to career betterment (via the district office of a government department, the branch of a bank or a stock and station agency, or the university department, for example), it has been a place where the stage of life shaped responses to the city's offerings. For students Palmerston North has presented a very particular experience, and their presence or absence over the cycle of the academic year has been noticeable.

The city has a reputation for being 'an easy place to live', a stronger selling point to some than to others. A 2013 survey by international urban authority Charles Landry noted how residents and outsiders 'agreed with the easy lifestyle moniker, the convenience and that it is a good place to bring up a family', but it was also regarded by critics as a place that was comfortable to the point of complacency. Landry put Palmerston North in the middle of his international 'creative cities' index, observing that it was on the cusp of a number of important choices.[17]

The tension between a desire for Palmerston North's continued growth

Te Peeti Te Aweawe's statue in The Square faces towards Te Āpiti (the Manawatū Gorge), keeping watch to ensure that Rangitāne are never again surprised by invasion from this direction. Te Peeti's sister, Ereni Te Aweawe, commissioned the statue in 1905. His brother, Hare Rākena Te Aweawe, performed the haka pōwhiri at its unveiling on 29 January 1907. Te Peeti's dying words, 'Kua kaupapa i au te aroha, ma koutou e whakaoti' ('I have laid the foundation of friendship for you to bring to completion'), are often invoked as an aspiration for relationships in the present. Manawatū Heritage P10331

on the one hand, and 'liveability' on the other, has remained a constant. In 2017 a new 'vision' emerged based on the slogan 'Small City Benefits, Big City Ambition'. The audience for this was local as well as external: citizen apology was passé, and 'Palmy Pride' was in. Marketing around these slogans did not reject growth, but it also emphasised sustainability and creativity. Internationally, small cities were seen as having positive attributes that their larger counterparts had lost, and, given the increasing environmental concerns in an uncertain world, growth was no longer a virtue in itself.[18] The energy of recent attempts at boosting Palmerston North rivals that of 150 years ago, when the settlement was rarely mentioned without the descriptor 'progressive' attached. But today's progressivism is tempered by notions of quality of life and questions about how widely benefits might be shared.

TIMELINE OF EVENTS

1500–1600	Arrival of Rangitāne in the Manawatū under leadership of Tamakere, Rākaumauī, Poutoa, Tāwhakahiku and Māngere
1820s	Arrival of Kāwhia and Taranaki hapū under leadership of Te Rauparaha
1824	Battle at Waiorua, and subsequent arrival of Ngāti Kauwhata under Te Ahu Karamū, and Ngāti Raukawa under Te Whatanui
1839	Arrival of the New Zealand Company, Kapiti Purchase
1864	Purchase of Te Ahu a Tūranga block from Rangitāne by the Crown
1866	Survey for township in Te Papaiōea clearing by John Tiffin Stewart
1871	Arrival of first substantial group of Pākehā settlers
1876	Completion of Foxton–Palmerston North railway
1877	Incorporation of Borough of Palmerston North Election unopposed of George Snelson as first mayor
1878	Conferment of the name Te Marae o Hine upon The Square; commencement of landscaping of The Square
1883	Formation of volunteer fire brigade
1886	Establishment of the Showgrounds by the Agricultural and Pastoral Association Completion of Wellington-to-Manawatū railway (incorporated into main trunk line 1908)

1889	Construction of first water supply weir and reservoir on the Turitea Stream Opening of gasworks
1890	Construction of sewerage system
1891	Completion of railway through Manawatū Gorge
1893	Opening of first hospital
1897	Naming of Victoria Esplanade (designated a reserve in 1876)
1902	Major flood of the Manawatū River Opening of the first high school for boys and girls
1907	Unveiling of Te Peeti Te Aweawe statue in The Square
1909	Opening of the 'lakelet' in The Square Construction of Technical School
1914	First biennial election of mayor and city councillors
1915	Establishment of military training camp at Awapuni Racecourse by the New Zealand Medical Corps
1920	Opening of Palmerston North Girls' High School
1924	Opening of electric power station
1926	Dedication of war memorial in The Square
1928	Donation of land for Massey Agricultural College by the Palmerston North Borough Council
1930	Incorporation of City of Palmerston North Opening of the Regent Theatre
1935	Opening of second Fitzherbert Bridge

1936	Great Easter storm Construction of Labour Government's state houses, continuing until 1944
1937	Purchase of Milson Aerodrome by city council (first opened 1931)
1938	Development of Fitzroy Park (opened as Memorial Park 1954)
1940	Māori Battalion first assembled in Palmerston North for training
1942	Establishment of Linton army camp
1950	Inclusion of Milson and Kelvin Grove within city boundary
1953	'Great flood' of the Manawatū River (January) — the largest since 1902
1957	Presentation of Hopwood clock tower to the city
1959	Opening of Milson railway deviation
1962	Election of Sam Mīhaere, the first Māori councillor, and Julia Wallace, the first woman councillor, to Palmerston North City Council
1964	Closure of railway through The Square Establishment of Massey University
1966	Opening of Lido swimming centre
1971	Opening of Manawatū Museum, which later moved to Church Street
1974	Centrepoint Theatre begins its first full season at 81 George Street, moving to Church Street site in 1978
1979	Completion of civic administration building
1980	Opening of convention centre
1983	Establishment of Te Āwhina Kōhanga Reo as the first local Māori 'language nest'
1987	Opening of third Fitzherbert Bridge

1988	Major flood (July)
1989	Extension of city boundary to include Ashhurst, Whakarongo, Aokautere and Linton
1990	Te Kura Kaupapa o Manawatū established, teaching at secondary level
1998	Election of Jill White as first woman mayor
2004	Major flood (February)
2019	Opening of He Ara Kotahi cycle and pedestrian bridge across the Manawatū River

NOTES

Abbreviations

AJHR	*Appendix to the Journals of the House of Representatives*
EP	*Evening Post*
IMCA	Ian Matheson City Archives
MJH	*Manawatū Journal of History*
MS	*Manawatu Standard* (*Manawatu Evening Standard*)
MT	*Manawatu Times* (also known as *The Manawatu Daily Times*)
NZH	*New Zealand Herald*
NZJH	*New Zealand Journal of History*
NZM	*New Zealand Mail*
NZT	*New Zealand Times*
PNCC	Palmerston North City Council
Te Ara	*Te Ara — the Encyclopedia of New Zealand* (includes *Dictionary of New Zealand Biography*)

01 Stories of a city

1 T. L. Buick, *Old Manawatu, or The Wild Days of the West* (Palmerston North: Buick and Young, 1903), 406.

2 *Bush Advocate*, 10 February 1891, 2; *Feilding Star*, 16 March 1895, 2.

3 *MT*, 13 February 1923, 4; *MS*, 18 September 1907, 4, 2 April 1927, 8, 13 February 1998, 1. For more on naming, see Ian Matheson, *Council and Community: 125 Years of Local Government in Palmerston North 1877–2002* (Palmerston North: Palmerston North City Library for PNCC, 2003), 7. The macron has appeared in more general usage over the past decade.

4 'Papaiōea' appears with and without a macron in recent usage, and those supporting it as a name for the town did not use one. Nevertheless, we have followed the usage of the Rangitāne contributors to the volume in subsequent chapters.

5 In 1930 an *Evening Post* article commented that it was a pity the European settlers did not adopt 'the aboriginal mode of nomenclature, and rather name the town after some local peculiarity' than after some celebrity of the time: *EP*, 18 June 1930, 17. Ethnographer Elsdon Best wrote to the *Manawatu Standard*, suggesting the name 'Papaihoea' be used, but also noting that several meanings could be attached to the name.

6 *MS*, 21 December 1926, 8; *MT*, 19 June 1906, 8.

7 *MS*, 18 September 1907, 4.

8 Ben Schrader, *The Big Smoke: New Zealand Cities 1840–1920* (Wellington: Bridget Williams Books, 2016), 17–18; Redmer Yska, *Wellington: Biography of a City* (Auckland: Reed, 2006); John Cookson and Graeme Dunstall, eds, *Southern Capital: Christchurch Towards a City Biography* (Christchurch: Canterbury University Press, 2000).

9 *Wairarapa Daily Times*, 15 August 1888, 2.

10 *Cyclopedia of New Zealand* (Wellington: Cyclopedia Company, 1897), 1140; *Feilding Star*, 18 January 1897, 2.

11 *MS*, 13 September 1907, 8.

12 *MS*, 16 August 1927, 6.

13 *MS*, 14 April 1966, 10.

14 *MS*, 13 September 1993, 1; PNCC, *Palmerston North Knowledge City: A View of Palmerston North* (Palmerston North: PNCC, 1999).

15 *MS*, 3 November 2018, https://www.pressreader.com/new-zealand/manawatu-standard/20181103/281539406962337.

16 'The Centre of an Island', Palmerston North 75th Anniversary Programme, 1952, *Manawatū Heritage*, https://

manawatuheritage.pncc.govt.nz/item/478f9248-f80a-44d0-8959-6ac3a02cc1e1?child=edba6d82-d4f3-4b6c-a8b7-942e0d5c01f6.

17 *Auckland Weekly News*, 2 October 1924, supplement, 40. The *Auckland Weekly* used similar phrasing in image captions on 1 November 1923, supplement, 43, and 29 November 1928, supplement, 43.

18 Palmerston North City Council Public Relations Committee, 'Foreword', *Palmerston North: A Garden City of New Zealand* [n.d.], Palmerston North Promotions Board, Misc. Publications 1960–1980, Series 9, Box 1, Folder 5, IMCA.

19 Schrader, *The Big Smoke,* 340–46.

20 Palmerston North Promotions Board, Misc. Publications 1960–1980, Series 9, Box 1, Folder 5, IMCA.

21 PNCC Town Planning Department, *Viewpoints: A Survey of Public Opinion About the Nature of Palmerston North Undertaken Prior to the Review of the District Plan*, PNCC 7/5/2, Box 5, No. 55, IMCA.

22 Peter Gibbons, *Astride the River: A History of Hamilton* (Hamilton: Whitcoulls/Hamilton City Council, 1977).

23 Matheson, *Council and Community,* 85. Many towns have presented themselves as a 'heartland', usually of surrounding rural areas.

24 Real estate agent Tim Mordaunt, quoted at http://www.stuff.co.nz/manawatu-standard/news/9224854/Slogan-captures-essence-of-city. The 'young heart' part did not prevent younger citizens from irreverently subverting the slogan into 'old farts, easy listening'! Personal communication, Helen Dollery, 6 June 2018.

25 https://www.stuff.co.nz/manawatu-standard/news/93359813/palmerston-north-small-but-ambitious.

26 On the history of Rangitāne, with a focus on the pre-1840 period, see J. M. McEwen, *Rangitāne: A Tribal History* (Auckland: Reed, 1986). See also 'Summary of the Historical Background to the Claims by Rangitāne o Manawatū', https://www.govt.nz/treaty-settlement-documents/rangitane-o-manawatu/.

27 See, especially, Val A. Burr, *Mosquitoes and Sawdust: A History of Scandinavians in Early Palmerston North and Surrounding Districts (Scandia 2)* (Palmerston North: Scandinavian Club of Manawatu Inc, 2017).

28 Matheson, *Council and Community.* Editing and appendices for the book were undertaken by city librarian Anthony Lewis, while the book has a very useful series of maps drawn by Ian Matheson and Sue Stirling.

29 The *Journal* was first edited by Cushla Scrivens, and included a number of prominent local historians on its first editorial committee: Lucy Marsden, Garry O'Neill, Dorothy Pilkington, Margaret Tate, Noelene Wevell, Tina White and Spencer Lilley. Russell Poole, a contributor to this volume, is the current editor.

30 Schrader, *The Big Smoke*, 22. Schrader's book also has an excellent historiographical discussion of the state of urban history in New Zealand, 12–20.

31 In Local History Week 2019 a range of master's and honours research exercises relating to Palmerston North's history was deposited in the Palmerston North Central Library.

32 Earlier histories of secondary centres of note include: Peter Gibbons, *Astride the River: A History of Hamilton* (Christchurch: Whitcoulls/Hamilton City Council, 1977); Mary Boyd, *City of the Plains: A History of Hastings* (Wellington: Victoria University Press, 1984). David Pearson's 1979 study of Johnsonville reflected sociological concerns about community and social stratification to study change over time in a smaller community: *Johnsonville: Continuity and Change in a New Zealand Township* (Auckland: George Allen & Unwin,

1979). Otago University's well-funded 30-year Caversham project, although focused on one part of Dunedin, remains the gold standard of urban histories in its theoretical and quantitative sophistication: see, for example, Erik Olssen, *Building the New World: Work, Politics and Society in Caversham 1880s–1920s* (Auckland: Auckland University Press, 1995).

33 An influential model for this approach was John Cookson and Graeme Dunstall's *Southern Capital.*

02 Tangata whenua

1 Elsdon Best, 'The Land of Tara and They Who Settled It', *Journal of the Polynesian Society* 26, no. 4 (1917): 143–69, at 151.

2 Rangitāne o Manawatū Deed of Settlement on 14 November 2015, 8, https://www.govt.nz/treaty-settlement-documents/rangitane-o-manawatu/.

3 J. M. McEwen, *Rangitāne: A Tribal History* (Auckland: Reed, 1986), 16–17.

4 Ibid., 21–22.

5 Ibid., 41–44.

6 Rangitāne o Manawatū Deed of Settlement, 8.

7 McEwen, *Rangitāne,* 51–54.

8 Rangitāne o Manawatū Deed of Settlement, 8.

9 A. E. Esler, in B. G. R. Saunders and A. G. Anderson, eds, *Introducing Manawatu* (Palmerston North: Department of Geography, Massey University, 1964), 39. Note: In the original text 'Rangitaane' was used, though for consistency we have used macrons throughout this quotation.

10 Ngāti Toa Rangātira Deed of Settlement on 7 December 2012, 7–12; https://www.govt.nz/treaty-settlement-documents/ngati-toa-rangatira/.

11 McEwen, *Rangitāne,* 121–22.

12 Ngāti Toa Rangātira Deed of Settlement, 7.

13 Ron Crosby, *The Musket Wars* (Auckland: Reed, 1999), 141–42.

14 Te Ahukaramū Charles Royal, 'Ngāti Raukawa', *Te Ara*, https://teara.govt.nz/en/ngāti-raukawa/print.

15 Crosby, *The Musket Wars*, 180.

16 Teremoana Sparks and W. H. Oliver, 'Waitohi', *Te Ara*, https://teara.govt.nz/en/biographies/1w3/waitohi.

17 McEwen, *Rangitāne,* 133–36; Robyn Anderson and Keith Pickens, *Wellington District: Port Nicholson, Hutt Valley, Porirua, Rangitikei, and Manawatu* (Wellington: Waitangi Tribunal, 1996), 34–35.

18 Robyn Anderson, *Porirua ki Manawatū Inquiry: Historical Issues Scoping Report for Hapū and Iwi Broadly Associated with Ngāti Raukawa*, 9 December 2014, Wai 2200, #A128, 14–15.

19 G. C. Petersen, *Palmerston North: A Centennial History* (Wellington: A. H. & A. W. Reed, 1973), 19.

20 Raeburn Lange, 'The Social Impact of Colonisation and Land Loss on the Iwi of the Rangitikei, Manawatu and Horowhenua Region, 1840–1960' (Wellington: Crown Forestry Rental Trust, December 2000), 4.

21 'Palmerston North', *An Encyclopaedia of New Zealand,* A. H. McLintock, ed., https://teara.govt.nz/en/1966/palmerston-north.

22 *Te Whanganui a Tara me ona Takiwa*, Wai 145 (Wellington: Waitangi Tribunal, 2003), 47.

23 Ibid., 47–48.

24 Ibid., 191.

25 Anderson and Pickens, *Wellington District*, 21–22.

26 For a discussion of the more general context, see Rosemary Tonks, '"A Difficult and Complicated Question": The New Zealand Company's Wellington, Port Nicholson Claim', in *The Making of Wellington 1800–1914,* ed. David Hamer and Roberta Nicholls (Wellington: Victoria University Press, 1990), 35–59, at 44–45.

27 *Te Whanganui a Tara me ona Tikanga*, 71–72.

28 Anderson, *Porirua ki Manawatū Inquiry*, 24–25.

29 Bryan Gillings, *'A Land of Fighting and Trouble': The Rangitikei – Manawatu* (Wellington: Crown Forestry Rental Trust, 2000), 18–19.

30 Anderson and Pickens, *Wellington District*, 30.

31 Ibid., 38–39.

32 Claudia Orange, 'Flags and Nations, 1839–1852', in *Frontier of Dreams: The Story of New Zealand,* eds Bronwyn Dalley and Gavin McLean (Auckland: Hodder Moa, 2005), 95–125, at 113–14.

33 T. J. Hearn, *One Past, Many Histories: Tribal Land in Politics in the Nineteenth Century* (Wellington: Waitangi Tribunal, 2015), 132–35.

34 Ibid., 161.

35 Ibid., 183.

36 Rangitāne o Manawatū Deed of Settlement, 10.

37 Ibid., 11.

38 Ibid., 12.

39 Catherine Love, Ngapera Moeahu and Shamia Love-Shariff, *New Zealand Māori Case Study: Wellington Tenths Trust and Palmerston North Māori Reserved Lands Trust* (Hamilton: Enhanced Wellbeing in an Ageing Society Programme, 2007), 26–27, http://www.ewas.net.nz/Publications/filesEWAS/EWAS%20CS%201%20TenthsTrust.pdf.

40 http://www.tekau.maori.nz/PalmerstonNorthMaoriReserveTrust/AboutUs/History.aspx; see Lucy Marsden, 'Six Minutes Walk to The Square: The Story of One City Block', *MJH* 14 (2018): 31–41 for the subsequent history of this area.

41 Mason Durie, 'Te Aweawe, Te Peeti', Volume One, *Dictionary of New Zealand Biography* (Wellington: Allen & Unwin/Department of Internal Affairs, 1990), 442–43.

42 Rangitāne o Manawatū Deed of Settlement, 15.

43 Durie, 'Te Aweawe, Te Peeti', 442–43.

44 Mason Durie, 'Te Rangiotū, Hoani Meihana', *Dictionary of New Zealand Biography. Te Ara*, https://teara.govt.nz/en/biographies/1t67/te-rangiotu-hoani-meihana.

45 Ibid.

46 Tina White, 'Who was the Daughter of Peace?', *MS,* 9 April 2016, 9.

47 Tūhuatahi Tui Adams and Paul Meredith, 'Ngāti Maniapoto', *Te Ara*, https://teara.govt.nz/en/ngati-maniapoto/print.

48 Historic Places Manawatu, 'An Inventory of Places Listed on the Register of the New Zealand Historic Places Trust Pouhere Taonga' (Palmerston North: Historic Places Manawatū-Horowhenua Inc, 2013), 17–18.

49 *MS,* 10 November 1906, 5.

50 '"New" Palmerston North Clock Tower, The Square', https://manawatuheritage.pncc.govt.nz/item/b363de9e-1ef6-41ed-beb1-33a22572411c#tab-item-description.

51 Malcolm McKinnon, 'Manawatū and Horowhenua region', *Te Ara*, https://teara.govt.nz/en/manawatu-and-horowhenua-region/print.

52 Ibid.

53 Mason Durie and Meihana Durie, 'Rangitāne', *Te Ara*, https://teara.govt.nz/en/rangitane/print.

54 *MS*, 10 March 1936, 6.

55 Claudia Orange, 'Mawhete, Rangiputangatahi', *Te Ara*, https://teara.govt.nz/en/biographies/4m48/mawhete-rangiputangatahi.

56 *MS*, 5 March 1940, 9.

57 Aroha Harris with Melissa Matutina Williams, 'Māori Affairs', in *Tangata Whenua: A History,* ed. Atholl Anderson, Judith Binney and Aroha Harris (Wellington: Bridget Williams Books, 2015), 382–413, at 395.

58 Ibid.

59 *Census,* 1926, 21. Ian Matheson, *Council and Community: 125 Years of Local Government*

in Palmerston North 1877–2002 (Palmerston North: Palmerston North City Library for the Palmerston North City Council, 2003), 60. Note that the 1926 figure is compromised by categorisation based upon degree of Māori blood; later statistics allow for self-identification.

60 Debi Marshall-Lobb, 'Young, Māori and Growing Up in Palmerston North', a talk presented at Palmerston North Local History Week 2008. Recording on *Manawatū Heritage*, https://manawatuheritage.pncc.govt.nz/item/821da539-386d-4cc7-90ca-96869a99af2c.

61 Pita King, Darrin Hodgetts, Mohi Rua and Mandy Morgan, 'When the Marae Moves into City: Being Māori in Urban Palmerston North', *City and Community* 17, no. 4 (December 2018): 1189–1208.

62 Marshall-Lobb, 'Young, Māori and Growing up in Palmerston North'.

63 Palmerston North City Council, *Palmerston North Māori Community Profile* (Palmerston North: PNCC, November 2011), 25.

64 Ibid.

65 'Matatini — Many Faces', https://www.tematatini.co.nz/.

66 *MS*, 25 February 2005, 1.

67 Ranginui Walker, 'Maori Studies — Ngā Tari Māori', *Te Ara*, https://teara.govt.nz/en/maori-studies-nga-tari-maori/print.

68 Talia Shadwell, *MS,* 21 December 2012.

69 For further information on Māori Studies at the Palmerston North Teachers' College, and the roles of Cliff Whiting, Frank Davis and John Tapiata, in particular, see Chapter 7 of Roger Openshaw, *Between Two Worlds: A History of the Palmerston North College of Education 1956–1996* (Palmerston North: Dunmore Press, 1996).

70 Mason Durie and Meihana Durie, 'Tūturu Pūmau meeting house', *Te Ara*, https://teara.govt.nz/en/photograph/1499/tuturu-pumau-meeting-house.

71 http://www.rangitaane.iwi.nz/page_1.htm.

72 *Te Ao Hou* 47 (June 1964): 32.

73 Mason Durie, 'Durie, John Mason', *Dictionary of New Zealand Biography*, first published in 1998. *Te Ara*, https://teara.govt.nz/en/biographies/4d25/durie-john-mason. There was also a link in this name to the mobile canteen Te Rau Aroha (Kai Truck) that delivered food to the Māori Battalion in the Second World War: https://www.facebook.com/MaoriBattalion/posts/te-rau-aroha-the-mobile-canteen-provided-the-28-with-comforts-in-every-campaign-/269716796375487/.

74 *Te Ao Hou 47* (June 1964): 32.

75 https://manawatuheritage.pncc.govt.nz/item/741ea9e8-7940-4acd-871b-03c80621fa70. For a floor plan and history of the subsequent uses of the hall, see Nicholas Rowell, 'The Māori Battalion Memorial Centre', *MJH* 9 (2013): 76–82 (Palmerston North Heritage Trust Prize for Year 12 History for 2012).

76 *MS,* 31 January 2009, http://www.stuff.co.nz/manawatu-standard/news/15748/18-years-in-the-making.

77 *MS*, 15 April 2010, http://www.stuff.co.nz/manawatu-standard/3579990/School-wins-design-award.

78 Michael Belgrave, *From Empire's Servant to Global Citizen: A History of Massey University* (Auckland: Massey University Press, 2016), 141.

79 Ibid., 334–36.

80 Professor Emeritus Sir Mason Harold Durie KNZM, Citation for Degree of Doctor of Health (Honoris Causa), M Durie 2018-11-30, K-4-9, Massey University Archives.

81 Belgrave, *From Empire's Servant,* 360–61.

82 http://www.massey.ac.nz/massey/about-massey/news/article.cfm?mnarticle_uuid=C2AA4F15-BE01-0964-8207-98124A241D41.

83 Jono Galuszka, 'Rangitaane o Manawatu signs treaty settlement with Crown', *Stuff*, 15 November 2015, https://www.stuff.

co.nz/national/74035296/null.

84 Rangitāne Deed of Settlement, 6.

85 https://www.radionz.co.nz/news/te-manu-korihi/115234/crown-urged-to-stop-rangitane-settlement.

86 https://www.parliament.nz/en/pb/hansard-debates/rhr/document/51HansD_20160318_00000012/rangit%C4%81ne-o-manawatu-claims-settlement-bill-first-reading.

87 Rangitāne Deed of Settlement, 22.

88 https://www.stuff.co.nz/manawatu-standard/news/113725938/palmerston-norths-first-female-mori-councillor-is-remembered#comments (Waana Davis); http://www.stuff.co.nz/manawatu-standard/lifestyle/obituaries/4092527/A-life-of-service-to-community (Yvonne Marshall).

89 Mīhaere blamed his loss of selection as the Labour candidate for the Ruāhine parliamentary seat in 1974 on his support for the urban marae. *MS*, 13 December 1974, 1.

90 Paul Spoonley, ed., *He Pātai? Racial Harmony in Palmerston North* (Palmerston North: PNCC, 1981); Ken Tremaine interviewed by Ian Matheson, 5 January 1992, tape 7, side 2, https://manawatuheritage.pncc.govt.nz/item/d6ef282e-8024-401a-87cf-ef5b70082f06.

91 'Discussion Document for Māori Ward Options', PNCC, https://www.pncc.govt.nz/media/3130212/maori-ward-discussion.pdf.

92 *MS*, 20 May 2018, https://www.stuff.co.nz/national/104055151/palmerston-north-mayor-disappointed-mori-wards-rejected#comments.

93 Ibid.

94 *MS*, 16 May 2018 (Steve Elers), 1–2; https://www.nzherald.co.nz/hawkes-bay-today/news/article.cfm?c_id=1503462&objectid=12055695.

95 http://archive.stats.govt.nz/Census/2013-census/profile-and-summary-reports/quickstats-about-a-place.aspx?request_value=14263&tabname=Culturaldiversity.

96 *Palmerston North Māori Community Profile*, 12.

97 https://www.stuff.co.nz/manawatu-standard/news/117362063/rangitne-invited-to-join-palmerston-north-council-committees.

Te Tānenuiārangi Flag

1 See, for example, *Auckland Star*, 17 June 1901, 5. This article also claims that the flag was given by Sir George Grey to Rangitāne.

2 *MS*, 11 November 1902, 2.

3 *MS*, 26 November 1912, 6.

4 *MS*, 27 January 1907, 4.

03 An environmental history

1 Ross Galbreath, 'Levy, Enoch Bruce', *Dictionary of New Zealand Biography*, first published in 2000. *Te Ara*, https://teara.govt.nz/en/biographies/518/levy-enoch-bruce.

2 *New Zealand Gardener*, 1 January 1948, 317.

3 The complexities of home gardens in the mid-twentieth century is laid out by Helen Leach, 'Exotic Natives and Contrived Wild Gardens: The Twentieth-Century Home Garden' in *Environmental Histories of New Zealand*, ed. Eric Pawson and Tom Brooking (Melbourne: Oxford University Press, 2002), 214–29.

4 E. Bruce Levy, 'The Grasslands of New Zealand 3. Steep Unploughable Forest Land,' *New Zealand Journal of Agriculture* 24 (1922): 147–58. The grasslands revolution is explored fully in Tom Brooking and Eric Pawson, eds, *Seeds of Empire* (London: IB Tauris, 2011). Levy also explained in 'Grasslands' that he was not an 'advocate of the indiscriminate clearing of forest on steep broken country for grassing purposes' (at 147).

5 'A Garden City' [Editorial], *MS*, 23

February 1912, 4. This was a reference to public gardens and not in anticipation of the garden suburbs of the early town-planning movement. For the latter, see Caroline Miller, 'Theory Poorly Practised: The Garden Suburb in New Zealand', *Planning Perspectives* 19 (2004): 37–55.

6 The built environment has its own environmental history, but space considerations and the overall structure of this chapter preclude further treatment of this theme.

7 Urban environmental history is in its infancy in New Zealand, although insightful statements have been made by Eric Pawson: 'On the Edge: Making Urban Places', *Making a New Land: Environmental Histories of New Zealand,* ed. Eric Pawson and Tom Brooking (Dunedin: Otago University Press, 2013), 226–40; and specifically for Christchurch, see Eric Pawson, 'Confronting Nature', *Southern Capital Christchurch: Towards a City Biography,* ed. J. Cookson and G. Dunstall (Christchurch: Canterbury University Press, 2000), 60–84. An urban wetland case study is provided by Katie Pickles, 'The Re-Creation of Bottle Lake: From Site of Discard to Environmental Playground?', *Environment and History* 4 (2003): 419–34. An earlier generation of quasi-environmental histories of Auckland and Christchurch are provided by Ken Cumberland, 'The Essential Nature of Auckland', *Auckland at Full Stretch*, ed. G. W. Bush and C. D. Scott (Auckland: University of Auckland and Auckland City Council, 1977), 17–28, and W. B. Johnston, 'The Place of Canterbury', *Canterbury at the Cross Roads,* ed. R. B. Bedford and A. P. Sturman (Christchurch: New Zealand Geographical Society, 1983), 6–19.

8 Many issues and events have been sacrificed in following this strategy; in particular, the restoration efforts at Pit Park, a former clay pit; the drainage of Awatapu Lagoon; efforts to manage the Mangaone Stream; the creation of treed avenues from 1892 that characterise parts of the city; the development of private gardens; and more recent green corridor initiatives and wetland restoration efforts, to list only a few.

9 Norman Whatman, 'Introduction: Landforms in the Manawatu', introduction to George C. Petersen, *Palmerston North: A Centennial History* (Wellington: A. H. & A. W. Reed for PNCC, 1973), 3–8.

10 Richard Heerdegen, 'Landforms of the Manawatu', *Landforms of New Zealand*, ed. Jane Soons and Michael Selby (Auckland: Longman Paul, 1982), 222–27.

11 Alistair Clement, Craig Sloss and Ian Fuller, 'Late Quaternary Geomorphology of the Manawatu Coastal Plain, North Island, New Zealand', *Quaternary International* 221 (2010): 36–45.

12 Robert Billens and Leslie Verry, *From Swamp to City: Official Souvenir 1887–1937: Commemorating the Diamond Jubilee of the City* (Palmerston North: K & B Print, 1937), 8. The term 'clearing' referred to land that was covered by light scrub, flax, fern and mānuka — it was not bare of vegetation: see Susan Forbes, *Archeological Survey Upper Manawatu River* (Porirua: Kotuku Consultancy, prepared for Te Kaunihera Kaumatua o Rangitane ki Manawatu and PNCC, 1997); Petersen, *Palmerston North*; G. C. Petersen, *The Pioneering Days of Palmerston North* (Levin: Kerslake, Billens and Humphrey, 1952), 24, puts the clearing at 900 acres (364 hectares). The smaller estimate seems to be more accurate.

13 Petersen, *Palmerston North*, 55.

14 Petersen in his centennial history was reluctant to accept that Māori could have used fires to produce the clearing, noting that 'there is nothing to explain the origins of the clearing which was too extensive to have been made by the stone implements of the Maoris [*sic*]. It may have been the result of an ancient conflagration': Petersen, *Palmerston North*, 53. He appears to have changed his opinion, for two decades earlier he had written of the

clearing that 'at one time fire had swept the clearing and probably enlarged it, for scattered about were the remains of large tree stumps': Petersen, *The Pioneering Days,* 24. The simplest explanation of Māori burning seems convincing enough.

15 T. L. Buick, *Old Manawatu, or The Wild Days of the West* (Palmerston North: Buick and Young, 1903; Christchurch: Capper Press, reprint, 1975), 326.

16 *Te Koha o Te Whenua / Karaka Grove* (information booklet) (Palmerston North: Massey University, 1988).

17 Petersen, *Palmerston North,* 34.

18 W. Moffat, 'A Paper on the Rangitane Tribe', Palmerston North Polynesian Discussion Group. n.d. Cyclostyled. Author's collection.

19 L. L. Pownall, 'The Origins of Towns in New Zealand', *New Zealand Geographer* 12 (1956): 173–88. The 10 types identified by Pownall included trading settlements, colonial settlements, mining settlements, accommodation settlements, whaling settlements, estate settlements, port settlements, military settlements, missionary settlements and spa settlements. To this might be added hydro and forestry towns. Pownall suggested that trading, colonial, mining or accommodation functions accounted for the origins of about 75 per cent of New Zealand towns.

20 Ibid., 175.

21 Some street or road names have changed over time. For ease of location, I have generally given the original and current name. Where I am endeavouring to pinpoint a location for present-day readers, I have typically made use of the current names.

22 Pownall, 'The Origins of Towns', 186.

23 Ian Matheson, 'Notes on Early Sawmills of Palmerston North District'. Typescript, 1971. Ian Matheson Papers, Series 2 'S' Sawmills, Box 39, IMCA.

24 Buick, *Old Manawatu*, 326. In 1878 this was purchased by Richter Nannestad and Co. See Val A. Burr, *Mosquitoes and Sawdust: A History of Scandinavians in Early Palmerston North and Surrounding Districts (Scandia II)* (Palmerston North: Scandinavian Club of Manawatu, 1995), 132.

25 Presumably having cut out their forests.

26 Rollo Arnold, 'The Virgin Forest Harvest and the Development of Colonial New Zealand', *New Zealand Geographer* 32 (1976): 105–26.

27 Burr, *Mosquitoes and Sawdust*. This volume includes a detailed account of the business activities of Richter Nannestad and Co.

28 The sawmillers had only a limited impact, with much of the nearby forest being felled and burnt for pastoral development. See Catherine Knight, 'Creating a Pastoral World Through Fire: The Case of the Manawatu, 1870–1910', *Journal of New Zealand Studies* NS16 (2013): 100–20.

29 His home, 'Totaranui', built in around 1875, was gifted to the city in 1970, and is now situated by Te Manawa. It stands as a reminder of the early sawmilling era, and is reputedly the oldest building in Palmerston North.

30 Burr, *Mosquitoes and Sawdust,* 132.

31 Matheson suggests financial difficulties prompted the sale, but Burr paints a more comprehensive picture of the firm's sawmills following the forest frontier, while it simultaneously developed and sold the cutover forest land. Richter Nannestad and Co. are comparatively rare in the New Zealand context as a sawmilling firm that owned its forests' land, as opposed to just having cutting rights, and subsequently developed the land for sale as farmland.

32 The Manawatū River features as a chapter in David Young, *Rivers: New Zealand's Shared Legacy* (Auckland: Random House, 2013). See also Catherine Knight, *New Zealand's Rivers: An Environmental History* (Christchurch: Canterbury University Press, 2016). See, for recent history, Jill White, 'An Uneasy Relationship:

Palmerston North City and the Manawatu River, 1941–2006' (MA thesis, Massey University, Palmerston North, 2007).

33 The town did not really begin to straddle the river until the suburban development of Summerhill took place in the 1990s.

34 Hokowhitu Native Reserve. MAI 857 1892/1638 Removal of Restrictions Hokowhitu No. 1 104-1892, Te Tiera Te Panau to Edwin Mitchelson Native Minister, 9 August 1888, Archives New Zealand, Wellington.

35 'Fighting the Manawatu', *MS,* 14 July 1908, 5. William Milverton at Brightwater Terrace had also constructed a log groyne by 1908: see 'Floods in the Manawatu', *MS,* 7 July 1908, 7. J. O. Batchelar had also earlier created groynes on his side of the river opposite the Esplanade. It is easy to imagine how these piecemeal efforts acted against each other.

36 Groyne was the term for a timber barrier intended to protect part of the riverbank by redirecting the river flow and trapping sediment.

37 *MS*, 26 June 1907, 6. Jickell considered the willows were also partly protecting the riverbank.

38 *MS*, 21 January 1908, 5.

39 'River Damage' [Editorial], *MS*, 10 July 1907, 4. Some 30,000 tonnes of rock were required for armouring the river channel and as part of stream alignment from Anzac Park cliff to the Fitzherbert Bridge in 2014–15 as proof against a 500-year flood: Janine Rankin, 'River Protection Work Continues', *MS*, 2 October 2013, 3.

40 Rivers board legislation dated back to 1884 and provided for the establishment of boards with rating powers and defined areas to construct river protection works. See A. R. Acheson, *River Control and Drainage in New Zealand* (Wellington: Ministry of Works, 1968), 15–17.

41 *MS,* 11 September 1922, 5.

42 Some delays were caused by legal challenges to the classification system that the catchment board sought to introduce: see Michael Roche, *Land and Water* (Wellington: Department of Internal Affairs, 1994), 48–51. For the river control and the Lower Manawatū Scheme more generally, see Knight, *New Zealand's Rivers,* 90–93, and Catherine Knight, *Ravaged Beauty* (Auckland: Dunmore Press, 2014), Chapter 7.

43 Westmont School (compilers), *Destructive Deluge: A Pictorial Coverage of the February Floods 2004* (Palmerston North: Westmont School, 2004). A decision in 1994 to raise the stopbanks in the city to contain a 4500 cu m/sec flood, and also to move the river channel at Fitzroy Bend away from the city, proved vital: John Saunders, '$7 Million Upgrade for City Stopbanks', *MS*, 22 June 1994, 1.

44 Knight, *New Zealand's Rivers*, 236–37.

45 In November 2018 the River Leaders Forum organised the first 'river festival' — to build community connections to the river. Effluent discharges and quantities of sediment eroding into the river had been much reduced. Rangitāne o Manawatū also lifted their 10-year rāhui on swimming in the river 'in acknowledgement of progress made in cleaning up the river': Janine Rankin and Paul Mitchell, 'River Deemed Safe for Swimmers', *MS,* 27 November 2018, 3.

46 Knight, *New Zealand's Rivers,* 237.

47 *The Tribune,* 25 June 2011.

48 'New Name for Steps', *MS,* 28 June 2018, 1. A section of the cliffs was dramatically reshaped into a steep slope as part of a river realignment project, which was part of the bigger project to protect the city from a 500-year flood. Some 30,000 tonnes of rock were used to form a berm to prevent further cliff erosion in the vicinity of Anzac Park: Rankin, 'River Protection Work Continues'.

49 *MS,* 3 May 2018, 1.

50 *MS*, 24 July 2018, 1.

51 John Hannigan, *History of the Manawatu*

River and the Manawatu Catchment Board (Palmerston North: Manawatu Catchment Board and Regional Water Board, 1982).

52 Space limitations preclude separate treatment of the Mangaone Stream.

53 *MT,* 13 April 1881, 2.

54 *MS,* 5 February 1885, 2.

55 *MS,* 7 May 1885, 2; for further on Snelson, see Roger Wigglesworth, 'Snelson, George Mathew and Snelson, Louisa Matilda', *Dictionary of New Zealand Biography*, first published in 1993. *Te Ara*, https://teara.govt.nz/en/biographies/2s34/snelson-george-mathew.

56 In New Zealand, from very early on the word 'creek' was used synonymously with 'stream', and not in its stricter British sense of an inlet running directly into the sea.

57 *MS,* 7 May 1885, 2.

58 Ibid.: a reference to the Manawatu Road Board.

59 *MS,* 3 June 1886, 2.

60 Ibid.

61 Comprised of councillors R. S. Abrahams, G. Hawkins, G. Snelson and L. G. West. 'Local and General News', *Feilding Star,* 29 March 1888, 2. At a Supreme Court trial in Whanganui, damages for £631 were sought for 'defective drainage'; the jury ruled in favour of Mr and Mrs Milverton, but awarded damages of only £178 — 'Borough Councils Beware', *Feilding Star,* 17 July 1888, 3.

62 *MS,* 24 September 1906, 5.

63 *MT,* 4 August 1909, 5.

64 *MS,* 27 January 1915, 2.

65 'Rate Payers Threaten Legal Proceedings', *MT,* 12 February 1927, 8.

66 *MT,* 22 February 1927, 8.

67 Other areas — such as Roy Street, Rongopai Street, St Johns Avenue and Tremaine Avenue — were also affected.

68 PNCC 1/5/2 43:2 Correspondence of Kawau Stream and Mangaone Stream Conferences, Secretary Takaro Progressive Association to City Council, 20 September 1939, IMCA.

69 PNCC 1/5/2 43:2 Correspondence of Kawau Stream and Mangaone Stream Conferences, J. R. Hughes City Engineer to Town Clerk, 28 August 1939, IMCA.

70 PNCC 1/5/2 43:2 Correspondence of Kawau Stream and Mangaone Stream Conferences, A. P. Grant (Public Works), J. R. Hughes (Palmerston North City Council) and L. C. Pickering (Kairanga County) to Town Clerk, 3 June 1940, IMCA.

71 PNCC 1/5/2 43:2 Correspondence of Kawau Stream and Mangaone Stream Conferences, A Petition, 18 December 1944, Archives Central, Feilding.

72 *MS,* 5 August 1972, 3.

73 *MS,* 10 December 1974, 1.

74 *MS,* 23 September 1977, 4.

75 *MS,* 17 July 2007, 3.

76 'Further Stage in Kawau Stream Restoration', *PNCC Newsletter,* 19 June 2006, n.p.

77 Garry O'Neill, 'Gravel Pits of Palmerston North', *MJH* 1 (2005): 69–73, at 70.

78 Cited in O'Neill, 'Gravel Pits of Palmerston North', 70.

79 Pit Park differs — it has now been developed with significant community involvement as a wetland and recreation area. However, from 1904 to the 1950s it was a source of clay for the nearby Hoffman Kiln — see Anna Wallis, 'Pit Park Could Include Wetland and Forest Area', *MS,* 8 November 2003, 6.

80 *MS,* 9 December 1936, 11.

81 Ibid.

82 *MS,* 17 July 1937, 2.

83 *MS,* 26 August 1937, 8.

84 *MS,* 17 May 1938, 8.

85 *MS,* 4 August 1938, 13.

86 In 1950, when Councillor Herb Jensen offered to remove 6000 yards of metal (valued at £300 to £450) and level and

batter the site, the Auditor-General advised the Council against accepting the offer. Memorial Park 1947 — 1956 PNCC 1/6/3 Box 17. City Treasurer to Controller and Auditor General Member's Contracts, 6 September 1950, IMCA.

87 Memorial Schemes (Fitzroy Park) 4/2/3 Box 27. G. F. Hogg and D. C. MacKenzie to Town Clerk Report on Memorial (Fitzroy Park), 6 August 1951, PNCC, IMCA.

88 In many New Zealand towns and cities, the First World War memorial doubled up as a memorial for the Second World War with the addition of extra names. In some places an additional utilitarian — as opposed to commemorative — memorial was constructed; for instance, a hall.

89 Memorial Schemes (Fitzroy Park) 4/2/3 Box 27. Form of Tender, 31 January 1952, PNCC, IMCA.

90 *MS,* 20 October 1952, 5.

91 Ibid.

92 Ibid. In 1954, in an official dedication ceremony, the Governor-General renamed the site, now with its modernist brick ceremonial entrance, 'Memorial Park'. See Tina White, 'First a Gravel Pit Then a Sports Ground', *MS,* 23 July 2011.

93 Reserves Memorial Park War Memorial (1963–1973) 83/14/12 part 1. Superintendent of Reserves to Town Clerk, 16 September 1963, PNCC, IMCA.

94 *MS,* 9 April 1968, 1.

95 Reserves Memorial Park War Memorial (1963–1973) 83/14/12 part 1. J. W. Bolton Director of Reserves to Town Clerk Re: War Memorials, 2 May 1968, PNCC, IMCA.

96 Indicative of the saga of the memorial, the newspaper also noted that the Latin inscription contained a mistake 'Palman' instead of 'Palmam': 'Memorial Repairs No Use', *MS,* 24 September 1968, 1.

97 Reserves Memorial Park War Memorial (1963–1973) 83/14/12 part 1. J. W. Bolton Director Reserves to Reserves and Recreation Committee Re: War Memorial Repairs Fitzroy Park, 4 September 1968, PNCC, IMCA.

98 *The Tribune*, 10 June 1973, 1; 2 September 1973, 3. Ironically, in noting that the memorial was to be scrapped, *The Tribune* mistakenly described it as 'the World War I obelisk'.

99 Paul Mitchell, 'Union: Still Too Many Worker Deaths', *MS,* 29 April 2016, 2. A plaque to former Council of Trade Unions President Helen Kelly was added in 2017: see Richard Mays, 'Kelly Honoured in City', *MS,* 29 April 2017, 2. In 1904 railway employee George Evans was killed in a shunting accident in the pit: see 'Gravel Pit Victim's Story Finally Told', *MS,* 28 April 2018, 3.

100 The name of the College Street and Kent Terrace lagoon has been lost. Hokowhitu Lagoon was sometimes known to Māori as Ruāhine Lagoon: Garry O'Neill, *Hokowhitu: The Story of Settlement and Development* (Palmerston North: Palmerston North Historical Society, 2012), 85.

101 O'Neill, *Hokowhitu,* 85.

102 Awapuni Lagoon was also an important source of eels, and of fruit from the surrounding karaka trees: see Moffat, 'A Paper on the Rangitane Tribe.'

103 In April of 1901 Jacob Nannestad wrote to the Colonial Secretary seeking sanctuary status for Hokowhitu Lagoon for the preservation of native birds, although he included swans. A petition signed by Nannestad, Richter and 10 others reiterating the request followed in November. The Wellington Acclimatisation Society supported the request. AAC W3179 46/29/52 Wildlife Service — Sanctuaries — Lake Hokowhitu or Te Ngutu Lagoon 1901–1962, Archives New Zealand, Wellington. The reserve was gazetted the following year: 'Acclimatisation Society', *MS,* 19 December 1902, 2.

104 *MS,* 16 July 1907, 4.

105 *MS,* 26 May 1904, 5.

106 Of particular concern was the 8½-foot (2.55-metre) fall of the land over 34 chains (680 metres) from the riverbank to Te Ngutu Lagoon. If the Manawatū River cut back to this point it was feared the river would change course through the suburb: see 'Flood Possibilities', *MS,* 6 July 1907, 4.

107 *MT,* 5 August 1916, 5. Regarded at the time as the largest since 1902.

108 *MT,* 16 June 1920, 5.

109 *MT,* 17 November 1920, 5. A Supreme Court judgment in 1905 had proven that Strang had title to the Hokowhitu Lagoon: see 'Wellington Supreme Court Palmerston Cases', *MS,* 6 March 1905, 5. This court decision caused Harold Mellsop — one of the petitioners who had supported sanctuary status for the lagoon in 1901 and whose section abutted it — to now seek to have the reservation removed 'as far as it affects my property'. AAC W3179 46/29/52 Wildlife Service — Sanctuaries — Lake Hokowhitu or Te Ngutu Lagoon 1901–1962, Harold Mellsop to James Carroll, 25 April 1906, Archives New Zealand, Wellington. The city council purchased the lagoon as a public reserve in 1939. See O'Neill, *Hokowhitu,* 85.

110 *MT,* 15 December 1920, 5. There is some ambiguity herein that previously the name 'Te Ngutu Lagoon' was used interchangeably with Hokowhitu Lagoon. Te Ngutu was also in the 1910s referred to as the 'Upper Main Lagoon' and sometimes the 'Scandia Street Lagoon'; Hokowhitu Lagoon was at times referred to as 'Strang's Lagoon'; and the newspapers refer to 'Hokowhitu lagoons' in the plural, taking in Hokowhitu Lagoon, Te Ngutu Lagoon and the unnamed lagoon at the corner of College Street and Kent Terrace.

111 *MS,* 8 August 1923, 2.

112 *MS,* 19 December 1923, 10.

113 Ibid.

114 By then owned by Mr William Caccia Birch: *MT,* 24 July 1923, 4.

115 *MT,* 18 August 1925, 5.

116 'Palmerston Nth First in N.Z. to Use New Weed Killer', *MT,* 10 October 1961, 6.

117 Reserves Hokowhitu Lagoon (Centennial Lagoon) Maintenance, Development Proposals and use of 1948–1974. 83/12/1/part 1 President Manawatu Golf Club to Town Clerk, 7 August 1950, IMCA.

118 See Bruce Wildblood-Crawford, 'Silent Spring: Re-reading the Agricultural Revolution in New Zealand', *New Zealand Geographer* 62:1 (2006): 65–72.

119 *MS,* 3 October 1961, 12.

120 Some eight weed species were targeted: 'Palmerston Nth First in N.Z. to Use New Weed Killer'. Later, in 1964, one of these species, *Anacharis canadensis,* had disappeared. Curly pond weed was most common along with New Zealand pond weed (*Potamotegon cheesemani*), which, along with the stonewart or tubular green algae, were the three main species. Milfoil weeds had also increased: see 'City Council to Spray Lagoon Soon', *MS,* 10 November 1964, 10. The surface area of the lagoon was 4.8 hectares.

121 See also Wildblood-Crawford, 'Grassland Utopia and the Silent Revolution', 62–75.

122 *MT,* 10 October 1961, 6.

123 *MS,* 3 October 1961, 12.

124 *MS,* 5 December 1962. Unpaginated clipping in Reserves Hokowhitu Lagoon (Centennial Lagoon) Maintenance, Development Proposals and use of 1948–1974. 83/12/1/part 1. Trout were introduced into the lagoon by the Wellington Acclimatisation Society in 1964: see *MS,* 16 November 1964, 12.

125 *MS,* 10 November 1964. Unpaginated clipping in Reserves Hokowhitu Lagoon (Centennial Lagoon) Maintenance, Development Proposals and use of 1948–1974. 83/12/1/part 1. Spraying continued annually into the 1970s, its timing being determined by the water temperature in the lagoon — 63° Fahrenheit (17.2°C)

being required: *MS,* 8 December 1976, 1.

126 Reserves Hokowhitu Lagoon (Centennial Lagoon) Maintenance, Development Proposals and use of 1948–1974. 83/12/1/part 1, W. S. Eatwell and seven residents of Montgomery Terrace to Town Clerk, 15 September 1969, IMCA.

127 Reserves Hokowhitu Lagoon (Centennial Lagoon) Maintenance, Development Proposals and use of 1948–1974. 83/12/1/part 1, J. C. Watt Deputy City engineer to Town Clerk Re: Centennial Lake — Request for improvements, 16 September 1969, IMCA.

128 The Chalet was built in 1962 by the council as a tea kiosk and storage space for canoes used on the lagoon.

129 Reserves Hokowhitu Lagoon (Centennial Lagoon) Maintenance, Development Proposals and use of 1948–1974. 83/12/1/part 1. G. W. Johansen City Engineer to Chairman Services Committee, 31 March 1970, IMCA.

130 Not until 2003 was a further desilting of the lagoon undertaken in order to reduce the smell brought on by low water levels in the previous summer: *MS,* 27 September 2003, 8.

131 *MS,* 1 February 1973, 1.

132 *MS,* 10 May 1983, 3.

133 *The Guardian*, 24 November 1987. Unpaginated clipping in Reserves Hokowhitu Lagoon (Centennial Lagoon) Maintenance, Development Proposals and use of 1975–1990. 83/12/1/part 2, IMCA.

134 *MS,* 26 May 2014, 3.

135 The alternative water sources identified included diverting water from stormwater channels, water from the golf club bore, drawing water from Manawatū River or drilling a second bore: see *MS,* 4 October 2014, 1.

136 Ibid.

137 *MS*, 4 December 2014, 4.

138 Reserves Hokowhitu Lagoon (Centennial Lagoon) Maintenance, Development Proposals and use of 1948–1974. 83/12/1/part 1. M. R. Jensen Public Relations Officer to Town Clerk, 2 September 1964, IMCA. Work on a jetty began in December 1964, and seating was installed in 1965: see 'Seats Installed for Lagoon', *MS*, 8 February 1965, 12.

139 This plan echoed some of the ideas put forward by local architect Peter Barter in 1972. Barter's plan was partly an alternative response to a proposed river weir in the Manawatū River, a financially prohibitive option, and was generated by his attendance at a powerboat racing event on the lagoon in 1971: see 'An Exciting Lagoon Development Planned', *Tribune*, 21 May 1972, 1. Powerboat racing took place on several occasions, but was administratively difficult to manage (involving the Marine Department) and unpopular with neighbours, so it ceased in 1975.

140 Reserves Hokowhitu Lagoon (Centennial Lagoon) Maintenance, Development Proposals and use of 1975–1990. 83/12/1/part 2. A. C. Jolley Centennial Lagoon Project Committee to Mayor and City Councillors, 18 August 1975, IMCA.

141 Reserves Hokowhitu Lagoon (Centennial Lagoon) Maintenance, Development Proposals and use of 1975–1990. 83/12/1/part 2. Rosemary Baragwanath and others to Reserves and Parks Committee [undated, but late November 1975], IMCA.

142 The results of the questionnaire, which had an 80 per cent response rate, indicated that residents generally considered the lagoon as a pleasant place, but favoured some form of change, mostly tree-planting and the provision of toilet and picnicking facilities. Reserves Hokowhitu Lagoon (Centennial Lagoon) Maintenance, Development Proposals and use of 1975–1990. 83/12/1/part 2. *Centennial Lagoon Survey March 1976,* IMCA.

143 *MS,* 25 May 1976, 3.

144 Peter Inder and Dick Rawstron, *'Five*

Thirty Wednesday': A History of the Rotary Club of Terrace End 1958–1998 (Palmerston North: Terrace End Rotary Club, 1998), 39–42.

145 Today the lagoon area perhaps resembles something closer to the amenity scheme than the more naturalistic landscape hopes of the protesters.

146 *MT*, 13 March 1922, 4.

147 Wellington Reserves Act 1876, s 5 and sch 4.

148 Further Acts of Parliament followed in 1890, 1901 and 1922. The 1890 Act also clarified that land originally intended to be used as roads was to be treated as a part of the reserve. The 1901 Act exempted the council from some of the leasing provisions of the Municipal Corporations Act 1900. The Palmerston North Reserves Act 1922 repealed the previous legislation to enable the council greater flexibility in leasing arrangements, particularly over expending revenue on reserves other than from the reserve from where the lease money was raised. It also gave the council powers to raise loans for fencing, planting and improvement of reserves.

149 This section concentrates on the Esplanade proper, rather than the remainder of the reserve that becomes Ongley Park and the associated sports grounds. On this, see Chapter 8. See also Garry O'Neill, *The West End of Palmerston North* (Palmerston North: self-published, 2018).

150 *MT*, 3 October 1921, 4; O'Neill, *The West End*.

151 D. E. Aldos, 'Native and Exotic Trees of the Esplanade Palmerston North, New Zealand', *Arboricultural Journal* 5 (1981): 291–300.

152 Katherine Raine and John P. Adam, '1860s–1900, Victorian Gardens', *A History of New Zealand Gardening*, ed. Matthew Bradbury (Auckland: Viking Penguin, 1995), 86–126; and Katherine Raine, '1900–1920, Early Twentieth-century Gardens', ibid., 127–34; Michael Roche, 'W. W. Smith and the Transformation of the Ashburton Domain "from a wilderness into a beauty spot", 1894 to 1904', *Studies in Garden History and Designed Landscapes* 36 (2016): 65–77.

153 *MT*, 29 April 1908, 5. Smith's career and credentials are further discussed in: Michael Roche, 'Seeing Scenic New Zealand: W. W. Smith's Eye and The Scenery Preservation Commission 1904–1906', *International Review of Environmental History* 3 (2017): 177–97; and Michael Roche, 'W. W. Smith (1852–1942): "Second to None in the Dominion as a Field Naturalist"', *Journal of New Zealand Studies* 25 (2017): 88–89.

154 *MS*, 20 June 1908, 5.

155 *MT*, 7 December 1910, 4.

156 *MS*, 24 June 1912, 6.

157 The nursery provided the elm trees planted on Cook Street in 1913: *MS*, 16 April 1913, 6; 14 August 1913, 5. Avenue planting also merits separate treatment for the fuller understanding of the environmental history of the city.

158 *MS*, 16 April 1913, 6.

159 *MS*, 6 January 1916, 5.

160 *MT*, 27 September 1916, 5. Black was possibly as much intent on creating a 'native garden' around the remnant bush in the Esplanade as endeavouring to preserve the forest.

161 'Exotic' and 'indigenous' can be tricky terms, in that what today may be termed 'exotic' was a familiar species from home — part of Black's 'indigenous' — while other plants used as ornamentals were not European although were from early on used in landscaping.

162 *MT*, 27 September 1916, 5; *MS*, 6 January 1917, 5. The tree trunks were presumably from the felled blue gums.

163 *MS*, 6 January 1917, 5.

164 *MT*, 6 November 1917, 4. The article continued: 'the brilliant scarlet briar, "Irish Engineer," climbs the live trees and mixes its brilliance with many hued leaves or clothes the bareness of the dead tree

pergola. Great masses of rhodendrons, pink, rose, scarlet and lavender, purple just past their prime, but still magnificent, scatter a shower of falling petals. Tall laburnums wave tassels of pale pink, and sweet scented shrubs, insignificant of flower but wealth of perfumes add sweetness to the air.'

165 The relative inaccessibility of the Esplanade except by foot, in the absence of trams, had attracted some adverse comment in previous years, especially from visitors. The Fitzherbert Avenue entrance to Victoria Drive was closed in the 1980s.

166 *MS,* 10 October 1919, 5. For similar articles, see: 'Our Esplanade', *MT,* 23 September 1923, 6; 'The Beauty of the Esplanade', *MT,* 22 October 1925, 6; 'Esplanade in Spring', *MT,* 22 October 1926, 6.

167 *MT,* 5 August 1922, 4.

168 *MS,* 1 November 1922, 15.

169 *MT,* 20 July 1926, 6.

170 *MT,* 11 May 1926, 8.

171 *MT,* 30 July 1927, 4.

172 As part of the New Zealand centennial celebrations in 1940 the city council initially planned an 'electronic fountain' in The Square, but decided instead to construct a winter garden. Under wartime stringencies this was downsized to a glass-house and propagation shed. Permits were obtained for the importing of construction steel from Australia, and glass and putty (2.03 tonnes of the latter) from the United Kingdom. This became the begonia house. PNCC 83/13/5 Reserves — Centennial Memorial Winter Gardens Esplanade [Peter Black Conservatory] 1939–1966, IMCA.

173 By ending the account in 1940, the opening of the Dugald MacKenzie Rose Garden in 1965 and the national rose trial garden (from 1970) escape attention; 'Rose City' was once one of the branding names for the city.

174 *MT,* 2 March 1927, supplement, 10.

175 AWH/1/5: Travel Diary: Australia and Java, 3 Nov 1927–15 March 1928, 267. Library, Kew Gardens, London.

176 As illustrated for the Brisbane River: Margaret Cook, 'A River with a City Problem, not a City with a River Problem: Brisbane and Its Flood-Prone River', *Environment and History* 24 (2018): 469–96.

Horticulturalists of Palmerston North

1 Information in this section is based on A. M. Hale, *Pioneer Nurserymen of New Zealand* (Wellington: Reed, 1955).

04 Building the city

1 This name for the municipality is used throughout the chapter, even though in the early years of the settlement it was known simply as 'Palmerston'.

2 'Manawatu', *New Zealand Spectator and Cook's Strait Guardian*, 11 June 1864, 6.

3 Jock M. McEwen, *Rangitāne: A Tribal History* (Auckland: Heinemann Reed, 1986), 148.

4 On the latter point, cf. Tony Ballantyne, 'On Place, Space and Mobility in Nineteenth-Century New Zealand', *NZJH* 45, no. 1 (2011): 50–70, at 63–64. On local tracks, see S. Percy Smith, *History and Traditions of the Maoris of the West Coast North Island of New Zealand Prior to 1840* (New Plymouth: Polynesian Society, 1910), 14.

5 G. C. Petersen, *Palmerston North: A Centennial History* (Wellington: A. H. & A. W. Reed for PNCC, 1973), 59.

6 The streets mentioned in this paragraph received their names subsequent to the survey.

7 Petersen, *Palmerston North*, 62.

8 Ibid., 58–59; Richard Mildon, *Kairanga: More Than One Hundred Years* (Waikanae: Heritage Press, 1989), 10–11, 86.

9 *EP,* 23 October 1866, 4; Ian Matheson, *Council and Community: 125 Years of Local*

Government in Palmerston North 1877–2002 (Palmerston North: Palmerston North City Library for PNCC, 2003), 7; Richard Mildon, *The People and the Land: Kairanga: An Alternative and Critical Look Into the Origins of a Manawatu Rural District* (Palmerston North: self-published, 2002), 138.

10 John Cookson, 'How British? Local Government in New Zealand to c.1930', *NZJH* 41, no. 2 (2007): 143–60, at 152.

11 *MT*, 11 July 1877, 2. For the situation in Fitzherbert, cf. 'General News', *NZT*, 9 April 1877, 2.

12 Mildon, *Kairanga*, 21, 23, 27, 159, 287.

13 T. L. Buick, *Old Manawatu, or, The Wild Days of the West* (Palmerston North: Buick and Young, 1903), 307–8; Petersen, *Palmerston North*, 70; cf. Garry O'Neill, *The West End of Palmerston North: Awapuni, Riverdale, Manawatu o Rangitane* (Palmerston North: self-published, 2018), 20; Matheson, *Council and Community*, 14; B. G. R. Saunders, *The South of the North: Manawatu and Its Neighbours* (Palmerston North: Massey University Geography Programme, 2000), 141.

14 'The Manawatu Land Sale', *Wellington Independent*, 10 November 1866, 4; 'Palmerston North', *NZM*, 19 August 1887, 14; 'Country News', *NZM*, 27 April 1888, 24; 'Up the Wellington-Manawatu Line', *NZT*, 9 January 1891, 4; cf. Clyde Griffen, 'Towards an Urban Social History for New Zealand', *NZJH* 20 (1986): 111–31, at 118; David Hamer, 'Towns in Nineteenth-Century New Zealand', *NZJH* 13 (1979): 5–24, at 8.

15 *MT*, 21 September 1878, 2; Petersen, *Palmerston North*, 68.

16 'Palmerston North Borough Council', *MT*, 9 January 1878; *MS*, 4 April 1905, 8, advertisements column 6.

17 Leigh Pownall, 'The Origins of New Zealand Towns', *New Zealand Geographer* 12 (1956): 173–88, at 175.

18 Brian Mather, *Lecture Notes 1994: Rangitikei Street*, with supplementary material and photos by Garry O'Neill (Palmerston North: Palmerston North Historical Society, 2011), 15; https://manawatuheritage.pncc.govt.nz/item/47e3a015-3958-4a83-bad7-1767f31ef111/pdf.

19 Cf. Hamer, 'Towns in Nineteenth-Century New Zealand', 12. For the use of the word 'urban' in this sentence, cf. P. J. Gibbons's commentary following Hamer's article, at 21.

20 See *MS*, 17 April 1901, 2.

21 Matheson, *Council and Community*, 28.

22 'Palmerston North Borough Council', *MT*, 9 January 1878, 2.

23 Garry O'Neill, *Terrace End: The Story of Palmerston North's First Suburb* (Palmerston North: Palmerston North Historical Society, 2009), 29–30.

24 The observed patterns in Palmerston North do not entirely fit with the class homogeneity posited for urban centres at this stage of New Zealand history by Griffen, 'Towards an Urban Social History', 127.

25 'Up the Wellington-Manawatu Line', *NZT*, 24 December 1890, 4.

26 Maurice Gilbert, pers. comm., 30 December 1990.

27 Adrian Broad, pers. comm., 29 October 2018.

28 'Protecting the Railway Line', *MS*, 5 March 1914, 6.

29 *MS*, 16 June 1920, 5.

30 'Which Deviation?', *Horowhenua Chronicle*, 23 February 1937, 8.

31 'Railway Deviation', *EP*, 1 March 1937, 10; 9 June 1938, 14; 'Deviation Commences', *MT*, 2 June 1926, 9; Matheson, *Council and Community*, 31.

32 'Soon as Possible', *EP*, 29 August 1945, 6.

33 'Mushroom Villas at Milson Suburb', *MT*, 15 February 1926, 9; Matheson, *Council and Community*, 31.

34 On this pattern in New Zealand towns,

cf. Hamer, 'Towns in Nineteenth-Century New Zealand', 9–10.

35 Matheson, *Council and Community*, 28.

36 PNCC 4/15/1 Folder 12, IMCA.

37 'New Destructor', *MS*, 15 December 1923, 2.

38 Griffen, 'Towards an Urban Social History', 118.

39 Petersen, *Palmerston North*, 99.

40 'Municipal Matters', *MT*, 6 March 1928, 10; Matheson, *Council and Community*, 36; Ben Schrader, *We Call It Home: A History of State Housing in New Zealand* (Auckland: Reed, 2005), 170; Margaret Tate, 'Design for Living: The Savage Crescent Conservation Area', *MJH* 6 (2010): 15–24.

41 Ben Schrader, 'City Planning – Planning Between the World Wars', *Te Ara*, http://www.teara.govt.nz/en/city-planning/page-3; W. B. Johnston, *Traffic in a New Zealand City* (Christchurch: Whitcombe & Tombs Ltd for the Christchurch Regional Planning Authority, 1965), 102; Caroline L. Miller, *The Unsung Profession: A History of the New Zealand Planning Institute 1946–2002* (Wellington: Dunmore Press, 2007), 11–22.

42 For this term, see Cookson, 'How British?', 152.

43 PNCC 4/15/3 Folder 1; Garry O'Neill, *Hokowhitu: The Story of Settlement and Development* (Palmerston North: Palmerston North Historical Society, 2012), 46.

44 Griffen, 'Towards an Urban Social History', 121.

45 PNCC 4/15/3 Folder 1; Matheson, *Council and Community*, 39, 46; cf. O'Neill, *Hokowhitu*, 46.

46 Griffen, 'Towards an Urban Social History', 121–23.

47 Matheson, *Council and Community*, 39.

48 City Development Loan Proposal Stage 1 1969–1972, G. F. Hogg, City Engineer, 27 August 1968, IMCA; Matheson, *Council and Community*, 39; Jill White, 'To Bridge or Not to Bridge . . . ?', *MJH* 12 (2016): 5–16.

49 Janine Rankin, 'Rearguard Action Mounted to Protect the Anzac Cliffs', *MS*, 7 September 2015, https://www.stuff.co.nz/manawatu-standard/news/71801271/.

50 Matheson, *Council and Community*, 56.

51 *PNCC Annual Report 2013–14.*

52 W. B. Sutch, *The Industrial Development of Palmerston North* (Palmerston North: Palmerston North City Corporation, 1971).

53 PNCC Archives, Oral Interview — Ken Tremaine, 2017Au_PNCC-S38_021005, sides 1 and 2.

54 PNCC Archives, Oral Interview — Ken Tremaine, 2017Au_PNCC-S38_021005, side 2; Matheson, *Council and Community*, 50, 68.

55 On this topic, see Leigh Pownall, 'Town and Region: A Comparison of Palmerston North, Wanganui and New Plymouth', *New Zealand Geographer* 9, no. 1 (1953): 1–16, at 14.

56 Ken Tremaine, pers. comm., 1988; Saunders, *The South of the North*, 146.

57 White, 'To Bridge or Not to Bridge . . . ?', 10; Matheson, *Council and Community*, 49; Margaret Tennant, 'The Elwood Mayoralty 1971–1985: Reflections From Oral Histories', *MJH* 14 (2018): 53–61, at 54; https://www.accelerate25.co.nz/distribution-and-transport.html.

58 Matheson, *Council and Community*, 31.

59 For comparisons between Whanganui and Palmerston North as developing market towns and regional centres, see Pownall, 'Town and Region'.

60 Cookson, 'How British?', 152–54; 'The Standard's Anniversary', *MS*, 29 November 1909, 5.

61 Cookson, ibid.; 'Local and General', *Wanganui Chronicle*, 17 July 1877, 2; 'Borough Loan Question', *MS*, 3 March 1885, 2; *MT*, 11 December 1884, 2.

62 'A Progressive Borough', *Wairarapa Daily Times*, 15 August 1889, 2. On the role and importance of 'boosterism', see Hamer, 'Towns in Nineteenth-Century New Zealand', 15–17; also Peter Holland and Bill Mooney, 'Wind and Water: Environmental Learning in Early Colonial New Zealand', *New Zealand Geographer* 62 (2006), 39–49, at 48.

63 'Country News', *NZM*, 2 February 1878, 16; Petersen, *Palmerston North*, 102–4; cf. *EP*, 18 May 1878, 2, Advertisements column 4.

64 'Palmerston North', *NZT*, 9 July 1888, 2; 'Manawatu News', *EP*, 8 August 1889, 2; [leading article], *MS*, 21 May 1884, 2.

65 See, for example, 'Commercial', *MS*, 24 October 1911, 5.

66 Matheson, *Council and Community*, 46, 77; *PNCC Annual Report 2015–16*; *PNCC Annual Report 2016–17*.

67 Petersen, *Palmerston North*, 101.

68 'Palmerston', *Wellington Independent*, 3 May 1872, 3.

69 O'Neill, *Terrace End*, 5.

70 City Development Loan Proposal Stage 1 1969–1972, G. F. Hogg, City Engineer, 27 August 1968.

71 *MT*, 1 September 1880, 3, advertisements column 4; 'Borough Council', *MS*, 5 March 1885, 2; 'Our Manawatu letter', *EP*, 21 March 1888, 4; [leading article], *MS*, 13 December 1904, 4; *MS*, 21 November 1906, 2; Report to Council from Inspector J. W. de Blois, 18 May 1897, PNCC 1/4/2, IMCA; 'Town News', *NZM*, 10 March 1877, 14; 'Our Manawatu letter', *EP*, 12 August 1887, 3; 'Borough Council', *Manawatu Herald*, 9 May 1890, 2; M. H. Holcroft, *The Line of the Road: A History of Manawatu County 1876–1976* (Dunedin: McIndoe for the Manawatu County Council, 1977), 131.

72 'Septic Tanks at Palmerston North', *NZM*, 21 June 1905, 28; 'Palmerston Sewerage System', *MS*, 22 February 1909, 2; Matheson, *Council and Community*, 26, 46.

73 'Palmerston Borough Council', *MT*, 4 October 1879, 2; 'The Rubbish Tip', *MT*, 1 May 1917, 4; 'The Rubbish Tip Again', *MT*, 4 May 1917, 5; 'River Board Meeting', *MS*, 15 June 1917, 2; 'Disposal of Refuse', *MS*, 7 February 1918, 5; 'New Destructor', *MS*, 15 December 1923, 2; 'Electric Trucks — A Query', *MT*, 26 July 1924, 6; 'A Destructor Saved', *EP*, 29 March 1930, 10; PNCC 4/15/3 Folder 1, IMCA.

74 See Chapter 1.

75 Matheson, *Council and Community*, 77.

76 *MT*, 10 October 1877, 2; 'Palmerston County Council', 12 October 1878, 2; 'Abattoirs', *MS*, 30 October 1900, 2; 'A Central Abattoir', *Feilding Star*, 24 October 1901, 2; 'The Abattoir Question', *The Bush Advocate*, 11 January 1902, 3; 'Palmerston Abattoir. Decision of a Public Meeting', *NZT*, 1 March 1902, 7; *The Cyclopedia of New Zealand [Taranaki, Hawke's Bay & Wellington Provincial Districts] Meat Trade*, http://nzetc.victoria.ac.nz/tm/scholarly/tei-Cyc06Cycl.html.

77 O'Neill, *Terrace End*, 62; 'Gas for Palmerston', *MS*, 22 June 1886, 3; 'Palmerston North', *NZT*, 19 February 1889, 2; Petersen, *Palmerston North*, 105; 'Manawatu News', *EP*, 25 February 1889, 2; 'Opening of Palmerston North Gas Works', *NZT*, 26 February 1889, 5; 'Economy in Gas', *EP*, 2 September 1890, 3; Matheson, *Council and Community*, 17, 46, 73; 'New Gas Works', *MS*, 21 December 1923, 5.

78 'Borough Council', *MT*, 8 May 1901, 4; 'Power from the Mangahao River. Palmerston's Lost Opportunity', *MS*, 16 June 1916, 5; 'Hydro Electricity. Bunnythorpe Sub-station', *MT*, 28 April 1925, 5; cf. R. E. Clevely, *Bunnythorpe and District: 1872–1952* (Wellington: Reed, 1953), 42–43; 'Electrical Energy', *MS*, 1 July 1920, 3; O'Neill, *Terrace End*, 65; Engineering Heritage New Zealand, 'Mangahao Power Station', http://www.ipenz.org.nz/heritage/itemdetail.

cfm?itemid=430; 'Electric Power Board', *MT*, 10 July 1923, 8.

79 O'Neill, *Terrace End*, 64–65; 'Palmerston Lives Within Its Means', *MT*, 13 April 1926, 8; 'The March of Progress', *MT*, 2 March 1927, supplement, 19; PNCC 4/15/1 Folder 7, with clippings from *MS*, 29 July 1935; Matheson, *Council and Community*, 22, 73.

80 James Watson, 'How Palmerston North Missed the Tram', *MJH* 10 (2014): 22–32; 'Busses [*sic*] for Palmerston', *MT*, 24 May 1920, 5; 'Which Bus?', *MT*, 29 September 1920, 5; Matheson, *Council and Community*, 45, 73.

81 On the importance of nodality for Palmerston North, see Pownall, 'Town and Region', 10–12, 15. On this phenomenon in New Zealand more generally, see Ballantyne, 'On Place, Space and Mobility', 57, cf. 60–61.

82 *MT*, 30 April 1920, 2; *MS*, 20 May 1922, 5; *Otago Daily Times*, 16 March 2018, https://www.odt.co.nz/news/national/new-route-replace-manawatu-gorge-road; Dorothy Pilkington, 'Refuge for Thousands: The Role of Manawatu After the Hawke's Bay Earthquake', *MJH* 4 (2008): 5–13.

83 *WI*, 25 September 1866, 3; Mildon, *Kairanga*, 84; Petersen, *Palmerston North*, 84; Mildon, *The People and the Land*, 125.

84 For this theme of 'opening up', see Cookson, 'How British?', 155.

85 *Wanganui Herald*, 14 March 1877, 2; 'General News', *NZT*, 9 April 1877, 2; 'Feilding', *NZT*, 14 September 1877, 2; [leading article], *MT*, 11 July 1877, 2; *MT*, 1 August 1877, 2; *MT*, 8 August 1877, 2; *MT*, 14 November 1877, 2; Carl Walrond, 'Roads — Funding Road Construction', *Te Ara*, http://www.TeAra.govt.nz/en/roads/page-5; 'Manawatu County Council', *MT*, 5 November 1881, 2; 'Palmerston North', *NZT*, 31 December 1877, 3; Peter Croad and Bill Dorreen, *The Fitzherbert Bridges, 1877–1987, Palmerston North* (Palmerston North: Rotary Club of Terrace End, 1986), 9, 14, 15; White, 'To Bridge or Not to Bridge . . . ?', 10.

86 Petersen, *Palmerston North*, 70, 76, 87–88; Matheson, *Council and Community*, 18; 'Ramblings by a Tramp', *NZH*, 12 April 1887, 6. For contemporary use of the term 'distributing port', see: *Wanganui Herald*, 2 June 1877, 2; 'Proposed Hutt, Waikanae, and Palmerston North Railway', *MT*, 29 December 1877, 3; 'Wellington-Manawatu Line', *Grey River Argus*, 1 December 1886, 2.

87 Jamie Gray, 'Longburn Inland Port Venture Announced', *NZH*, 13 August 2014, https://www.accelerate25.co.nz/distribution-and-transport.html.

88 'Transpacific Airmen', *NZH*, 13 June 1928, 11; 'Crowd Welcomes the First Aeroplane to Land in Palmerston North', Public Photograph Collection Av 33, *Manawatū Heritage*; 'Manawatu Airport', *Poverty Bay Herald*, 6 June 1930, 4; 'Palmerston Aerodrome', *EP*, 28 November 1931, 6; 'Manawatu Aerodrome', *NZH*, 7 December 1931, 10; 'Southern Cross at Palmerston North', *EP*, 2 February 1933, 13; 'Centre for Air Service', *EP*, 14 June 1937, 15; Matheson, *Council and Community*, 33, 73; 'Completion of First Official Flight in New Service', *Otago Daily Times*, 16 January 1936, 10; Graham Parsons, '"Cleared to Land": Early Days of Aviation in Palmerston North', *MJH* 6 (2010): 5–14.

05 A city at work

1 G. C. Petersen, *Palmerston North: A Centennial History* (Wellington: A. H. & A. W. Reed for PNCC, 1973), 34, 45, 56.

2 R. G. Oliver, 'The Impact of Communications in Manawatu-Kairanga 1874–1916' (MA thesis, Victoria University of Wellington, 1963), 21–22.

3 Val A. Burr, *Mosquitoes and Sawdust: A History of Scandinavians in Early Palmerston North and Surrounding Districts (Scandia II)* (Palmerston North:

Scandinavian Club of Manawatu, 2017 reprint), 29.

4 Report by Arthur Follett Halcombe, Wellington Provincial Secretary in Papers Relating to the Introduction of Scandinavian Immigrants, *AJHR*, 1871, D-3A, 13.

5 Ibid.

6 The standard iteration of the 'colonial helpmeet' argument is Raewyn Dalziel's 'The Colonial Helpmeet: Women's Role and the Vote in Nineteenth-Century New Zealand', *Women in History: Essays on European Women in New Zealand,* eds Barbara Brookes, Charlotte Macdonald and Margaret Tennant (Wellington: Allen & Unwin/Port Nicholson Press, 1986), 55–68. See also James Belich, *Making Peoples: A History of the New Zealanders From Polynesian Settlement to the End of the Nineteenth Century* (Auckland: Allen Lane/The Penguin Press, 1996), 394–97, on the 'sturdy yeowoman'.

7 Descriptors such as 'settler', 'farmer' or 'engineer' could signify many different relationships with the workplace. For discussion of occupation as an indicator of skill, status, social mobility and community, see, for example: Melanie Nolan, 'Constantly on the Move, But Going Nowhere? Work, Community and Social Mobility', *The New Oxford History of New Zealand,* ed. Giselle Byrnes (Melbourne: Oxford University Press, 2009), 363–87; Miles Fairburn, 'Social Mobility and Opportunity in Nineteenth-Century New Zealand', *NZJH* 12, no. 1 (1979): 43–60; Rebecca Lenihan, '"Jocks"-of-all-trades: Genealogical Methods, Occupational Profiles and New Zealand's Scots, 1840–1920', *NZJH* 46, no. 2 (2012): 157–85. Erik Olssen's study based on more than 20 years of research from the well-resourced Caversham study is especially rich in its combination of theoretical sophistication, quantitative data derived from the study, and understandings of the cultures of work. See, for example, Erik Olssen, *Building the New World: Work, Politics and Society in Caversham 1880s–1920s* (Auckland: Auckland University Press, 1995).

8 Nolan, 'Constantly on the Move', 363–67.

9 Tina White, 'The Bushman Was King', *MS*, 7 April 2007, digital edition, https://www.pressreader.com/new-zealand/manawatu-standard/20070407/281560876347114.

10 Ian Matheson, *Council and Community: 125 Years of Local Government in Palmerston North 1877–2002* (Palmerston North: Palmerston North City Library for PNCC, 2003), 12, 20.

11 See Lenihan, '"Jocks"-of-all-trades', 162–64; Miles Fairburn, *The Ideal Society and its Enemies: The Foundations of Modern New Zealand Society 1850–1900* (Auckland: Auckland University Press, 1989), 12, 42.

12 Matheson, *Council and Community*, 17.

13 *MS,* 17 July 1884, 2. A chain is approximately 20 metres, and a yard 0.91 metres.

14 *Statistics of New Zealand*, 1883, 188. To give a sense of what this might purchase in the 1880s, a loaf of bread sold for 6d to 8d, milk for 4d per pint.

15 Petersen, *Palmerston North*, 96. Richter, Nannestad and Jensen Notes by Val Burr used at WEA History Group 15.7.93 by B. Mather. Burr, Val, Series 1 folder 16, Community Archive, IMCA.

16 'Michael Rosanowski, Recollections About His Life As a Boy in Palmerston North' [1956], Rosanowski, Michael, Series 1, Folder 1, IMCA. Rosanowski (c.1876–1968) was the son of a Polish family that settled at Stoney Creek. The amount is lower than that given for labourers in *Statistics of New Zealand*, but it is unclear whether this included board and keep, which was common at the time in many work situations.

17 Roger Wigglesworth, 'Snelson, George Mathew and Snelson, Louisa Matilda', *Dictionary of New Zealand Biography*, first published in 1993. *Te Ara*, https://teara.govt.nz/en/biographies/2s34/snelson-george-mathew.

18 Report of Registrar for Friendly Societies, *AJHR*, 1886, H-01, 1; *Wanganui Herald*, 4 March 1876, 2; *EP*, 27 June 1887, 2; 19 August 1887, 2; *MS*, 12 December 1883, 3.

19 *MT*, 26 March 1883, 2; 26 October 1883, 2.

20 *The Star*, 12 December 1889, 4; *The New Zealand Mail*, 1 August 1890, 33; *Wanganui Chronicle*, 18 August 1888, 2. The Knights of Labour originated in the United States, and its membership extended beyond manual workers to include farmers and small businessmen. The Knights were at their strongest in New Zealand during the 1890s.

21 Erik Olssen, *The Red Feds: Revolutionary Industrial Unionism and the New Zealand Federation of Labour 1908–1913* (Auckland: Oxford University Press, 1988), 88. For further on the flax industry in the Manawatū and nationally, see Zara Jane Burnett, 'Men of Fibre: The New Zealand Flax Industry and Its Workers 1860–1939' (MA thesis, University of Auckland, 2012).

22 Olssen, *The Red Feds*, 89.

23 Tina White, *A History of the Manawatu Club's 135 Years in Palmerston North* (Palmerston North: Manawatu Club, 2019), 5, 17–18, 64.

24 *Census of New Zealand*, 1886, Part V, s. 60, Conjugal Condition by Boroughs.

25 Stevan Eldred-Grigg, *New Zealand Working People 1890–1990* (Palmerston North: Dunmore Press, 1990), 39. See also Rollo Arnold, *New Zealand's Burning: The Settlers' World in the Mid 1880s* (Wellington: Victoria University Press, 1994), 154–55.

26 Charlotte Eliot Warburton, *Changing Days and Changing Ways: Collections and Recollections of Palmerston North and the Manawatu District* (Palmerston North: Keeling and Mundy Print, 1954), 82. See, for example, advertisement *MS*, 5 September 1883, 2.

27 On the history of domestic service in New Zealand, see Charlotte Macdonald, 'Strangers at the Hearth: The Eclipse of Domestic Service in New Zealand Homes, 1830s–1940s', *At Home in New Zealand: History Houses People*, ed. Barbara Brookes (Wellington: Bridget Williams Books, 2000), 41–56.

28 *MT*, 24 November 1885, 3. A 'monthly nurse' was a woman employed to look after mother and baby in the weeks after childbirth.

29 *MT*, 31 May 1883, 3; 9 October 1884, 3.

30 See *MT*, 6 November 1883, 3; *MS*, 2 February 1885, 2.

31 Valerie Burr and Vera Lydia McLennan-Boman, 'Lydia Burr', *The Book of New Zealand Women Ko Kui Ma Te Kaupapa*, ed. Charlotte Macdonald, Merimeri Penfold and Bridget Williams (Wellington: Bridget Williams Books, 1991), 109–11.

32 Jill White, 'Women at Work in the Manawatu Knitting Mills', *MJH* 3 (2007): 20.

33 *New Zealand Post Office Directory*, 1892–93, 590. Emma Belk was Margaret Tennant's great-great-grandmother.

34 See *New Zealand Post Office Directory*, 1902, Pt 1, 699–712; and, more generally, Catherine Bishop, *Women Mean Business: Colonial Businesswomen in New Zealand* (Dunedin: Otago University Press, 2019), 185–94.

35 Wigglesworth, 'Snelson, George, and Snelson, Louisa'.

36 *MS*, 12 May 1885, 3; 20 May 1885, 3.

37 Bishop, *Women Mean Business*, 198.

38 *EP*, 28 August 1894, 2.

39 Jeanine Graham, 'Child Employment in New Zealand', *NZJH* 21, no. 1 (1987): 62–78, at 69. 'Breadwinner' meant earning a wage, not sole breadwinner.

40 *New Zealand Post Office Directory*, 1902, Pt I, 699–712. For a description of businesses around The Square, see G. C. Petersen, *The Pioneering Days of Palmerston North* (Levin: Kerslake, Billens and Humphrey, 1952), 98–102.

41 1898 figure from *NZT*, 16 April 1898, supplement, 2; see also Annual Report, Department of Labour, *AJHR*, 1895, H-06, 15; 1897, H-11 (S2), xxi; 1902, H-11, xvii; 1905 (S1), H-11, xx. Workshops came under the Factories Act if they employed more than three workers.

42 Despite the proliferation, statistics are not comparable over time. The categorisation of occupations has shifted, and, on a local basis, some figures refer to the Palmerston North local government area (which itself changed boundaries), others to the larger Palmerston North urban area, and others again to boundaries determined by government departments, there being differences between the spatial boundaries adopted by the Labour and Statistics Departments, for example. The distribution of the workforce is variously given as a proportion of total population, population over 15, or workforce.

43 Jim Lundy's history of the Hoffman Kiln is especially strong in showing workers' experiences: Jim Lundy with editorial assistance from Dorothy Pilkington and Margaret Tate, *Nine Thousand Bricks a Day: The Hoffman Kiln and the Brickworks of Palmerston North* (Palmerston North: Manawatu Branch of the Historic Places Trust, 2005). Other business-focused histories that shed light on the nature of work within their operations are Julia Millen, *Glaxo: From Joseph Nathan to Glaxo Wellcome: The History of Glaxo in New Zealand* (Auckland: Glaxo Wellcome NZ, 1997); Herbert H. Hammond, *Challenge and Enterprise: Manawatu Co-operative Dairy Company Ltd* (Palmerston North: self-published, 2009). See also Dan Higgins, *Fragments of a Journey as Told to Dorothy Pilkington* (Palmerston North: Higgins Group Ltd, 2008).

44 Peter Crawford, *Labour Force: A Survey of the Growth and Potential of the Labour Force of Palmerston North and Some Future Considerations*, Report No. 25 (Palmerston North: PNCC, 1970), 1, 5, 14.

45 Copies of the reports can be found in PNCC archives 7/5/2.

46 Peter Crawford, *Industrial Employment and Occupational Survey of the Labour Force of Palmerston North 1951–1966*, Report No. 3 (Palmerston North: PNCC, 1968), 4; *Census of New Zealand 1916*, Occupations and Unemployment Grades by Boroughs, 168.

47 Susan M. Shipley, *Women's Employment and Unemployment: A Research Report* (Palmerston North: Massey University, Society for Research on Women, 1982), 58, Appendix H. See also Donna Ferretti, *Palmerston North Economic Base* (Palmerston North: Manawatu Employment Advisory Committee, 1982), 5, 15.

48 Peter Crawford, *Unemployment: A Discussion and Approach to the Unemployment Problem in Palmerston North*, Report No. 44 (Palmerston North: PNCC, 1972), 16–18.

49 Crawford, *Industrial Employment and Occupational Survey*, 1.

50 W. B. Sutch, *The Industrial Development of Palmerston North* (Palmerston North: Palmerston North City Corporation, 1971), 62–4.

51 Ken Tremaine, interviewed by Ian Matheson, 30 December 1993, Tape 1, side 2, https://manawatuheritage.pncc.govt.nz/item/d6ef282e-8024-401a-87cf-ef5b70082f06.

52 Peter Crawford (economic policy adviser PNCC), pers. comm., 23 January 2019. Manufacturing employment has increased since the 2000s, but its proportion is affected by the dominance of other sectors.

53 Figures estimated from *New Zealand Post Office Directory*, 1902, Pt 1, 699–712; *AJHR* 1900, F5, 7; *AJHR*, E.1, 26. A photograph in *The New Zealand Mail*, 27 August 1902, 6, shows 29 railways employees in Palmerston North, but that may not be the full number.

54 Ferretti, *Palmerston North Economic Base*, 31–33.

55 Palmerston North City Council Strategic Planning Unit, *Government Sector Employment Levels in Palmerston North* (Palmerston North: PNCC, 2001), 3.

56 Crawford, *Labour Force*, 4; *Census of New Zealand* 2013, Regional Summary Tables 9 and 10.

57 *New Zealand Core Cities Report: Palmerston North. Competitive Advantage and Distinctiveness Technical Report* (Palmerston North: PNCC, 2014), 15, https://www.pncc.govt.nz/media/2626204/core_cities_report_-_full__2014_.pdf. See also Shipley, *Women's Employment and Unemployment*, 58–59.

58 Peter Crawford, *Maori Population of the Manawatu Region 1956–1986*, Report No. 32 (Palmerston North: PNCC, 1971), 22–23, Ian Matheson Collection 4/1, Box 13, IMCA.

59 Palmerston North City Council, *Sector Profile Defence Industry for Manawatū Region 2016* (Palmerston North: PNCC, 2016), https://www.pncc.govt.nz/media/3129473/defence-sector-profile-2016.pdf [n.p.]. Māori made up 47 per cent of the population of Linton camp when families were included, compared with 16.5 per cent of the city's population as a whole.

60 https://www.pncc.govt.nz/media/1726593/maori-profile-2011-pdf.pdf, 13. This report (at 12) gives a 2006 breakdown of iwi affiliations, with Ngāti Raukawa being the most common (13.7 per cent). Those identifying as Rangitāne comprised 4.8 per cent of the city's Māori population.

61 Palmerston North City Council, *New Zealand Core Cities* (Palmerston North: PNCC, 2014), 28, https://www.pncc.govt.nz/media/2626204/core_cities_report_-_full__2014_.pdf. See also Palmerston North City Council, *Palmerston North Māori Community Profile November 2011* (Palmerston North: PNCC, 2011), https://www.pncc.govt.nz/media/1726593/maori-profile-2011-pdf.pdf.

62 See, for example: A. Grant Anderson, 'The Element of Change in Palmerston North', *New Zealand Geographer* 15, no. 2 (October 1959): 115–29; Brian Mather, 'Lecture Notes: Cuba Street', https://manawatuheritage.pncc.govt.nz/item/57185d37-3352-47bc-8c7f-f40b5c79183d; Brian Mather, 'Lecture Notes 1994: Rangitikei Street, with supplementary notes by Garry O'Neill', https://manawatuheritage.pncc.govt.nz/item/47e3a015-3958-4a83-bad7-1767f31ef111.

63 There were 78 dairy groceries in Palmerston North in 1969: J. B. Mercer, *Palmerston North: A Survey of Dairy-Groceries 1969,* Report No. 16 (Palmerston North: PNCC, 1970), 3. Listings in the 2018 *Yellow Pages* now suggest fewer than 20 remain, even allowing for expanded city boundaries.

64 Palmerston North City Council Town Planning Office, *Commuting to Palmerston North* (Palmerston North: PNCC Town Planning Office, 1970), PNCC Archives, 7/5/2, Box 3; pers. comm. re. the 2013 census from Peter Crawford, PNCC Economic Policy Advisor, 16 April 2019.

65 Other workplaces could equally have been used as examples. Martin Engineering, Robêrt Embroideries, and the Manawatu Knitting Mills, in particular, are all more than 100 years old: see, for example, for Robêrt Embroideries, Tina White, 'Shifts in Time for Family Company', *MS*, 27 August 2011, digital edition, https://www.pressreader.com/new-zealand/manawatu-standard/20110827/281539402659167; and Jill White, 'Women at Work in the Manawatu Knitting Mills', *MJH* 3 (2007): 20–29.

66 'Reliving Longburn', *Spectrum with Jack Perkins*, RNZ National, 13 October 2013, https://www.radionz.co.nz/national/programmes/spectrum/20131013. Other impressions drawn on include Laurie McCallum, 'Longburn Freezing Works', A175/185, Palmerston North Ian Matheson Community Archive Research File; IC&A Act – Strikes –

Cooperative Wholesale Society Ltd, Longburn Freezing Works General File 1972–4, AANL W3580 947 Box 113, Archives New Zealand; *Longburn Freezing Works 1890–1946* (Palmerston North: Longburn Freezing Works Reunion Committee, 2000); *MS*, 26 February 2000, 10–11; Kerry Taylor, 'Longburn Freezing Workers' Singlets', *Te Hao Nui The Great Catch*, ed. Fiona McKergow and Kerry Taylor (Auckland: Random House, 2011), 180–85.

67 McCallum, 'Longburn Freezing Works', 4, 6.

68 *MS*, 26 February 2000, 10; *Longburn Freezing Works*, 33–34.

69 *MS*, 26 February 2000, 10; Toby Boraman, 'Indigeneity, Dissent and Solidarity: Māori and Strikes in the Meat Industry in Aotearoa New Zealand During the Long 1970s', *International Review of Social History* 64, no. 1 (April 2019): 1–35.

70 'Reliving Longburn', *Spectrum*, 13 October 2013.

71 John Muirhead, pers. comm., 19 May 2019.

72 Dick Earle, 'The Longburn Tunnel: Development of a New Freezing Technology in the Manawatū', *Plains Science 3*, ed. V. E. Neall (Palmerston North: Royal Society of New Zealand Manawatū Branch and the Science Centre Inc.), 51–57; Dick and Mary Earle, interviewed by Margaret Tennant, 20 April 2017. I would also like to thank Denis and Dorothy Pilkington for comments on this section.

73 'Longburn Freezing Works', research file, A175/185, IMCA; *MS*, 22 November 1986, 4–5.

74 Gordon Parry, *N.M.A.: The Story of its First 100 Years. The National Mortgage and Agency Company of New Zealand Ltd, 1864–1964* (Dunedin: NMA, 1964), Chapter 11.

75 The chain was based on the moving assembly line processes associated with the motor industry in the United States, but involved the deconstruction of animals rather than the construction of a product – hence 'dis-assembly'. See, for example, Toby Boraman, 'Wildcat Homers, Gamifying Work, and Workplace-Whānau in the Meat Industry: Re-examining the Subversiveness of Informal Resistance', *Journal of Labor and Society* 20 (December 2017): 467–85.

76 Boraman, 'Wildcat Homers', 471–72; Taylor 'Longburn Freezing Workers' Singlets', 183.

77 The quote about Middlemass is from *Committee of Inquiry into the Longburn Freezing Works*, Wellington, 1974, and Hastie from press cutting, *Tribune*, 27 April 1969, AANL W3580 947 Box 113, Archives New Zealand. *MS,* 22 November 1986, 4–5, has interviews with Middlemass and manager Brian Cuff. More generally, see Taylor, 'Longburn Freezing Workers' Singlets', 182–85.

78 Reference to the 'grand old lady of Palmerston North retailing' is made in an article by Richard Trow from *The Dominion Post*, 11 April 2003, A10, Collinson and Cunninghame research file, A175/125, IMCA.

79 Helen B. Laurenson, quoting other works on the history of the department store, *Going Up, Going Down: The Rise and Fall of the Department Store* (Auckland: Auckland University Press, 2005), 1. See also Gail Reekie, *Temptations: Sex, Selling and the Department Store* (Melbourne: Allen & Unwin, 1994); Fiona McKergow, '"Just the Thing": Shopping for Clothes in Palmerston North', *Looking Flash: Clothing in Aotearoa New Zealand,* ed. Bronwyn Labrum, Fiona McKergow and Stephanie Gibson (Auckland: Auckland University Press, 2007), 132–53.

80 Brian Mather, 'Collinson and Cunninghame', Research file A175/125, IMCA. On Collinson, see Dorothy Pilkington, 'Collinson, Leopold Henry', *Dictionary of New Zealand Biography*, first

published 1998. *Te Ara*, https:teara.govt.nz/en/biographies/4c26/collinson-leopold-henry. Mention is also made of Leo and Humphrey Collinson and their Methodist connections in Jill White, 'The Methodist Church and the Early Development of Palmerston North', *MJH* 15 (2019): 29–40.

81 Quoted by Tony Rasmussen, 'Celebrating a Milestone: 100 Years of Santa's Cave', unpublished paper in author's possession, 4. Various papers and memorabilia relating to the store were deposited in Te Manawa in the years after the store's closure.

82 Former staff of Collinson and Cunninghame interviewed by Margaret Tennant, 14 March 2017: Bryan Gaskin, Sylvia Bentley, Chris Blair and Helen Mullinger. Information in this and the following paragraph is based on this group interview, as well as newspaper clippings in Collinson and Cunninghame research file, A175/125, IMCA. For other memories, see https://manawatuheritage.pncc.govt.nz/item/8fcc1418-78d7-4c2a-b1ba-f2679282174f.

83 *MS,* 5 June 1934, 2; *Auckland Star,* 25 October 1927, 6.

84 Tony Rasmussen, pers. comm., 30 May 2019; *MT*, 28 March 1922, 5; Fiona McKergow, 'Through the Shop Window: Claude Dixon's Original and Artistic Window Displays', *MJH* 3 (2007): 5–12.

85 *MT*, 13 April 1926, 2.

86 'Manawatu — Hub of Industry' supplement, *MT*, 12 March 1960, 5.

87 Margaret Berry, quoted by Tina White, 'Integrity, Ideas and Faith', *MS*, 3 November 2007, 2.

88 *The Dominion*, 18 February 1958, 15.

89 *NZ Truth*, 26 August 1926, 1.

90 *The Tribune,* 10 July 1977, 14.

91 Early figures from: *NZ Truth*, 26 August 1926, 1; *MT,* supplement, 12 March 1960, 5; 'Berry Engineering Works Reunion 1988', Series 8, folder 1, IMCA.

92 Quoted in Tina White, 'Integrity, Ideas and Faith', 2.

93 'Berry Engineering Works Reunion 1988', 4.

94 *MT,* supplement, 12 March 1960, 5, shows Mrs P. Walker and Mrs D. Barclay assembling refrigeration components 'under the supervision of the foreman, Mr. K. Bycroft'.

95 Tina White, 'Integrity, Ideas and Faith', 2.

96 On this firm, see http://archivescollection.anu.edu.au/index.php/mauri-brothers-and-thomson-limited.

97 Brian Crews, pers. comm., 27 May 2019. On the 'Cheddarmaster' and 'Curdmaster' collaborations with the Dairy Research Institute, see Sheelagh A. Hewitt, 'The Cheddarmaster', *Plans Science 1,* ed. G. W. Yeates and V. E. Neall (Palmerston North: Royal Society, Manawatu Branch/The Science Centre), 75–82; *The Tribune,* 10 July 1977, 14.

98 *MS,* 31 July 1986, 1.

Tragedy in the shunting yards, 1925

1 For reports on the accident and inquest, see: *MT,* 3 August 1925, 6; *NZH*, 5 August 1925, 8; *EP*, 13 August 1925, 7; *Northern Advocate*, 9 September 1925, 5.

2 *MT*, 3 June 1925, 7; *The Waihi Daily Times*, 4 June 1925, 2.

3 See Special Inquiry into the Work and Conditions at Palmerston North, *AJHR* 1926, D-2 Annexure to Appendix E. Material in this and the following paragraphs is based on evidence recorded on 124–91.

4 *EP*, 2 November 1926, 13. This article contains a detailed description of the proposed Milson deviation, already under way.

5 See, for example, *EP*, 4 April 1936, 8; *The Gisborne Herald*, 23 May 1941, 7; *The Gisborne Herald*, 6 May 1949, 6.

06 Towards a political biography

1 *MS,* 22 November 1934, 2. See also Robert Billens and Leslie Verry, *From Swamp to City: Official Souvenir 1887–1937: Commemorating the Diamond Jubilee of the City* (Palmerston North: K & B Print, 1937), 14.

2 G. C. Petersen, *Palmerston North: A Centennial History* (Wellington: A. H. & A. W. Reed for Palmerston North City Council, 1973), 68; Ian Matheson, *Council and Community: 125 Years of Local Government in Palmerston North 1877–2002* (Palmerston North: Palmerston North City Library for PNCC, 2003), 16; *New Zealand Official Year-Book, 1902* (Wellington: Government Printer, 1902), 211.

3 T. L. Buick, *Old Manawatu, or The Wild Days of the West* (Palmerston North: Buick and Young, 1903; Christchurch: Capper Press, reprint, 1975), 321.

4 G. M. Snelson, Research File A 175/28, IMCA.

5 *MS,* 1 November 1901, 2; G. M. Snelson, Research File A 175/54, IMCA.

6 Roger Wigglesworth, 'Snelson, George Mathew and Snelson, Louisa Matilda', *Dictionary of New Zealand Biography,* first published in 1993. *Te Ara,* https://teara.govt.nz/en/biographies/2s34/snelson-george-mathew.

7 James Belich, *Making Peoples: A History of the New Zealanders From Polynesian Settlement to the End of the Nineteenth Century* (Auckland: Allen Lane/The Penguin Press, 1996), 349.

8 Petersen, *Palmerston North,* 101.

9 Ibid., 102.

10 Election results, Research File A 175/34/1, IMCA.

11 *MT,* 20 August 1879, 2; 23 August 1879, 2. At this time party lines were very loose, and the term 'liberal' was used by many candidates.

12 Election results, Research File A 175/34/1, IMCA; *MT,* 20 December 1883, 2.

13 *MS,* 18 December 1884, 2; 13 October 1884, 2. The term 'Long Depression' refers to an economic downturn that began in the late 1870s and continued until the early 1890s. Historians are divided as to its severity, but there is a general consensus that the economy was significantly affected. James Belich, *Paradise Reforged: A History of the New Zealanders from the 1880s to the Year 2000* (Auckland: Allen Lane/The Penguin Press, 2001), 32–38.

14 *Wanganui Chronicle,* 10 March 1891, 2.

15 *MS,* 30 March 1901, 2, 4.

16 *MT,* 1 November 1901, 2.

17 *MS,* 15 April 1901, 4; 8 May 1901, 3.

18 *MS,* 4 November 1901, 3; *MT,* 11 November 1901, 2.

19 Wigglesworth, 'Snelson, George Mathew and Snelson, Louisa Matilda'; *MT,* 1 November 1901, 2.

20 *NZ Truth,* 23 September 1922, 1; 2 December 1922, 5.

21 *MT,* 25 April 1907, 5. Jim Lundy, *James Alfred Nash 1871–1952: Businessman and Politician, Mayor and Member of Parliament of this City* (Palmerston North: Palmerston North City Library, 2001), 2.

22 Jim Lundy, 'Nash, James Alfred', *Dictionary of New Zealand Biography,* first published in 1998. *Te Ara,* https://teara.govt.nz/en/biographies/4n1/nash-james-alfred. For example: the Terrace End School Committee, the Beautifying Society, and the Chamber of Commerce. Nash was also a dedicated Freemason. J.A. Nash, A 175/28, IMCA.

23 *MS,* 9 November 1907, 3. For further detail see *MT,* 3 September 1907, 5; 4 December 1907, 5; 31 January 1908, 4, 5; 10 March 1908, 4; *MS,* 3 February 1908, 6; 18 April 1908, 5–6; 28 April 1908, 5. See also Ross Galbreath, 'Smith, William Walter', *Dictionary of New Zealand Biography,* first published in 1996. *Te Ara,* https://teara.govt.nz/en/biographies/3s27/smithwilliam-walter. For election results

of 1908 Mayoral Election, see Election Results, A 175/34/1, IMCA.

24 J. A. Nash, A 175/54, IMCA. Election results, A 175/34/1, IMCA.

25 J. A. Nash, A 175/54, IMCA; *MS,* 19 November 2005, 21.

26 Elizabeth Ward, 'For Life and Liberty: The Origins and Early Development of the Reform Party, 1887–1915' (PhD thesis, Massey University, 2019), 197–99. On 10 March 1920, James wrote to Prime Minister William Massey stating he had written articles for the *Manawatu Evening Standard* criticising the record of the Labour Government in Queensland, which had helped James Nash counter the growing appeal of the Labour Party in his 1919 election campaign: letter from E. A. James to W. F. Massey, 10 March 1920, PM9 2 9 r22281271, Archives New Zealand.

27 Lundy, *James Alfred Nash*, 14.

28 Matheson, *Council and Community,* 20.

29 *MS,* 15 August 1914, 5; *MT,* 11 August 1914, 5; *MS,* 25 May 1915, 6.

30 Tim Shoebridge, 'Manawatū's First World War Camps, 1914–1919', *MJH* 9 (2013): 11–21, at 11.

31 *MT,* 1 September 1917, 5.

32 *MS,* 11 August 1914, 7.

33 Matheson, *Council and Community,* 25.

34 Palmerston North Loan Polls 1878–1973, A 175/51, IMCA. For example, on 6 September 1920 ratepayers voted in favour of a loan of £70,000 for roading and drainage, and on 21 August 1922 they voted in favour of a £500,000 loan to establish the power plant owned by the Manawatu–Oroua Electric Power Board: A175/51/1, IMCA.

35 James Watson, 'How Palmerston North Missed the Tram', *MJH* 10 (2014): 22–32.

36 Matheson, *Council and Community,* 27.

37 Karen J. Morgan, '"Power to the People?" The Palmerston North Municipal Electricity Department 1910–1996' (MA thesis, Massey University, Palmerston North, 1996), 15.

38 Palmerston North Loan Polls 1878–1973, A 175/51, IMCA.

39 Morgan, '"Power to the People?"', 21, 25.

40 *MT,* 7 April 1923, 4.

41 Lundy, *James Alfred Nash,* 6.

42 J. W. Clevely, *Manarua Memoirs: A Short History of the Manawatu–Oroua Electric Power Board 1920–1972* (Palmerston North: The Manawatu–Oroua Electric Power Board), 48.

43 James Nash, *Reminiscences,* unpublished typescript, James Nash Series 1, Folder 1, IMCA.

44 *MS,* 14 June 1962, 8.

45 These were 1933, 1935 and 1944. See: Election results, Research file A 175/34/1, IMCA.

46 *MS,* 24 April 1931, 5; 29 April 1931, 4; 2 May 1931, 2.

47 *MS,* 27 April 1931, 7.

48 Bruce Webster, 'The Palmerston North Political Labour Movement, 1916–1935' (BA Hons research exercise, Massey University, Palmerston North, 1980), 53; *MS,* 29 January 1934, 8.

49 Webster, 'The Palmerston North Political Labour Movement', 53–57, has details of the issue and the meeting held to resolve it.

50 *MS,* 23 May 1934, 9. Malcolm McKinnon credits this meeting as possibly influencing a change in government policy: Malcolm McKinnon, *The Broken Decade: Prosperity, Depression and Recovery in New Zealand* (Dunedin: Otago University Press, 2016), 299.

51 *MS,* 30 November 1939, 8.

52 *MS,* 3 November 1939, 6.

53 This was the forerunner to Civil Defence; see Ministry of Internal Affairs, *History of Civil Defence in New Zealand* (Palmerston North: Ministry of Internal Affairs, 1990), 3; *MS,* 1 May 1941, 6.

54 *MS,* 7 January 1942, 6; 9 January 1942, 8.

55 *MS,* 23 September 1947, 3; *MS,* 14 June 1962, 8.
56 Matheson, *Council and Community,* 102.
57 Election results, A 175/34/1, IMCA.
58 *MS,* 29 September 1971, 1.
59 Margaret Tennant, 'The Elwood Mayoralty 1971–1985: Reflections from Oral Histories', *MJH* 14 (2018): 53–61, at 53.
60 Matheson, *Council and Community,* 45.
61 Joyce Dunmore, *The Cobweb: A Torpid Neglect* (Waikanae: Heritage Press, 1992), 185–87. Dunmore's memoir details the sexist behaviour she encountered during her term on council.
62 Tennant in 'The Elwood Mayoralty' notes (at 60) that 'vision' was one of the themes of the oral history interviews she did with Elwood.
63 Ibid., 53.
64 Ibid., 58.
65 Matheson, *Council and Community,* 51.
66 Tennant, 'The Elwood Mayoralty', 59.
67 Ibid., 57–58.
68 Ibid., 58.
69 Ibid., 57.
70 Ibid., 55.
71 *MS,* 21 September 2019, 17.
72 *MS,* 22 June 1985, 2.
73 *MS,* 27 June 1985, 9.
74 *MS,* 28 June 1985, 2.
75 *MS,* 1 July 1985, 1.
76 Matheson, *Council and Community,* 56.
77 *MS,* 13 August 1988, 1; 11 August 1988, 1; 23 August 1988, 1; 15 August 1988, 1.
78 Matheson, *Council and Community,* 56.
79 Jo Myers, 'Quiet Captain Leaves the Team', *MS,* 10 October 1998, 8.
80 Matheson, *Council and Community,* 66.
81 *MS,* 10 August 1988, 3.
82 Jill White, 'To Bridge or Not to Bridge . . . ?', *MJH* 12 (2016): 5–16, at 14.
83 *MS,* 29 September 1992, supplement, 1.
84 *MS,* 8 January 1997, 11.
85 White, 'To Bridge or Not to Bridge . . . ?', 14.
86 *MS,* 16 September 1995, 1.
87 *MS,* 16 October 1995, 1.
88 *MS,* 28 November 1996, 2.
89 White, 'To Bridge or Not to Bridge . . . ?', 14.
90 *MS,* 10 October 1998, 8; 12 October 1998, 1; 9 January 1997, 1.
91 Matheson, *Council and Community,* 69; *MS,* 3 May 2003, 2.
92 Matheson, *Council and Community,* 69.
93 Marianne Tremaine, 'Her Worship the Mayor: Women's Leadership in New Zealand Local Government' (PhD thesis, Massey University, Palmerston North, 2007), 163.
94 Ibid., 166.
95 Ibid., 168.
96 *MS,* 1 December 1998, 1.
97 Tremaine, 'Her Worship the Mayor', 175–81.
98 Matheson, *Council and Community,* 73.
99 Tremaine, 'Her Worship the Mayor', 188–94.
100 Matheson, *Council and Community,* 82; Tremaine, 'Her Worship the Mayor', 198, 207–8.
101 Council Election Results, A175/34/1 Part 3, IMCA.
102 Matheson, *Council and Community,* 82.
103 Ibid., 73.
104 Ibid., 83–85.
105 Merv Hancock, *The First Sixteen Members of Parliament for Palmerston North 1871–2005: Lectures Presented in Association with the Workers' Educational Association (WEA)* (Palmerston North: Manawatu Workers' Educational Association 2005), 11.
106 Alan McRobie, *New Zealand Electoral Atlas* (Wellington: GP Books, 1989), 39.
107 Hancock, *The First Sixteen Members*, 11.
108 McRobie, *New Zealand Electoral Atlas,* 51.

109 Ibid., 55.

110 Len Richardson, 'Parties and Political Change', *The Oxford History of New Zealand,* second edition, ed. G. W. Rice (Auckland: Oxford University Press, 1992), 201–9.

111 Hancock, *The First Sixteen Members,* 90–92.

112 http://www.pncossieclub.co.nz/home; *MT,* 10 December 1927, 5. The Working Men's Club was established in 1884: *MS,* 2 September 1884, 2.

113 B. Symondson, 'Frederick Pirani. M.H.R. Palmerston North, 1893–1902: A Study of his Political Career' (MA thesis, Massey University, Palmerston North, 1977), 19–25; Steven Oliver, 'Pirani, Fredrick', *Dictionary of New Zealand Biography,* 1993. *Te Ara,* https://teara.govt.nz/en/biographies/2p19/pirani-frederick.

114 Hancock, *The First Sixteen Members,* 101.

115 D. A. Hamer, *The New Zealand Liberals: The Years of Power, 1891–1912* (Auckland: Auckland University Press, 1988), 216–18.

116 After the 1905 election, Reform held two North Island seats south of Lake Taupō. After the 1908 election this increased to 10: Hamer, *The New Zealand Liberals,* 185; Ward, 'For Life and Liberty', 116.

117 *EP,* 28 January 1908, 7; *MS,* 12 February 1909, 6; Ward, 'For Life and Liberty', 131–35.

118 *MS,* 22 February 1924, 2.

119 Matheson, *Council and Community,* 94; McRobie, *New Zealand Electoral Atlas,* 87.

120 Hancock, *The First Sixteen Members,* 239–43.

121 Ibid., 239; Neill Atkinson, 'Hodgens, Joseph', *Dictionary of New Zealand Biography. Te Ara,* https://teara.govt.nz/en/biographies/4h31/hodgens-joseph.

122 Mansford declared he would vote against the government but would not caucus with Labour: see *MS,* 2 November 1935, 9.

123 Alaric Bragg, '"The Model Suburb": The Savage Crescent State Housing Precinct, Palmerston North' (BA Hons research exercise, Massey University, Palmerston North, 2004); Margaret Tate, *Palmerston North Heritage Trails: The Savage Crescent Walk* (Palmerston North: PNCC, 2012), https://manawatuheritage.pncc.govt.nz/item/2e7b5497-7214-4fa2-b42b-496518da9518?child=2e7b5497-7214-4fa2-b42b-496518da9518.

124 Wilson was the grandson of James Wilson: see Hancock, *The First Sixteen Members,* 281.

125 Barry Gustafson, *The First 50 Years: A History of the New Zealand National Party* (Auckland: Reed Methuen, 1986), 2–17.

126 Hancock, *The First Sixteen Members,* 314–18.

127 *MS,* 2 November 1949, 8; 25 November 1949, 3; 26 November 1949, 4.

128 *MS,* 1 November 1949, 6; 11 November 1949, 6.

129 Hancock, *The First Sixteen Members,* 323.

130 Ibid., 350–53; Denis Duffy, *Phil Skoglund* (Auckland: Rugby Press, 1983), 15.

131 Hancock, *The First Sixteen Members,* 381–82.

132 Massey University Archives, newspaper clippings, files K-7-2; K-7-3.

133 Hancock, *The First Sixteen Members,* 406–9. The Jaycees were a service club for young men between the ages of 18 and 40. National membership of the organisation peaked at c.6400 in the early 1970s. In 1966 there were 5915 members. https://teara.govt.nz/en/graph/31289/lions-and-jaycees-membership-1944-2006.

134 *MS,* 27 November 1975, 1.

135 *MS,* 12 November 1975, 3; 13 November 1975, 1, 3.

136 *MS,* 23 November 1978, 17.

137 *MS,* 24 November 1978, 2, 15.

138 Hancock, *The First Sixteen Members,* 487–94.

139 *MS,* 30 November 1981, 12.

140 Steve Maharey interviewed by Margaret

Tennant, 7 July 2017, transcript, A175/28 'M', IMCA.

141 Janine Rankin, 'Palmerston North Mayoral Profiles: Grant Smith', *MS*, 4 January 2015, digital edition, https://www.stuff.co.nz/manawatu-standard/news/64642640/palmerston-north-mayoral-profiles-grant-smith.

142 Tremaine, 'Her Worship the Mayor', 59, 158.

143 Tennant, 'The Elwood Mayoralty', 57; *MS*, 21 September 2019, 17. Other high-profile mayors who stood unsuccessfully for Parliament include Gus Mansford in 1935 and 1949. Jono Naylor, who contested the 2014 election as the National Party candidate for Palmerston North, did not win the electorate vote but did enter Parliament as a list MP.

144 Tennant, 'The Elwood Mayoralty', 56–57.

145 Janine Rankin, 'Labour Chooses Four Party Candidates for Palmerston North City Council', *MS*, 22 March 2016, digital edition, https://www.stuff.co.nz/manawatu-standard/news/78100740/labour-chooses-four-party-candidates-for-palmerston-north-city-council.

146 *MS*, 14 October 2019, 1; 22 October 2019, 5.

147 Janine Rankin, 'Palmerston North Keeps Grant Smith as Mayor', *MS*, 12 October 2019, digital edition, https://www.stuff.co.nz/manawatu-standard/news/116513312/palmerston-north-keeps-smith-as-mayor; Janine Rankin, 'Green and Red Colours Intensify', *MS*, 15 October 2019, 11.

148 *MS*, 14 October 2019, 1. Renee Dingwall, born in Sāmoa, also has German, Swedish, Scottish, English and Chinese heritage. Janine Rankin, 'Greens Endorse Two Candidates for Palmerston North City Council', *MS*, 20 June 2019, digital edition, https://www.stuff.co.nz/manawatu-standard/news/113628408/greens-endorse-two-candidates-for-palmerston-north-city-council.

149 Figures for female councillors compiled by Elizabeth Ward. On women's role in politics more generally during this period, see Barbara Brookes, *A History of New Zealand Women* (Wellington: Bridget Williams Books, 2016), 379–414.

150 Hancock, *The First Sixteen Members*, 314–15, 341.

151 *Feilding Star*, 2 November 1901, 2; *MS*, 29 April 1916, 3. Mansford was also involved with St Peter's Anglican Church: *MS*, 25 April 1919, 6.

152 A. G. S. Bradfield, *The Precious Years: Further Stories of the Pioneering Days of Palmerston North and Districts in the Manawatu* (Levin: Kerslake, Billens and Humphrey, 1962), 56–62; Lundy, *James Alfred Nash*, 4.

153 *MS*, 7 July 1938, 8; Matheson, *Council and Community*, 18; Jill White, 'The Methodist Church and the Early Development of Palmerston North', *MJH* 15 (2019): 38–40; *MS*, 31 January 2009.

154 *MS*, 7 July 1938, 8; Matheson, *Council and Community*, 18; Jill White, 'The Methodist Church', 38–40; *MS*, 14 April 1905, 6; *MT*, 11 April 1912, 5; *MS*, 18 April 1912, 3.

155 Janine Rankin, 'Religion Downplayed as an Issue for Council', *MS*, 31 January 2009, digital edition, http://www.stuff.co.nz/manawatu-standard/news/36532/Religion-downplayed-as-issue-for-council. The article noted that in the 2006 census 14 per cent of Palmerston North's population identified as active church-goers. Statistics on turnout at Palmerston North's local elections compiled by Elizabeth Ward.

Mayoresses and consorts of Palmerston North

1 Roger Wigglesworth, 'Snelson, George Mathew and Snelson, Louisa Matilda', *Dictionary of New Zealand Biography*, first published in 1993. *Te Ara*, https://teara.govt.nz/en/biographies/2s34/snelson-george-mathew.

2 *MT,* 29 March 1917, 4.

3 *MT,* 16 December 1919, 4.

4 *MT,* 20 July 1909, 3.

5 *MS,* 23 July 1909, 4.

6 *MS,* 10 March 1910, 5.

7 *MS,* 11 February 1911, 7.

8 *MS,* 16 July 1915, 6.

9 *MT,* 12 November 1918, 4.

10 Brookes, *A History of New Zealand Women,* 308–15.

11 *MS,* 23 July 2010, 3.

12 Pascal Street Community Trust, 'Initiatives', https://www.psct.org.nz/initiatives/.

Julia Wallace and the many facets of politics

1 *Reflections: Palmerston North Girls' High School 1902–2002* (Palmerston North: Palmerston North Girls' High School Centenary Committee, 2002). For further information, see Chapter 7. See also Mary D. Davies, 'Wallace, Julia Nannie', *Dictionary of New Zealand Biography, Te Ara,* https://teara.govt.nz/en/biographies/5w3/wallace-julia-nannie.

2 *MS,* 11 October 1962, 8.

3 *MS,* 15 October 1962, 10.

4 *MS,* 20 January 1988, 2; *The Tribune,* 3 March 1977, 8.

5 *The Tribune,* 6 March 1977, 8; *MS,* 20 January 1988, 2; *Reflections,* 92–93.

6 See, for example, Marilyn Lake, *Getting Equal: The History of Australian Feminism* (Melbourne: Allen & Unwin, 1999), 9–13, 139–42.

7 *MS,* 20 January 1988, 2.

8 *Reflections,* 90.

07 Educating the city

1 Anne Hilson, *Palmerston North City Council Education Policies* (Palmerston North: PNCC, 1995), 5.

2 *EP,* 16 August 1927, 11.

3 The emphasis in this chapter is on patterns of education in the city rather than on developments in education and the curriculum more generally. For further information on national trends, see, for example: Ian McLaren, *Education in a Small Democracy: New Zealand* (London: Routledge and Kegan Paul, 1974); I. Cumming & A. Cumming, *History of State Education in New Zealand 1840–1975* (Wellington: Pitman's Pacific Books, 1976); Roger Openshaw and Ian McKenzie, eds, *Reinterpreting the Educational Past: Essays in the History of New Zealand Education* (Christchurch: NZCER, 1987).

4 *Manawatu Herald,* 25 February 1879, 3.

5 The 1878 *Census of New Zealand,* Part III, 111, shows 87 children aged 5–15 at the public school, with a further 22 attending private schools. Under the 1877 Education Act attendance was required between the ages of seven and 13, but only for those within 2 miles by road of a school, and the Act was not binding on Māori. Other exemptions meant that schooling did not become truly compulsory until the early twentieth century: see Colin McGeorge, 'Childhood's Serious Business: The Long Haul to Full School Attendance', *NZJH* 40, no. 1 (2006): 25–38.

6 Rollo Arnold, 'New Zealand Education 1871–1877: "The Great Leap Forward"', *New Zealand Journal of Educational Studies* 8, no. 2 (1973): 112–31.

7 Ibid., 116–17.

8 Rollo Arnold, *New Zealand's Burning: The Settlers' World in the Mid 1880s* (Wellington: Victoria University Press, 1994), 120.

9 See Education Act 1877, *Statutes of New Zealand,* 1877, No. 21, especially ss 84(1) and 89–90.

10 *The Wanganui Herald,* 24 October 1872, 2; G. C. Petersen, *Palmerston North: A Centennial History* (Wellington: A. H. & A. W. Reed for PNCC, 1973), 119–20.

An unidentified press cutting based on research by Ian Matheson and John Grigg confirms that the first teacher commenced duty in March 1873. 'Palmerston North: Historical newspaper cuttings 1955–77', Pq 993.1 Pal 1952-7, Alexander Turnbull Library, Wellington.

11 *NZT*, 24 July 1917, 7. This number was probably exaggerated, as the deputation was making a case for a separate girls' high school. Former Wanganui Education Board member G. H. Bennett suggested in the deputation that the high number was because there were few large landholdings in the district — and by implication, many smaller farms generating pupils for rural primary schools.

12 Petersen, *Palmerston North*. Dorothy Pilkington suggests that there may have been children who experienced French, German, Gaelic and Māori in their homes (pers. comm., 22 December 2018).

13 A report in *MS*, 26 February 1927, 26, repeated in Petersen, *Palmerston North*, at 121, indicates that the first school structure, a building without windows or chimney, burned down, but newspaper searches have not found any reports of this, despite the extensive reporting of building fires. See also Ian Matheson's historical survey, *Centennial Celebrations: Central Normal School Centenary 1873–1973* (Palmerston North: Offset Publications, 1973), 10.

14 *Wanganui Chronicle*, 13 July 1886, 2.

15 *Wanganui Herald*, 19 October 1880, 2.

16 *MS*, 3 March 1923, 4; *MT*, 1 April 1927, 3.

17 Palmerston North School Committee Minutes, 2 March 1891, Series 1, Box 1, IMCA.

18 *College Street School Palmerston North 1893–1993: Souvenir of Centenary Celebrations October 22nd, 23rd, 24th 1993* (Palmerston North: College Street School, 1993).

19 Reminiscences of Irene Wilton in *Ashhurst School Reunion 1879–2004* [n.d.], 35.

20 Judgement of J. Ongley, 20 December 1983, ABFI W3540, Box 515 34/1/29/12 pt. 4, Archives New Zealand; *MS*, 20 December 1983, 1.

21 Newspaper cutting [1893] pasted at back of Palmerston North School Committee Minute Book 1890–1894, Series 1, Box 1, IMCA.

22 Matheson, *Centennial Celebrations*, 13.

23 *Wanganui Chronicle*, 1 June 1892, 3.

24 See McGeorge, 'Childhood's Serious Business', 25; 'Child Labour 1925–6', H1 35/75, Archives New Zealand.

25 *Horowhenua Chronicle*, 1 November 1930, 5.

26 *MS*, 24 October 1998, cutting with A175/320, Palmerston North City Library Research Files, IMCA.

27 *MT*, 14 April 1923, 5; 11 July 1924, 4; *MS* 24 March 1925, 5.

28 Undated cutting, with Palmerston North Intermediate School Log Book, week of 17–21 February 1941, Series 1, Box 1, IMCA.

29 Unidentified cutting, with Palmerston North Intermediate School Log Book, 4 February 1947, IMCA, Series 1, Box 1. On Whibley, see *Palmerston North Intermediate Normal 50th Jubilee 1991* (Palmerston North: Palmerston North Intermediate Normal, 1991), 3.

30 *MT*, 4 February 1884, 2.

31 Information taken from Nicholas Simmons, *110 Years of Catholic Education in Palmerston North* (Palmerston North: Grant Smith Printing, 1985).

32 See list attributed to Garry Hermansson in Garry O'Neill, *Our Lady of Lourdes Palmerston North: Five Decades* (Palmerston North: OLOL Golden Jubilee Committee, 1999), 4–5.

33 Dorothy Pilkington, 'Accomplishments and Other Educational Advantages: Private Schools in 19th Century Palmerston North and Feilding', *MJH* (2006): 2, 23–31.

34 Ibid., 29; *MS*, 26 May 1908, 5.

35 Dorothy Pilkington, *Carncot — The First Hundred Years* (Palmerston North: Friends of Carncot, 2006), 22, 24, 163, 169. I would like to thank Mrs Pilkington for her expert comments on this paragraph in particular.

36 www.cornerstone.ac.nz/our-school/special-character.

37 Hilson, *Palmerston North City Council Education Policies,* 20, 37.

38 'Suburban Planning — A planning assessment of the provision of education facilities in Palmerston North, City Planning Department 1982', Awatapu Special School Series 19, Folder 2, IMCA.

39 John E. Murray, *Palmerston North High School Historical Survey 1902–1951* (Palmerston North: H. L. Young Print, 1952), 4.

40 Rollo Arnold, 'The Village and the Globe: Aspects of the Social Origins of Schooling in Victorian New Zealand', *Australian and New Zealand History of Education Society Journal* 5, no. 2 (1976): 1–12, at 10.

41 Rory Sweetman, *'Above the City': A History of Otago Boys' High School 1863–2013* (Dunedin: Otago Boys' High School Foundation, 2013), 101.

42 Tom Brooking, *Richard Seddon: King of God's Own: The Life and Times of New Zealand's Longest-Serving Prime Minister* (Auckland: Penguin, 2014), 351, 359.

43 Steven Oliver, 'Pirani, Frederick', *Dictionary of New Zealand Biography*, first published in 1993, updated January 2012. *Te Ara,* https://teara.govt.nz/en/biographies/2p19/pirani-frederick. See also B. Symondson, 'Frederick Pirani M.H.R. Palmerston North, 1893–1902: A study of his political career' (MA thesis, Massey University, Palmerston North, 1977), especially Chapter 10.

44 *MS*, 26 September 1900, 3; Symondson, 'Frederick Pirani, M.H.R.', 195–203; Brooking, *Richard Seddon,* 354.

45 Zelda K. Tucker, 'The Establishment of Public Secondary Education in Palmerston North' (BA Hons research exercise, Massey University, Palmerston North, 1979), 7–8.

46 Symondson, 'Frederick Pirani, M.H.R.', 199–200.

47 For more detail about the 'correspondence, deputations, conferences, lobbying and ambuscades' that led to the emergence of a separate high school, see Bruce Hamilton, *Palmerston North Boys' High School 1902–2001* (Palmerston North: Palmerston North Boys' High School, 2001), 25–27.

48 *Census of New Zealand*, 1901, Table X, 288; 1906, Table X, 332.

49 Hamilton, *Palmerston North Boys' High School*, 24.

50 Unpaginated clipping, *MS*, 3 June 1977, with 'Palmerston North: historical newspaper cuttings [1952–77]', Pq 993.1 Pal 1952–7, Alexander Turnbull Library, Wellington.

51 On these and other personalities, see Hamilton, *Palmerston North Boys' High School.*

52 See, for example, deputation to Minister of Education from Palmerston North and Dannevirke High Schools Boards, *MS*, 17 July 1917, 5.

53 Hamilton, *Palmerston North Boys' High School*, 56.

54 Evidence to Education Commission, *AJHR*, 1912, E-12, 479. Forms 3 and 4 were the equivalent of Years 9 and 10.

55 *Palmerstonian*, May 1918, 41. See also the editorial in that issue of *Palmerstonian*, 6–7. For further on girls' activities in the combined school, see *Reflections: Palmerston North Girls' High School 1902–2002* (Palmerston North: Palmerston North Girls' High School Centenary Committee, 2002), 5–11.

56 *Palmerstonian*, 1918, 25.

57 Hamilton, *Palmerston North Boys' High School*, 83. Such disparities in the size of boys' and girls' school grounds were common in New Zealand, with girls' needs for physical activity being seen as less than boys'.

58 *Reflections,* 13.

59 *Reflections*, 42. Comment from former pupil and teacher M. P. Daphne Eilers.

60 See, for example, Colonel Powles to the 1927 prizegiving, *MT*, 12 December 1927, 10. More generally, see Margaret Tennant, 'Natural Directions: The New Zealand Movement for Sexual Differentiation in Education During the Early Twentieth Century', *Women in History: Essays on European Women in New Zealand*, ed. Barbara Brookes, Charlotte Macdonald and Margaret Tennant (Wellington: Allen & Unwin/Port Nicholson Press, 1986), 87–100.

61 *The Colonist,* 28 January 1920, 3; *MT*, 17 April 1924, 8.

62 *Reflections*, 37.

63 Tucker, 'The Establishment of Public Secondary Education', 28–29.

64 Ibid., 30.

65 Report of Queen Elizabeth College Committee, 9 August 1966, Palmerston North High Schools Board Minutes, 1966, IMCA; Edward Body, 'Gone: A Study of the Demise of Technical High Schools in New Zealand, including a Case Study of the Transition of Palmerston North Technical High School into Queen Elizabeth College' (BA Hons research exercise, Massey University, Palmerston North, 2010), Chapter 3.

66 Body, 'Gone', 25–6.

67 F. E. Conway in *MS*, 19 July 1974, quoted in Body, 'Gone', 32.

68 *Queen Elizabeth College Palmerston North Technical School 90th Jubilee 1996* [n.d.].

69 Body, 'Gone', 36.

70 Palmerston North High Schools Board Minutes, 6 November 1983, IMCA.

71 Gary McCulloch, 'School Zoning, Equity and Freedom: The Case of New Zealand', *Education Policy* 6, no. 2 (1991): 155–68.

72 Correspondence March–November 1974, ABFI W3544 Box 166 35/2, Archives New Zealand.

73 Palmerston North High Schools Board Minute Book 1983–4, IMCA; Hamilton, *Palmerston North Boys' High School*, 326.

74 Hamilton, *Palmerston North Boys' High School*, 325.

75 Correspondence and cuttings, ABFI W3540 Box 515 34/1/29/12 Pt 4, Archives New Zealand.

76 Martin Thrupp, 'School Admissions and the Segregation of School Intakes in New Zealand Cities', *Urban Studies* 44, no. 7 (June 2007): 1393–1404.

77 *MS*, 15 April 2005, 3.

78 *MS*, 21 March 2016, https://www.stuff.co.nz/manawatu-standard/news/78300200.

79 *MS*, 2 December 1998, 2. The Manawatu Polytechnic offered a Bachelor of Nursing degree from 1993 after the 1989 Education Act enabled polytechnics to award degrees. For a useful review of tertiary sector reforms since the late 1980s, see: https://www.tec.govt.nz/assets/Publications-and-others/4a3e011554/A-brief-history-of-Institutes-of-Technology-and-Polytechnics.pdf and https://www.productivity.govt.nz/sites/default/files/nzpc-rn-2016-1-history-of-tertiary-education-reforms.pdf.

80 https://www.twoa.ac.nz/?sc_lang=en.

81 See Roger Openshaw, *Between Two Worlds: A History of the Palmerston North College of Education 1956–1996* (Palmerston North: Dunmore Press, 1996). As the title suggests, in *From Empire's Servant to Global Citizen: A History of Massey University* (Auckland: Massey University Press, 2016), Michael Belgrave also stresses Massey's international links.

82 Belgrave, *From Empire's Servant,* 68–70.

83 Ibid., 71–72.

84 *MT*, 28 July 1926, 6.

85 Tom Brooking makes the point that this circle of people with similar interests proved helpful to English staff wives who knew no one on arrival: T. W. H. Brooking, *Massey: Its Early Years: A History of the Development of Massey Agricultural*

College to 1943 (Palmerston North: Massey University Alumni Association, 1971), 72. Street directories confirm the residential location of Massey staff.

86 *Massey College Calendar*, 1938, 2; 1958, 13.

87 Pers. comm. from Helen Dollery, research assistant for Belgrave, *From Empire's Servant*, 22 November 2018.

88 *Bleat*, July 1939, numbered 2.

89 *MT*, 24 August 1927, 6.

90 Openshaw, *Between Two Worlds*, 28–32. The college later moved to new premises at Hokowhitu.

91 Roger Openshaw, pers. comm., 1 May 2017. See also Openshaw, *Between Two Worlds*, 53.

92 Belgrave, *From Empire's Servant,* 194.

93 Ibid., 204–5; Lucy Marsden, '"Massey Seems to be in His Blood": Sir Alan Stewart and the Development of University Education in Palmerston North', *MJH Commemorative Issue* (2014): 29–37.

94 Council for the Development of University Education in the Manawatu, 11/21/1, Boxes 1–4, IMCA.

95 Merv Hancock, interviewed by Margaret Tennant, 14 July 1999, N-3-3-8, Massey University Archives.

96 Helen Dollery, '"Fools Abroad": The Town–Gown Relationship Between Massey University Students and Palmerston North at Capping Time 1963–1973' (BA Hons research exercise, Massey University, Palmerston North, 2003), 5. This excellent research exercise has a sophisticated analysis of changing public attitudes to student activities around graduation.

97 Adrian Gover, 'Massey University and Palmerston North: An Impact Study of Some Relationships Between University and City' (MA thesis, Massey University, Palmerston North, 1978), 60, 63.

98 Ibid., 123.

99 Palmerston North High Schools Board, Minutes, 16 February 1966, Minute Book 1966–71, IMCA.

100 Gover, 'Massey University and Palmerston North', 85–87.

101 *MS,* 27 October 2018, digital edition, https://www.pressreader.com/new-zealand/manawatu-standard/20181027/281487867340273.

102 Merv Hancock, interviewed by Margaret Tennant, 16 March 1999, 7 April 1999, N-3-3-8, Massey University Archives.

103 https://www.facebook.com/PNCityCouncil/ (posting dated 21 December 2019).

104 Dorothy Pilkington, *Playing On: A History of the Manawatu Youth Orchestra and Manawatu Sinfonia 1987–2011* (Palmerston North: Manawatu Youth Orchestra, 2011), 16.

105 Lucy Marsden, 'Keith Westhead Thomson – Weaving the Strands', *MJH Commemorative Issue* (2014): 53–54; '"Enthusiastic, Talented People": Fifty Years of Drama at Massey University', ibid., 72; Jean Corbin Thomas interviewed by Margaret Tennant, 12 September 2018.

106 Pers. comm., Helen Dollery, 30 November 2018.

107 Dollery, '"Fools Abroad"', 58.

108 Gover, 'Massey University and Palmerston North', 113; Sector Profiles 2012 Manawatu Region, https://www.pncc.govt.nz/media/1978140/education_sector_profile_2012__full_profile_.pdf.pdf, 23, 27.

109 PNCC City Future Unit, *Tertiary Education. A View of Palmerston North* (Palmerston North: PNCC, 2003), 38.

110 *MS,* 16 January 2014, digital edition, www.stuff.co.nz/manawatu-standard/news/9611978/Palmy_folk_a_brainy_lot. See also comments by new Mayor Grant Smith in 2016, *MS*, 27 October 2016, digital edition, https://www.stuff.co.nz/manawatu-standard/news/85781724/palmerston-north-new-zealands-smartest-city.

111 *MS*, 13 September 1993, 1; Hilson,

Palmerston North City Council Education, 5; Palmerston North City Council, *Palmerston North Knowledge City. A View of Palmerston North* (Palmerston North: PNCC, 1999).

'The spaces between'

1 *MS*, 9 December 1915, 5.

2 Simon Johnson, pers. comm., 15– 16 August 2018; Jill White, recounting Tim Forde's memories, 'Whose River Is It, Anyway? Recreation on the Manawatū', *MJH* 13 (2017): 12–13.

3 Val Mills, pers. comm., 30 August 2018.

4 Tina White, pers. comm., 7 January 2019.

5 Mervyn Dykes, *Confessions of a State House Kid* (Palmerston North: self-published, 2015), 81–83.

6 Merv Hancock interviewed by Margaret Tennant, 'A Palmerston North Childhood, 1926–1939', *MJH* 1 (2005): 20–24, at 21, 22.

7 Alan Crews, interviewed by Simon Johnson, 11 July 2017.

Educating downwards

1 https://www.pncc.govt.nz/media/1978140/education_sector_profile_2012__full_profile_.pdf.pdf, 3.

2 John Grigg, *The Last Ripple: A Century of Methodism in the Manawatu* (Palmerston North: self-published, 1972), 54; Frank Hanson, *The Sunday School in New Zealand Methodism*, Wesley Historical Society Proceeding No. 66 (Auckland: Wesley Historical Society, July 1998), http://www.methodist.org.nz/files/docs/wesley%20historical/66%20sunday%20school%20in%20nz.pdf.

3 Information in this paragraph is based on articles and letters in *Maoriland Worker*, 24 November 1920, 8; 14 December 1921, 5; 22 February 1922, 4; *MS*, 18 October 1921, 6.

4 *Maoriland Worker*, 24 November 1921, 8.

5 Information in this paragraph is from Kerry Bethell, '"The Second Frontier of Education": Community-based Preschool Education in Manawatū 1939–1979', *MJH* 14 (2018): 70–79. 'Play Centre' and 'Playcentre' both appear at various times.

6 *MS*, 6 October 1972, 5.

7 https://www.pncc.govt.nz/media/1978140/education_sector_profile_2012__full_profile_.pdf.pdf, 9.

8 *MS*, 3 February 1983, 20.

9 *MS*, 21 September 2013, 3, covers the thirtieth anniversary of Te Āwhina Kōhanga Reo; *MS*, 31 October 2009, 5, the twenty-fifth anniversary of Roslyn's Te Ao Marama.

08 Sport and leisure

1 Geoff Watson, 'An Age of Expansion: The Widening Sporting World in Palmerston North and New Zealand', *New Zealand Between the Wars*, ed. Rachael Bell (Auckland: Massey University Press, 2017), 308–33.

2 *Manawatu Herald*, 15 April 1879, 2.

3 James Belich, *Making Peoples: A History of the New Zealanders from Polynesian Settlement to the End of the Nineteenth Century* (Auckland: Allen Lane/The Penguin Press, 1996), 367–75.

4 Ian Matheson, *Council and Community: 125 Years of Local Government in Palmerston North 1877–2002* (Palmerston North: Palmerston North City Library for PNCC), 12.

5 Palmerston North City Council, *Palmerston North City Heritage Trail* (Palmerston North: PNCC, 2008), 18.

6 Greg Ryan and Geoff Watson, *Sport and the New Zealanders: A History* (Auckland: Auckland University Press, 2018), 33–37.

7 *MT*, 15 December 1877, 3.

8 *MT*, 16 April 1879, 2.

9 'Popular airs' was the contemporary term given to songs of the day. *MS*, 14 January 1885, 3.

10 Dorothy Pilkington, *Playing On: A History of the Manawatu Youth Orchestra and Manawatu Sinfonia 1987–2011* (Palmerston North: Manawatu Youth Orchestra, 2011), 3.

11 Ibid., 3.

12 Ibid., 3–4; *MT*, 16 May 1877, 2.

13 *MT*, 29 September 1877, 2.

14 Pilkington, *Playing On*, 5.

15 *MT*, 16 May, 1877, 2. The *Manawatu Times* reported that the Georgia Minstrels were 'the only real troupe of Negro Minstrels which have ever exhibited in public, all of them being escaped slaves': *MT*, 4 June 1879, 2.

16 Pauline Knuckey, 'Flea Houses and Picture Palaces — Cinema Life Before the Downtown Multiplex', *MJH* 10 (2014): 5–13.

17 *MT*, 23 October 1880, 2; *MT*, 22 June 1881, 2; Clive Akers, *Manawatu Rugby: The First 100 Years* (Palmerston North: Offset, 1986), 17; *Wanganui Herald*, 22 July 1886, 2; Keith Cunningham, *Palmerston North Bowling Club 100 Year 1889–1989: Short History and Centennial Programme* (Palmerston North: Styles Print for Palmerston North Bowling Club, 1989), 13.

18 *Feilding Star*, 20 November 1886, 2. Figures calculated using Reserve Bank Inflation Calendar: https://www.rbnz.govt.nz/monetary-policy/inflation-calculator.

19 T. L. Buick, *Old Manawatu, or The Wild Days of the West* (Palmerston North: Buick and Young, 1903), 405.

20 Manawatu and West Coast Agricultural and Pastoral Association, *An Account of the Proceedings of the Twelfth Annual Meeting of the Manawatu and West Coast Agricultural and Pastoral Association, 30 April 1898* (Palmerston North: Manawatu Daily Times, 1898), 6; Manawatu and West Coast Agricultural and Pastoral Association, *An Account of the Proceedings of the Fourteenth Annual Meeting of the Manawatu and West Coast Agricultural and Pastoral Association, 28 April 1900* (Palmerston North: Hunt and Keeling, 1900), 6.

21 Geoff Watson, 'The Rise and Fall of the Manawatu Sports Association 1894–1900', *MJH* 10 (2014): 69–76.

22 H. A. Seifert, *The First 75 Years of the Manawatu Golf Club* (Palmerston North: Simon Printing Company, 1970), 11–25.

23 *Feilding Star*, 1 April 1896, 2. The Manawatū representative rugby team had played in maroon jerseys prior to 1896, but selected new colours at the request of the New Zealand Rugby Union because Southland, formed earlier, also played in maroon. Clive Akers, *Manawatu Rugby, The First 100 Years, 1886-1986* (Palmerston North: Offset, 1986), 21.

24 Dorothea Joblin, *The Colonial One: Lorna Monckton of Newstead* (Wellington: Whitcombe & Tombs, 1975), 107–14.

25 *EP*, 5 September 1902, 7.

26 Jessica McLean, 'Social Bonding Through Faith: The Catholic Community of Pre-WWI Palmerston North' (Unpublished history exercise, Massey University, Palmerston North, 2012), 1–9.

27 *NZT*, 4 June 1886, 2.

28 Palmerston North City Council, *Palmerston North City Heritage Trail* (Palmerston North: Palmerston North City Council, 2008), 20.

29 Val Mills, *Down at the Baths: The Story of the Palmerston North Municipal Baths 1917–1966* (Palmerston North: self-published, 2017), 1–30.

30 *MS*, 12 July 1905, 5.

31 *New Zealand Official Yearbook* (Wellington: Government Printer, 1902), 211.

32 http://www.regent.co.nz/history-of-the-regent.html.

33 A. G. S. Bradfield, *Forgotten Days: Pioneering Experiences of the Early Citizens of Palmerston North and Settlers of the Manawatu* (Levin: Kerslake, Billens and Humphrey, 1956), 54.

34 A. G. S. Bradfield, *The Precious Years: Further Stories of the Pioneering Days of Palmerston North and Districts of the Manawatu* (Levin: Kerslake, Billens and Humphrey, 1962), 19.

35 Buick, *Old Manawatu,* 369.

36 *MS,* 28 October 1909, 6.

37 'Anti-Rowdy Driving Group Now Active', *Scoop,* 21 February 2002, digital edition, http://www.scoop.co.nz/stories/AK0202/S00039/anti-rowdy-driving-group-now-active.htm.

38 Robin McConnell, 'Māori, the Treaty of Waitangi and Sport: A Critical Analysis', *Sport in New Zealand Society,* ed. Chris Collins (Palmerston North: Dunmore Press, 2000), 227–40, at 228; Brendan Hokowhitu, 'Māori Sport: Pre-colonisation to Today', *Sport in Aotearoa/New Zealand Society,* ed. Chris Collins and Steve Jackson (Auckland: Thomson, 2007), 78–95, at 81.

39 Tina White, 'Who was the Daughter of Peace?', *MS,* 9 April 2016, 9.

40 *MT,* 30 March 1878, 2.

41 *MT,* 21 September 1904, 2.

42 Ben Schrader has noted that this was broadly characteristic of Māori engagement with urban areas in New Zealand by the late nineteenth century: Ben Schrader, *The Big Smoke: New Zealand Cities 1840–1920* (Wellington: Bridget Williams Books, 2016), 202–12.

43 *MS,* 30 March 1910, 6.

44 *MT,* 26 December 1911, 4.

45 Watson, 'An Age of Expansion', 320–22.

46 Ibid., 322.

47 Ibid., 322–24.

48 *Manawatu Heritage,* https://manawatuheritage.pncc.govt.nz/item/a7e629a4-8b36-4671-bc4b-d8cc34fa709b.

49 P. S. Larcomb, J. P. McDavitt and H. Greenwood, *You Must Come and See Us Too! All Railways, Highways, Airways Lead You to Palmerston North: The Model Modern City* (Palmerston North: PNCC, Keeling and Mundy, 1939), n.p.

50 *Manawatu Heritage,* 'Cherry Blossom', https://manawatuheritage.pncc.govt.nz/item/7890306b-66c1-4dce-aeba-35e7564cc476. Dorothy Pilkington, *Heritage Trails: Palmerston North Esplanade Walk* (Palmerston North: PNCC, 1994), 3, 5, 7.

51 *MT,* 15 December 1925, 4.

52 Larcomb, McDavitt and Greenwood, *You Must Come and See Us Too!*, n.p.

53 Watson, 'An Age of Expansion', 324.

54 Allan Batt, *The Big Thrill: Speedway at the Palmerston North Showgrounds 1930–69* (Christchurch: Speedway Classics, 2012), 1–2.

55 Ibid., 11–18.

56 Geoff Watson, *Sporting Foundations of New Zealand Indians: A Fifty Year History of the New Zealand Indian Sports Association* (Wellington: New Zealand Indian Sports Association, 2012), 7–21.

57 Geoff Watson, '"Gentlemen On and Off the Field": The 1924 Chinese Universities Soccer Team in New Zealand', *New Zealand Journal of Asian Studies* 13, no. 2 (2011): 1–17, at 14–16.

58 *MS,* 29 March 2019, digital edition, https://www.stuff.co.nz/manawatu-standard/news/111643849/expanded-federation-league-to-kick-off-next-weekend.

59 *MS,* 7 July 1938, 2; *MT,* 5 July 1938, 5, 8.

60 According to the 1921 census there were 98 Chinese in Palmerston North in 1921, and a further 60 living in Manawatū, Ōroua and Kairanga: *New Zealand Census,* 1921, Pt VI, 'Race', 14–17, 20–21.

61 Pauline Knuckey, 'A Global Province? The Development of a Movie Culture in a Small Provincial City' (MA thesis, Massey University, Palmerston North, 2012), 77.

62 Ibid., 95.

63 Ibid., 113.

64 Philip Fleming, 'Radio Broadcasting in Palmerston North 1924–37' (BA Hons

research exercise, Massey University, Palmerston North, 1980), 35–38.

65 Monte Holcroft, *The Line of the Road: A History of Manawatu County 1876–1976* (Dunedin: John McIndoe, 1977), 167–76.

66 J. V. T. Baker, 'Population', *Encyclopaedia of New Zealand,* vol. 2, ed. A. H. McLintock (Wellington: Government Printer, 1966), 825; Ryan and Watson, *Sport and the New Zealanders,* 195–96.

67 Ian Matheson, *Council and Community: 125 Years of Local Government in Palmerston North 1877–2002* (Palmerston North: Palmerston North City Library for PNCC), 38.

68 Bill Greenwood, 'Sports Tables 512', unpublished Excel worksheet, 2010.

69 P. Crawford, *Participation in Recreation Groups, Clubs and Societies: A Study of Cultural and Social Groupings in Palmerston North in 1968/69,* Palmerston North City Council Town Planning Office Report No. 14 (Palmerston North: PNCC Town Planning Office, November 1969), 3, 16–23.

70 Grant Smith, 'Palmerston North Squash Club: The Golden Early Years', *MJH* 5 (2009): 63–69.

71 I. M. Gurr, *Manawatu Netball Association: The First 60 Years* (Palmerston North: Keeling and Mundy, 1983), 91–93.

72 Palmerston North City Council, *The Opening of the New Public Library, 4th November 1965* (Palmerston North: Palmerston North Printing Company, 1965), https://manawatuheritage.pncc.govt.nz/item/fb61a632-c24d-4b25-84e1-dea14565c368?child=ff71105e-06fe-467b-97e5-5264aee88647; *MS,* 20 May 2017, 19.

73 *Palmerston North's Lido* (Palmerston North: Palmerston North City Council, c.1966).

74 Leanne Croon Hickman, 'Palmerston North Showgrounds History', 2018, *Manawatu Heritage*, https://manawatuheritage.pncc.govt.nz/item/7c9a0c03-5975-4935-a555-8dbe3544077b. At the time of writing the Showgrounds were known as the Central Energy Trust Arena.

75 Grant Rosvall, *Stock-Car Racing: 25 Years at Palmerston North, 1963–1988* (Palmerston North: Manawatu Stock and Saloon Car Club, 1988), 3; Palmerston North City Council, *Palmy Proud* 1 (2018): 17.

76 *MS,* 4 March 1982, 13. See also *Manawatu Heritage*, https://manawatuheritage.pncc.govt.nz/item/d1cd4599-4aee-478f-be4a-ec4e5df44200.

77 The survey found 46 youth groups — mainly Scouts — and 51 cultural groups — including music groups: Crawford, *Participation in Recreation Groups, Clubs and Societies*, 24–25.

78 New Zealand Rugby Museum Souvenir Programme, *Inaugural Exhibition,* 16 April 1969.

79 *MS,* 29 April 1970, 6.

80 *MT,* 13 December 1901, 2.

81 *MT,* 30 June 1904, 2; 7 February 1908, 4; *MS,* 30 March 1922, 4; Fiona McKergow, 'Veteran Curator: Charles Hirtzel and the Manawatu Philosophical Society Museum', *MJH* 5 (2009): 17–22.

82 Fiona McKergow and Kerry Taylor, 'Introduction', *Te Hao Nui: The Great Catch,* ed. Fiona McKergow and Kerry Taylor (Auckland: Random House, 2011), 13–18.

83 *'The Birth of Palmerston North', MS,* 13 March 1971, 3. Frank Davis was married to Waana Davis, who became the first Māori woman elected to the Palmerston North City Council.

84 Cliff Whiting and John Bevan Ford are discussed in more detail in Chapter 2.

85 McKergow and Taylor, 'Introduction', 13–18.

86 http://rugbymuseum.co.nz/about-us/; https://www.temanawa.co.nz/about/.

87 G. C. Petersen, *Palmerston North: A Centennial History* (Wellington: A. H. & A. W. Reed for PNCC, 1973); Holcroft, *The Line of the Road.*

88 Graham Parsons, 'The Choral Societies of Palmerston North', *MJH* 5 (2009): 40–48. The Choral Society went into recess between 1933 and 1945 and 1955 and 1956. Earlier Palmerston North Choral Societies existed in about 1880–83 and 1908–10.

89 There is a website devoted to listing creative people from Palmerston North: http://www.creativegiants.co.nz/view/artist-index/c/. By the end of August 2019 Laura Daniel's anthem on Palmerston North had been viewed more than 44,000 times on YouTube: https://www.youtube.com/watch?v=tf_UPi30aoQ.

90 Mills, *Down at the Baths,* 2–5.

91 Jill White, 'Whose River Is It Anyway? Recreation on the Manawatu', *MJH* 13 (2017): 5–14.

92 Garry O'Neill, *Hokowhitu* (Palmerston North: Palmerston North Historical Society, 2012), 88.

93 Phil Gifford and Armin Lindenberg, *The Lion Brown Kiwi Sports Book* (Auckland: Burnham House, 1985), 72.

94 *Manawatu Guardian,* 9 May 2019, 1–2; 13 June 2019, 3, 5.

95 Palmerston North City Council, 'Huge Numbers on He Ara Kotahi Opening Weekend', 11 June 2019, https://www.pncc.govt.nz/news-events/news/huge-numbers-on-he-ara-kotahi-opening-weekend/?fbclid=IwAR33LgI2l88nDnrOy8E3fP4sA-AjdQf6WEH2kcTCwobX0vnCyB0GDkqqGK4.

96 *Manawatū Heritage*, '"More Than One" Hula Hooping in the Square', https://manawatuheritage.pncc.govt.nz/item/8b0efceb-57db-42fd-b817-5f32b4d3ed41; *Manawatū Heritage*, 'Carnival of the Lake, Palmerston North', https://manawatuheritage.pncc.govt.nz/item/52ab35e4-d4a0-4595-8bf9-73b6d09c6c76.

97 In 2019 the Palmerston North City Council received a Local Government New Zealand Excellence Award for Social Wellbeing for the Festival of Cultures: Palmerston North City Council, 'Festival of Cultures wins National Award', 9 July 2019, https://www.pncc.govt.nz/news-events/media-releases/festival-of-cultures-wins-national-award/.

98 *Manawatu Guardian,* 15 February 2018, 6.

99 'Records Broken and Record Crowds for the Hilux New Zealand Rural Games', https://www.ruralgames.co.nz/records-broken-record-crowds-hilux-new-zealand-rural-games/.

100 Palmerston North City Council, *Palmerston North City Council Ratepayers Newsletter 2019* (Palmerston North: PNCC, 2019), 6–8.

101 Janine Rankin, 'Reservations Explored About the Value of Empty Spaces', *MS,* 29 April 2019, digital edition, https://www.stuff.co.nz/manawatu-standard/news/112269383/reservations-explored-about-the-value-of-empty-spaces.

102 Watson, *Sporting Foundations of New Zealand Indians*, 25–26, 162–65.

103 Debi Marshall-Lobb, 'Young, Māori and Growing Up in Palmerston North', a talk presented at Palmerston North Local History Week 2008. Recording on *Manawatū Heritage*: https://manawatuheritage.pncc.govt.nz/item/821da539-386d-4cc7-90ca-96869a99af2c.

09 An organised city

1 George C. Petersen, *Palmerston North: A Centennial History* (Wellington: A. H. & A. W. Reed for PNCC, 1973), 130–33; *NZT*, 28 November 1877, 2; 2 December 1877, 3; *MT*, 5 December 1877, 2. On the wider context of fires and their effects on new towns and countryside, see Rollo Arnold, *New Zealand's Burning: The Settlers' World in the Mid 1880s* (Wellington: Victoria University Press, 1990).

2 Ben Schrader, *The Big Smoke: New Zealand Cities 1840–1920* (Wellington: Bridget Williams Books, 2016), 51.

3 Ian Matheson, *Council and Community: 125 Years of Local Government in Palmerston North 1877–2002* (Palmerston North: Palmerston North City Library, for PNCC, 2003), 16.

4 *MT*, 4 August 1914, 4.

5 Val A. Burr, *Early Manawatu Scandinavians (Scandia 1)* (Palmerston North: Scandinavian Club of Manawatu Inc, 1995), 68–70.

6 Both quotes are from Peter Lineham, 'The History of the Churches of Palmerston North', typescript of lecture c.1990 in writer's possession, 4, 6. See also Geoffrey Troughton, 'Christianity and Community: Aspects of Religious Life and Attitudes in the Wanganui-Manawatu Region, 1870–1885' (MA thesis, Massey University, Palmerston North, 1995).

7 Lineham, 'The History of the Churches of Palmerston North', 6.

8 Ibid., 7.

9 G. C. Petersen, *The Pioneering Days of Palmerston North* (Levin: Kerslake, Billens and Humphrey, 1952), 39.

10 'Frontier' settlements in New Zealand, as in other empire outposts, were often initially male-dominated, whether for bush-clearing or extractive industries. Within the Scandinavian community, the gender balance was much more even, due to planned immigration. See Burr, *Early Manawatu Scandinavians*.

11 *Wellington Independent*, 4 April 1873, 3.

12 For more on gendered leisure in colonial New Zealand, see Caroline Daley, *Girls and Women, Men and Boys: Gender in Taradale 1886–1930* (Auckland: Auckland University Press, 1999); and Barbara Brookes, Annabel Cooper and Robin Law, eds, *Sites of Gender: Women, Men and Modernity in Southern Dunedin, 1890–1939* (Auckland: Auckland University Press, 2003).

13 Tina White, *A History of the Manawatu Club's 135 Years in Palmerston North* (Palmerston North: Manawatu Club, 2019), 17–20.

14 *Palmerston North Cosmopolitan Club Centennial: A Recorded History of the Club 1889–1989*, 17–18; Steven Oliver, 'Pirani, Frederick', *Dictionary of New Zealand Biography*, first published in 1993. *Te Ara*, https://teara.govt.nz/en/biographies/2p19/pirani-frederick. Pirani was an early member of bodies as diverse as the fire brigade, the Knights of Labour, the A & P Association and the Operatic Society, as well as various public bodies.

15 Dorothy Page, 'Dalrymple, Learmonth White', *Dictionary of New Zealand Biography*, first published in 1990. *Te Ara*, https://teara.govt.nz/en/biographies/1d2/dalrymple-learmonth-white.

16 *Feilding Star*, 29 March 1892, 3; 11 October 1893, 2.

17 *Feilding Star*, 11 October 1893, 2; *Poverty Bay Herald*, 25 May 1895, 2; *NZT*, 12 May 1897, 3.

18 *MT*, 28 May 1920, 5; *Waipa Post*, 21 March 1931, 5.

19 On the All Saints' Church Ladies' Guild, see *MS*, 2 September 1885, 2; and St Peter's Church Ladies' Guild, *MT*, 28 August 1901, 2.

20 For more on this, see Margaret Tennant, *The Fabric of Welfare: Voluntary Organisations, Government and Welfare 1840–2005* (Wellington: Bridget Williams Books, 2007).

21 *MT*, 8 May 1880, 3.

22 For local references to the need for a benevolent society, see: *MT*, 8 October 1881, 2; *MT*, 6 September 1883, 2; *MS*, 17 October 1883, 2.

23 For examples of the Palmerston North Hospital and Charitable Aid Board acting in a welfare capacity rather than in a strictly medical role, see Margaret Tennant, *Paupers and Providers: Charitable Aid in New* Zealand (Wellington: Allen & Unwin/Historical Branch, Department of Internal Affairs, 1989), 71, 79, 95–97.

24 The St John organisation in New Zealand began in 1885, and, at a time before most

hospital services included first-aid outreach and district nursing, had been taken up in many centres by the turn of the century.

25 *MS*, 14 March 1901, 3; Percy Harris, *History of the St John Ambulance Association Manawatu, 1900–1975* (Palmerston North: The Association, 1975), 5.

26 For a description of women's fundraising for this public institution, see Margaret Tennant, 'The End of the Road: The Early Years of the Awapuni Home', *MJH* 12 (2016): 64–73. The DPA Society was active in Palmerston North by 1910 (*MS*, 13 July 1910, 6). The SPCA had a presence before 1905 (*MS*, 14 October 1905, 4), yet experienced lapses in its organisational life over the following 20 years (*MS*, 16 January 1909, 4; *MT*, 23 April 1926, 8).

27 For further information on both the institutional life of the home and its community support, see Elizabeth Ward, '"Such a Work As This": A Case Study of the All Saints' Children's Home, Palmerston North' (MA thesis, Massey University, Palmerston North, 2015).

28 See Chapter 7, ibid., for a discussion of All Saints' children's experiences, largely based on reminiscences.

29 See, for context, James Belich, *Paradise Reforged: A History of the New Zealanders from the 1880s to the Year 2000* (Auckland: Allen Lane/The Penguin Press, 2001), 356–67.

30 *MT*, 15 December 1909, 4.

31 *MS*, 26 June 1914, 2. Girl Peace Scouts constituted a distinctly New Zealand form of girl's Scouting established shortly after Boy Scouting in New Zealand in 1908, and before British Girl Guiding's formal establishment in 1910. On the wider history of Scouts and Guides, see Helen Dollery, 'Making Happy, Healthy, Helpful Citizens: The New Zealand Scouting and Guiding Movements as Promulgators of Active Citizenship, c.1908–1980' (PhD thesis, Massey University, Palmerston North, 2012).

32 As an example of Wellington Queen Carnival press coverage, see *MS*, 20 May 1915, 6.

33 *MS*, 22 May 1915, 6. On the participation of Mayor Nash and his wife, Elizabeth, see Chapter 6.

34 *MS*, 2 June 1915, 6.

35 Simon Johnson, 'The Final Battle', *MJH* 12 (2016): 25–33.

36 The Savage Club was named after its English founder Richard Savage, and had the versatile Dr Arthur Martin as one of its first two presidents: Noel Watts, *Entertaining the Manawatu: The Manawatu Savage Club's Century of Achievement* (Palmerston North: self-published, 2009), 1, 42.

37 *MS*, 2 August 1917, 6; 29 September 1921, 6; *MT*, 30 May 1918, 5; 18 December 1918, 4; 7 October 1921, 7. The WCTU opened a hostel for visiting soldiers' wives in wartime.

38 Ian Malcolm and Arthur Hall, *The First 75 Years: A Brief History 1924–1999* (Palmerston North: Palmerston North Rotary Club, 1999).

39 Rotary was seeded in New Zealand by politician George Fowlds, with Auckland and Wellington chartered in 1921. Histories of local Rotary Clubs include Ian Malcolm and Arthur Hall, *The First 75 Years,* and Peter Inder and Dick Rawstron, *'Five Thirty Wednesday': A History of the Rotary Club of Terrace End 1958–1998* (Palmerston North: Palmerston North Rotary Club of Terrace End, 1998).

40 *EP*, 17 September 1924, 7.

41 *MS*, 29 November 1928, 8.

42 The Women's Institute movement was founded in 1921 in New Zealand, following the British model, and is still active; founded in 1925, the Women's Division of the New Zealand Farmers' Union (established in 1899 and subsequently renamed Federated Farmers) is now entitled Rural Women. 'Kainga Moe' was formerly the Strang family home 'Shalimar'.

43 See *MS*, 7 November 1938, 11, for an obituary detailing McLagan's many spheres of social service.

44 See a review of the League's activities in *MS*, 2 July 1936, 11.

45 Helen Dollery, 'From Wild Child to Future Citizen? Children and Youth in Interwar New Zealand', *New Zealand Between the Wars*, ed. Rachael Bell (Auckland: Massey University Press, 2017), 232–55. YWCA's Girl Citizens were active in Palmerston North from 1924 as part of a combined Australia–New Zealand mission: *MT*, 2 August 1924, 4; 12 June 1925, 4. Girl Guides' troop leaders in this period in New Zealand were often young women, intent on providing girls with opportunities for civic service, camping and skills development.

46 *MT*, 12 August 1924, 3.

47 For a discussion of national fitness in New Zealand, see Charlotte Macdonald, *Strong, Beautiful and Modern: National Fitness in Britain, New Zealand, Australia and Canada, 1935–1960* (Vancouver: University of British Columbia, 2013).

48 *MT*, 15 February 1927, 6.

49 *MS*, 24 February 1927, 10. See also the programme for the jubilee, detailing events for 27 February to 4 March 1927: Palmerston North 1927 Jubilee Souvenir Programme, *Manawatū Heritage*, 2016Pa_A175-20-1_013140, https://manawatuheritage.pncc.govt.nz/item/ac8396a6-db3d-40ea-8765-bd3afc87f594?child=be758359-8f91-47c8-862b-ce2d9c821db2.

50 For an overview of this period, see Malcolm McKinnon, *The Broken Decade: Prosperity, Depression and Recovery in New Zealand, 1928–1939* (Dunedin: Otago University Press, 2016).

51 Malcolm and Hall, *The First 75 Years,* 8.

52 *MS,* 10 June 1931, 4.

53 *MT,* 17 June 1931, 6.

54 *MS*, 10 August 1931, 8.

55 See, for example, 'Work for Boys: Welfare and Employment', *MS,* 29 June 1932, 3; 'Progress League: Organisation Formed', *MS,* 8 October 1932, 2.

56 Bruce Webster, 'The Palmerston North Political Labour Movement 1916–1935' (BA Hons research exercise, Massey University, Palmerston North, 1990), 45–46.

57 *MS,* 27 March 1935, 12.

58 New Zealand's Home Guard was formed in 1940, on the model of the British Home Guard. *MS*, 7 September 1940, 5.

59 On specific activities see, for example, on Girl Guides net-making, *MS,* 25 November 1941, 6; 'Poland's Gratitude', *MS*, 26 March 1943, 2.

60 Local organisations provided support and entertainments for the troops while in the city. See, for example, *MS*, 3 April 1940, 13; 19 April 1940, 9; 30 May 1940, 11; 16 February 1940, 8.

61 *MS*, 13 April 1940, 9.

62 Margaret Weir, 'Warburton, Charlotte Eliot', *Dictionary of New Zealand Biography*, first published in 1998. *Te Ara*, https://teara.govt.nz/en/biographies/4w5/warburton-charlotte-eliot.

63 Freda Larsen, *The Overseas Ladies' Club in Palmerston North: A Memoir* (Palmerston North: Sundial Productions, 2003), 4–6, 12–13, 16, 22.

64 Peter Clayworth, 'Weekends — The Great Kiwi Weekend', *Te Ara*, http://www.TeAra.govt.nz/en/weekends/page-3.

65 See Margaret Tennant, Mike O'Brien and Jackie Sanders, *The History of the Non-Profit Sector in New Zealand* (Wellington: Office for the Community and Voluntary Sector, 2008), 23. In *Jaycee: Developers of People; Builders of Communities* (Wellington: Ngaio Press, 2007), 81, 93, Graham and Susan Butterworth suggest that in New Zealand international service clubs attained a level of adult male participation unequalled in the world.

66 The 1966 *Encyclopaedia of New Zealand* gave national figures for Scouts at an

impressive 42,000, Guides at 33,198, Boys' Brigade at 12,000 and Girls' Life Brigade at 19,000: https://teara.govt.nz/en/1966/youth-organisations.

67 *MS*, 19 October 1943, 2; 23 August 1945, 8.

68 The 1961 census recorded 723 Māori residents of Palmerston North and in 1966, 1376: Peter Crawford, *Maori Migration in the Manawatu Region and Palmerston North*, Palmerston North Town Planning Office Report No. 43 (Palmerston North: PNCC, November 1971), 5. The same report notes that some Māori moved on, fitting a pattern of migration from rural homes to smaller centres to larger cities as noted in Aroha Harris and Melissa Matutina Williams, 'Maori Affairs, 1945–1970', *Tangata Whenua*, ed. Atholl Anderson, Judith Binney and Aroha Harris (Wellington: Bridget Williams Books, 2015), 333–57, at 343. See also Matheson, *Council and Community*, 41, 60–61.

69 P. Crawford, *Participation in Recreation Groups, Clubs and Societies: A Study of Cultural and Social Groupings in Palmerston North 1968/69*, Palmerston North City Council Town Planning Office Report No. 14 (Palmerston North: PNCC Town Planning Office, 1969), 8–15.

70 Ibid., 9.

71 See Sue Forde, '"Grand Men of the Road": The Early Decades of the Automobile Association in the Manawatū', *MJH* 13 (2017): 44–52.

72 Crawford, *Participation in Recreation Groups*, 1.

73 See also A. G. Anderson, 'The Community', *Report on Proceedings at the Industrial Promotion Seminar Held in Palmerston North, on 7th October 1961*, Palmerston North Industrial Promotions Committee, 3. Anderson drew a distinction between those with career mobility who might be less concerned with local affairs and community problems, and those who built a life in one city.

74 Crawford, *Participation in Community Groups*, 34. See also J. Park, *Social Welfare and the Community* (Palmerston North: PNCC Town Planning Office, 1971), 15.

75 Former city planner Ken Tremaine gives an interesting perspective on such debates. See Ken Tremaine interviewed by Ian Matheson, 5 January 1994, https://manawatuheritage.pncc.govt.nz/item/d6ef282e-8024-401a-87cf-ef5b70082f06.

76 Palmerston North Community Services Council (CSC), *Sharing Our Stories: Palmerston North Community Services Council, 1971 to 1996: 25 Years of Working in Community — A Celebration* (Palmerston North: CSC, 1996).

77 John Thornley, 'Role of Local Government: The History of the Palmerston North Support Model', in *Sharing Our Stories*, 51–52, at 51.

78 Merv Hancock interviewed by Margaret Tennant, 8 July 1998, N-3-3-8, Massey University Archives.

79 Establishment dates include Barnardos Family Day Care Project (1981) and Barnardos Family Support Service (1984), Parent to Parent (1985) and Tough Love (Kapiti–Manawatu) (1989).

80 On the 1981 tour protests, see Geoff Kaandorp, 'The 1981 Springbok Tour and the Anti-Apartheid Movement in Palmerston North' (BA Hons research exercise, Massey University, Palmerston North, 2000).

81 Larsen, *The Overseas Ladies' Club*, 29.

82 http://www.historicmanawatuhorowhenua.org.nz/Records/United%20Lodge%20(Aqaba).pdf.

83 Craig Black, 'The Stomach: 25 Years of Musical Gestation in Palmy', https://nzmusician.co.nz/features/25-years-of-musical-gestation-in-palmy/.

84 Jarrod Gilbert, *Patched: The History of Gangs in New Zealand* (Auckland: Auckland University Press, 2013), 33, 35–36. For a 1996 *20:20* television item on the Mothers, see https://www.youtube.com/watch?v=1bqItgOCZrI.

85 Women's organisations expanded nationally — one source has identified 24 new women's organisations in the 1960s, and 101 emerging in the 1970s: Tennant, O'Brien and Sanders, *The History of the Non-Profit Sector*, 24.

86 Histories of the Palmerston North and Terrace End Rotary Clubs make this point: see Malcolm and Hall, *The First 75 Years*, 32, 38; Inder and Rawstron, *'Five Thirty Wednesday'*, 118.

87 See Palmerston North CSC, *Sharing Our Stories*, 1996, for similar organisations.

88 Palmerston North Town Planning Office, *A Preliminary Report on Halls and Meeting Places in Palmerston North*, Report No. 20 (Palmerston North: Palmerston North Town Planning Office, March 1970), 3.

89 'Siting of Centennial Pavilion at Kaimanawa Park, Kelvin Grove, 1980', Folder 6, 7/1/2, IMCA. See also Jackie Sayers, *Highbury Whānau: The Early Years: Collected Stories* (Palmerston North: Massey University School of Sociology, Social Policy and Social Work, 2006). The quote comes from an article by L. Knight, *MS*, 2 July 2015, digital edition, https://www.stuff.co.nz/manawatu-standard/news/69862148/.

90 Community Support Plan, Palmerston North, 2018/21, PNCC, adopted June 2018, https://www.pncc.govt.nz/media/3130997/community-support-plan-2018.pdf.

91 See Tennant, O'Brien and Sanders, *The History of the Non-Profit Sector*, 30–33, for an overview.

92 *MS*, 31 January 2009, digital edition, http://www.stuff.co.nz/manawatu-standard/news/36532/Religion-downplayed-as-issue-for-council.

93 Margaret Tennant, *Across the Street, Across the World: A History of the Red Cross in New Zealand 1915–2015* (Wellington: New Zealand Red Cross, 2015), 238–39.

94 Ian Ritchie, 'The Voluntary Welfare Sector in Palmerston North — Overviewing 25 Years', in *Sharing Our Stories*, 45–46. Other essays in this collection elaborate on funding issues, training requirements, and tensions between volunteer boards and paid staff.

95 *MS*, 12 March 2001, 1.

Leaders and joiners

1 Information in this and previous paragraph from: *MS*, 3 October 1942, 6; David Abraham, *Abraham and His Seed Forever: The Life and Times of Lionel Augustus Abraham and Constance Palgrave Abraham 1863–1942* (Marton: self-published, 2007); Margaret Weir, 'Abraham, Constance Palgrave', *Dictionary of New Zealand Biography*, first published in 1996. *Te Ara*, https://teara.govt.nz/en/biographies/3a1/abraham-constance-palgrave.

Akela Collins: West End Scout Group cub pack leader, 1941–54

1 For further information, see Helen Dollery, 'Akela Collins and the West End Boys: A 1940s–1950s Palmerston North Cub Pack', *MJH* 10 (2014): 61–68.

Merv Hancock (1926–2016): Sharing time and knowledge

1 Helen Dollery, 'Social Service, Social Justice or a Matter of Faith? The Palmerston North Methodist Social Service Centre, 1963–2000' (MA thesis, Massey University, Palmerston North, 2005).

2 Tennant, *Fabric of Welfare*, 220–21; Professor Emeritus Graeme Fraser, Citation for Doctor of Literature (Honoris Causa), Massey University Graduation, 2012, Massey University Archives, K-4-9; *MS*, 15 May 2016, digital edition, www.stuff.co.nz/manawatu-standard/news/79912477/palmerston-north-has-farewelled-a-social-worker-and-dear-friend.

3 Merv Hancock interviewed by Margaret Tennant, 8 and 22 July 1998, speaks about

the social background of the time. In further interviews on 16 March 1999, 7 April 1999 and 14 July 1999, he discusses his time on the Palmerston North City Council. Massey University Archives, N-3-8-8.

Conclusion

1 James Belich, *Making Peoples: A History of the New Zealanders from Polynesian Settlement to the End of the Nineteenth Century* (Auckland: Allen Lane/The Penguin Press, 1996), 349–75.

2 Malcolm McKinnon, *The Broken Decade: Prosperity, Depression and Recovery in New Zealand, 1928–39* (Dunedin: Otago University Press, 2016), 27.

3 'The Community', *Report on Proceedings at the Industrial Development Seminar held in Palmerston North on 7th October 1961*, Palmerston North Industrial Promotions Committee, 1961. For a sense of some of these businesses, see, for example, cuttings relating to 'The Golden Oldies of Palmerston North Business', 1984, 1985, Ian Matheson Papers, Series 2, Folder 6, IMCA.

4 Ian Matheson, *Council and Community: 125 Years of Local Government in Palmerston North 1877–2002* (Palmerston North: Palmerston North City Library for PNCC, 2003), 33.

5 Jill White, 'Hokowhitu and Floods', in Garry O'Neill, *Hokowhitu* (Palmerston North: Palmerston North Historical Society, 2012), 26. The phrase 'uneasy relationship' featured in the title of White's 2007 MA thesis, 'An Uneasy Relationship: Palmerston North City and the Manawatū River'.

6 Matheson, *Council and Community*, 35.

7 Palmerston North City Council Public Relations Committee, 'Foreword', in *Palmerston North: A Garden City of New Zealand* [n.d.], Palmerston North Promotions Board, Misc. Publications 1960–1980, Series 9, Box 1, Folder 5, IMCA.

8 The sections in major histories of New Zealand, such as Geoffrey Rice, ed., *The Oxford History of New Zealand*, 2nd edition (Auckland: Oxford University Press, 1992) and James Belich, *Paradise Reforged: A History of the New Zealanders from the 1880s to the Year 2000* (Auckland: Allen Lane/The Penguin Press, 2001) present the 1960s as heralding a period of rapid change on many fronts, as do the more thematic chapters in Giselle Byrnes, ed., *The New Oxford History of New Zealand* (Melbourne: Oxford University Press, 2009).

9 'Nature Calls', https://www.pncc.govt.nz/get-involved/have-your-say/nature-calls/.

10 Ken Tremaine interviewed by Ian Matheson, 30 December 1993 (tape 1, side 2), https://manawatuheritage.pncc.govt.nz/item/d6ef282e-8024-401a-87cf-ef5b70082f06.

11 Ibid.

12 https://www.facebook.com/PNCityCouncil/.

13 A point noted also by Charles Landry, *Creative Cities Index: Comfortable or Captivating: An Assessment of Palmerston North* (Palmerston North: PNCC, 2013), 33, https://www.pncc.govt.nz/media/2096880/creative_city_index_report__web_document_.pdf.

14 *New Zealand Core Cities Report: Palmerston North: Competitive Advantage and Distinctiveness Technical Report* (Palmerston North: PNCC, 2014), https://www.pncc.govt.nz/media/2626204/core_cities_report_-_full__2014_.pdf, 70.

15 Matheson, *Council and Community*, 41; *New Zealand Core Cities Report*, 36, 40.

16 *New Zealand Core Cities Report*, 40.

17 Charles Landry, *Creative Cities Index*, 21, 24, 28, 48.

18 See Peter Karl Kresl and Daniele Ietri, *Smaller Cities In a World of Competitiveness* (New York: Routledge, 2016).

BIBLIOGRAPHICAL NOTE

Historians researching the Manawatū are well served for primary and secondary sources. Staff of the Heritage section of the Palmerston North City Library host a comprehensive set of online and digital resources. *Manawatū Heritage* is an excellent online repository, not just for its rich collection of images, but also for its increasingly diverse holdings of interviews, digitised texts and film clips, although information pertaining to donated images may need cross-checking. Complementing the online holdings is the Ian Matheson City Archives, which includes both official Palmerston North City Council records and an extensive series of folders relating to community groups and individuals. Among them is Ian Matheson's personal research collection, the result of many years of immersion in the history of the Manawatū.

Publications by the Palmerston North City Council are another valuable resource, particularly the more than 30 reports produced by its planning section in the 1970s and 1980s on a rich range of topics, and more recent reports and city profiles available in digital form. Histories commissioned by the council — including Arthur Bradfield's *Forgotten Days* (1956) and George Petersen's *Palmerston North: A Centennial History* (1973) — offer a wealth of historical detail, albeit weighted heavily towards Palmerston North's formative years. Notwithstanding its title, Ian Matheson's *Council and Community* (2003) provides a thoughtful, interpretive social history of Palmerston North, drawing on the author's extensive knowledge of local history. Its coloured maps detailing the emergence of new suburbs are particularly valuable. Palmerston North is also well covered by *Papers Past*, the first port of call for many historians, and a useful tool for verifying other sources of information. The *Manawatu Standard* and the *Manawatu Times* are digitised for the years 1883 to 1945 and 1877 to 1936, respectively, with further years to follow.

Palmerston North has also been well served by its local historians. *Rangitāne: A Tribal History* (1986) by former Secretary for Māori Affairs Jock McEwen was based on informant information, whakapapa books and Māori Land Court records, and is still well used. Published in 1903, *Old Manawatu* by Lindsay Buick also remains a valuable authority on the early history of Palmerston North. Other local historians have written focused studies on aspects of Palmerston North's past, some not formally published but now appearing on *Manawatū Heritage*. In the early 2000s Brian Mather produced a series of microhistories of central city streets, which charted change over time. Although framed primarily with reference to politics, Merv Hancock's *The First Sixteen Members of Parliament for Palmerston North* (2005) affords valuable insights into its social history. Garry O'Neill has published histories of Terrace End (2009), Hokowhitu (2012) and West End (2018), which give a rich description of suburban identities in Palmerston North.

The *Manawatū Journal of History*, first published in 2005, covers a wide range of specialist topics. Under the direction of Professor Bill Oliver and successive teachers of New Zealand history, the Massey University history programme produced a number of theses and research exercises on Palmerston North. The majority were presented to the City Library in Local History Week 2019. Tina White's weekly 'Memory Lane' column in the *Manawatu Standard* has proven a popular success since its inception in 2004, with topics ranging from personal profiles to snapshots of particular years and events.

The book has been fully referenced so that those wishing to read more specifically on themes and topics relating to Palmerston North can follow through via the extensive endnotes of each chapter.

ABOUT THE CONTRIBUTORS

Helen Dollery is a historian whose research reflects her interest in New Zealand's civil society, and how people choose to group themselves around shared interests at local and national levels. She enjoys teaching BA students about New Zealand identity and citizenship at Massey University. Her PhD research focused on the history of the Scouting and Guiding movements in New Zealand.

Simon Johnson is a former library manager with a life-long interest in history (and watch-collecting). He has researched First World War patriotic activity in the Manawatū at master's level, and has more recently written articles for the *Manawatū Journal of History.*

Peter Meihana is of Ngāti Kuia, Rangitāne, Ngāti Apa and Ngāi Tahu descent. He is a past trustee of Te Rūnanga a Ngāti Kuia and a present trustee of Te Rūnanga a Rangitāne o Wairau. Peter's research interests include the oral traditions and history of the Kurahaupō tribes of the northern South Island. Peter holds a doctoral degree, and teaches history at Massey University's Manawatū campus.

Hone Morris is of Ngāi Te Rangitotohu ki Rangitāne and Ngāti Mārau ki Kahungunu descent, and is an associate professor in Te Pūtahi a Toi at Massey University. A former teacher and editor, he is a licensed interpreter and translator of te reo Māori, and is working on a major MBIE-funded project entitled 'He Tātai Whenua: A Te Ao Māori Land Classification 2017–2020'.

Russell Poole is a distinguished professor emeritus of medieval studies, of the University of Western Ontario, having previously taught for many years at Massey University. He holds fellowships of the Royal Society of Canada and the Royal Society of New Zealand, and has published numerous books and articles on British and Scandinavian history and literature. Since retirement he has extended his research to local and regional New Zealand history, and currently edits the *Manawatū Journal of History.*

Professor Michael Roche is a graduate of the University of Canterbury and of Massey University. His research interests include historical geography, especially colonial forestry, landscape transformation and the history of geographical thought. Previously he has contributed to the *New Zealand Historical Atlas*, the *Dictionary of New Zealand Biography*, and *Te Ara*. He is a Life Fellow of the New Zealand Geographical Society.

Associate Professor Kerry Taylor is Head of the School of Humanities at Massey University, and a historian of labour, dissent and political surveillance. On the local history front, he was a contributor to, and co-editor of, *Te Hao Nui: The Great Catch* (2011).

Emeritus Professor Margaret Tennant's past publications have mainly been in the areas of women's history and the history of social policy. Most recently she has published articles, chapters and books on the non-profit sector, including a history of the New Zealand Red Cross. She is a Fellow of the Royal Society of New Zealand Te Apārangi.

Elizabeth Ward teaches in the history programme at Massey University, and has a PhD based on her research into the Reform Party in New Zealand.

Geoff Watson is an associate professor in the history programme in the School of Humanities, Massey University. He grew up in Palmerston North. His specialist field is sports history, and he has authored and co-authored a number of books and articles in this field, including *Sport and the New Zealanders: A History* (2018) and *Will to Win: New Zealand Netball Greats on Team Culture and Leadership* (2020). He has also contributed articles on sport in Palmerston North to the *Manawatū Journal of History*.

ACKNOWLEDGEMENTS

A volume such as this does not come to fruition without the input of a good many people, beyond those whose words appear in the text. The editors would nonetheless like to acknowledge the colleagues who voluntarily wrote up chapters, often at a busy time, and at personal cost. Sharing ideas with them at our monthly Friday-morning sessions over coffee was an example of the value added to a project through companionable teamwork and brainstorming.

All historical projects depend on the resources of a research infrastructure, including, in the case of this book, Massey University's W. H. Oliver Humanities Research Academy and the School of Humanities. The assistance of the Heritage team in the Palmerston North City Library was critical. It was given unstintingly and professionally, and we are hugely grateful to all involved. Lesley Courtney's secretarial support for the Palmerston North Heritage Trust, the body overseeing the project, was particularly important, as was Adam Melville's assistance in providing images from *Manawatū Heritage*. Without this digital resource, our pictorial research would have been far more lengthy, onerous and expensive. At the Massey University Archives, Louis Changuion was similarly helpful in meeting all of our requests.

The Palmerston North History Project has financial support from the Lotteries Commission, whose liaison person, Joanne Becker, was always accessible and encouraging. The Palmerston North City Council also provided funding for publication, and we wish to acknowledge, most especially, the ongoing interest of Mayor Grant Smith, and also Rachel Bowen.

The *Manawatu Standard* very generously gave access to images from its archival and in-house collections, and here we wish to thank *Stuff*'s Jude Tewnion, two successive editors, Jonathon Howe and Matthew Dallas, and also news director Jimmy Ellingham, for facilitating this. It was an ideal way for *Stuff* to acknowledge Palmerston North's 150 years from township to city, and the *Standard*'s journey alongside since 1880.

Trieste and Wiremu Te Awe Awe very kindly met with us and gave us a steer from a Rangitāne perspective early in the project. Wiremu Te Awe Awe, Nuwyne Te Awe Awe, Meihana Durie, Jon Proctor, Huataki Whareaitu, Mark Moses and Richard Bradley also provided valuable assistance, particularly for the chapter on tangata whenua. We acknowledge Professor John Cookson for early discussions on urban history, and those community historians who attended initial meetings to discuss possible content. For assistance in the later stages, we wish to thank Peter Crawford from the Palmerston North City Council's planning section for discussion of content and figures on recent developments; Todd Taiepa, Principal Māori Advisor, for advice on Māori place names from a Palmerston North City Council perspective; Dr Jane Richardson for preparing the maps used in Chapters 2 and 3; Kate Elliott and Graham Slater for Centrepoint images; Brian Crews for images and information relating to Berry Engineering; Jeff Fox and Cindy Lilburn for retrieving images from Te Manawa's collections; the Art Gallery Society, as well as the artist, John Coley, for permission to use *Around the Square* as our very beautiful cover image; and Tina White and Dorothy Pilkington for so generously sharing their knowledge of Manawatū history. Dorothy, in particular, gave initial chapter drafts an extensive and professional review (but cannot be held responsible for any errors that have inadvertently crept in during subsequent iterations).

Leanne Hickman provided research assistance, and was fully involved in discussions about the shape and content of the book along the way. Jessica McLean and Therese Crocker were also part of the research team in its early phases. We were privileged to have such competent historians working alongside us.

Nicola Legat, Tracey Borgfeldt and Anna Bowbyes from Massey University Press have been excellent to work with, as was Kate Stone, our editor, and Kate Barraclough, whose elegant design has enhanced this book.

We are grateful to Hone Morris for providing the whakataukī incorporated into the title page of this book.

Margaret Tennant would like to thank Bettina Bradbury, Charlotte Macdonald, Kate Hunter and Bronwyn Labrum — the 'wayward girls' of her Wellington-based research group — for comments on drafts of her chapters along the way, and for the intellectual support and aroha that have characterised the group over its 10 years of existence.

We would all like to thank our families for their love, support and tolerance.

Finally, we dedicate the book to Ian Matheson, Palmerston North City Archivist (1971–2002). Without his dedicated and enthusiastic collection of community as well as local body archives, our work would have been so much harder. He has been an inspiration to us.

Margaret Tennant, Geoff Watson and Kerry Taylor
October 2020

INDEX

Page numbers in **bold** refer to images

A

B

D

E

F

G

H

I

J

K

L

M

N

Q

R

T

U

V

W

Y

Z

MASSEY UNIVERSITY PRESS

First published in 2020 by Massey University Press
Private Bag 102904, North Shore Mail Centre
Auckland 0745, New Zealand
www.masseypress.ac.nz

Design by Kate Barraclough
Cover artwork: John Coley, *Around the Square* (1999), used with permission of the artist
Back cover (from top): Workers at the Manawatu Knitting Mills, early 1920s (Manawatū Heritage 2011N-P137_006066); Terrace End School cadets, 1905 (Manawatū Heritage 2014N_Sc62_007928); West End Plunket gala day, 1960 (Manawatū Heritage 2017N_2017-20_015767); Te Piringa kapa haka group, performing at Freyberg High School, 2008 (Warwick Smith, *Manawatu Standard*).

A catalogue record for this book is available from the National Library of New Zealand

Printed and bound in China by Everbest Investment Ltd

ISBN: 978-0-9951135-2-7